Baby & Child Health

Everything you need to know

Baby & Child Health

Everything you need to know

Dr Philippa Kaye

DK

London • New York • Munich • Melbourne • Delhi

Dedication

For my parents, who love and support me, always

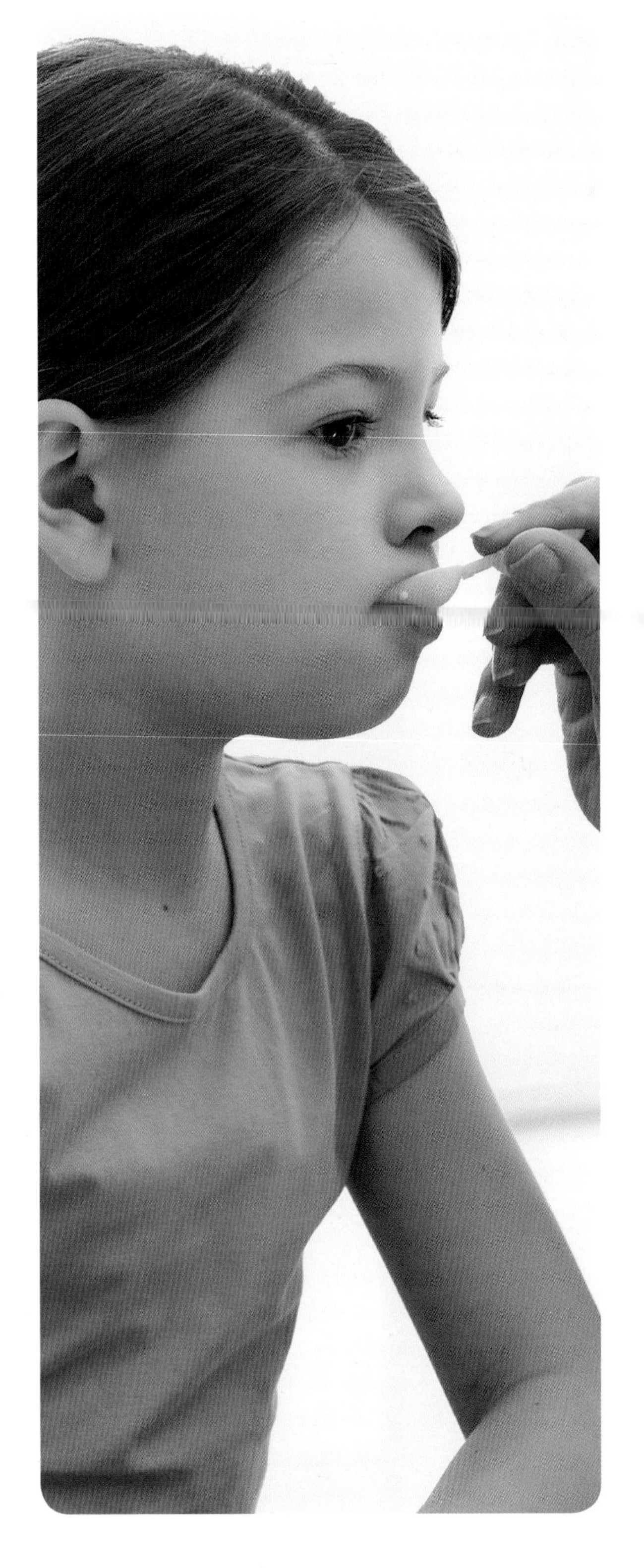

Project editor Andrea Bagg
Designer Louise Dick
Design assistant Charlotte Johnson
Senior editor Mandy Lebentz
Senior art editor Sara Kimmins
Managing editor Penny Warren
Managing art editor Glenda Fisher
Production editor Maria Elia
Production controller Alice Sykes
Creative technical support Sonia Charbonnier
Art director Lisa Lanzarini
Category publisher Peggy [illegible]
Photographer Ruth Jenkinson
Photography art direction Peggy Sadler

First published in Great Britain in 2012 by Dorling Kindersley Limited, 80 Strand, London, WC2R 0RL Penguin Group (UK)

2 4 6 8 10 9 7 5 3 1

001–178167 – March/2012

A CIP catalogue of this book is available from the British Library

ISBN 978-1-4093-8301-7

Colour reproduction by Colourscan
Printed and bound in Singapore by Tien Wah Press

Discover more at
www.dk.com

Contents

First aid

About the author
Dr Philippa Kaye is a London GP, medical writer and new mother. Her areas of interest include children's, women's and sexual health. She writes about parenting and children's health issues for **Junior** magazine, and contributed regularly as the health expert for the teenage magazine **Sugar**. She contributed to Dorling Kindersley's **The Day-by-Day Pregnancy Book** (2009). For more information, see **www.drphilippakaye.com**

Introduction

As a parent, I understand the anxiety and fear that you feel when your child is unwell, or when your child is physically well but you are concerned that he is not developing appropriately, or even when you are worried but not sure what, if anything, is wrong.

This book aims to dispel some of the anxieties you may have in these circumstances. It tells you what symptoms to look out for, when to seek medical advice, and clearly describes and shows self-help treatment you can give for a wide range of problems. Being able to manage a fever and other conditions (such as diarrhoea, or even simple bumps and scrapes after an accident) will mean a happier (and hopefully) healthier child – as well as less worry for you.

Of course, the book is not a replacement for contact with your doctor. If you are concerned about your child, seek medical advice from your GP, who will ask questions about your child's illness and examine him or her before deciding on the appropriate course of action.

The book gives general information about child development, healthy eating, exercise, immunizations, and safety. It also includes a series of symptom charts to help you identify what your child's symptoms may mean; these refer you to conditions in the disorders section of the book where you will find more detail.

There is also a section on first aid. I would recommend looking at this section carefully, even before any accidents occur so that you are aware of the techniques used in an emergency. There is also a glossary of other medical conditions, which are not included in the main body of the book, either because they are rare, or because their treatment requires a lot of input from medical professionals.

Parents and carers know their children better than anyone else, so you are in the best position to recognize when your child is unwell and to support and comfort him. I hope this book will provide the reassurance and practical help you need.

P. Kaye

Dr Philippa Kaye

Health essentials

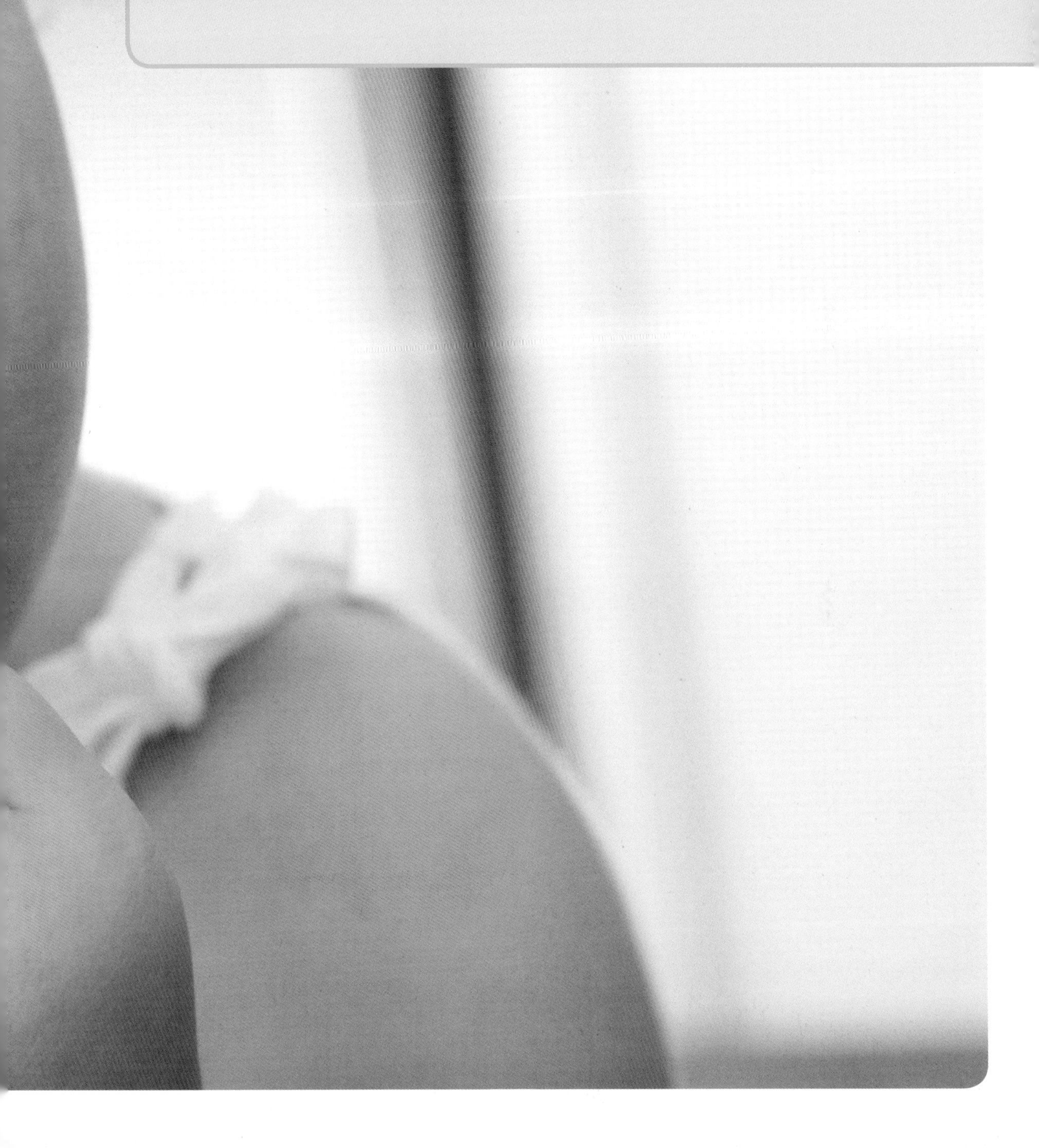

YOUR CHILD'S WELLBEING

From her very first moments your baby looks upon you for protection and care – you are the centre of her world. You have to guide her through her early years, caring for her physical and emotional needs.

With time, all newborn babies develop into fully mature adults so they have a lot of developing to do! Not only does your child grow in size, but she acquires new skills, progressing from holding up her head to walking and from making coo-ing noises to giving speeches.

MEDICAL CHECKS

The first year of life is a period of massive change and growth – the average baby grows 25cm (10in). Development is split into various areas: gross motor or physical skills; fine motor or manual dexterity; and speech and language, and social skills. From birth, your child will be offered a variety of screening tests to monitor her health. Every newborn is assessed by a doctor or midwife. A Guthrie or "heel-prick" test is given 5 to 6 days after the birth to check for chronic diseases such as hypothyroidism (a thyroid deficiency that causes learning difficulties and growth problems), sickle cell anaemia (affects red blood cells), phenylketonuria (which can cause brain damage), cystic fibrosis (mainly affecting the lungs and pancreas) and medium-chain-acyl-CoA dehydrogenase (MCADD, a condition that means the body can't turn fat into energy).

Every newborn is also offered a hearing test, as the earlier hearing loss is diagnosed the sooner appropriate treatment can begin. All babies are invited for a check-up at 6–8 weeks, at which they are weighed and given a thorough physical examination. You will be asked about any feeding problems, about your baby's hearing and vision, and whether you have any concerns. You will also be informed about and offered immunization against some serious diseases (see p.21). If as your child grows older she isn't developing the skills expected for her age, she may be given further tests, such as a hearing test if speech is delayed. A child who is not walking by 18 months should be seen by a doctor.

If you have any concerns about your child's health or wellbeing always seek medical advice; it is better to be safe.

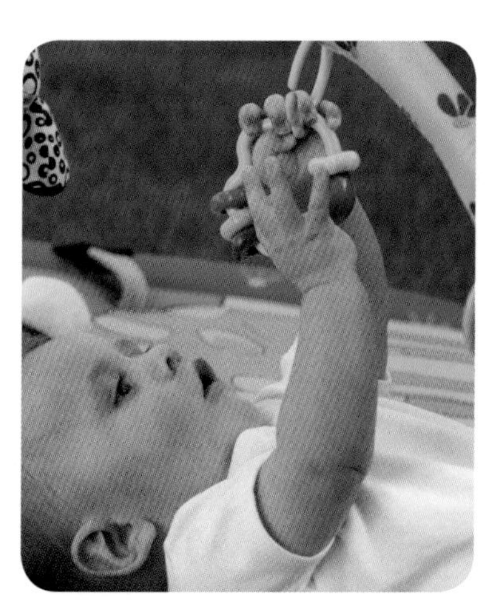

Encourage skill development Toys can help a young baby's development. Brightly coloured rattles in a baby gym, for example, encourage hand–eye coordination.

Fresh air and exercise Almost as soon as your toddler is on her feet she will be running everywhere. Physical activity is good for her, so encourage the habit!

A healthy diet If you want your child to eat healthily, you need to serve the right balance of foods that contain all the nutrients he needs to grow.

A HEALTHY START

You can play an important part in your child's physical wellbeing by building the foundations for lifelong good health. Provide good nutrition (see pp.18–19) and plenty of exercise (see p.20) from the outset. Also make sure that your child gets enough sleep; not only are growth hormones released during sleep but children who sleep well are more able to concentrate, accomplish tasks, and handle minor irritations.

EMOTIONAL WELLBEING

Your child is completely dependent on you for all her emotional as well as physical needs. As a newborn she needs to be held close to feel loved and secure. As she grows, you are her most important role model and playmate. As she becomes more independent, she will need your emotional support as well as firm boundaries. Praising her achievements will help her confidence, as will talking, listening, and supporting her when she is anxious or fearful. Nurturing, loving, and guiding her to help her become a happy, resilient adult can be very rewarding.

Drinking water Make water the drink of choice whenever possible. It's much better for your child than sugary or fizzy drinks and far kinder to her teeth.

Life can be a game Your baby's development, especially in the early months and years, will centre around play. For a young baby play can be as much about learning where his hands and feet are and looking at you as playing with a brightly coloured toy. By about six months he will be enjoying social games and giggle in response to your actions.

Your growing baby

The first year of life is a time of change. A newborn can see and hear, and is equipped with simple reflexes. By his first birthday he'll have tripled his birthweight and will be ready to begin walking and talking.

Developmental milestones

Every baby develops at a different rate, but skills appear in a specific order as the nervous system develops:

★ **From birth** A baby sees objects up to 20–25cm (8–10in) away and startles at loud sounds.

★ **2 to 8 weeks** He begins to smile responsively and turn towards your voice; he can grasp your finger; he makes noises such as coos and gurgles.

★ **3 to 4 months** He can support his head; starts to roll over; looks at his hands, which are now open, and can hold them together; he may be able to lift his head to 45 degrees when lying on his tummy.

★ **4 to 6 months** He can sit supported and bear weight on his legs; he will reach for an object and hold it in the palm of his hand –"palmar grasp"; he smiles at familiar people.

★ **6 to 8 months** He now sits unsupported; he can pass an object from one hand to the other; he finds his feet and plays with them; he enjoys sociable games like "peek-a-boo".

★ **8 to 10 months** He begins to crawl; he can pick up objects with finger and thumb (early pincer movement); he can eat with his fingers.

★ **10 to 12 months** Your baby can stand unsupported and may cruise around furniture; he makes noises such as "mamama, dadadada, babababababa", initially without meaning.

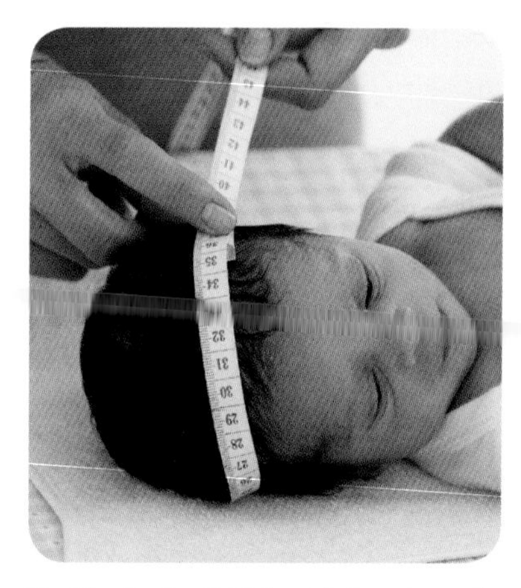

Health checks At birth, at 6–8 weeks, and at 8 months your baby will be checked by a health professional. Head circumference is measured to monitor brain development.

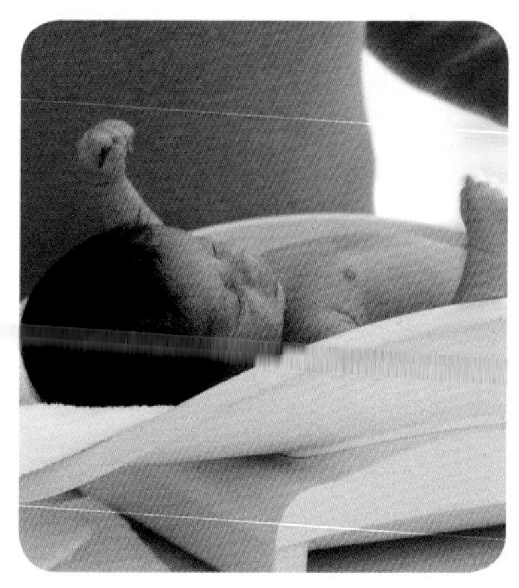

Monitoring development Babies are weighed and measured regularly in the first year. The measurements are plotted on a chart to monitor the rate of growth.

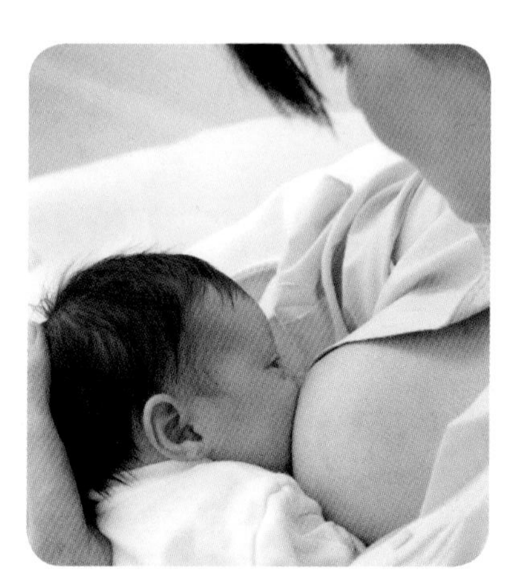

Breastfeeding Breast milk is the perfect baby food. It's readily available at the right temperature, it protects your baby from infection, and changes to meet his needs.

Bottle-feeding If breastfeeding isn't an option, formula meets all a baby's nutritional needs. Bottles, teats, and feeding equipment must be sterilized to avoid bacteria growing.

Teething Babies generally cut their first tooth at around 6 months, and teething continues for most of the second year. Giving your baby something to chew on can help to soothe sore, swollen gums.

Weaning At about 6 months old, your baby will need solid foods as well as milk to satisfy her nutritional needs. Most babies are weaned on cereals and purées first and progress to lumpier textures and finger foods.

Becoming mobile As your baby's bones grow stronger and she gains more muscle control she will start to crawl, enabling her to start to explore her world. You will need to take a look at how safe your home is.

Sudden Infant Death Syndrome (SIDS)

SIDS, or cot death, still isn't fully understood. It occurs most in babies under 4 months old. The way you put your baby to bed can reduce the risks.

Do put your baby on his back with his feet to the foot of the cot, and have him sleep in your room for the first 6 months, so you can notice if there are any problems. You could offer a dummy (there are pros and cons to using these); research indicates that their use can help to prevent SIDS. Keep the temperature of your baby's room at about 18°C (64.4°F). Breastfeed if you can – breastfed babies are less likely to die from SIDS than bottle-fed babies.

Don't share your bed with your baby. Don't sleep with your baby on a sofa or chair. Don't smoke in pregnancy, or let anyone smoke near your baby. Don't let your baby get too hot: use a nursery thermometer to check the room temperature and adjust your baby's clothing or bedding appropriately; keep your baby's head uncovered. Don't let a baby under 1 year old sleep with a pillow or duvet.

Sleeping feet to foot Always place your baby on her back with her feet touching the foot of the cot. Tuck in the bedclothes so she can't overheat by wriggling under the blankets.

Your growing toddler

One of the most exciting moments for parents is when their baby takes her first steps and becomes a toddler. Over the next couple of years she will become more independent, and master many new skills.

Developmental milestones

The progression from baby to toddler is exciting and rapid. All children achieve milestones at different times, but general guidelines are as follows:

★ 12 to 18 months Your child learns to sit herself down from standing; she begins to walk unaided; she can build a tower made of two bricks; she eats finger food; she can hold a spoon, but food drops off before it reaches her mouth; she says mama/dada specifically to her parents.

★ 18 months to 2 years She learns to climb stairs unaided; she can run and attempts to kick a ball; she can build a tower of four blocks; she can undress herself; she eats with a spoon, and progresses to using a fork too; she holds a pencil in her fist and scribbles; she will have about 20 recognizable words that she uses with meaning.

★ 2 to 3 years She can now jump; she starts to use the potty and may be dry in the daytime (with occasional accidents); she will now have over 50 recognizable words and she starts to link two words together to form a sentence – about 50 per cent of her speech is understood by her parents; she still holds a pencil in her fist but can draw straight lines; she starts to enjoy pretend play such as cooking games or dressing up; she begins to socialize with other children; she starts to differentiate between right and wrong.

Drinking from a cup Once your baby is eating solid food, give him his own cup to drink from while you are feeding him. Offer him water to drink rather than juice.

Feeding herself By the time your child is about 2 years old she will be able to feed herself with a spoon and will enjoy family meals with you.

Using the potty As soon as your child expresses an interest in the potty let her sit on one – never force her. At first, nothing may happen, but she'll soon get the idea.

Read to your toddler It's never too early to start looking at books with your child. Reading to him helps his vocabulary and communication skills – and it's fun.

Comforting a toddler Always take a child's tears seriously. At this age children are constantly exploring and learning, but they need plenty of reassurance from a parent when something goes wrong.

Learning to share Toddlers enjoy seeing other children. At first, they play alongside each other. Gradually they learn to share their toys, which is an important part of social development.

Sleep is essential Toddlers need at least 10 to 12 hours' sleep per 24 hours, as most of their growing – about 6cm (2½in) a year – takes place as they sleep. More than ever, toddlers need a consistent bedtime routine.

From walking to running

Children take their first steps any time between the ages of 9 and 18 months, when their bones and muscles have developed sufficiently.

Early problems It is normal for toddlers to be bow-legged at first. This generally resolves by the age of 3. Children then commonly become knock-kneed, which also resolves itself, though it can take a while. If either condition only affects one leg, see your doctor. Some children also walk with their feet turned inwards or outwards. Again, they usually grow out of this, but see your doctor if only one leg is affected.

The right footwear Once your child is walking she needs professionally fitted shoes to reduce the risk of problems developing later. Children up to the age of 2 or 3 often have flat feet, but this does not generally cause problems.

Walking unaided At first a child's gait is very unlike an adult's. She will walk with her legs spread apart and arms outstretched for balance and will take very short steps. She is likely to fall over a lot in the early days.

New skills After a few months, your toddler will be running about, able to stand on one leg and kick a ball. She may even attempt to jump, although she won't succeed straight away.

Your growing child

Children experience many challenges over the next few years as they grow and learn about life outside the home. It is essential that they have a healthy diet, plenty of exercise, emotional support, and enough sleep.

Developmental milestones

This is the stage where you start to let your "baby" go as he begins his schooling and path to independence.

★ 3 to 4 years He is now coordinated enough to be able to pedal and use a trike; he can dress without help; he can talk in full sentences; he'll copy a circle shape; he will play with other children and is learning to taking turns; he begins to understand letters and numbers.

★ 4 to 5 years He becomes more and more coordinated now, he can hop on one leg, and walk along narrow bars; he may now be dry at night (with occasional accidents); he can copy a square.

★ 6 to 7 years Your child could now learn to ride a push bike; he can hold a pencil correctly, draw a simple man, and write letters and numbers; he will be able to use scissors; his level of understanding means he can now play complex games.

★ From 7 onwards His handwriting becomes more legible; he will be reading fluently; he now understands the concept of time (a watch can be useful now); he works successfully in teams and enjoys more competitive games; he will also enjoy more complex games.

Using the toilet As your child grows she will want to use a toilet like her parents. Stay with her at first and teach her about the importance of good hygiene.

Starting school Many children are nervous about starting school. Talk about what is going to happen, focusing on all the positives such as the exciting new activities.

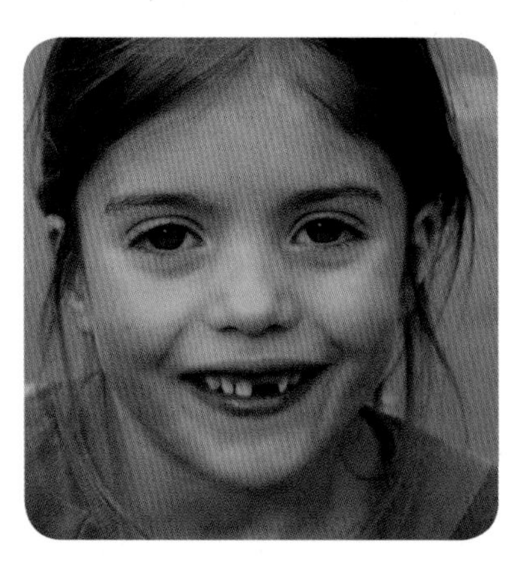

Toothless smile A child will have all 20 of her first teeth by the time she's 3 years old. When she is about 6, these teeth start to fall out to make way for permanent teeth.

Healthy snacking Encourage your child to eat heathy snacks such as fresh fruit. It's another way to make sure she gets her five portions of fruit and vegetables a day.

Stimulating the brain As children's understanding and ability to reason develops they enjoy intricate construction games, sewing or threading beads. These activities also encourage hand–eye coordination, accuracy and patience.

Friends and peers Friends become more important to your child as she starts to experience life outside the home. At first, children choose friends of the same gender.

Keep talking It's important to keep lines of communication open so that your child feels able to discuss any worries. Be ready to listen and value what she has to say.

Rate of growth

Young children grow on average 6cm (2½in) a year. Some grow steadily throughout the year while others grow in bursts, known as growth spurts.

Various changes occur in a child's bones to allow growth to take place. Many bones, especially the long ones, contain bone and areas of cartilage called growth centres, where growth can take place. Over time these cartilage areas gradually ossify, or turn into bone. Children undergo a major growth spurt during puberty, which starts between 8 and 13 in girls and 10 and 15 in boys, when the rate of growth speeds up dramatically. It slows down later, and continues into late teens. A child's final height will be determined by his genes.

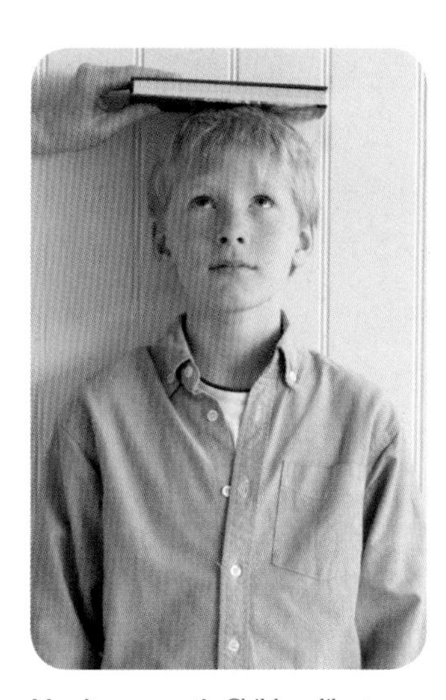

Monitor growth Children like to see how fast they grow. Try standing your child against a wall, mark his height, and measure from the floor. Date the spot and repeat in a few months.

Eating a healthy diet

Make healthy eating a choice for the whole family and you will all see the benefits. A balanced diet will help your child grow and develop and hopefully encourage good food habits that she will keep for life.

Childhood obesity

This increasingly common problem can lead to obesity in adulthood and all its associated health risks.

Feeling the effects Obesity in children results in health problems just as it does in adults. It causes breathlessness and other breathing difficulties, leads to high blood pressure, and puts extra strain on the hip and knee joints. Some overweight children will even develop type 2 diabetes. Overweight children also face emotional and social challenges – they may be teased at school or ignored by their peers, making them feel excluded.

Taking action If you think your child is overweight, talk to your doctor, who can assess your child's weight, height, and body mass index (BMI). If necessary your doctor may refer you to a nutritionist who can assess your child's food intake and help you both make any necessary changes. Prevention is the best "cure". Encourage your child to eat a healthy balanced diet from the beginning. Give your child the right amounts of the right types of foods (see box, opposite) and encourage daily exercise.

Packed lunch Providing a healthy packed lunch for school is a good way to make sure your child is eating well and has enough energy for the afternoon activities.

Drinking water Give your child plenty to drink at mealtimes. Water is best. Offer fruit diluted juice occasionally at mealtimes, but avoid sugary drinks.

Family mealtimes Make time to eat together as a family. Seeing you eating healthy food sends out good messages to the children and picky eaters may be encouraged to try new foods. Children also come to see mealtimes as a time for socializing and sharing.

What is a balanced diet?

Children need a balanced diet – one that has elements from all the different foods groups. This does not have to be adhered to every day; children may eat more of one thing one day and another the next. What's important is that it balances out over the week. Involve your child in choosing and cooking foods; it's fun for both of you and it helps her learn about healthy eating.

★ **Starting solid foods** The current guidelines recommend that weaning should start at about 6 months old. Some parents start with baby rice, and move onto fruit and vegetable purées, followed by proteins. As babies become used to solid food, change the texture, for example chop or mash food and give finger foods. Some parents prefer to start with finger foods.

★ **Serving sizes** As a toddler your child should be eating a varied diet with foods from all five food groups. She needs more carbohydrates than anything else for energy (see below for recommendations for each group). A serving for a toddler, for example, would be a slice of bread or a heaped tablespoon of rice, a matchboxed-sized piece of cheese, or 50–70g (2–3oz) lean meat or fish.

★ **Five a day** Everyone needs to eat a variety of fruit and vegetables; the current guidelines recommend a minimum of five servings a day. One serving is an apple, two satsumas, a heaped tablespoon of dried fruit, a medium salad or three tablespoons of peas. Younger toddlers may need smaller portion sizes. Vegetable or fruit juice counts as one portion, however much you have. Potatoes do not count as one of your five a day.

★ **Some fats are important** Children need fats in their diets because they are the building blocks of hormones, are essential for nerve development, and help with the absorption of some vitamins. However, what's needed is not lots of fried foods, but more of the healthy fats found in nuts and vegetable oils. Milk, cheese, and yogurts also contain bone-building calcium. Children under the age of 2 should have full-fat milk and yogurts. After that, you can switch to semi-skimmed varieties.

★ **Healthy proteins** Give your child lean meats and try to include fish in her diet at least twice a week, especially oily fish like salmon as it contains omega-3 fatty acids. Beans and pulses are also healthy proteins.

★ **Variety** Try lots of different foods. Don't worry about using strong flavours such as spices or fish as many children like these. If your child does not like something, don't get stressed or force her – mealtimes should be relaxed and not turned into battles. Avoid foods that are high in sugar or salt. Don't give salt or honey to children under 1 year old.

★ **Fluids** Give your child plenty to drink but stick to water – avoid sugary drinks. Offer more water when it's hot, as well as before, during, and after exercise.

★ **Snacks** Young children have small stomachs so need to eat little and often. Choose healthier snacks such as a homemade oat and dried fruit flapjack, a bowl of sliced fruit, a handful of dried apricots, or a box of raisins.

Carbohydrates Foods like wholegrain pasta, cereals and bread provide energy. Young children need four small servings; older children need double the amount per serving.

Protein foods Fish, meat, poultry, eggs, beans, pulses, and nuts all contain protein, which is essential for growth. Children need about two to three servings a day.

Dairy foods This group includes cheese, yoghurt, and milk, which provide protein, vitamins, and minerals, especially calcium. Children need at least two servings a day.

Vegetables Packed with vitamins, minerals, and fibre, vegetables can be blended into sauces, or piled onto home-made pizza. Aim for at least two to three servings a day.

Fruit Fresh, frozen, dried, purēed, juiced, or in smoothies, fruit also contains vitamins, minerals, and fibre. Aim for two to three servings to make up five fruit and veg a day.

Being active

Exercise has many benefits. Children who exercise develop strong bones and muscles, sleep better and have more confidence. In addition they are less likely to be overweight or develop diet-related health problems.

TOP TIP

Children over the age of 2 should exercise for at least an hour every day. This does not have to be in one go; 15 minutes, four times a day is fine.

Social exercise A trip to the playground is a good opportunity for your child and you to socialize. You can both get exercise from running around and playing together in the playground. Remember to take water to drink and a healthy snack.

Family outings Exercising as a family can be part of a healthy lifestyle. Try a weekly cycle ride, a game of football, a trip to the swimming pool, or even a walk to the park.

Dancing Activities such as dancing or martial arts help increase a child's flexibility, strength, and control, which is excellent for bone and muscle development.

Swimming Aerobic exercise like swimming improves the way the body uses oxygen. After exercise, your child should be slightly out of breath, but still able to talk to you.

Immunizing your child

One of the most important things that you can do for your child is to make sure that he has his immunizations. It's the most effective way of protecting him from infectious diseases. Your doctor may postpone an injection if your child has a fever(but not if he has a slight cold) or he is undergoing medical treatment.

KEY FACT

Any vaccine that is offered to children or adults will have undergone rigorous safety testing before its use is authorized.

Immunization timetable

Below is a checklist of the vaccines offered to children in the UK, the age at which they should have them, and the diseases they protect against.

Immunizations have few side effects, although there may be some inflammation around the injection site, or a mild fever.

AGE	DISEASES PROTECTED AGAINST
2 months (two injections)	★ Diphtheria/tetanus/pertussis (whooping cough)/polio/*Haemophilus influenzae* type b (Hib) – known as the 5-in-1 vaccine ★ Pneumococcal infection (PVC)
3 months (two injections)	★ Diphtheria/tetanus/pertussis (whooping cough)/polio/Haemophilus influenzae type b (Hib) ★Meningitis C
4 months (three injections)	★ Diphtheria/tetanus/pertussis (whooping cough)/polio/*Haemophilus influenzae* type b (Hib) ★Meningitis C ★Pneumococcal infection (PVC)
Around 12 months (two injections)	★ *Haemophilus influenzae* type b (Hib) ★Meningitis C
Around 13 months (two injections)	★ Measles, mumps, and rubella (MMR) ★Pneumococcal infection (PVC)
3 years and 4 months or soon after (two injections)	★ Diphtheria/tetanus/pertussis (whooping cough)/polio ★Measles, mumps, and rubella (MMR)
Girls aged 12 to 13 years (three injections over 6 months)	★ Cervical cancer caused by human papillomavirus types 16 and 18
13 to 18 years (one injection)	★ Tetanus/diphtheria/polio

Keeping your child safe

Children have lots of energy and are curious so they will take risks. It is essential to let your child learn, but it is also important to take sensible precautions to prevent serious accidents.

Safety checklist

★ **Hall and stairs** Install safety gates on the stairs, and even across the kitchen doorway if necessary. Put non-slip mats under rugs on wood floors. Check that banisters are secure.

★ **Cupboards** Fix safety catches to any cupboards that contain breakable or potentially dangerous items.

★ **Medicines and household chemicals** Keep these locked in high cupboards out of reach of children. Return old medicines to a pharmacy when they are out of date.

★ **Kitchen safety** Use the back rings of the hob and turn pan handles inwards. Warn your child that the oven is hot. Keep knives out of reach. Always strap your child securely into her highchair.

★ **Garden safety** Check the garden for poisonous plants (dig them up if necessary); don't leave garden tools lying around; keep the shed locked; and make sure pools or ponds are fenced off.

★ **Car seats** By law all children under the age of 12 need to be restrained in a car seat. Babies up to 13kg (28lb) should sit in rear-facing car seat, which can go in a back seat or in the front seat provided the air bag is switched off. Older babies 9–18kg (20–40lb) should be in the back in a forward-facing seat. Older children of 15–25kg (33–55lb) can sit on a booster seat.

★ **Cycling** Children should wear a helmet and reflective or fluorescent clothing so that they are visible. Young children should not ride on the road.

Safe play Use a cushioned play ring or put lots of pillows around your baby, especially in the early days. That way she can sit up and see the world and she won't hurt herself if she falls. Make sure she has age-appropriate toys – check the label if you are unsure. If you have children of different ages, keep their toys separate.

Safety on the stairs Put safety gates at the top and bottom of your stairs. Keep them closed, and don't climb over them yourself – your child will copy you. Teach your child how to go up and down stairs safely; at first she'll find it easier to crawl backwards, later she can learn to walk.

Out and about Before you put your baby in a pushchair make sure that it's fully open and the brake is on. Always use the safety harness even when the baby is older. Put your shopping in the basket underneath the seat not on the handles as the weight can cause the buggy to tip over backwards.

Safety in the sun Apply a high sun protection factor (SPF) sunscreen – at least SPF 30 – and reapply it throughout the day. Dress your child in clothing made of natural fibres, protect her face and neck with a wide-brimmed hat, and put on sunglasses to protect her eyes.

Road safety Teach your child about the dangers of roads as well as how to cross a road safely. Encourage her to stay away from the edge of pavements. Hold her hand when you are near a road or you are crossing one, and use a pelican or zebra crossing where possible.

Travelling abroad

Away from home all the same safety rules apply, but your destination may not be child-friendly. It's worth checking the rooms when you arrive and, if necessary, removing any hazards.

Medication Make sure that your child's immunizations are up-to-date (see p.21). Find out whether she needs anything specific for the countries you are travelling to. Take all your medication with you. If you need insect repellents make sure they are safe for children.

Sun protection Dress your child in loose cotton clothes to keep her cool and give her plenty to drink. This prevents dehydration and reduces the risk of heat exhaustion (see p.217). Take sunglasses for you and your children; those with a European Standard mark will protect against ultraviolet rays. Stay in the shade as much as possible, but especially between 12 and 3pm when the sun at its highest to avoid sunburn (see p.130), and apply sunscreen.

Car safety Child car seats are essential wherever you are; if you are hiring a car check that the hire company can supply one. If you are in any doubt take your own with you.

Food and drink Take baby milk or snacks for the journey in case of delays. While you are away, boil water used to make formula and check the local water is safe to drink. If you're unsure, stick to bottled water, don't let your children have ice in their drinks, and peel fruit and veg.

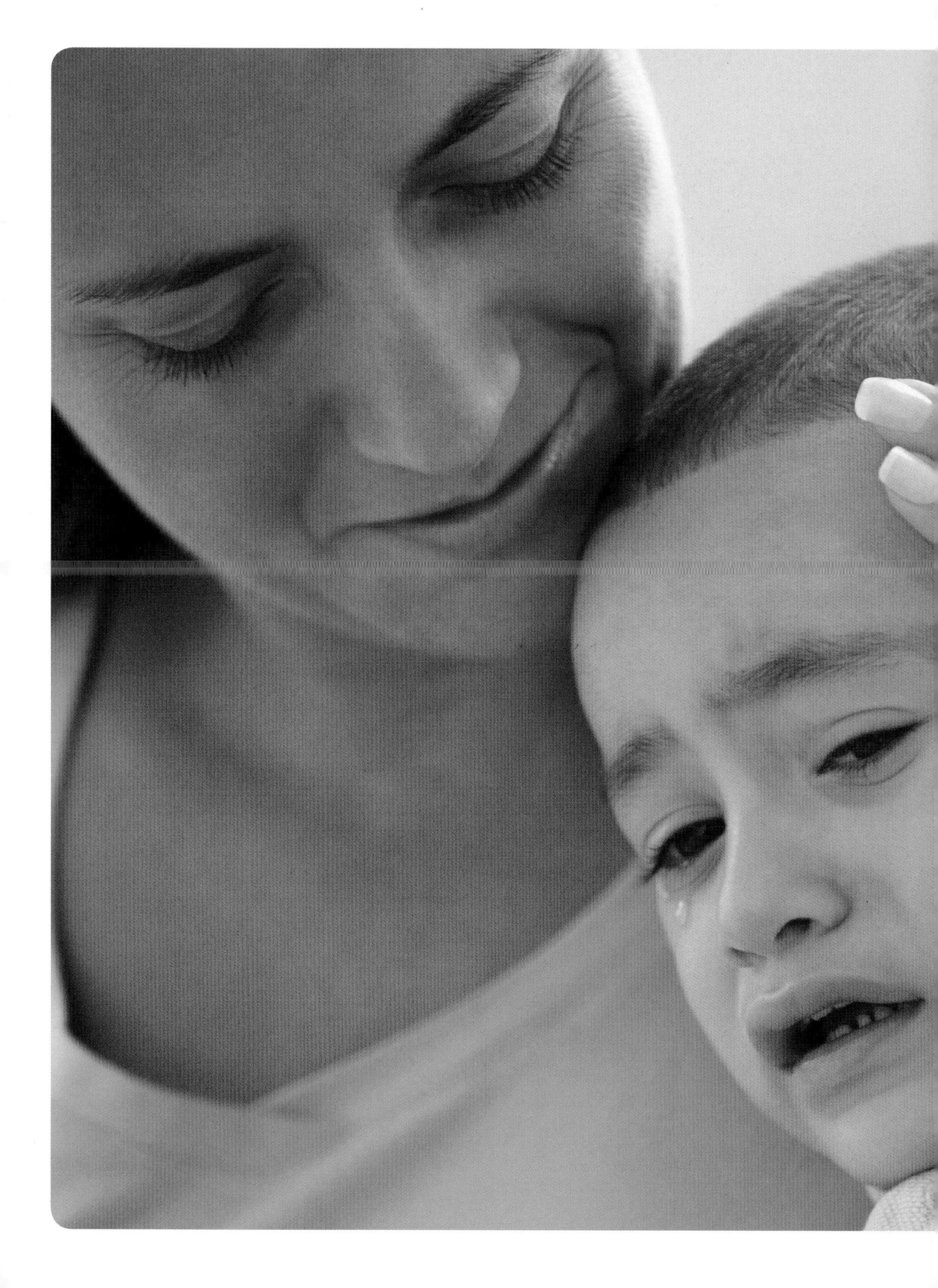

When your child is ill

DEALING WITH A SICK CHILD

Children get many minor illnesses, such as coughs and colds, and these usually get better in a few days without medical treatment. However, it is important to know when your child's symptoms may indicate a more serious problem.

ASSESSING SYMPTOMS

When a child seems unwell and lacking her normal energy, it can be worrying for parents and carers. It may be difficult to assess what the problem is, especially in babies and very young children who may not be able to tell you their symptoms and in whom the signs that they are unwell can be very non-specific, for example they may just be off their food or unusually irritable or short-tempered.

USING THE SYMPTOM CHARTS

The symptoms charts included in this section can help you identify what might be wrong with your child and how serious it is. By answering questions about your child's symptoms you arrive at an endpoint that gives the possible cause or causes of your child's symptoms. In most cases, the causes refer you to conditions in the *Childhood disorders* section for more detail. Endpoint also tells you if you need to seek medical advice immediately or if the situation is an emergency, requiring an ambulance. If medical advice is advised but not urgent, you'll find this information in the disorder article you're referred to, or you will be given this information on the chart itself.

BEING PREPARED

Many childhood illnesses can be treated at home and it is important that you keep your home medicine cabinet stocked up with certain basic items. You also need to know how to give your child medicine (see p.30). One indication of illness is a fever, so if your child shows signs of being unwell, take her temperature (see p.28). If you are concerned about your child; if she has a fever that doesn't come down; if she's not drinking or urinating or her illness is prolonged, see your doctor.

Unwell baby If your baby or young child seems unwell, it can be very hard to know what is wrong as she will not be able to describe her symptoms. If you have any concerns, seek medical advice from your doctor or NHS Direct.

Home treatment If your child is unwell she will probably feel tired and may want to rest in bed. Make sure that she drinks plenty of fluids, especially if she has a fever.

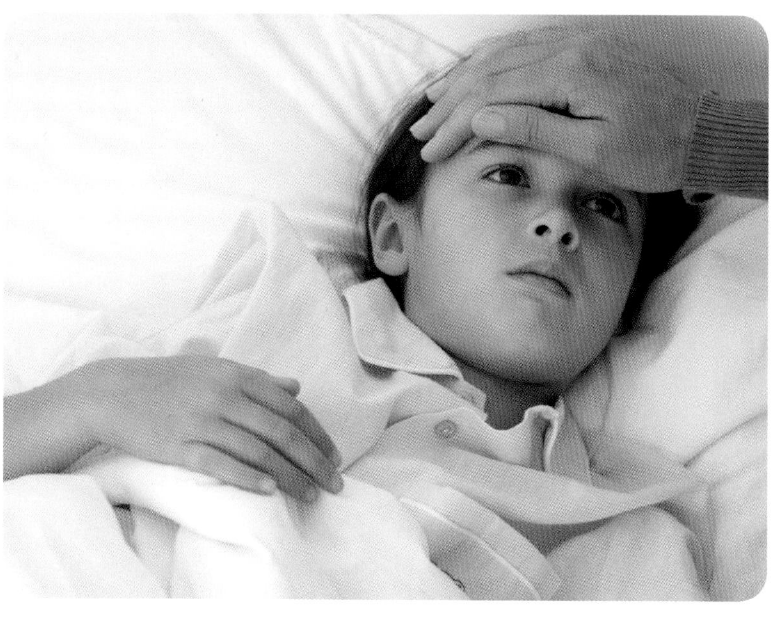

Seeking medical help

When your child is unwell, you'll probably wonder whether you need to call your doctor. The sections of this book that follow will help you decide if medical advice is needed and how urgently. There are three different levels of urgency, depending on your child's symptoms.

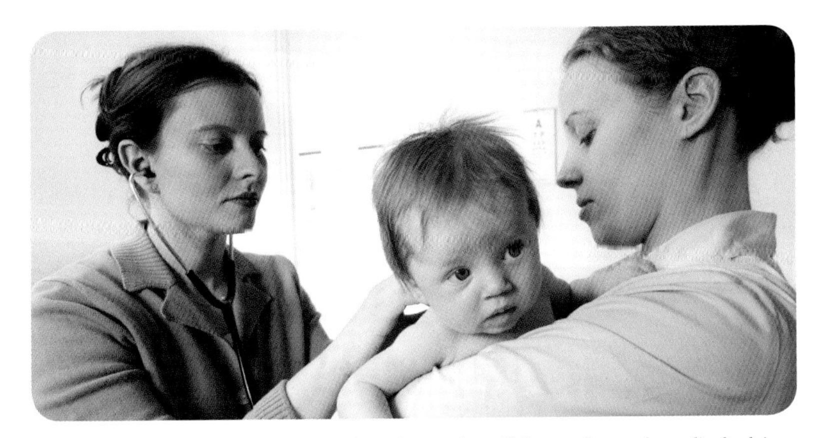

Seek medical advice You'll be given these instructions if the need to seek medical advice is not initially urgent. For example, a child with diarrhoea who is drinking enough water or a child with a sore throat who is eating and drinking can be looked after at home for a few days before seeking medical advice. Of course, if you have concerns do seek advice earlier.

Seek medical advice immediately This instruction means that you should contact your doctor or other medical provider such as your local out-of-hours service, walk-in clinic, or NHS Direct, for example if your baby is under 3 months old and has a fever.

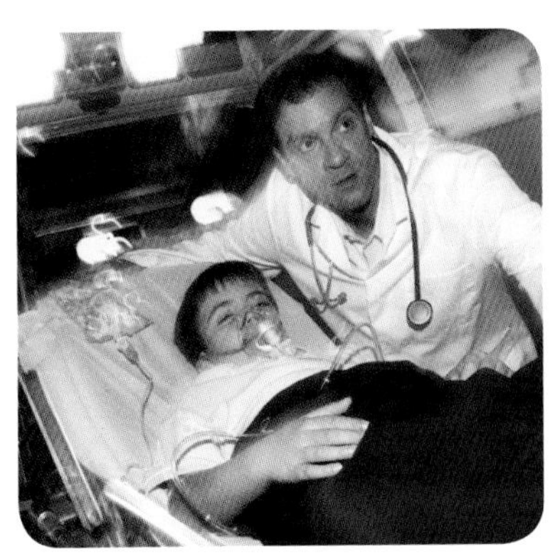

Call an ambulance If your child's symptoms indicate a serious problem that could be life-threatening, you'll be told to call an ambulance (phone 999). In some cases, it may be quicker to take your child to the nearest A&E department.

If your child has an accident

There are a number of different options for getting help if your child has an accident, depending on the severity of the injury.

Minor injuries unit If your child's injury is not serious and she is over 3 years, you can take her to a minor injuries unit. Such units can treat sprains and strains, broken bones, minor burns and scalds, minor head injuries, insect and animal bites, minor eye injuries, and injuries to the back, shoulders, and chest.

Walk-in centre These centres treat minor illnesses and ailments without the need for an appointment. Many centres are open 365 days, outside office hours.

Ambulance Phone 999 for an ambulance if your child's injury is very serious or could be life-threatening, for example she has lost a lot of blood or has a severe burn.

Accident and Emergency (A&E) department If your child is badly injured, you may prefer to take her to your nearest A&E department. A doctor or nurse will assess your child and decide what action is needed.

Taking your child's temperature

If your child is flushed and sweaty, feels hot, or seems unwell, you should take his temperature. Measure it every few hours until it returns to normal.

KEY FACT

A normal body temperature is between 36°C (97°F) and 37°C (99°F). Your child is considered to have a fever if his temperature is 38°C (100°F) or above.

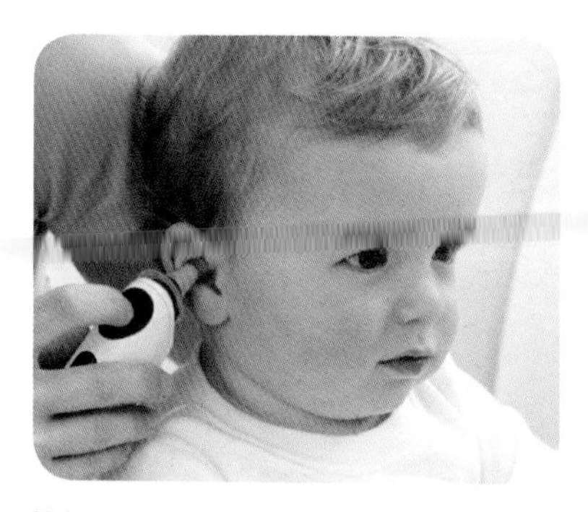

Using an ear thermometer Fit a new plastic tip and place in your child's ear. You may need to first gently pull your child's ear upwards slightly to straighten the ear canal. Hold steady for the recommended time, then remove to take a reading.

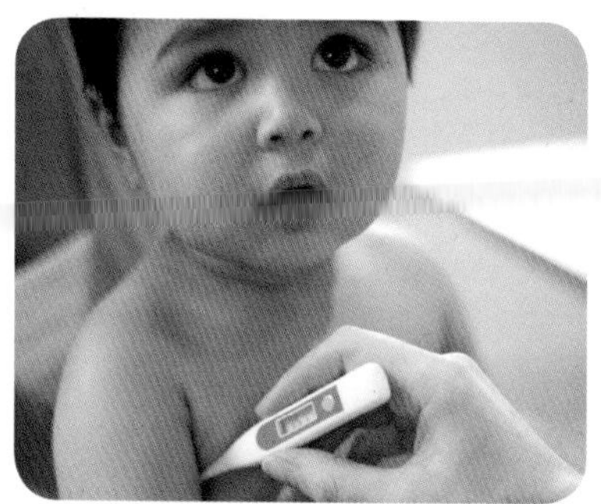

Probe thermometer: armpit method Place the thermometer under the armpit and keep it in place by holding the arm against the body for 5 minutes. Armpit readings are lower than ear or mouth; add 0.5°C (0.9°F) to get an accurate result.

Probe thermometer: oral method Place the thermometer in your child's mouth, just under the tongue and leave it there for 3–5 minutes. If your child has recently eaten something hot or cold, wait 10 minutes before taking a temperature.

Obtaining an accurate reading

Depending on the type of thermometer, you can take a child's temperature in the ear, under the armpit, on the forehead or, for older children, in the mouth. (The oral method is not suitable for young children who may bite the thermometer.) So what are the pros and cons of each method?

Ear thermometers These are the most accurate provided they are placed correctly in the ear.. If your child has been out in the cold, or lying on a pillow, wait 10-15 minutes before taking a reading. Excess earwax can cause incorrect readings. Ear thermometers give a reading very quickly and are good if a child is fidgety.

Probe thermometers: armpit method Armpit readings are not the most reliable. However, this method is safer than the oral method for taking a small child's temperature.

Probe thermometers: oral method Readings from the mouth are accurate and this method is a good way to take an older child's temperature.

Forehead strips These measure the skin – rather than body – temperature, so are not particularly accurate. However, they are quick and convenient, especially if your baby doesn't like to sit still. Place the strip on your baby's forehead, being careful not to touch the heat sensitive strips with your fingers, and hold it in place for a couple of minutes.

Bringing down a fever

Not all children with a fever require treatment. However, if your child looks unwell or appears to be in discomfort he will need some help to bring the fever down. All babies less than 3 months old with a fever should be seen by a doctor.

Give medicine You can use a children's formula of paracetamol or ibuprofen to bring down a fever, but don't give ibuprofen if your child has asthma. Always give the appropriate dose for your child's age. Do not give aspirin to children under 16.

Remove clothing As long as the room is of normal temperature take off some clothes, for example strip a toddler down to his vest or even just his nappy and cover him with a light sheet. You can put a fan on in the room, but don't aim it directly at your child.

Apply a cool flannel An older child may enjoy the sensation of a cool flannel on his hot forehead. Sponging with tepid or cool water is no longer recommended because if the water is too cool the body may try to conserve heat by increasing its temperature.

Offer plenty of fluids Make sure that your child drinks plenty of liquids to prevent dehydration. If he doesn't want to drink, treat the fever with medications and keep offering fluids. As the fever comes down he may be more willing to drink.

Monitoring your child

Although many fevers are due to minor coughs and colds, it is important to monitor your child for signs of a more serious illness, for example meningitis. Call an ambulance if your child has any of the following symptoms:

- ★ Flat, pink or purple spots that don't disappear when pressed (see p.102)
- ★ Stiff neck
- ★ Intolerance to bright light
- ★ Blue lips or nails
- ★ Abnormal drowsiness or floppiness
- ★ Extreme irritability
- ★ Difficulty breathing

Seek medical advice immediately if your child has either of the following:

- ★ Fever lasting longer than 3 days
- ★ A febrile convulsion (p.187), a seizure due to high fever (if it's the first occurrence or the seizure lasts longer than 5 minutes, call an ambulance)

TOP TIP

If your instinct tells you that something is wrong and that your child is not himself, or is not getting better and you are concerned, see your doctor.

Medicines for babies and children

Liquid medicine is easier for children to swallow than tablets. Shake the bottle before each use, and always measure it carefully so you give the right dose. Follow the manufacturer's storage instructions.

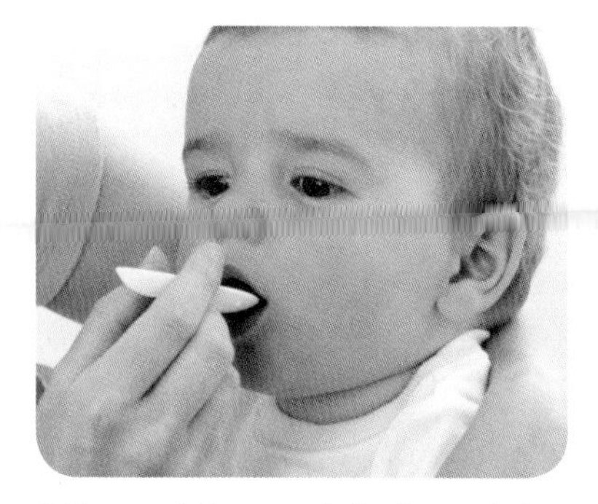

Giving medicine to a baby Sit your baby on your lap and talk to her calmly. Give the medicine on a spoon or use a syringe to squirt medicine into the side of your baby's mouth, between her teeth and cheek.

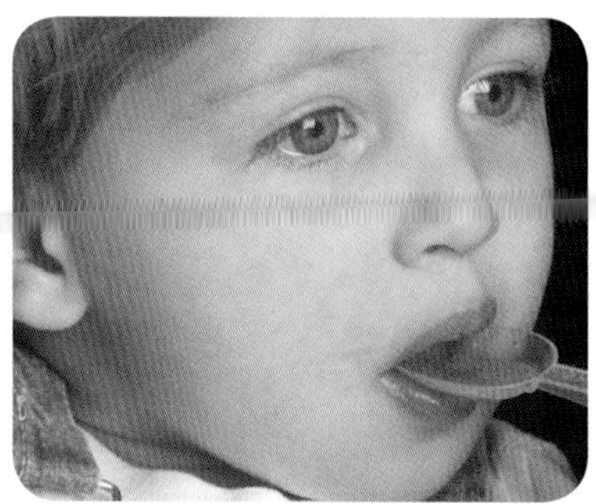

Giving medicine to an older child Give liquid medicine on a spoon. Sometimes you may have to resort to bribery if a child won't take his medicine, such as awarding a sticker or a sweet treat for taking the medication.

Mixing medication with food You may be able to hide some medications in your child's food, for example by mixing it with fruit purée, although check with your pharmacist first before trying this.

Your medicine cabinet

Given below are recommendations for what to have in your medicine cabinet, which must be kept locked and out of reach of children. Put medicines back in their packaging after use and check regularly for out-of-date medication, which should be returned to a pharmacist for safe disposal.

Thermometers Various types are available (see p.28).

Paracetamol and ibuprofen For treating pain and fever. Do not give ibuprofen to children with asthma. (Do not give aspirin to children under 16).

Measuring spoon or syringe Used for giving medicine.

Antihistamine In case of allergic reactions.

Oral rehydration solution Most children will drink orange or blackcurrant flavours, or add a small amount of sugar-free squash or juice to a natural-flavoured solution.

Sunscreen See p.130 for details.

Teething gel Helps ease pain of teething.

Insect repellent Only use products approved for children.

First aid kit Should include antiseptic or cleansing wipes, plasters, crêpe bandages, gauze pads, tweezers, medical sticky tape, round-ended scissors, triangular bandage to make a sling, distilled/sterile water to use to wash out wounds or to wash out the eyes.

Symptom charts

These charts will help you identify what might be causing your child's symptoms. Choose the chart that corresponds with your child's main symptom, then answer "yes" or "no" to the questions until you reach an endpoint, where you'll find the possible cause or causes of the symptoms. In most cases, you will be referred to the appropriate pages in *Childhood disorders* or the *Glossary of other medical conditions* where you can find more detail about the condition giving rise to the symptoms and what to do. The chart endpoints also include instructions about the level of urgency in seeking medical advice (see p.27 for more information).

For some symptoms there are separate charts for children under and over 1 as the symptoms can have a different significance or require different actions depending on the child's age. If a chart does not specify an age, it applies to children of all ages.

Fever (Children under 1)

Fever is a temperature of 38°C (100°F) or above and is usually caused by infection. If your baby feels hot or seems listless or unusually irritable, take his temperature.

Danger signs

Call an ambulance if your baby has any of the following symptoms:

- ★ Abnormally rapid breathing
- ★ Noisy or difficult breathing
- ★ Abnormal drowsiness or irritability
- ★ Mottled or blue skin, including lips

Seek medical advice immediately if your baby has any of the following symptoms:

- ★ Refusing to drink
- ★ Persistent vomiting
- ★ Temperature above 39°C (102°F)

START HERE

Is your baby under 6 months old?

POSSIBLE CAUSE Fever in babies younger than 6 months is unusual; it may indicate a serious illness.
URGENT Seek medical advice immediately
See also *Bringing down a fever* (p.29).

NO

Does your baby have a rash?

See chart: RASH WITH FEVER (p.50).

Does your baby cry and pull at one ear or wake up screaming?

POSSIBLE CAUSE *Middle-ear infection* (p.139).

Is your baby's breathing rate faster than normal (see panel: *Breathing rates*, p.70)?

POSSIBLE CAUSES *Pneumonia* (p.157) or *Bronchiolitis* (p.158).
URGENT Seek medical advice immediately

NO

Does your baby have a cough or runny nose?

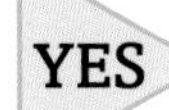

POSSIBLE CAUSES *Common cold* (p.153), or possibly *Influenza* (p.154) or, more rarely, *Measles* (p.106).

Does your baby have any of the following symptoms: vomiting without diarrhoea, abnormal drowsiness, unusual irritability?

POSSIBLE CAUSES *Meningitis* (p.102) or *Urinary tract infection* (p.178).
URGENT Seek medical advice immediately

Is your baby reluctant to eat solid food?

POSSIBLE CAUSE *Throat infection* (p.147).

Is your baby suffering from vomiting with diarrhoea?

POSSIBLE CAUSE *Gastroenteritis* (p.168).

Is your baby wearing a lot of clothing or is the room very warm?

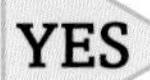

POSSIBLE CAUSE Your baby may have become overheated.
SELF-HELP Babies do not usually need to be much more warmly dressed than adults in a similar environment. If you think your baby might be overheated, remove some clothes and lower the room temperature. If your baby's temperature is not normal within an hour or your baby shows any Danger signs (opposite), seek medical advice.

NO

If you cannot identify your baby's problem from this chart or you are worried about your child, seek medical advice.

Fever (Children over 1)

Fever – a temperature above 38°C (100°F) – is usually an indication of an infection. If your child seems unwell, take her temperature.

Danger signs

Call an ambulance if your baby has any of the following symptoms:

- ★ Difficulty breathing
- ★ Abnormal drowsiness
- ★ Mottled or blue skin, including lips

START HERE

Does your child have a rash?

YES → See chart: Rash with fever (p.50).

NO ↓

Does your child seem unwell and does she also have any of the following: stiff neck, headache, abnormal drowsiness, unusual irritability, pain in arms or legs, cold hands or feet?

YES → **POSSIBLE CAUSE** *Meningitis* (p.102). **EMERGENCY Call an ambulance**

NO ↓

Is your child's throat sore or is he refusing solid food?

YES → **POSSIBLE CAUSE** *Throat infection* (p.147).

NO ↓

Does your child have a cough or runny nose?

YES →

NO ↓

Does your child have a swelling on the side of her face?

YES → **POSSIBLE CAUSES** *Mumps* (p.108) or *Dental abscess* (p.161).

NO →

Is your child's breathing unusually noisy?

YES → **POSSIBLE CAUSES** *Croup* (p.155) or *Bronchitis* (p.156).
URGENT Seek medical advice immediately

NO ↓

Is your child's breathing unusually rapid?

YES → **POSSIBLE CAUSE** *Pneumonia* (p.157).
URGENT Seek medical advice immediately

NO → **POSSIBLE CAUSES** *Common cold* (p.153) or *Influenza* (p.154).

Is your child passing urine more often than usual or complaining of pain or a burning sensation when passing urine?

YES → **POSSIBLE CAUSE** *Urinary tract infection* (p.178).

NO ↓

Is your child vomiting with or without diarrhoea?

YES → **POSSIBLE CAUSE** *Gastroenteritis* (p.168).

NO ↓

Does your child have an earache or is she pulling at one ear or waking up screaming in the night?

YES → **POSSIBLE CAUSE** *Middle-ear infection* (p.139).

NO ↓

Has your child been outside in the sun or in a hot room for several hours?

YES → **POSSIBLE CAUSE** Your child may have become overheated.
SELF-HELP Follow self-help measures for *Bringing down a fever* (p.29). If these do not succeed in lowering your child's temperature within one hour seek medical advice at once.

NO → If you cannot identify your child's problem from this chart or you are worried about your child, seek medical advice.

Diarrhoea

(Children under 1)

Diarrhoea is the passage of runny stool more often than normal. However, babies who are entirely breastfed pass semi-fluid stool and this is not diarrhoea. A baby who has diarrhoea must be given plenty of fluids in order to prevent dehydration.

Danger signs

Call an ambulance if your baby has the following symptom:

★ Abnormal drowsiness or irritability

Seek medical advice immediately if your baby has any of the following:

★ Refusing fluids

★ Persistent vomiting

★ Sunken eyes

★ Passing small amounts of urine or no urine

START HERE

Does your baby have a fever?

POSSIBLE CAUSE *Gastroenteritis* (p.168).

NO

Has the diarrhoea lasted for 2 weeks or more?

POSSIBLE CAUSES *Food intolerance* (p.163) is the most likely cause of persistent diarrhoea in infants. Other possible causes include *Food allergy* (p.164), *Giardiasis* (p.170), *Coeliac disease* (p.166), and *Cystic fibrosis* (p.204), but these are much less common.

NO

Has your baby had any of the following symptoms in the past few days: vomiting, poor feeding, lethargy?

POSSIBLE CAUSE *Gastroenteritis* (p.168).

NO

Have you been giving your baby prescribed medicine for any other disorder?

POSSIBLE CAUSE Side-effect of medicine. **Seek medical advice** about whether the medicine could be causing your baby's symptoms and whether you should stop giving it.

Have you been including more fruit juice or squash than usual in your baby's diet?

POSSIBLE CAUSE In large quantities, the sugar in fruit juice or squash can lead to diarrhoea.
SELF-HELP Always mix fruit juice with at least an equal quantity of cooled, boiled water or try giving your baby cooled, boiled water instead of fruit juice. Don't give squash.

Have you introduced a new food into your baby's diet within the last 24 hours?

POSSIBLE CAUSE New foods may cause diarrhoea. Such episodes are usually short-lived.
Seek medical advice if your baby's diarrhoea persists or if the diarrhoea seems to be associated with particular foods.
SELF-HELP If you can identify the food causing the diarrhoea, stop offering it until you have seen the doctor.

POSSIBLE CAUSES Mild *Gastroenteritis* (p.168), *Food intolerance* (p.163), or *Food allergy* (p.164).

Preventing dehydration

A baby who is dehydrated does not have enough fluid in his body, and this can have serious effects. Dehydration can occur if a baby has diarrhoea, is vomiting persistently, or has a fever. If your baby has these symptoms, you need to give him extra fluids to compensate for those lost.

★ The best form in which to give your baby extra fluids is as an oral electrolyte rehydrating solution, available over the counter. For as long as your baby has symptoms, make sure she drinks small amounts of the solution every 2–3 hours.

★ If you are breastfeeding, continue to give your baby breast milk.

★ If your child is vomiting in addition to having diarrhoea, give small amounts of fluid regularly, for example 5ml every 5 minutes; if this is tolerated you could increase the time and volume, for example 10ml every 10 minutes, then 15ml every 15 minutes, and so on. You may find it easier to use a syringe for giving very small amounts of fluid.

★ Treat your child's fever if she has one.

Diarrhoea

(Children over 1)

Frequent, loose stools are usually caused by infection and do not normally continue for more than a few days. If your child drinks plenty of fluids while the diarrhoea lasts, there should be no ill-effects. If the diarrhoea recurs or persists for over a week, seek medical advice.

Danger signs

Call an ambulance if your child is:

★ Abnormally drowsy

Seek medical advice immediately if your child has any of the following:

★ Severe abdominal pain

★ Persistent vomiting and not able to keep fluids down

★ Refusing to drink for 6 hours

★ Sunken eyes

★ Passing no urine for more than 6 hours during the day

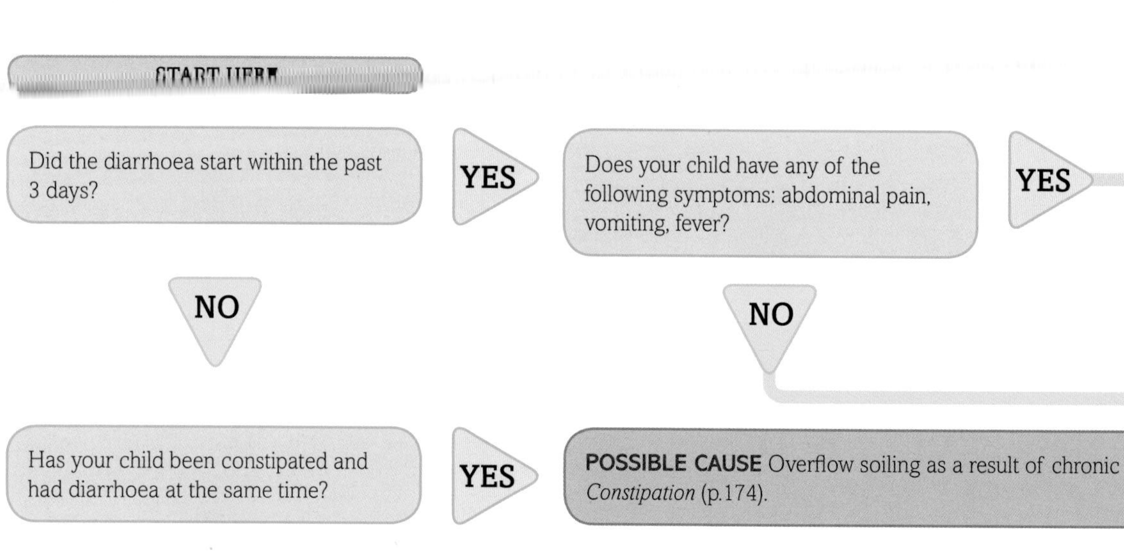

Have you been giving your child any medicine?

YES

POSSIBLE CAUSE Your child's diarrhoea could possibly be a side-effect of the medicine she is taking.
Seek medical advice to find out if the medicine may be causing your child's symptoms and whether you should stop giving it.

NO

POSSIBLE CAUSE *Gastroenteritis* (p.168).

Did the diarrhoea start just before an exciting or stressful event or period of time?

YES

POSSIBLE CAUSE Excitement or emotional stress. The diarrhoea is likely to clear up quickly.
Seek medical advice if the diarrhoea continues or is distressing to your child.

NO

POSSIBLE CAUSE *Gastroenteritis* (p.168).

POSSIBLE CAUSE *Toddler's diarrhoea* (p.176).

Do your child's faeces contain recognizable morsels of food?

YES

Is your child under 3 years old?

YES

NO

NO

POSSIBLE CAUSES The most likely causes of diarrhoea in children are *Food intolerance* (p.163), *Food allergy* (p.164), or *Giardiasis* (p.170). Other possibilities include *Coeliac disease* (p.166) and *Cystic fibrosis* (p.204) but these are rare.

Vomiting

(Children under 1)

In young babies, it is important not to confuse vomiting, which might indicate an illness, with posseting, which is the effortless regurgitation of small amounts of milk. However, a single episode of vomiting is common in infants and is unlikely to have a serious cause.

Danger signs

Call an ambulance if your baby is:

★ Abnormally drowsy or irritable

Seek medical advice immediately if your baby has any of the following symptoms:

★ Persistent vomiting

★ Sunken fontanelle or eyes

★ Passing very small amounts of dark, concentrated urine

★ Loose skin

★ Greenish vomit

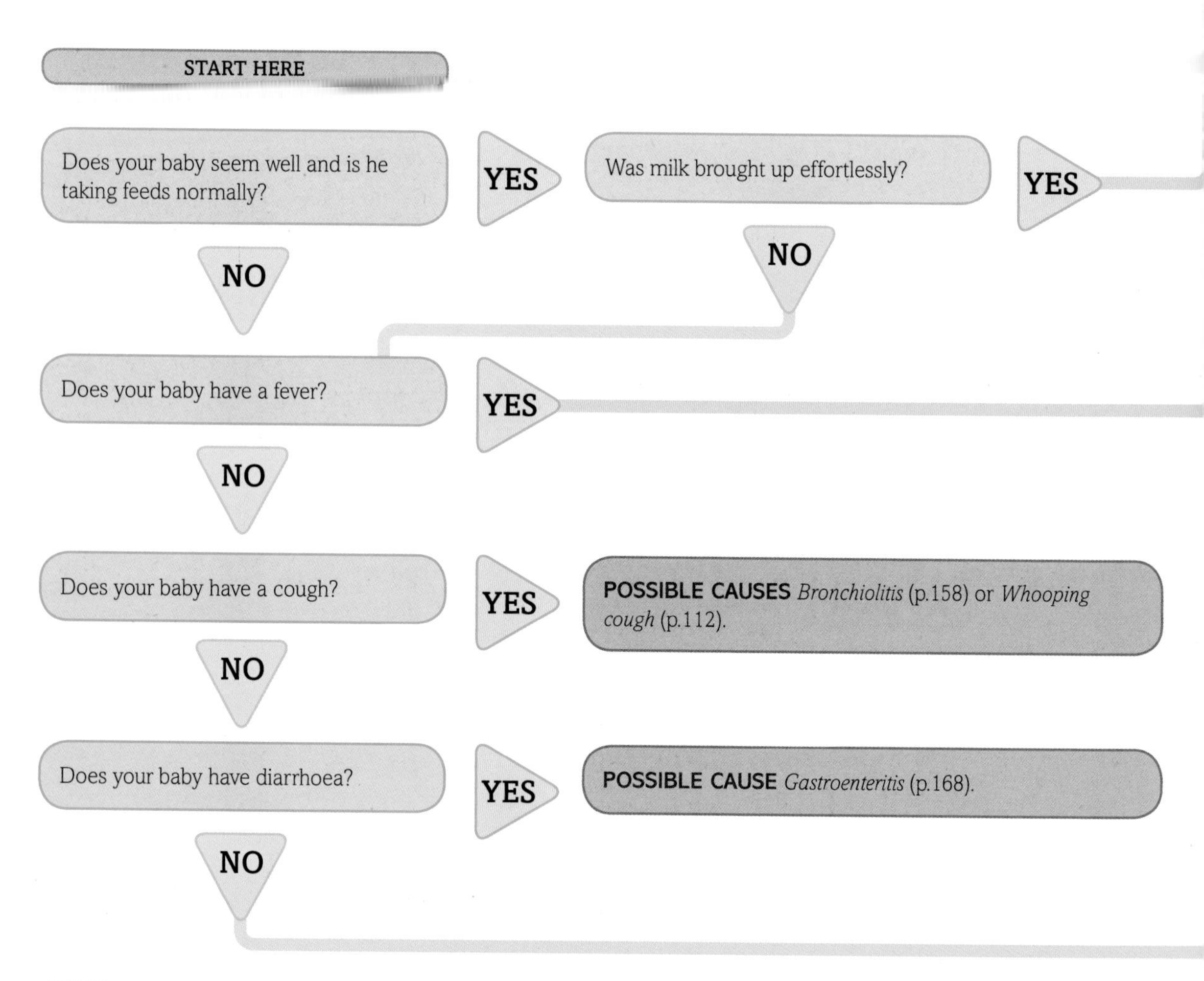

POSSIBLE CAUSES Posseting (regurgitation), which may be due to *Wind* (p.97) or *Reflux* (p.96).

Is your baby abnormally drowsy or is he refusing feeds?

YES

POSSIBLE CAUSES *Roseola infantum* (p.110), *Meningitis* (p.102), or *Urinary tract infection* (p.178).
URGENT Seek medical advice immediately

NO

Does your child have two or more of the following symptoms: fever, pain on passing urine, abdominal pain, bed-wetting?

YES

POSSIBLE CAUSE *Urinary tract infection* (p.178).

NO

Does your baby have diarrhoea?

YES

POSSIBLE CAUSE *Gastroenteritis* (p.168).
URGENT Seek medical advice immediately

NO

Does your baby have a cough?

YES

POSSIBLE CAUSES *Bronchiolitis* (p.158) or *Whooping cough* (p.112).

NO

See chart: FEVER (CHILDREN UNDER 1), p.32.

Is your baby's vomit greenish in colour?

YES

POSSIBLE CAUSE *Intestinal obstruction* (p.205).
EMERGENCY Call an ambulance While waiting, do not give your baby anything to eat or drink.

NO

If your baby has vomited only once and otherwise seems quite well, he is unlikely to be seriously ill. However if your baby vomits repeatedly or if any other symptoms develop, seek medical advice.

Vomiting

(Children over 1)

In children, an episode of vomiting without other symptoms is unlikely to indicate a serious disorder. Repeated vomiting is often caused by a digestive tract infection but can be due to infection elsewhere.

Danger signs

Call an ambulance if your child has any of the following symptoms:

- ★ Greenish vomit
- ★ Abdominal pain for 6 hours
- ★ Flat, pink, or purple spots that do not disappear when pressed
- ★ Abnormal drowsiness

Seek medical advice immediately if your child has any of the following symptoms:

- ★ Vomiting for 12 hours
- ★ Refusing to drink for 6 hours
- ★ Sunken eyes
- ★ Dry tongue
- ★ Passing no urine for more than 6 hours during the day

START HERE

Has your child had continuous pain for 6 hours?

POSSIBLE CAUSE *Appendicitis* (p.172). **EMERGENCY Call an ambulance** While waiting, do not give your child anything to eat or drink.

NO

Is your child's vomit greenish?

YES

POSSIBLE CAUSE *Intestinal obstruction* (p.205). **EMERGENCY Call an ambulance** While waiting, do not give your child anything to eat or drink.

NO

Is your child abnormally drowsy?

YES

Has your child had a blow to the head in the past few days?

YES

NO

NO

Is your child passing pale faeces and unusually dark urine?

YES

POSSIBLE CAUSE *Hepatitis* (p.168).

NO

POSSIBLE CAUSE *Head injury* (p.186).
EMERGENCY Call an ambulance While waiting, do not give your child anything to eat or drink.

Does your child have have any of the following symptoms: headache; stiff neck; flat, pink or purple spots that do not disappear when pressed?

YES

POSSIBLE CAUSE *Meningitis* (p.102).
EMERGENCY Call an ambulance

Does your child have any of the following symptoms: fever, pain on passing urine, abdominal pain, bed-wetting?

POSSIBLE CAUSE *Urinary tract infection* (p.178).

NO

Does vomiting follow bouts of coughing?

POSSIBLE CAUSE *Whooping cough* (p.112).

NO

Was your child very excited or upset just before vomiting?

POSSIBLE CAUSE Vomiting when excited or before stressful events is common in children.
Seek medical advice if the vomiting persists.

NO

Did the vomiting occur during or soon after a journey?

POSSIBLE CAUSE *Travel sickness* (p.167).

NO

If you cannot identify your child's problem from this chart or you are worried about your child, seek medical advice.

Skin problems (Children under 1)

Young babies have very sensitive skin that can be irritated easily. Rashes confined to the nappy area are particularly common and can be distressing for your baby. If the skin inflammation or irritation is persistent or if it is accompanied by other symptoms, your baby should be seen by a doctor.

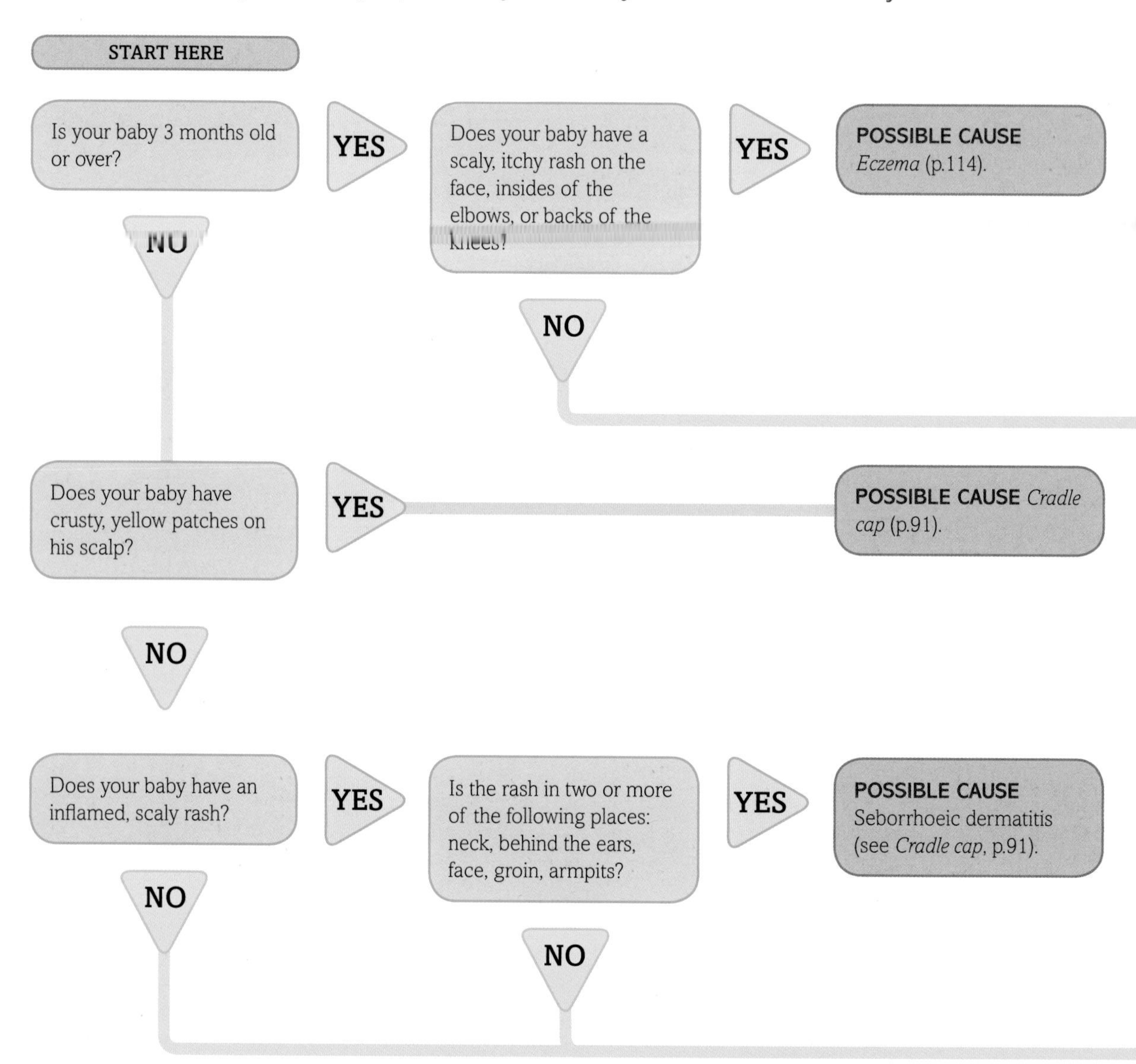

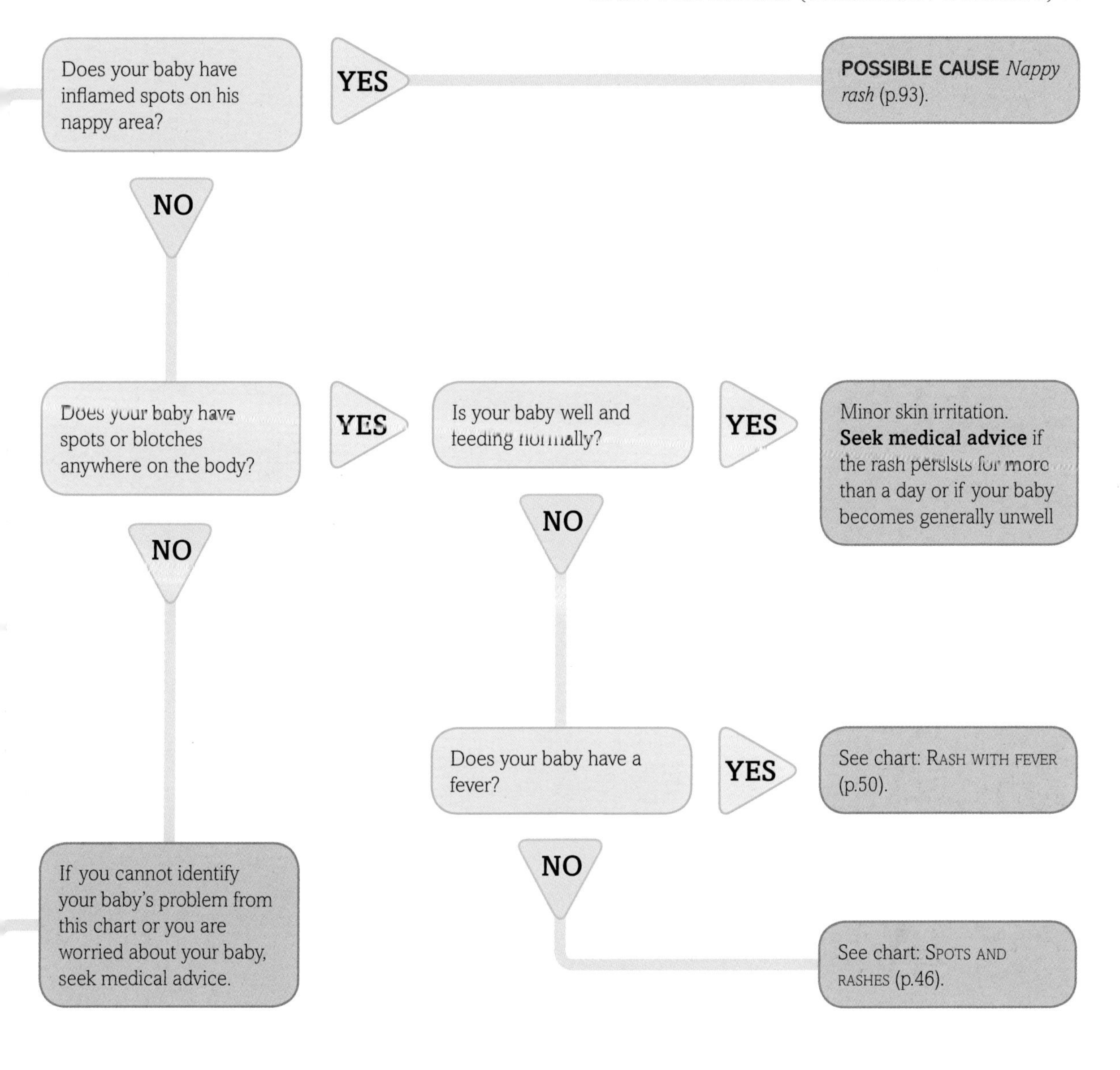

Relieving itchiness

If your baby has itchy skin, try to discourage him from scratching since this may lead to infection. Keep his nails short and you could put mitts on his hands at night to stop scratching. If your child has dry skin, which is often the cause of itchiness, the following measures may help.

★ Avoid soaps as these can be drying to the skin and cause irritation and itchiness. Try using soap substitutes, such as a water-based (aqueous) cream, to clean your baby's skin instead.

★ Don't add bubble bath or bath oil to the water when bathing your child as these are drying. Instead, you can add a specially formulated oil (bath additive), which forms a waterproof barrier on the skin.

★ If your child's skin is very dry, itchiness may be more severe. Try to keep the skin well moisturized by applying an emollient cream or ointment to his skin regularly.

Spots and rashes

Most spots and rashes are due to infection or an allergic reaction. They are unlikely to be serious if your child is otherwise well. If skin is very itchy or sore or your child is distressed, see your doctor.

Danger signs

Call an ambulance if your child develops any of the following symptoms:

- ★ Swelling of the face or mouth
- ★ Noisy or difficult breathing
- ★ Difficulty swallowing
- ★ Abnormal drowsiness
- ★ Flat, pink or purple spots that do not disappear when pressed

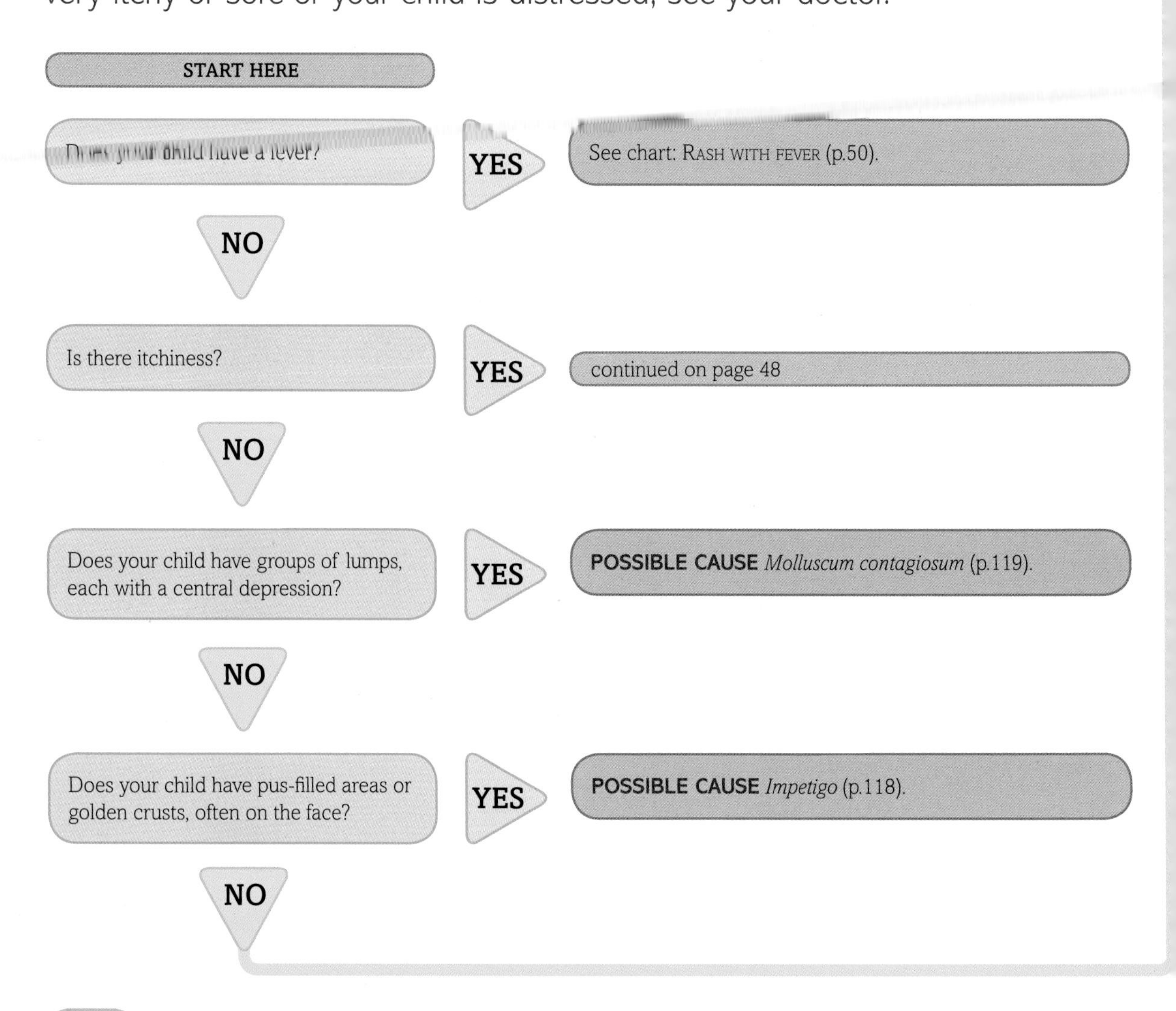

Does your child have one or more firm, rough lumps?

YES → **POSSIBLE CAUSE** *Warts* (p.120).

NO ↓

Does your child have a painful red lump, possibly with a yellow top?

YES → **POSSIBLE CAUSE** *Boil* (p.117).

NO ↓

Does your child have tiny, red, itchy spots or fluid-filled blisters?

YES → **POSSIBLE CAUSE** Heat rash.
SELF-HELP Take your child to a cooler place and/or remove some of her clothing.

NO ↓

Are you giving your child any medicine?

YES → **POSSIBLE CAUSE** Medication reaction.
URGENT Seek medical advice immediately to find out whether the medicine may be causing your child's symptoms and whether to stop giving it.

NO ↓

If you cannot identify your child's problem from this chart or you are worried about your child, seek medical advice.

continued from page 46

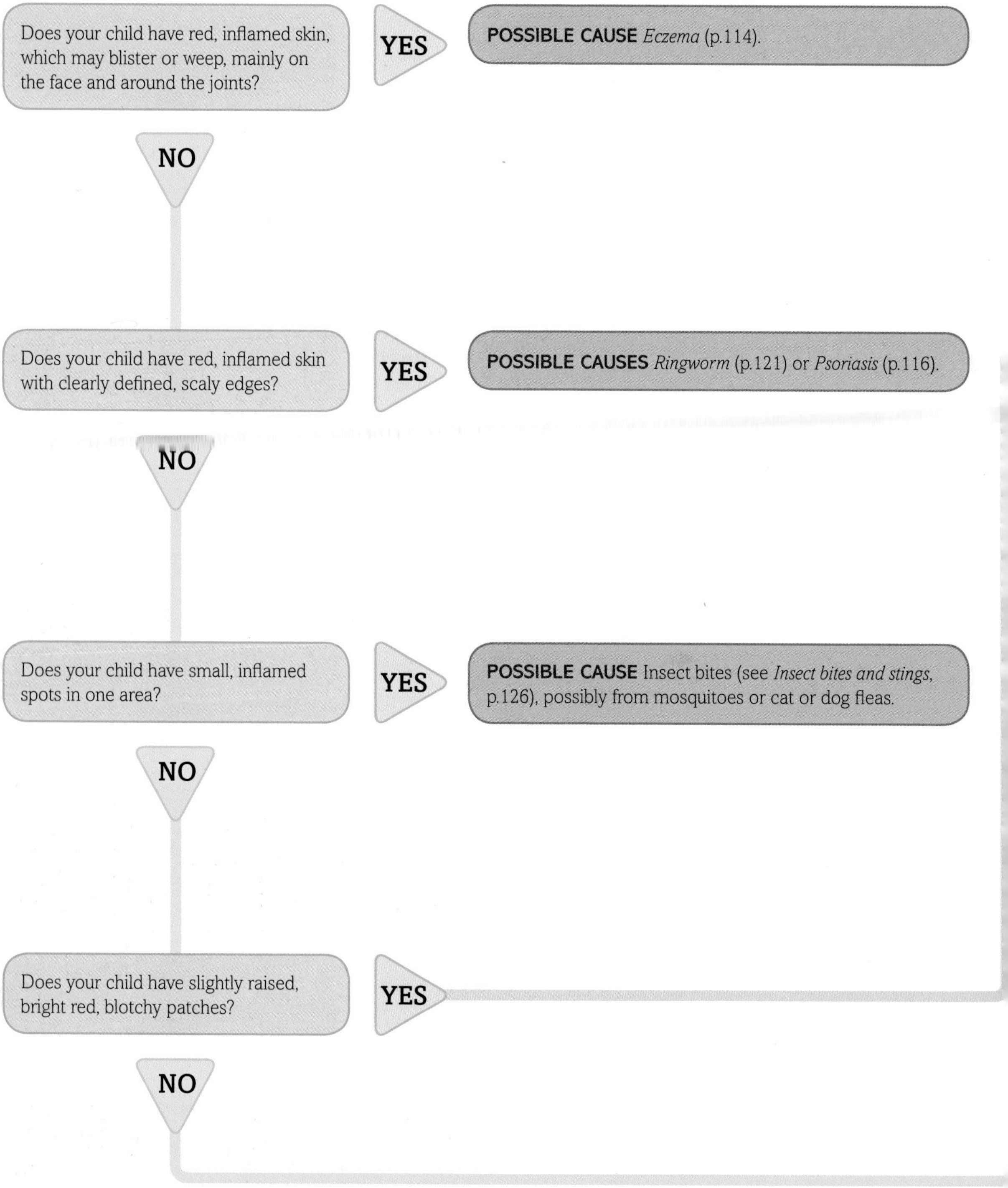

Does your child have red, inflamed skin, which may blister or weep, mainly on the face and around the joints?

YES

POSSIBLE CAUSE *Eczema* (p.114).

NO

Does your child have red, inflamed skin with clearly defined, scaly edges?

YES

POSSIBLE CAUSES *Ringworm* (p.121) or *Psoriasis* (p.116).

NO

Does your child have small, inflamed spots in one area?

YES

POSSIBLE CAUSE Insect bites (see *Insect bites and stings*, p.126), possibly from mosquitoes or cat or dog fleas.

NO

Does your child have slightly raised, bright red, blotchy patches?

YES

NO

Allergic reactions

In an allergic reaction, the body's immune system reacts inappropriately to a substance, causing a number of different symptoms, one of which may be a rash. The first allergic reaction to a substance may be mild, but repeated exposure can cause increasingly severe reactions.

★ Substances that can produce an allergic reaction in susceptible people include certain foods, such as peanuts, airborne particles such as pollen, the venom from an insect sting, insect bites (rarely), and some medicines.

★ Symptoms of an allergic reaction are wide-ranging and may include: a rash; nausea and vomiting; diarrhoea; bloating; runny nose; and itchy, watery eyes.

★ In a few cases, a very severe, potentially life-threatening reaction called anaphylactic shock, can develop. Symptoms of anaphylactic shock include: swelling of the mouth, lips, tongue, and throat; increased heart rate; difficulties breathing or shortness of breath, such as wheezing; and a feeling of anxiety. If your child develops any of these symptoms, call an ambulance at once.

★ A child who has previously had a severe allergic reaction may have an injector containing medication to give in an emergency (see p.218).

Is your child's face or mouth swollen?

POSSIBLE CAUSE Allergic reaction, which may be caused by an insect sting, peanuts, or other factors, and can lead to *Anaphylactic shock* (p.218).
EMERGENCY Call an ambulance

NO

POSSIBLE CAUSE *Urticaria* (p.127).

Are you giving your child any medicine?

POSSIBLE CAUSE Medication reaction.
URGENT Seek medical advice immediately to find out whether the medicine may be causing your child's symptoms and whether to stop giving it.

NO

If you cannot identify your child's problem from this chart or you are worried about your child, seek medical advice.

Rash with fever

The combination of rash and fever is usually caused by an infectious disease. Most of these diseases clear up quickly without special treatment but see your doctor for a diagnosis.

Danger signs

Call an ambulance if your child has any of the following symptoms:

- ★ Flat, pink or purple spots that do not disappear when pressed
- ★ Abnormal drowsiness or irritability
- ★ Seizures
- ★ Abnormally fast, noisy, or difficult breathing
- ★ Mottled or blue skin

Seek medical help immediately if your child has any of the following symptoms:

- ★ Temperature of 40°C (104°F) or above
- ★ Severe headache
- ★ Refusing to drink for 6 hours

START HERE

Does your child's rash consist of flat spots that don't disappear when pressed?

POSSIBLE CAUSES Septicaemia (blood infection) resulting from the bacterium that causes *Meningitis* (p.102).
EMERGENCY Call an ambulance

NO

Is the rash a fine red rash or a blotchy raised red rash that fades when pressed?

NO

Are there crops of itchy spots that blister and dry into scabs?

POSSIBLE CAUSE *Chickenpox* (p.104).

NO

Does the rash consist of flat, pink spots starting on the face or trunk?

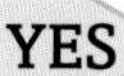

NO

Before the rash appeared, did your child also have any of these symptoms: runny nose, cough, red eyes?

YES

POSSIBLE CAUSES *Measles* (p.106) or, rarely, *Kawasaki disease* (p.206).

Does your child have a sore throat and/or is he vomiting?

YES

POSSIBLE CAUSE *Scarlet fever* (p.103).

Has your child taken any medicine during the past week?

YES

POSSIBLE CAUSE Medication reaction.
URGENT Seek medical advice immediately to find out whether the medicine may be causing your child's symptoms and whether you should stop giving it.

NO

If you cannot identify your child's problem from this chart or you are worried about your child, seek medical advice.

Was your child's temperature 38°C (100°F) or above 3 to 4 days before the rash appeared?

YES

POSSIBLE CAUSE *Roseola infantum* (p.110).

POSSIBLE CAUSE *Rubella* (p.107).

Is your child's rash bright red and confined to the cheeks?

YES

POSSIBLE CAUSE *Slapped cheek syndrome* (p.110).

NO

If you cannot identify your child's problem from this chart or you are worried about your child, seek medical advice.

Itchiness

The whole of your child's body or just one area may be affected by itchiness. The causes of itchiness are varied and range from allergic reactions to infestation by parasites. Intense itchiness can be very distressing and scratching may lead to infection, so prompt treatment of any underlying disorder is essential.

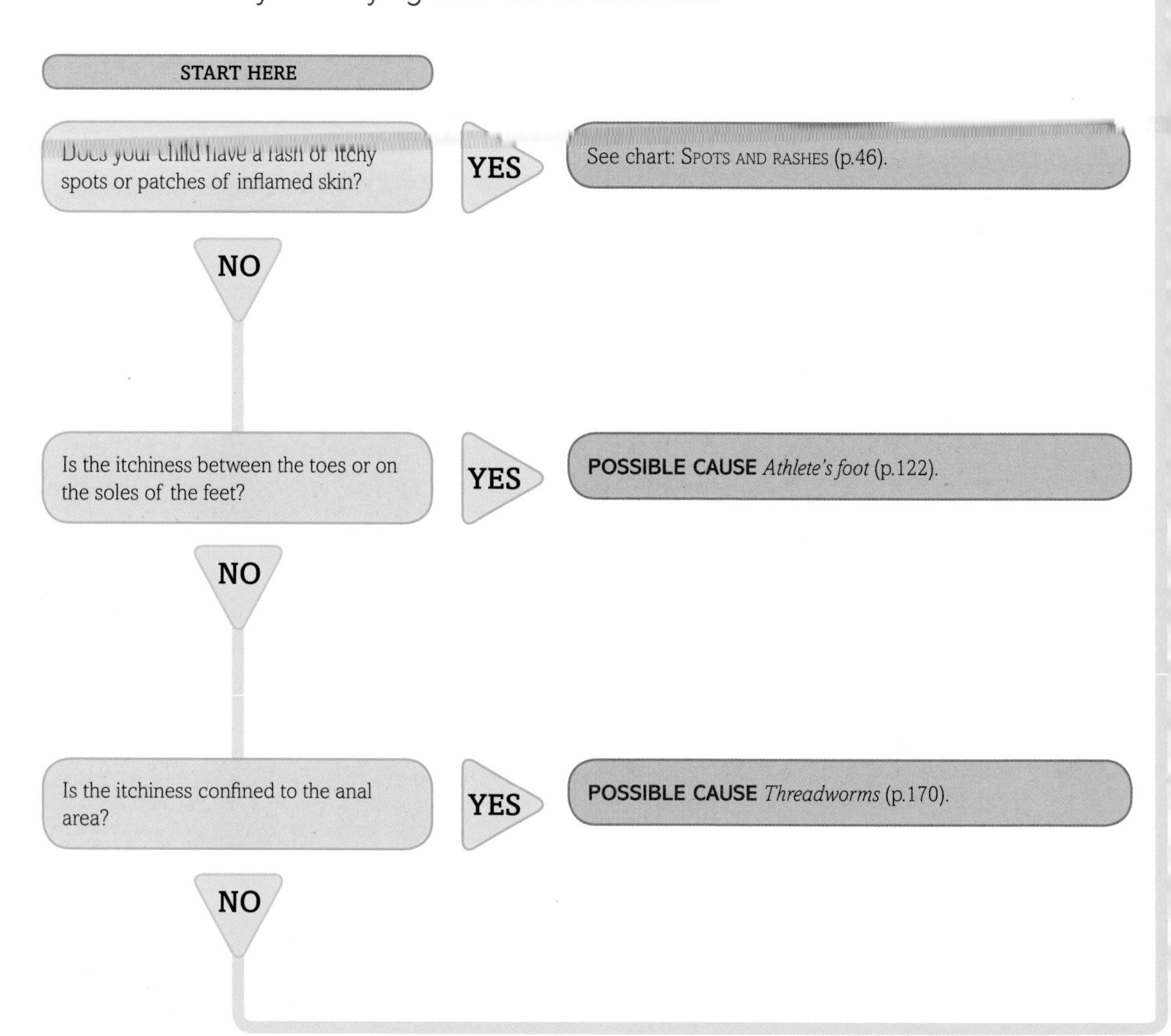

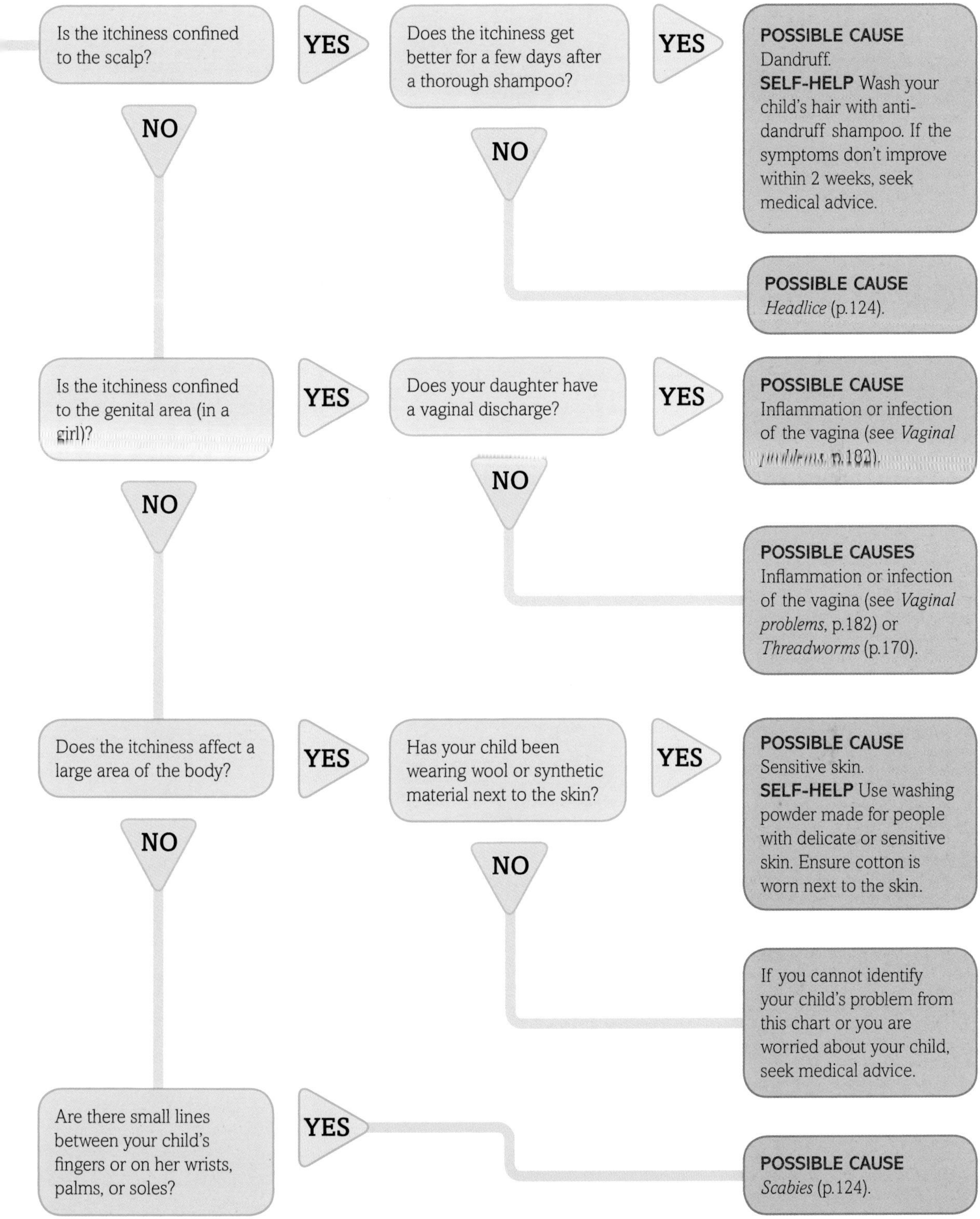

Is the itchiness confined to the scalp?

YES → Does the itchiness get better for a few days after a thorough shampoo?

YES → **POSSIBLE CAUSE** Dandruff. **SELF-HELP** Wash your child's hair with anti-dandruff shampoo. If the symptoms don't improve within 2 weeks, seek medical advice.

NO → **POSSIBLE CAUSE** *Headlice* (p.124).

NO ↓

Is the itchiness confined to the genital area (in a girl)?

YES → Does your daughter have a vaginal discharge?

YES → **POSSIBLE CAUSE** Inflammation or infection of the vagina (see *Vaginal problems*, p.182).

NO → **POSSIBLE CAUSES** Inflammation or infection of the vagina (see *Vaginal problems*, p.182) or *Threadworms* (p.170).

NO ↓

Does the itchiness affect a large area of the body?

YES → Has your child been wearing wool or synthetic material next to the skin?

YES → **POSSIBLE CAUSE** Sensitive skin. **SELF-HELP** Use washing powder made for people with delicate or sensitive skin. Ensure cotton is worn next to the skin.

NO → If you cannot identify your child's problem from this chart or you are worried about your child, seek medical advice.

NO ↓

Are there small lines between your child's fingers or on her wrists, palms, or soles?

YES → **POSSIBLE CAUSE** *Scabies* (p.124).

Lumps and swellings

Lumps and swellings occur on, or just below, the skin surface. Swellings may be lymph glands that have swollen to fight infection. Injuries, bites, and stings can also cause lumps and swellings. Any lump that persists should be seen by a doctor.

START HERE

Does your child have a painful red lump on the skin?

POSSIBLE CAUSES *Boil* (p.117) or an insect sting (see *Insect bites and stings*, p.126).

NO

Does your child have a soft lump in the groin or at the navel?

POSSIBLE CAUSES *Inguinal hernia* (p.100) or *Umbilical hernia* (p.100).

NO

Does your child have a tender swelling near an infected cut or graze?

POSSIBLE CAUSE The swelling is probably a nearby lymph gland, which has become swollen as it helps to fight the infection.
Seek medical advice If your child's swelling or pain persists for more than a week.

NO

Does your child have a tender lump on the head?

Did your child have a recent accident or injury that involved banging the head?

POSSIBLE CAUSE *Head injury* (p.186).

NO

NO

If you cannot identify your child's problem from this chart or you're worried about your child, seek medical advice.

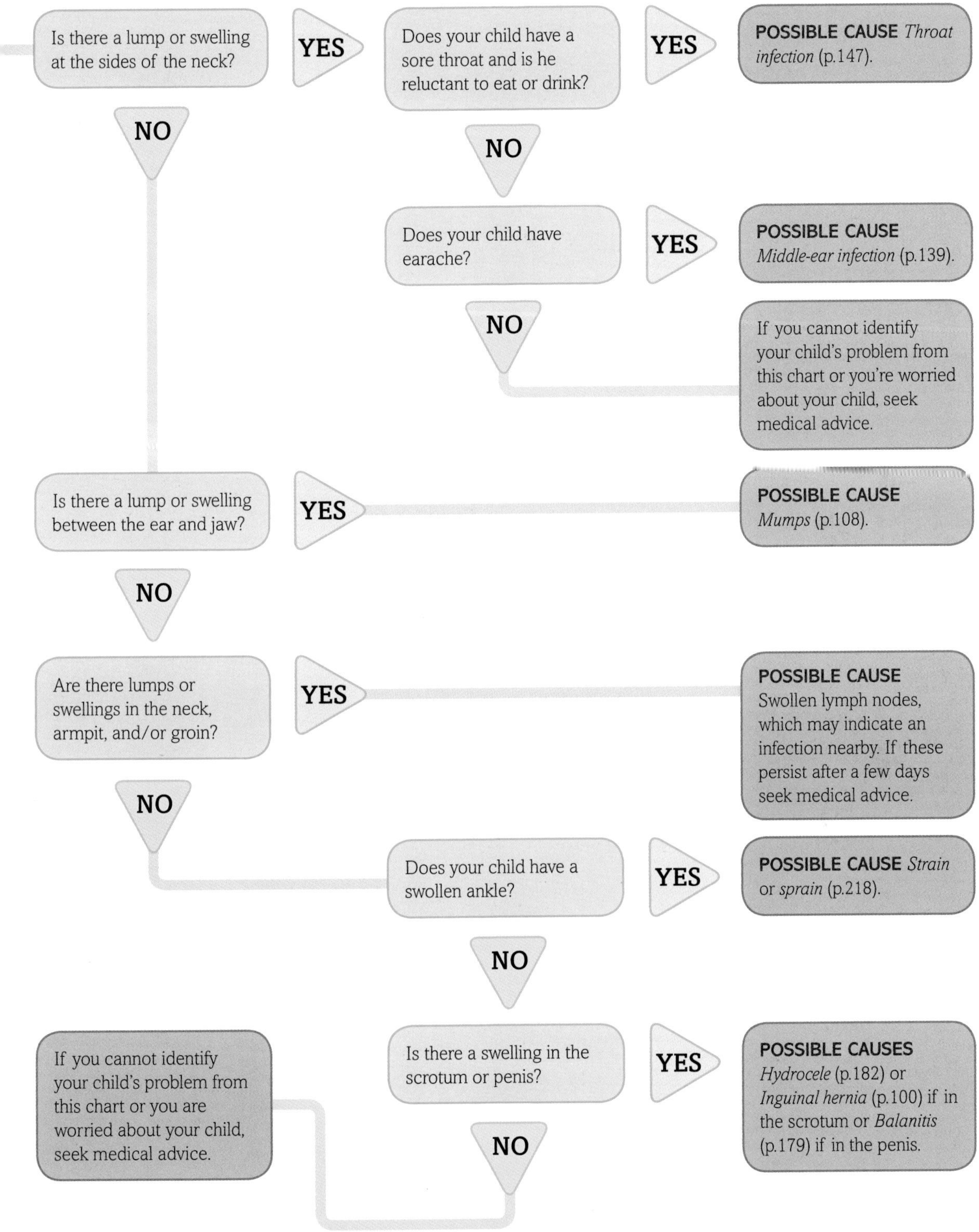

Is there a lump or swelling at the sides of the neck?

YES → Does your child have a sore throat and is he reluctant to eat or drink?

YES → **POSSIBLE CAUSE** *Throat infection* (p.147).

NO → Does your child have earache?

YES → **POSSIBLE CAUSE** *Middle-ear infection* (p.139).

NO → If you cannot identify your child's problem from this chart or you're worried about your child, seek medical advice.

NO → Is there a lump or swelling between the ear and jaw?

YES → **POSSIBLE CAUSE** *Mumps* (p.108).

NO → Are there lumps or swellings in the neck, armpit, and/or groin?

YES → **POSSIBLE CAUSE** Swollen lymph nodes, which may indicate an infection nearby. If these persist after a few days seek medical advice.

NO → Does your child have a swollen ankle?

YES → **POSSIBLE CAUSE** *Strain* or *sprain* (p.218).

NO → Is there a swelling in the scrotum or penis?

YES → **POSSIBLE CAUSES** *Hydrocele* (p.182) or *Inguinal hernia* (p.100) if in the scrotum or *Balanitis* (p.179) if in the penis.

NO → If you cannot identify your child's problem from this chart or you are worried about your child, seek medical advice.

Feeling generally unwell

If your child complains of feeling unwell, check his temperature and look for a rash. A symptom, such as being tired, may clear up with self-help measures, or it may be the first sign of an infection, such as flu.

Danger signs

Call an ambulance if your baby has either of the following symptoms:

★ Abnormal drowsiness or irritability

★ Flat, pink or purple spots that do not disappear when pressed

★ Fast or noisy breathing

Seek medical advice immediately if your baby has any of the following:

★ Temperature over 39°C (102°F)

★ Persistent vomiting

★ Refusing to drink for 6 hours

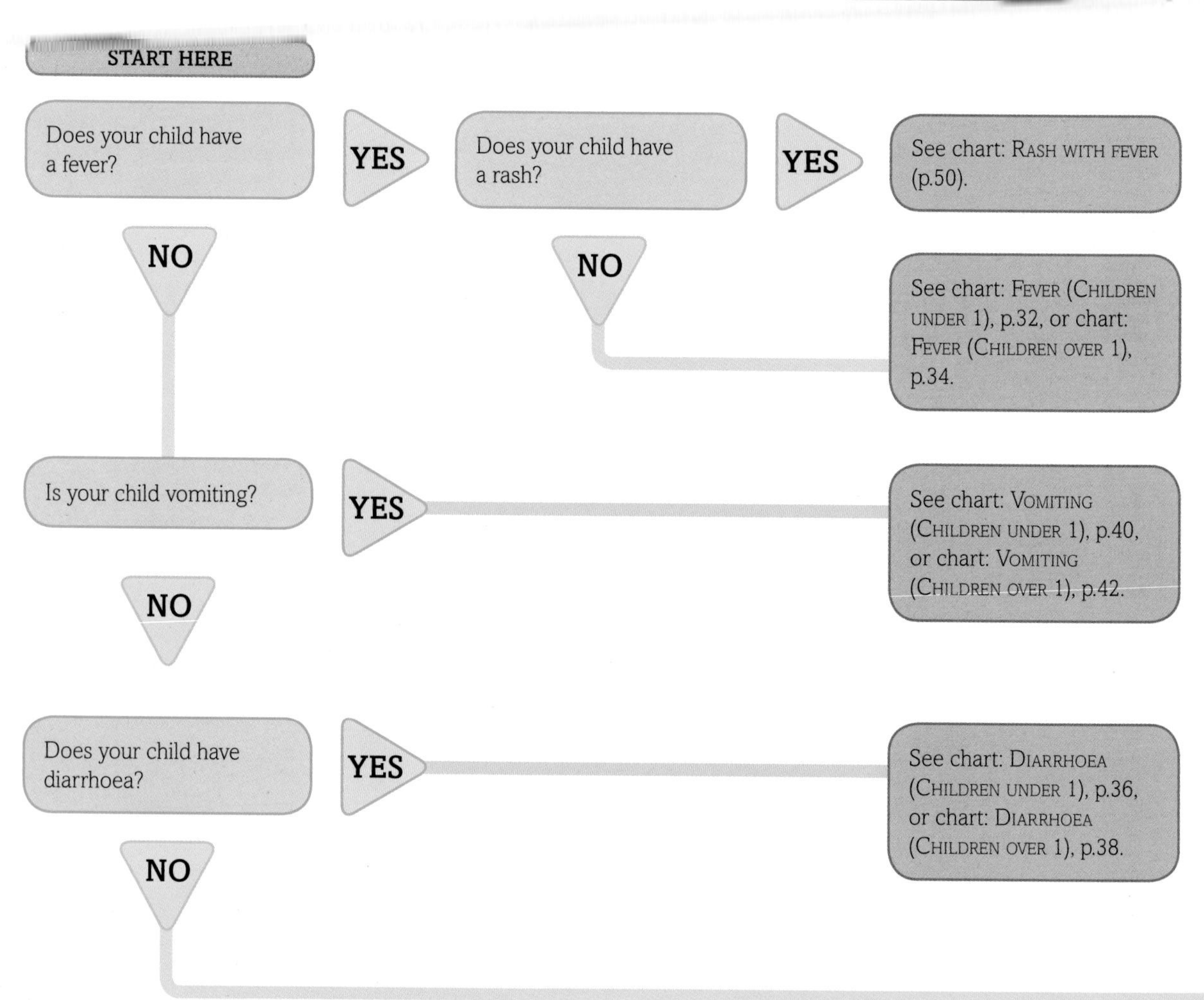

Is your child suffering from abdominal pain?

YES

See chart: ABDOMINAL PAIN (p.76).

Is your child eating and/or drinking less than usual?

YES

POSSIBLE CAUSE Your child may be developing an infectious disease, particularly if she has other signs of illness, such as irritability or listlessness.
Seek medical advice if your child feels no better after 24 hours or if she develops other symptoms.

NO

In the past 3 weeks is it possible that your child had contact with someone who has an infectious disease?

YES

POSSIBLE CAUSE One of the childhood infectious diseases in its incubation period may causing your child to feel unwell.
Seek medical advice if your child feels no better after 24 hours or if she develops other symptoms.

NO

Could your child be worried or anxious about something?

YES

POSSIBLE CAUSES Anxiety or problems at school can cause a child to feel unwell (see *Anxiety and fears*, p.195).

NO

If you cannot identify your child's problem from this chart or you are worried about your child, seek medical advice.

Abnormal drowsiness or confusion

Drowsiness may simply be a result of lack of sleep or a minor illness, or it may be a symptom of a serious disease, such as meningitis. Confusion – which includes appearing dazed or agitated, or talking nonsense – is always a serious symptom that requires immediate medical attention.

START HERE

Did your child have a recent accident or fall that involved banging the head?

POSSIBLE CAUSE *Head injury* (p.186)
EMERGENCY Call an ambulance While waiting, do not give your child anything to eat or drink.

Do you think your child might have swallowed any poisonous plants or fungi, household cleaners, alcohol, or other harmful substance?

EMERGENCY Call an ambulance
See also p.217 for first aid advice on poisoning.

Does your child have a fever?

POSSIBLE CAUSE A high fever, resulting from any infection, can cause confusion and abnormal drowsiness, particularly if your child's temperature exceeds 39°C (102°F).
EMERGENCY Call an ambulance
See also *Bringing down a fever* (p.29).

NO

Does your child have diarrhoea with or without vomiting?

POSSIBLE CAUSE Your child may be suffering from dehydration as a result of *Gastroenteritis* (p.168).
EMERGENCY Call an ambulance

Does your child have any of the following symptoms: headache; vomiting; stiff neck; flat, pink or purple spots that do not disappear when pressed?

POSSIBLE CAUSE *Meningitis* (p.102).
EMERGENCY Call an ambulance

Has your child lost weight or seemed unusually tired during the last few weeks?

NO

Does your child seem to be suffering from excessive thirst?

Has your child been passing urine with increased frequency?

POSSIBLE CAUSE *Diabetes mellitus* (p.188). **EMERGENCY Call an ambulance**

NO

EMERGENCY Call an ambulance if you cannot identify your child's problem from this chart.

Have you been giving your child over-the-counter or prescribed medicines?

POSSIBLE CAUSE Certain medicines, such as antihistamines given for allergies, can cause confusion or have a sedative effect on some children. **Seek medical advice** to find out whether the medicine may be causing your child's symptoms and whether you should stop giving it.

Dizziness, fainting, and seizures

Danger signs

Call an ambulance if your child loses consciousness (does not respond to external stimuli, such as a tap on the shoulder) and:

★ Breathing becomes slower, irregular, or noisy

★ Twitching of the face or limbs, passing urine, or injury such as biting the tongue occurs

Dizziness is a reeling or spinning sensation, which may be accompanied by faintness or light-headedness. Fainting is a brief loss of consciousness caused by a fall in blood pressure. In a seizure, consciousness may also be lost, but it is a result of abnormal electrical activity in the brain.

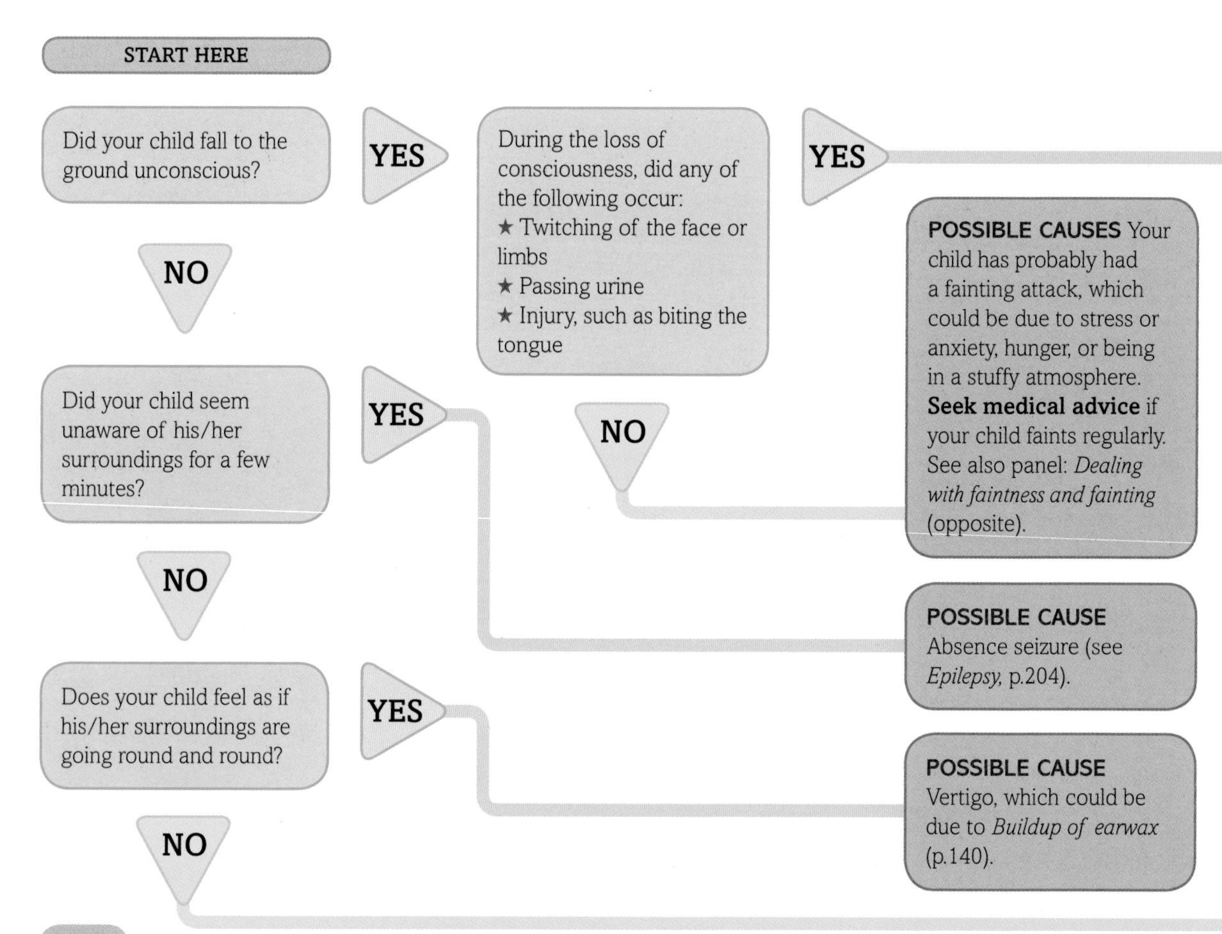

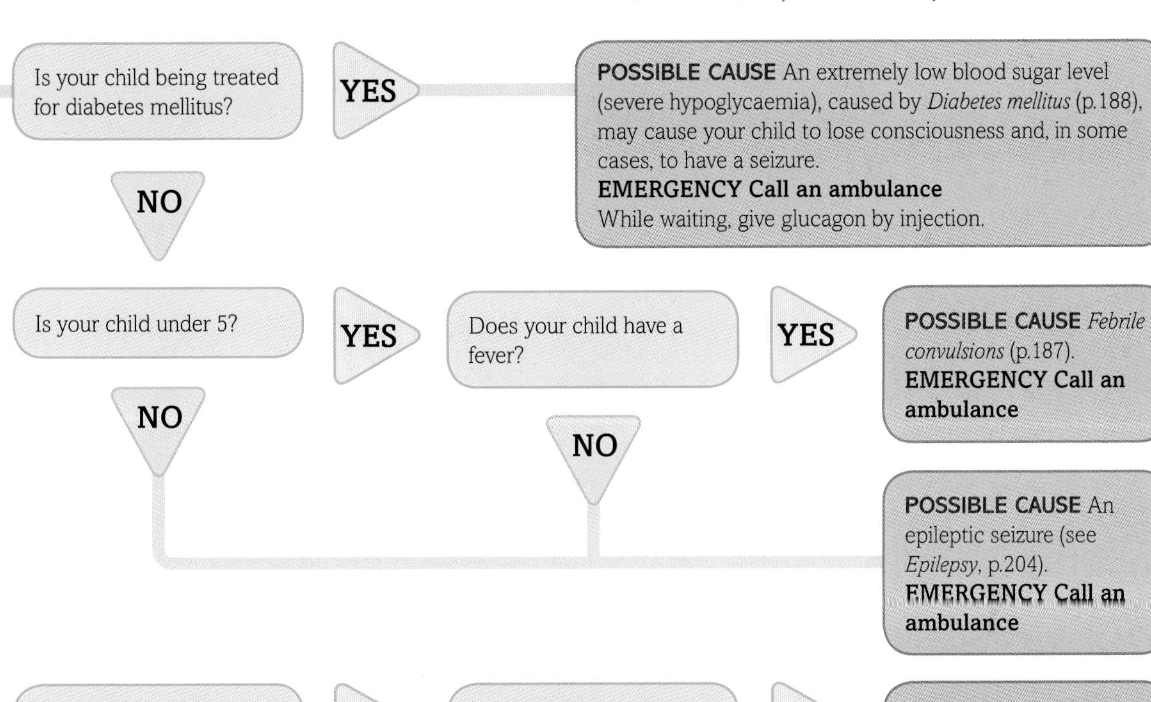

Does your child feel faint or unsteady?

YES

Is your child being treated for diabetes mellitus?

YES

POSSIBLE CAUSE Low blood sugar level due to *Diabetes mellitus* (p.188).

NO

NO

If you cannot identify your child's problem from this chart or you are worried about your child, seek medical advice.

POSSIBLE CAUSES Hunger, anxiety, or being in a stuffy atmosphere are all possible causes of faintness.
URGENT Seek medical advice immediately if your child has not shown signs of recovery within 30 minutes.
See also panel: *Dealing with faintness and fainting* (left).

Dealing with faintness and fainting

Feeling faint or fainting can occur if not enough blood and oxygen reach the brain If your child feels faint, take the following measures.

★ Lay her down with her legs propped up on several cushions to increase the blood supply to the brain.
★ Loosen tight clothing and make sure there is plenty of fresh air.
★ Calm and reassure her.
★ Faintness can be caused by low blood sugar, so a sugary drink or small snack may help. Do not offer food or drink if your child is not fully conscious.
★ If your child loses consciousness, follow the first aid advice on pp.210–213.
★ If your child faints frequently or without an obvious cause seek medical advice.

Disturbed or impaired vision

Any problem with a child's vision should be investigated promptly. Usually, any defects are picked up in the routine eye tests most children have at school. Alternatively, it may be you or the teacher who notices a problem.

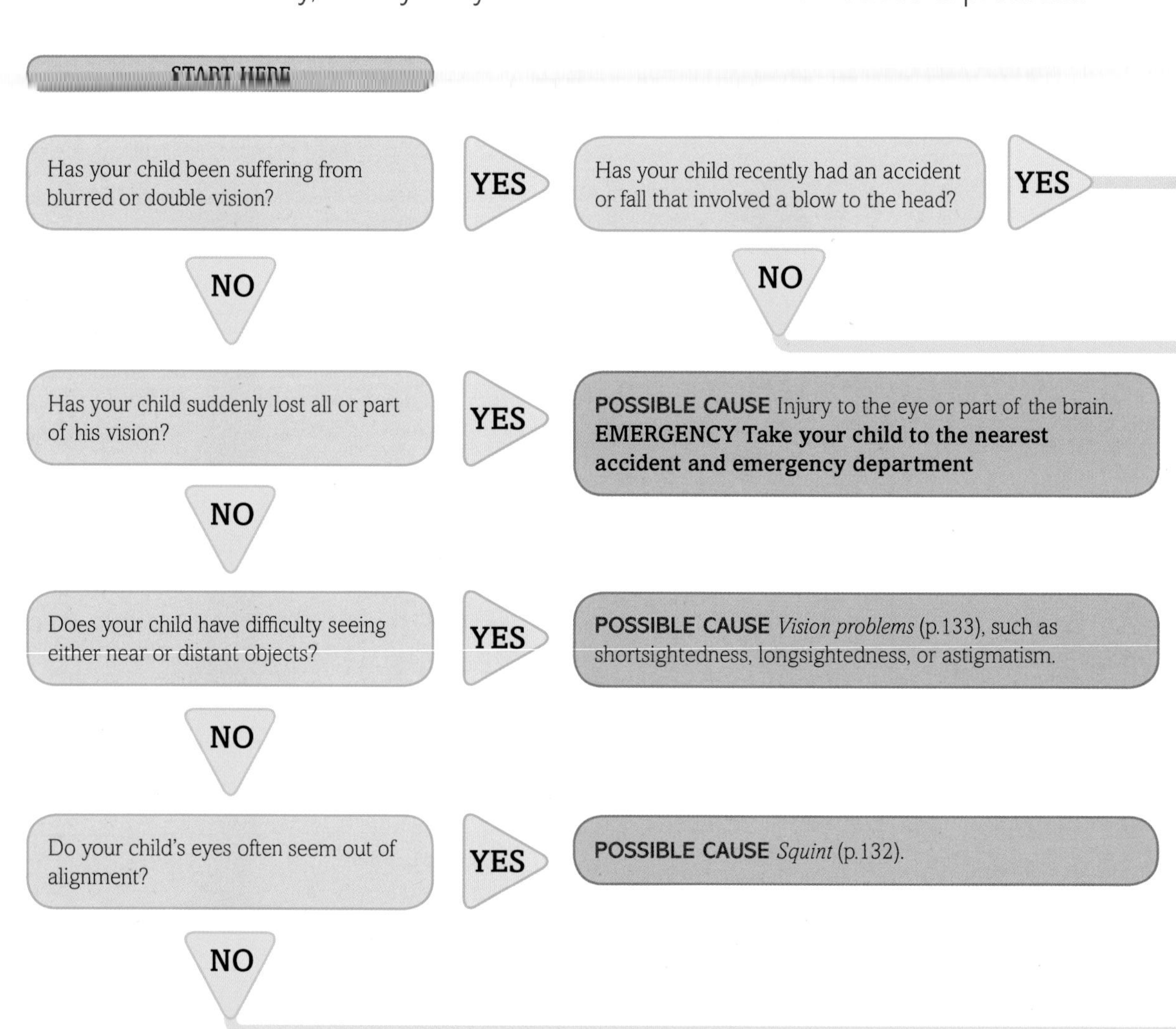

POSSIBLE CAUSE *Head injury* (p.186).
EMERGENCY Take your child to the nearest accident and emergency department

Does your child have vision problems associated with headaches?

YES

POSSIBLE CAUSE *Migraine* (p.185).

NO

Are you giving your child any medicine?

YES

POSSIBLE CAUSE Some drugs may cause blurred vision. **Seek medical advice** to find out whether the medicine may be causing your child's symptoms and whether you should stop giving it.

NO

Could your child have taken someone else's medicine?

YES

POSSIBLE CAUSE Accidental poisoning by drugs, especially some antidepressants, may cause blurred vision.
URGENT Seek medical advice immediately
See also p.217 for first aid advice on poisoning.

NO

POSSIBLE CAUSES *Vision problems* (p.133), such as shortsightedness, longsightedness, or astigmatism, or a *Squint* (p.132).

Does your child have recurrent attacks of seeing flashing lights or floating spots, with a severe headache afterwards?

YES

POSSIBLE CAUSE *Migraine* (p.185).

NO

If you cannot identify your child's problem from this chart or you are worried about your child, seek medical advice.

Painful or itchy ear

Earache is usually caused by infection. Young children are particularly prone to middle-ear infections because the tubes connecting the ears and nose are shorter and more horizontal than in adults and can become easily blocked. The outer ear canal can be affected by disorders that cause symptoms such as itchiness or discharge.

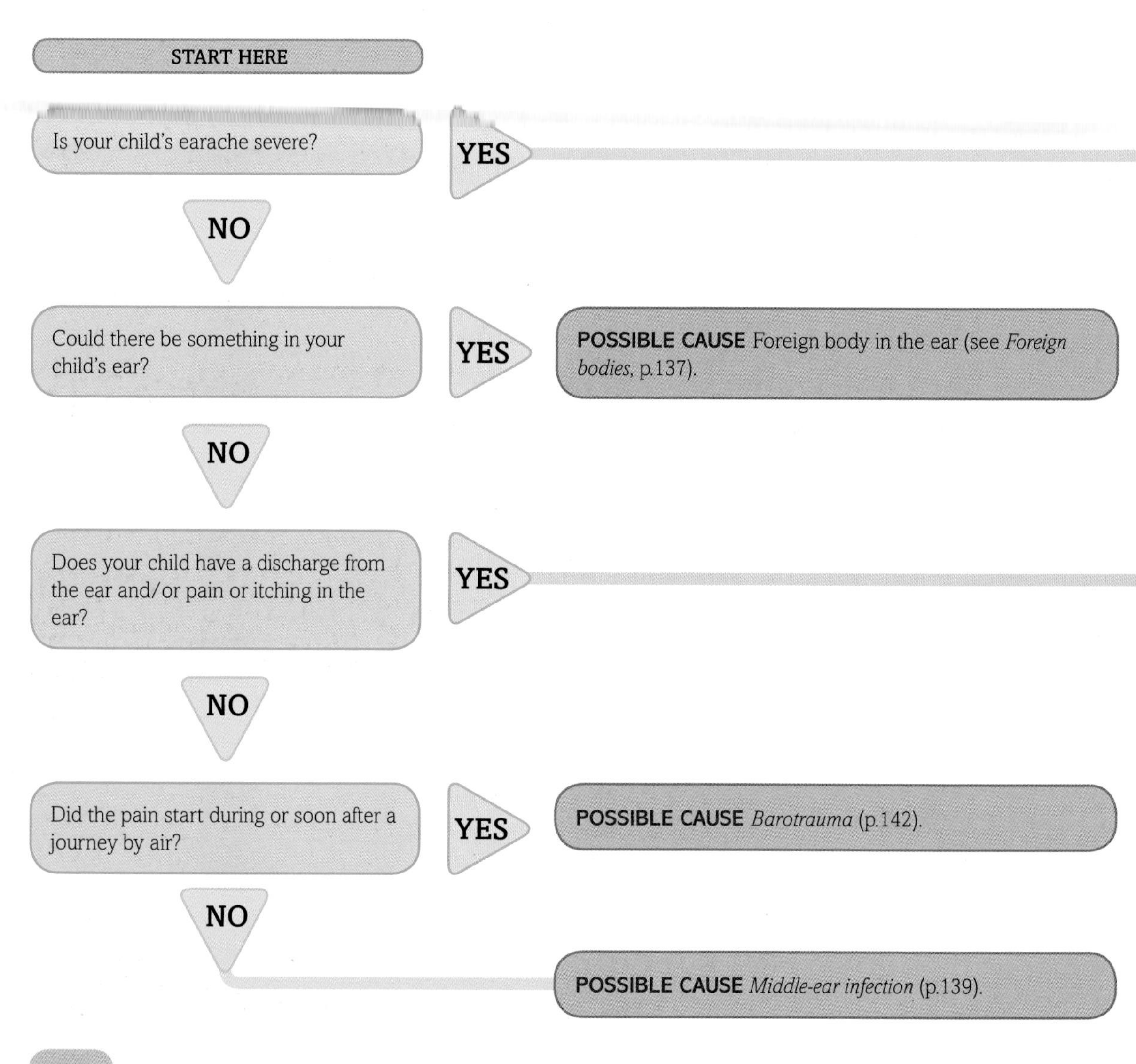

Does your child have a cold or sore throat or seem generally unwell?

YES

POSSIBLE CAUSE *Middle-ear infection* (p.139).

NO

Does your child have a red lump inside his ear?

YES

POSSIBLE CAUSE *Boil* (p.117) in the outer ear canal.

NO

POSSIBLE CAUSE *Inflamed ear canal* (p.138).

Does gently tugging on your child's earlobe make pain worse?

YES

POSSIBLE CAUSES *Eczema* (p.114), *Inflamed ear canal* (p.138), *Middle-ear infection* (p.139), or an unsuspected foreign body that has been in the ear for a while and caused an infection (see *Foreign bodies*, p.137).

NO

POSSIBLE CAUSE *Middle-ear infection* (p.139).

Hearing problems

Hearing defects are often first noticed by a child's parents. In babies, the first sign of deafness is a failure to respond to sounds. In older children, hearing problems may cause school work to deteriorate. Although hearing loss may be only temporary, it should be checked by your doctor.

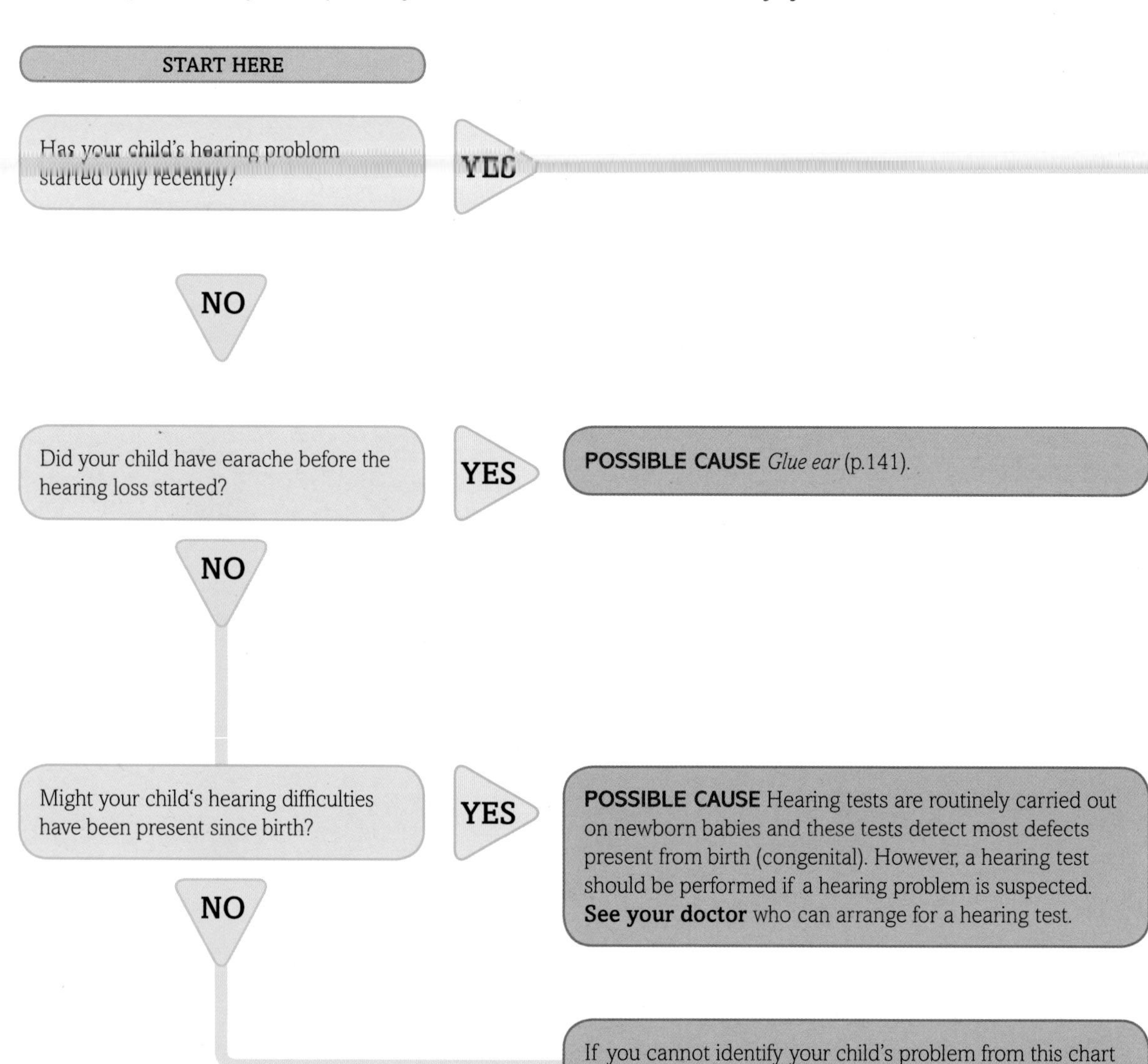

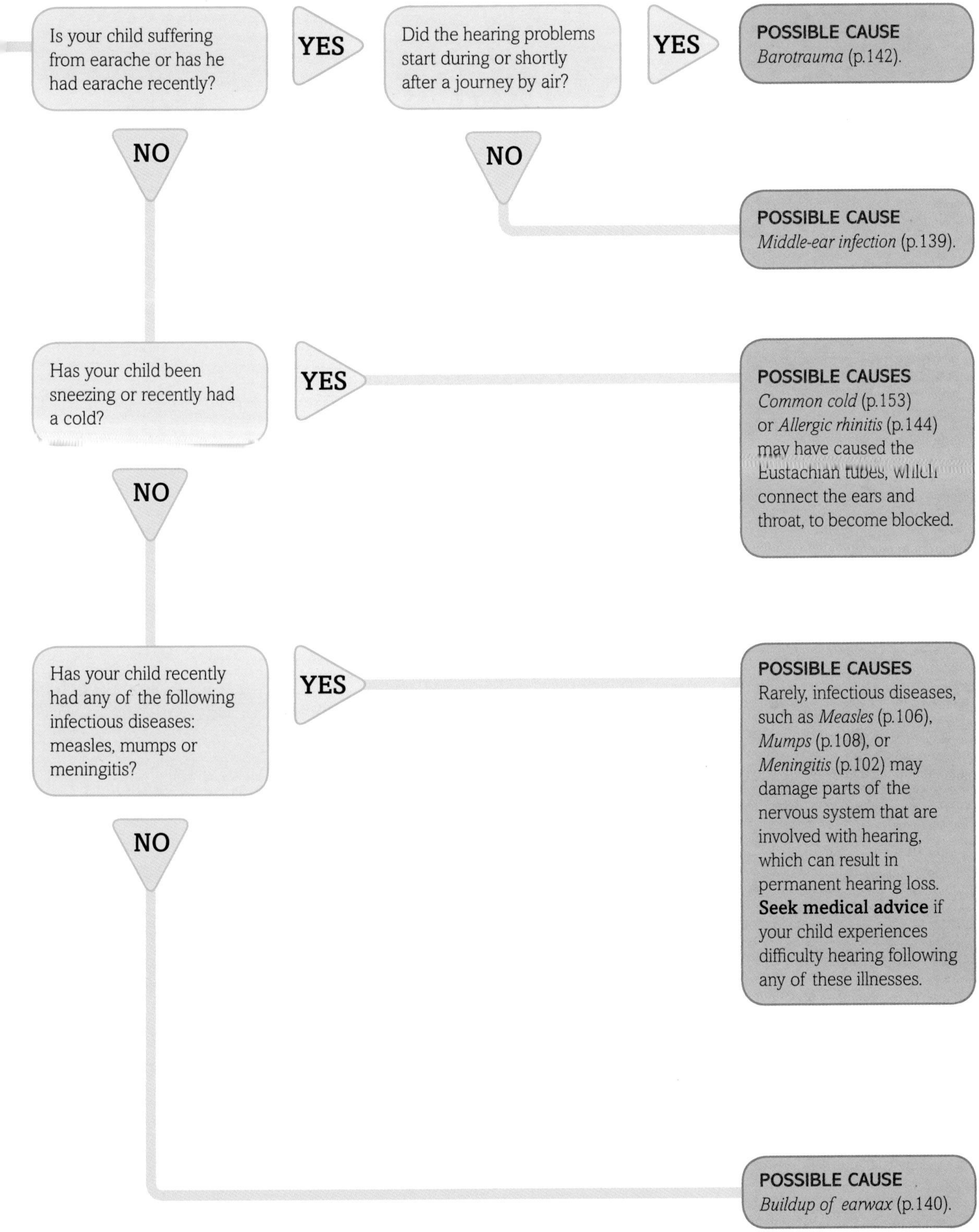

Is your child suffering from earache or has he had earache recently?

YES → Did the hearing problems start during or shortly after a journey by air?

YES → **POSSIBLE CAUSE**
Barotrauma (p.142).

NO → **POSSIBLE CAUSE**
Middle-ear infection (p.139).

NO ↓

Has your child been sneezing or recently had a cold?

YES → **POSSIBLE CAUSES**
Common cold (p.153) or *Allergic rhinitis* (p.144) may have caused the Eustachian tubes, which connect the ears and throat, to become blocked.

NO ↓

Has your child recently had any of the following infectious diseases: measles, mumps or meningitis?

YES → **POSSIBLE CAUSES**
Rarely, infectious diseases, such as *Measles* (p.106), *Mumps* (p.108), or *Meningitis* (p.102) may damage parts of the nervous system that are involved with hearing, which can result in permanent hearing loss. **Seek medical advice** if your child experiences difficulty hearing following any of these illnesses.

NO → **POSSIBLE CAUSE**
Buildup of earwax (p.140).

Coughing

In very young babies, coughing is rare and may indicate a serious lung infection. In older children, it is usually caused by a minor respiratory infection, such as a cold. Sudden coughing in an otherwise well child could indicate an airway obstruction.

Danger signs

Call an ambulance if your child has any of the following symptoms:

★ Blue-tinged lips or tongue

★ Abnormal drowsiness

★ Inability to talk or produce sounds

★ Laboured breathing – areas between and under the ribs drawing in and nostrils flaring with each breath

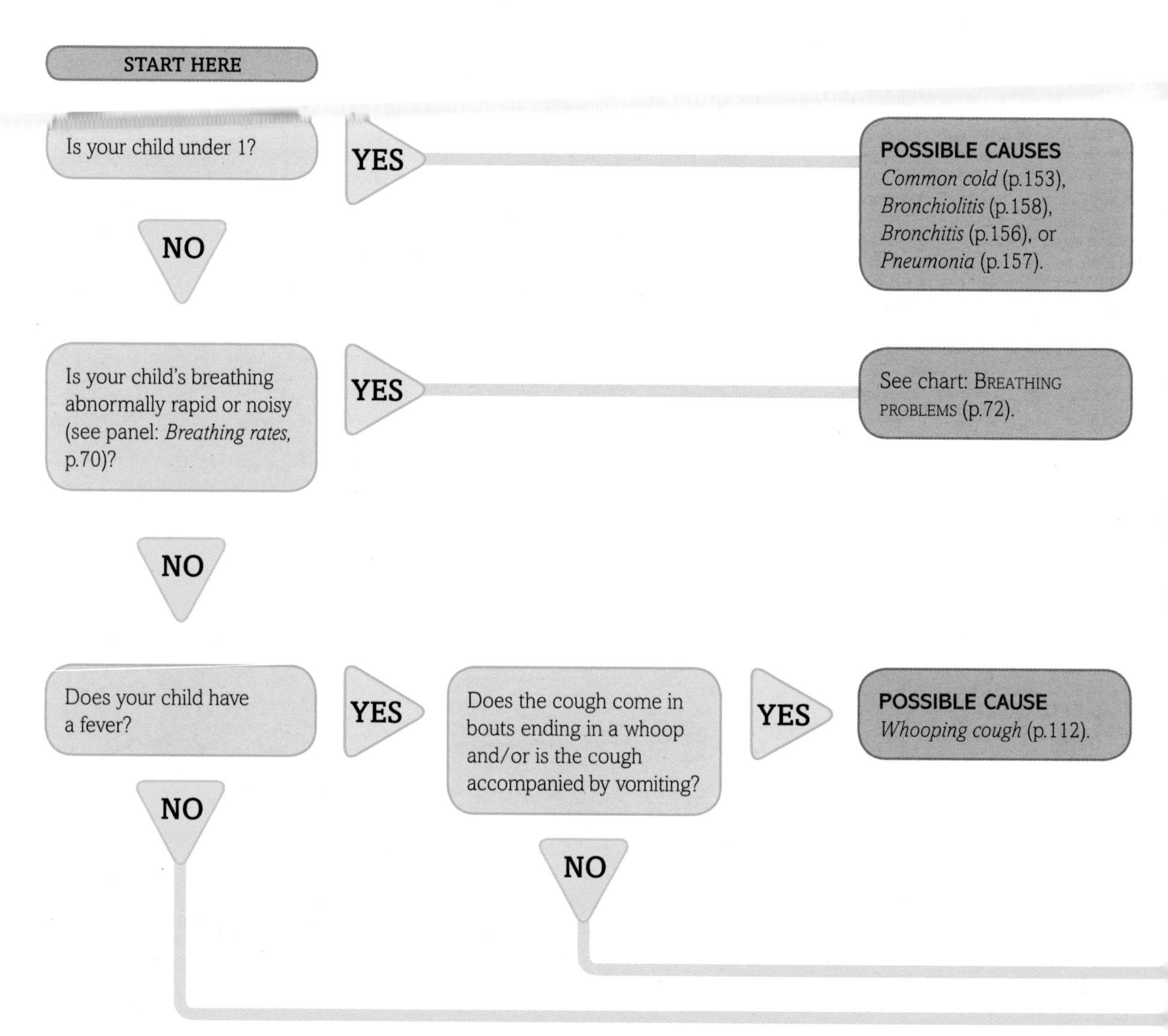

Does your child have a rash, or has your child recently been exposed to measles?

YES → **POSSIBLE CAUSE** *Measles* (p.106).

NO → **POSSIBLE CAUSE** *Common cold* (p.153).

Does your child cough mainly at night rather than during the day and night?

YES → **POSSIBLE CAUSE** *Asthma* (p.150).

NO

Does the cough come in bouts ending in a whoop and/or is the cough accompanied by vomiting?

YES → **POSSIBLE CAUSE** *Whooping cough* (p.112).

NO

Has your child been coughing for 24 hours or more?

YES → continued on page 70

NO

Does your child have a stuffy or runny nose?

YES → **POSSIBLE CAUSES** *Common cold* (p.153) or *Influenza* (p.154).

NO → **POSSIBLE CAUSE** Your child may be choking on an object he has put in his mouth and inhaled.
URGENT Seek medical advice immediately
See pp.214–215 for first aid advice on choking.

continued from page 69

Is your child's nose persistently runny?

YES

POSSIBLE CAUSES *Enlarged adenoids* (p.146), Recurrent colds (see *Common cold*, p.153), or *Allergic rhinitis* (p.144).

NO

Has your child had whooping cough within the last few months?

YES

POSSIBLE CAUSE Cough persisting after *Whooping cough* (p.112).

NO

Has your child been diagnosed with asthma?

YES

POSSIBLE CAUSE *Asthma* (p.150).

NO

Are there smokers in your home, or might your child have been smoking?

YES

POSSIBLE CAUSE Irritation of the throat and lungs as a result of being in a smoky atmosphere. **SELF-HELP** Make sure no one smokes around your child.

NO

If you cannot identify your child's problem from this chart or you are worried about your child, seek medical advice.

Breathing rates

A child whose breathing rate is unusually rapid may need medical attention. To check your child's breathing, make sure she is resting, then count the number of breaths over one minute. Normal rates are:

- ★ Up to 1 year: 30–60 breaths per minute.
- ★ 1 to 3 years: 24–40 breaths per minute
- ★ 3 to 6 years: 22–34 breaths per minute
- ★ 6 to 12 years: 18–30 breaths per minute

Sore throat

Most sore throats in children are caused by minor viral infections that clear up quickly without treatment. Occasionally, however, a sore throat may indicate a more serious problem, such as scarlet fever. In very young children, reluctance to eat or drink may be a sign of a sore throat.

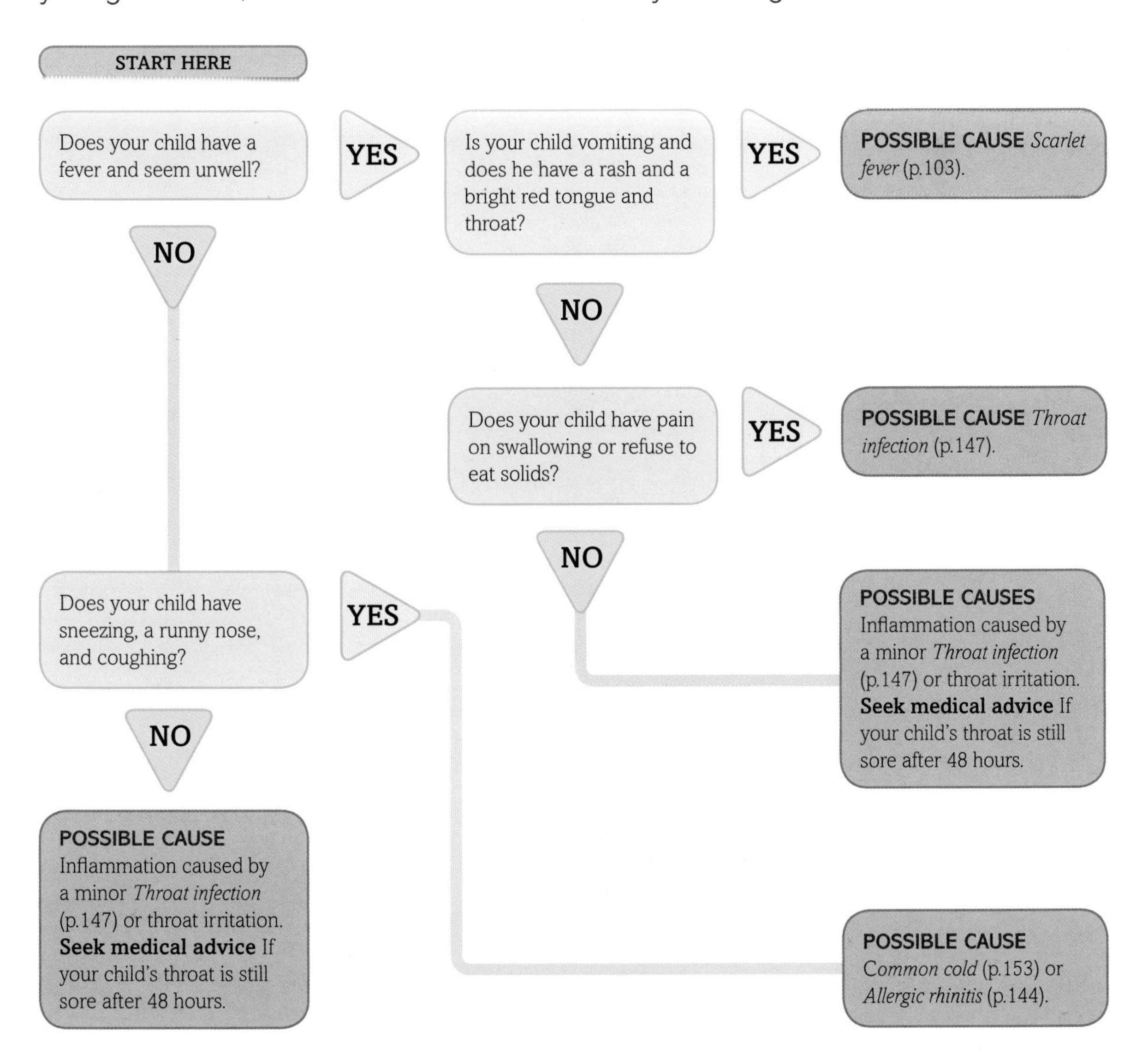

Breathing problems

Breathing problems range from noisy or fast breathing to difficulty breathing. Many babies and children wheeze slightly when they have a minor respiratory infection. However, breathing problems can be serious.

Danger signs

Call an ambulance if your child has any of the following symptoms:

- ★ Blue-tinged lips or tongue
- ★ Abnormal drowsiness
- ★ Inability to talk or produce sounds normally
- ★ Laboured breathing – muscles in between and under the ribs drawing in and nostrils flaring with each breath

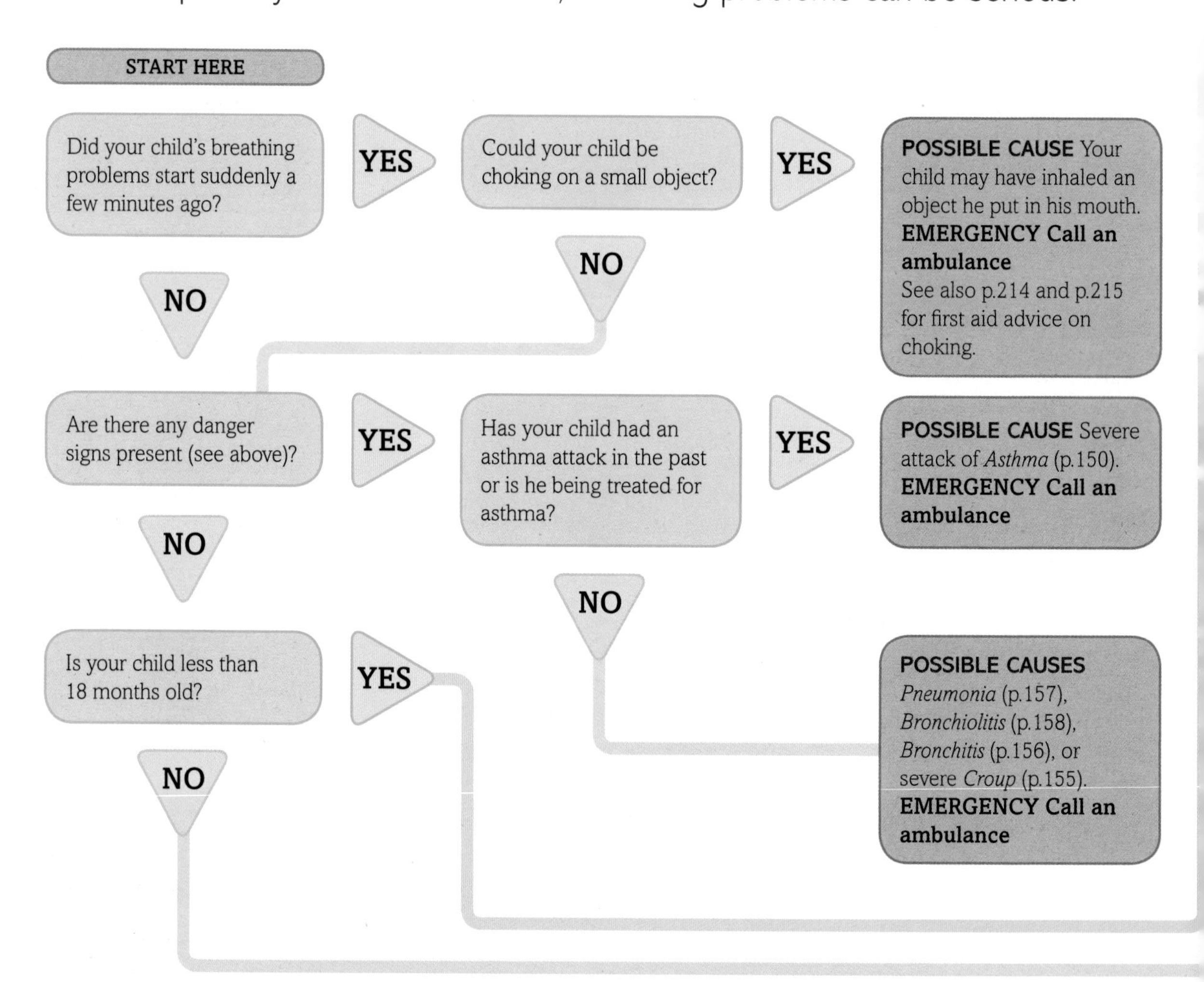

Has your child had noisy breathing since birth but otherwise been well?

YES

POSSIBLE CAUSE Your baby's voice box (larynx) may be flopping in on itself during inhalation, causing a noise. This is called congenital laryngeal stridor. In most cases no treatment is needed and it improves by between 18 months and 2 years of age. However, if you are concerned about your baby's breathing take her to see your doctor immediately.

NO

Does your child suffer from repeated episodes of any of these symptoms?

- Wheezing
- Shortness of breath
- Coughing at night

YES

POSSIBLE CAUSE *Asthma* (p.150).

NO

Does your child have fast breathing, fever, and a cough?

YES

POSSIBLE CAUSES *Pneumonia* (p.157), *Bronchiolitis* (p.158), *Bronchitis* (p.156), or *Croup* (p.155).
URGENT Seek immediate medical advice

NO

Does your child have a hoarse voice, noisy breathing, and a barking cough?

YES

POSSIBLE CAUSE *Croup* (p.155).

NO

POSSIBLE CAUSES *Asthma* (p.150) or *Bronchitis* (p.156).

Mouth problems

Most problems affecting the lips, tongue, gums, and inside of the mouth are minor. However, a sore mouth may make your child miserable and eating and drinking painful. In an infant, mouth pain may be due to teething, which may be relieved by chewing on a hard or cold object.

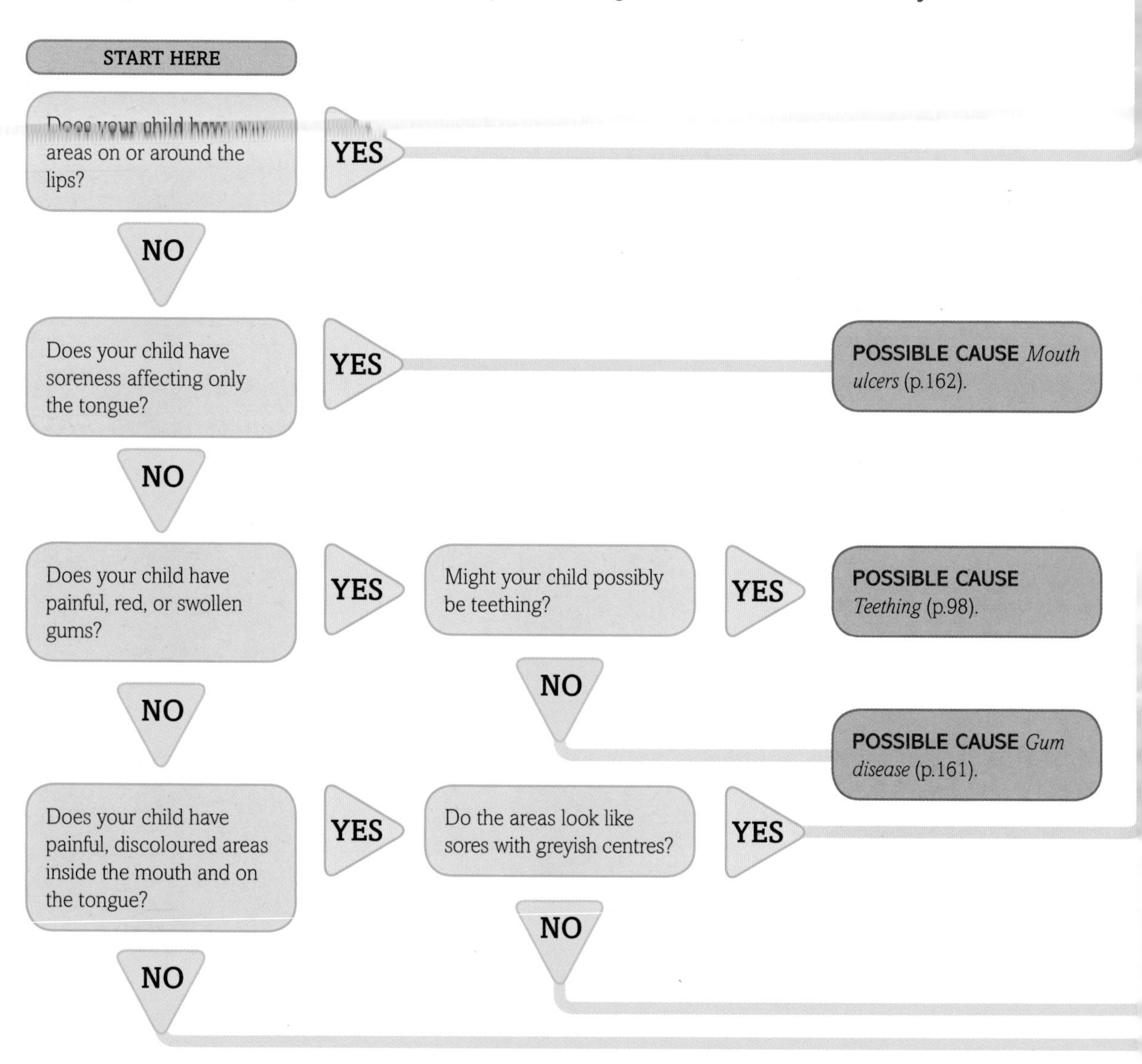

Are there tiny blisters or sores on or around the lips?

YES

POSSIBLE CAUSE *Cold sores* (p.119).

NO

Is there redness around the mouth or cracks at the corners of the lips?

YES

POSSIBLE CAUSE Lick eczema, which is skin irritation around the mouth due to drooling, continually licking the area, or thumb sucking.
SELF-HELP Apply petroleum jelly to the affected area every few hours. Use a lip salve to moisturize and protect the lips themselves. Children usually grow out of their lip-licking habit or thumb-sucking habits by the time they go to school and the eczema then disappears.

NO

Are there straw- or honey-coloured crusts around the lips?

YES

POSSIBLE CAUSE *Impetigo* (p.118).

NO

If you cannot identify your child's problem from this chart or you are worried about your child, seek medical advice.

Does your child have spots on her hands and feet?

YES

POSSIBLE CAUSE *Hand, foot, and mouth disease* (p.109).

NO

POSSIBLE CAUSE *Mouth ulcers* (p.162).

Are the spots creamy-yellow and easily scraped off?

YES

POSSIBLE CAUSE *Oral thrush* (p.99).

NO

If you cannot identify your child's problem from this chart or you are worried about your child, seek medical advice.

Abdominal pain

Every child has occasional abdominal pain and some children have recurrent bouts. Usually the cause is minor and the pain disappears quickly without treatment. Rarely, there may be a serious cause requiring medical attention.

Danger signs

Call an ambulance if your child has any of the following:

- ★ Abdominal pain for 6 hours
- ★ Pain or swelling in the groin or testes
- ★ Greenish-yellow vomit
- ★ Red material (blood) in faeces

START HERE

Does your child have a painful swelling in the groin or scrotum?

YES → **POSSIBLE CAUSES** Strangulated *Inguinal hernia* (p.100) or *Testicular torsion* (p.207). **EMERGENCY Call an ambulance** While waiting, do not give your child anything to eat or drink.

NO

Has your child had continuous pain for 6 hours?

YES → **POSSIBLE CAUSES** *Appendicitis* (p.172) or *Swollen abdominal glands* (p.172). **EMERGENCY Call an ambulance** While waiting, do not give your child anything to eat or drink.

NO

Is the pain aggravated when the abdomen is gently pressed?

YES → **POSSIBLE CAUSE** *Appendicitis* (p.172). **URGENT Seek medical advice immediately**

NO

Has your child been vomiting?

YES

Has your child been in continuous pain for 3 hours?

YES

POSSIBLE CAUSE *Appendicitis* (p.172).
URGENT Seek medical advice immediately

NO

Has your child been bringing up greenish-yellow vomit?

YES

POSSIBLE CAUSE *Intestinal obstruction* (p.205).
EMERGENCY Call an ambulance While waiting, do not give your child anything to eat or drink.

NO

NO

Does your child have either of the following symptoms?
- Diarrhoea with or without vomiting
- Pain that is relieved by vomiting or passing faeces

YES

POSSIBLE CAUSE *Gastroenteritis* (p.168).

NO

Does your child have red material (blood) in his faeces?

YES

POSSIBLE CAUSE Intussusception (see *Intestinal obstruction*, p.205).
EMERGENCY Call an ambulance While waiting, do not give your child anything to eat or drink.

NO

continued on page 78

continued from page 77

Does your child have any of the following symptoms?
- Sore throat
- Cough
- Stuffy or runny nose

POSSIBLE CAUSES *Common cold* (p.153), *Influenza* (p.154), *Throat infection* (p.147), or *Swollen abdominal glands* (p.172).

NO

Does your child have two or more of the following symptoms?
- Fever
- Pain on passing urine
- Bed-wetting (after being dry at night)
- Frequent urination

YES

POSSIBLE CAUSE *Urinary tract infection* (p.178).

NO

Does your child often have bouts of recurrent abdominal pain without seeming otherwise unwell?

YES

POSSIBLE CAUSES Anxiety (see *Anxiety and fears*, p.170) or *Food intolerance* (p.163) may be the explanation, but often there is no obvious cause (see *Recurrent abdominal pain*, p.174).

NO

If you cannot identify your child's problem from this chart or you are worried about your child, seek medical advice.

Abnormal-looking faeces

The colour, smell, consistency, and content of a baby's faeces are highly variable. However, if there is a sudden change in faeces accompanied by other symptoms, or faeces are white, red (contain blood), or black you should seek medical advice.

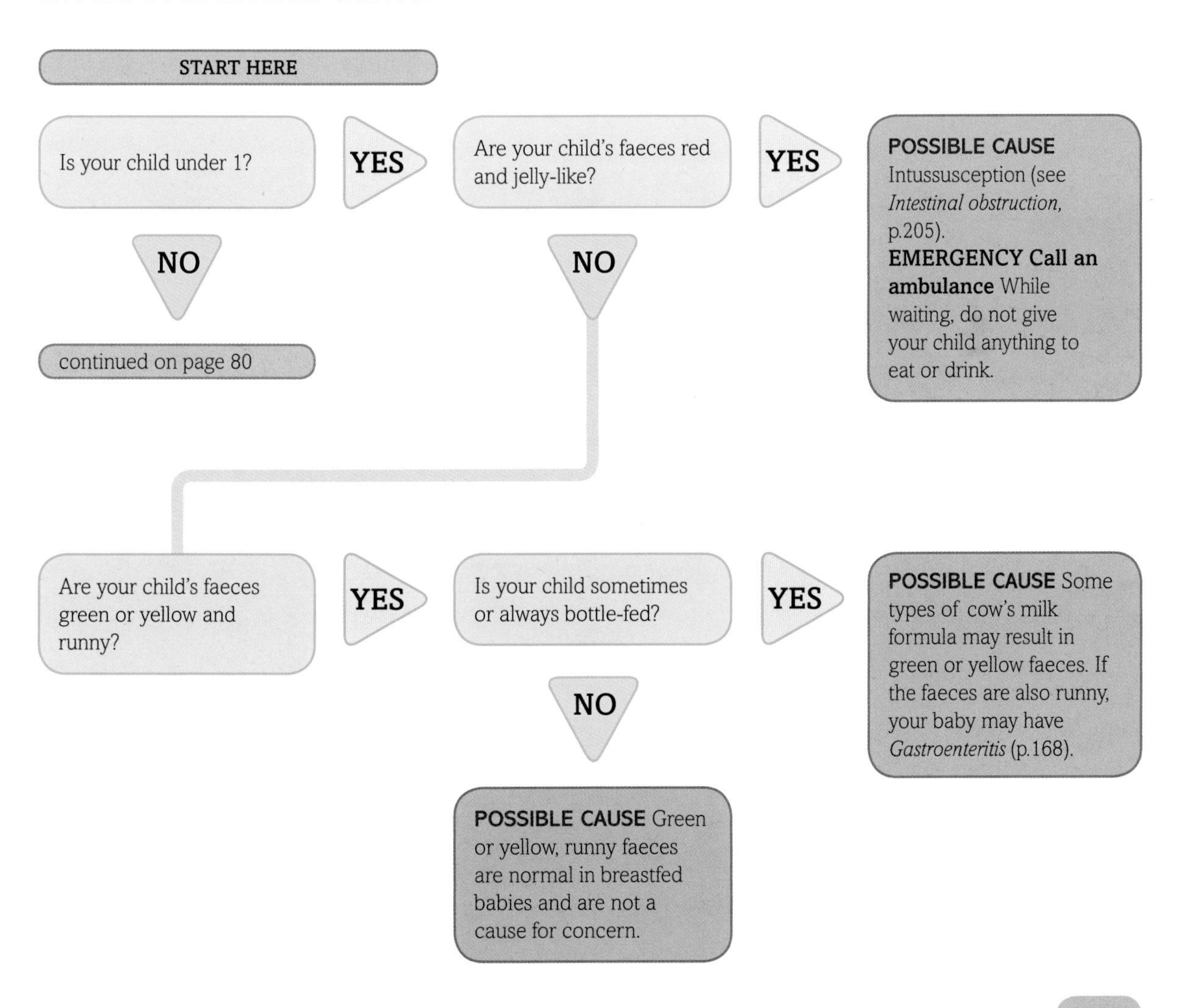

continued from page 79

Is your child taking any medicine?

YES

POSSIBLE CAUSE Many medicines can affect the appearance of faeces.
Seek medical advice to find out if the medicine may be causing your child's symptoms and if you should stop giving it.

NO

Are your child's faeces very pale but otherwise unchanged?

YES

NO

Are your child's faeces pale and foul-smelling and do they float in the toilet and are hard to flush away?

YES

POSSIBLE CAUSES Failure of the intestines to absorb nutrients from food, which could be due to *Food intolerance* (p.163), *Food allergy* (p.164), or *Cystic fibrosis* (p.204).

NO

Do your child's faeces have blood on them?

YES

POSSIBLE CAUSES *Gastroenteritis* (p.168), Anal fissure (see *Constipation*, p.174), or inflammatory bowel disease, which includes Crohn's disease and ulcerative colitis, both of which cause inflammation in the bowel.
URGENT Seek medical advice immediately

NO

Are your child's faeces runny?

YES

See chart: DIARRHOEA (CHILDREN OVER 1), p38.

NO

Your baby's faeces: what's normal and what isn't

The appearance and smell of a baby's faeces are very variable. Most are normal and nothing to worry about, but is important to know what changes could indicate there is a problem. If you are concerned about your baby's faeces, then speak to your health visitor or doctor.

The following are normal:

★ In breastfed babies, faeces may be browny-green, greenish-yellow, or bright yellow and are loose, with a grainy texture.

★ In bottle-fed babies, faeces are usually browner and more formed than those of breast-fed babies and they may have a stronger smell.

The following are not normal, and you should seek medical advice:

★ White or putty-coloured faeces could mean there is a problem with the liver.

★ Red material (blood) in the faeces can be a sign of an infection or can occur as a side effect of constipation.

★ Black faeces can mean there is bleeding in the upper part of the digestive tract.

Has your child recently recovered from a bout of diarrhoea or vomiting?

POSSIBLE CAUSE *Gastroenteritis* (p.168) may sometimes cause faeces to be pale for several days.

Does your child have any of the following symptoms?

★ Yellowish skin

★ Yellowish whites of the eyes

★ Dark urine

POSSIBLE CAUSES *Hepatitis* (p.168) or *Neonatal jaundice* (p.88).

NO

If you cannot identify your child's problem from this chart or you are worried about your child, seek medical advice.

Urinary problems

If your child is passing urine rarely or very frequently or she has pain when passing urine, seek medical advice, as there could be an underlying disorder.

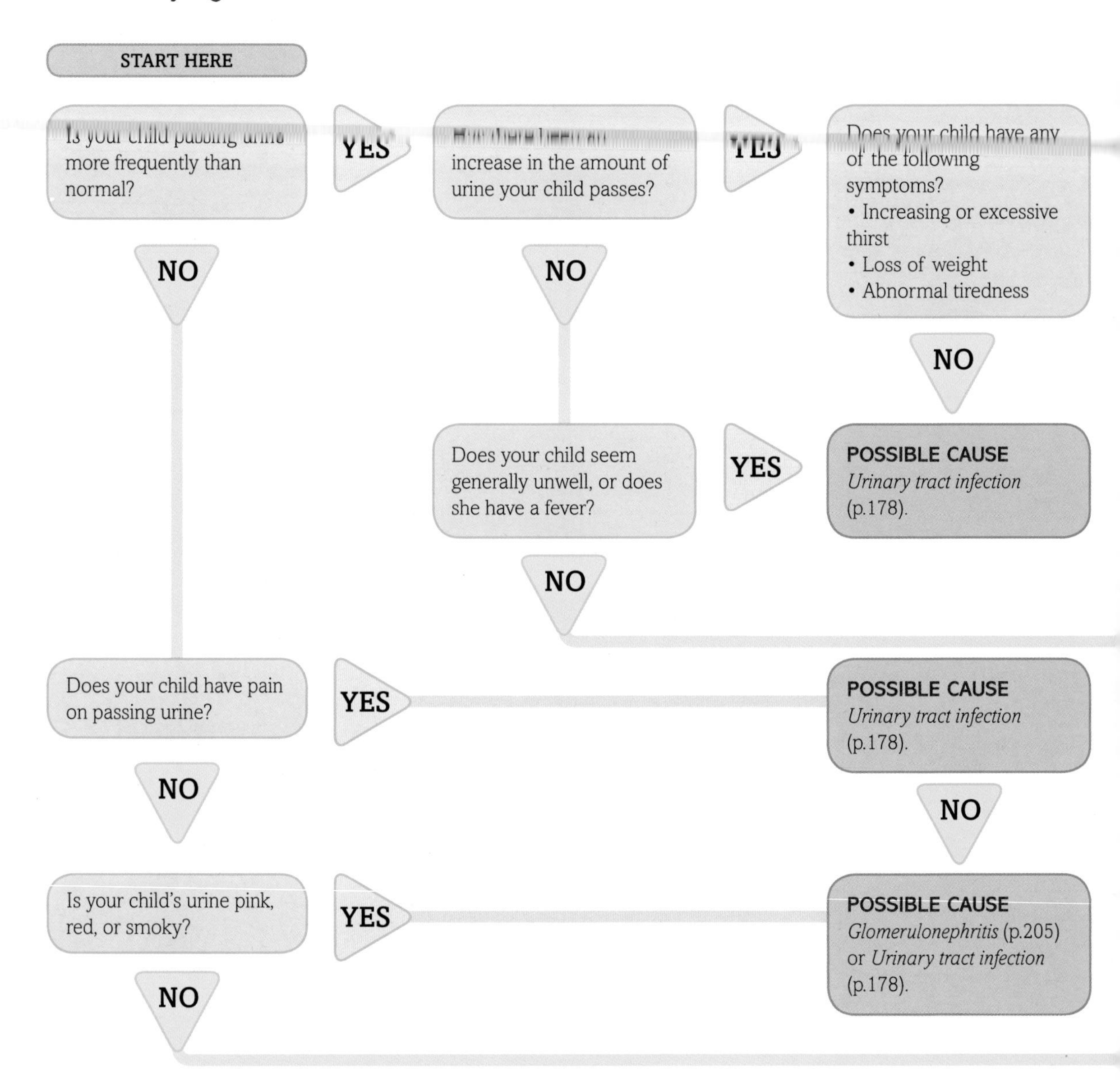

YES

POSSIBLE CAUSE *Diabetes mellitus* (p.188).

Has your child been taking any medications recently?

YES

POSSIBLE CAUSE Some drugs may cause frequent passing of urine. **Seek medical advice** to find out whether the medicine may be causing your child's symptoms and whether you should stop giving it.

Is your child's urine dark brown and clear?

YES

Are your child's faeces paler than normal?

YES

POSSIBLE CAUSE *Hepatitis* (p.168) *or Neonatal jaundice* (p.88).

NO

NO

POSSIBLE CAUSE The urine has probably darkened because it has become concentrated as a result of low fluid intake or of excessive loss of fluids from fever, vomiting, and/or diarrhoea, possibly due to *Gastroenteritis* (p.168).
SELF-HELP Make sure that your child has plenty to drink and the urine should soon return to its normal colour.

Is your child's urine dark yellow or orange?

YES

NO

POSSIBLE CAUSE Artificial colouring in food, drink, or medicine is almost always the cause of such discoloration. **Seek medical advice** if urine hasn't returned to its normal colour within a few days.

Is your child's urine green or blue?

YES

NO

If you cannot identify your child's problem from this chart or you are worried about your child, seek medical advice.

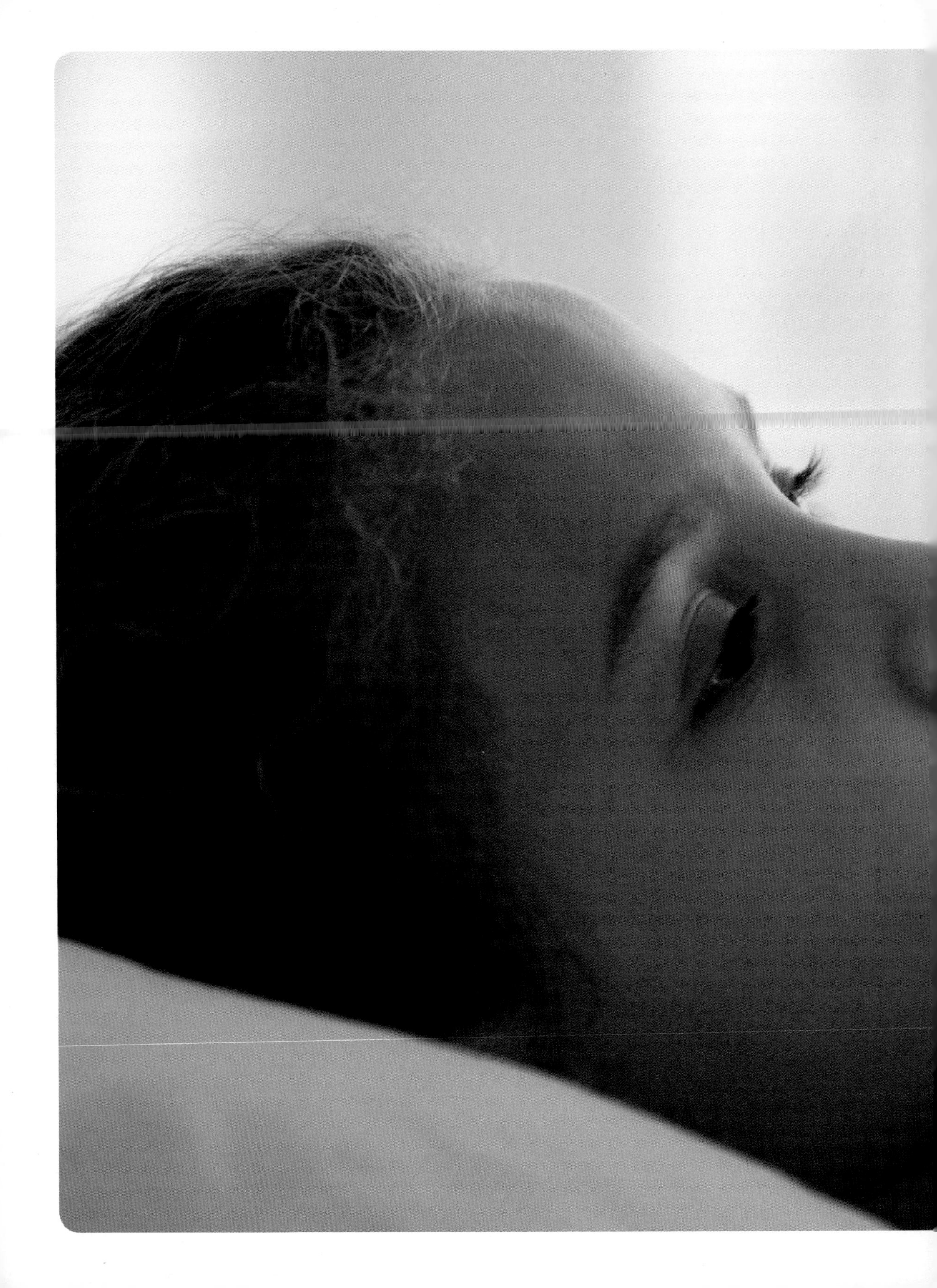

Childhood disorders

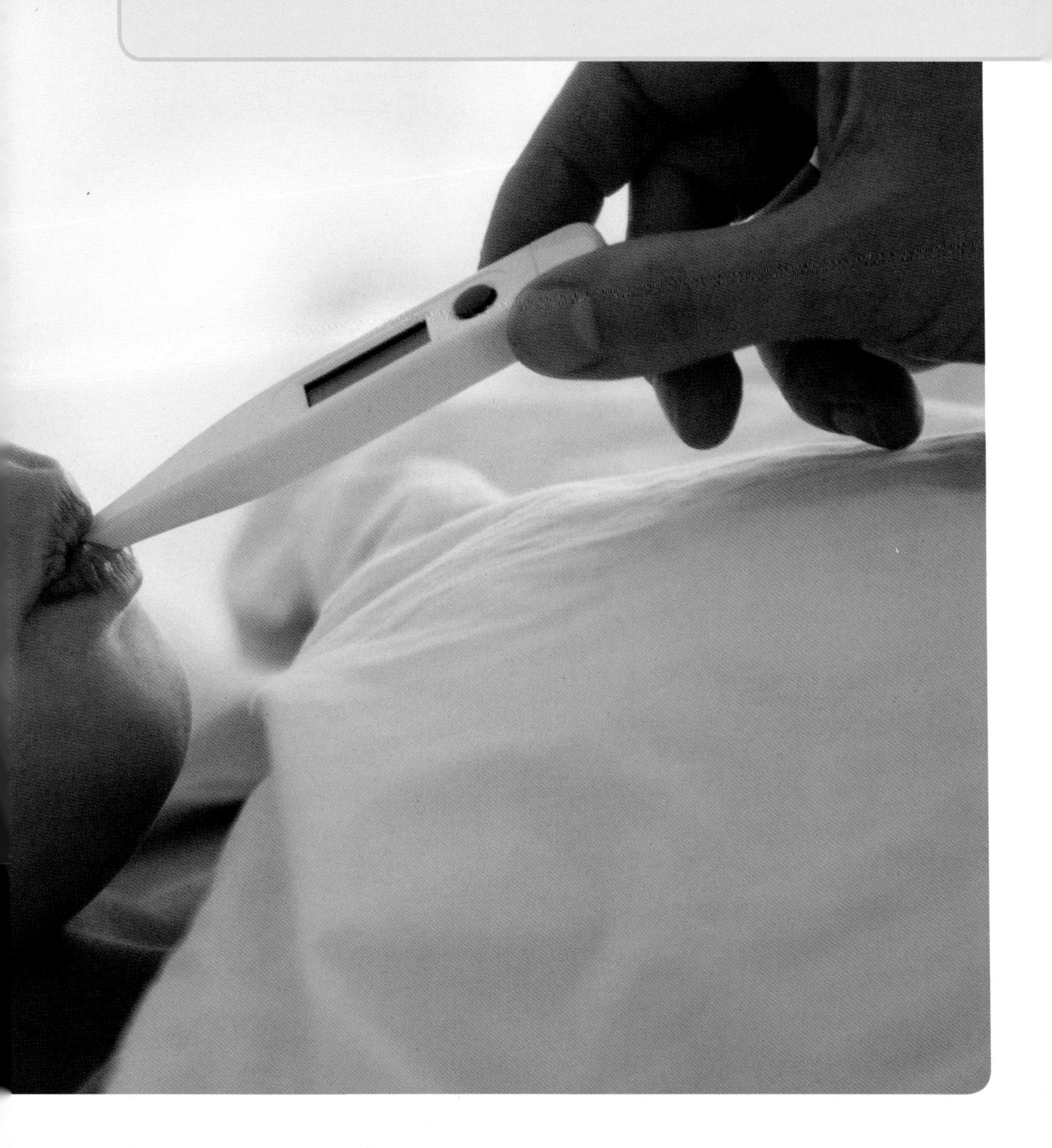

ALL ABOUT ILLNESS

In this section you will find information, with the emphasis on self-help advice, about the most common and important disorders that can affect children from birth up to the age of 10.

HOW THE SECTION IS ORGANIZED

Diseases and disorders starts with common conditions in babies, followed by infectious diseases. Conditions are then split into chapters according to the parts or systems of the body they affect, for example the respiratory system or the nervous system. Disorders affecting the eyes, ears, nose, and throat are considered together.

Some conditions could have been in various chapters, for example the common cold, a viral infection of the nose and throat, could be under respiratory system; eyes, ears, nose and throat; or infectious diseases. It has been included in the respiratory system so that it is near influenza, with which it shares symptoms and is sometimes confused. Chickenpox could be under infectious diseases or skin as it is accompanied by a rash, but because its effects are not restricted to the skin, it is included under infectious diseases.

FINDING YOUR WAY AROUND

The opening page of each chapter lists all the conditions included in the chapter with their page references. If you are not sure where to find a condition, you can refer to the index at the back of the book. You can also use the symptom charts to help you identify what disorder your child may have, which you can then read about.

AIMS OF THE SECTION

The aim of this part of the book is to give you information about each condition: what it is, what it is caused by (if known), what the symptoms are, how it is treated, and what the outlook is for the future. There is advice on treatment and self-help that you can do at home, for example putting on emollients (moisturizers) for eczema or other dry skin conditions, or using reward charts for bed-wetting. There is also guidance about when to seek medical advice. No book can replace the face-to-face contact of seeing a doctor so if you are concerned about your child, make an appointment with your GP.

ADDITIONAL DISORDERS

An alphabetically arranged glossary follows the main *Childhood disorders* chapters and includes less common and generally serious childhood disorders for which medical treatment is usually needed.

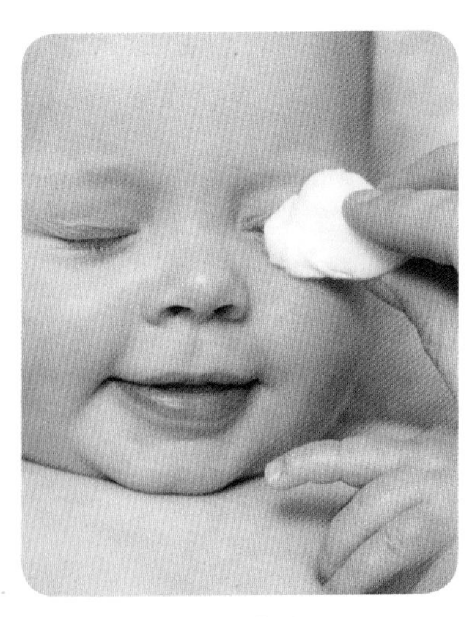

Conditions in babies Sticky eye is one of the problems that mainly affect babies under 1 year old. You can help by wiping away the discharge with clean cotton wool. Cradle cap, colic, nappy rash, reflux and wind are other common complaints.

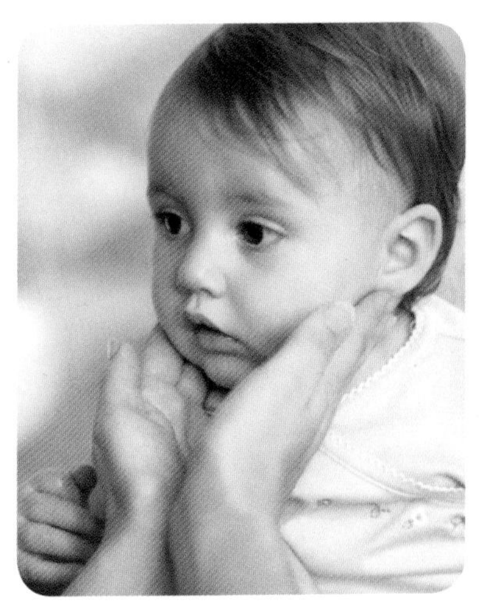

Infectious diseases Mumps is an infectious disease that affects more than one body system or part of the body. One symptom of mumps is enlarged glands, which you may be able to feel. Chickenpox and rubella are also infectious illnesses.

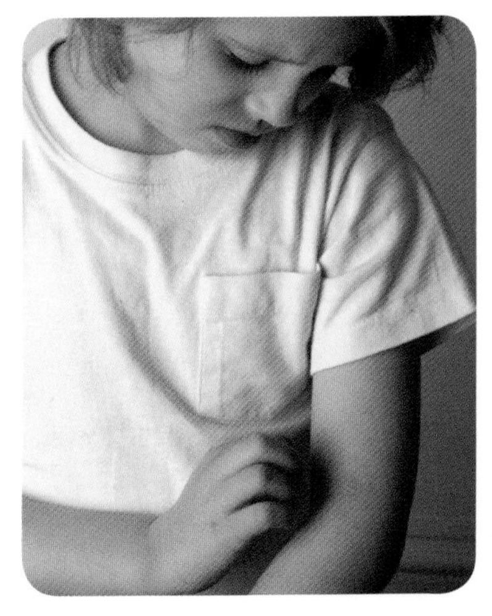

Skin disorders Eczema, seen here on the inner elbow, is a common complaint that can affect the skin anywhere on the body. It can often be relieved with self-help measures. Other skin disorders, such as cold sores, tend to affect only one area.

Common conditions in babies

The problems discussed in this section exclusively or mainly affect babies under the age of 1 year. Many of these problems are related to immaturity or the need to adjust to a new environment. Other conditions that can affect babies but are not specific to them are discussed under the body system or part of the body affected. Genetic disorders and serious abnormalities present from birth (congenital disorders) are included in the *Glossary of other medical conditions* (see pp.203–7).

Umbilical cord problems

After a baby is born, the umbilical cord, which connected the baby to the placenta, is cut. In the majority of cases, the cord stump heals without problems but it can become infected or a collection of scar tissue (called a granuloma) may form.

WHAT ARE THE CAUSES?

After the umbilical cord has been cut and clamped, a stump of 2–3cm (about 1in) is left. This dries out and may turn black before it falls off. Once it has fallen off, the baby's bellybutton may look red and takes about another week to heal fully. Until the cord stump has fully healed, infection can occur as the moist area around it can harbour potentially harmful bacteria.

The exact cause of granulomas is not known but it may be more likely to occur if healing takes longer than usual.

SHOULD I SEE A DOCTOR?

If you think the cord stump is infected, see your doctor who may prescribe an antibiotic cream. Generally no action is needed for granulomas as these tend to disappear on their own. If a granuloma persists, then see your doctor.

ARE THEY PREVENTABLE?

It is important that you keep the cord stump clean and dry until the bellybutton is fully healed. Keep the top of your baby's nappy folded down so that the cord stump is outside the nappy and does not get urine or stool on it. If urine or stool does get onto the cord, wash it off with water. Use a piece of gauze to do this. Do not use cotton wool because bits of fluff could stick to the stump. You do not need to apply alcohol or antiseptic to the stump.

There's nothing you can do to prevent a granuloma from forming.

Possible symptoms

Infection:

★ **Redness** around base of stump

★ **Discharge or pus** from stump

★ **Fever, feeding poorly, or irritability**

Granuloma:

★ **Red/pink, raised, moist area** where the stump was

★ **Yellowish fluid** draining from the stump

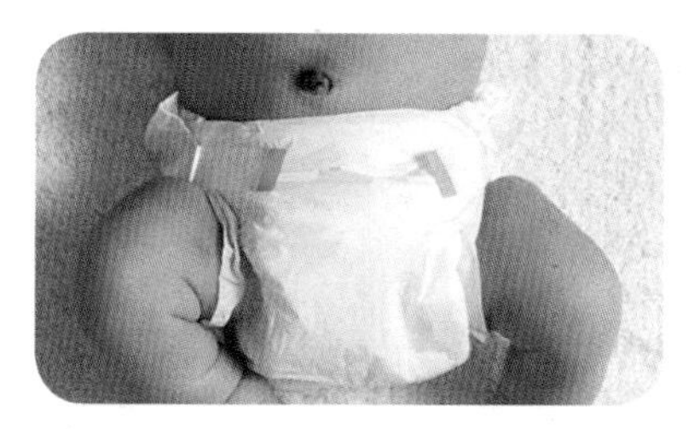

Cord stump care Fold the top of your baby's nappy down so that the cord is exposed to the air and stays dry.

Neonatal jaundice

In jaundice, the skin and eyes have a yellowish tinge. It is common in newborns, affecting about 6 out of 10 babies, and is usually not serious.

Possible symptoms

★ **Yellowish skin** and whites of the eyes

★ **Itchy skin**

★ **Sleepiness** or poor feeding

WHAT CAUSES IT?

The yellowish tinge is due to a build-up of bilirubin in the blood. Bilirubin is a waste product formed by the liver when red blood cells are broken down. There are several different causes of jaundice in newborns. The most common type is known as physiological jaundice. It occurs because newborns have more red blood cells and the removal of bilirubin from the blood is slower than in adults as their livers are immature. This type develops within the first week and generally gets better by day 10–14 after birth without treatment.

Other forms of jaundice may be more serious, for example if there is incompatibility between the mother's and the baby's blood, resulting in rapid breakdown of red blood cells. This comes on within 24 hours of the birth and needs urgent treatment. Jaundice that lasts longer than 2 weeks can be due to a harmless reaction to hormones in the mother's milk but it could have a more serious underlying cause. Jaundice is more common in premature and breastfed babies.

SHOULD I SEE A DOCTOR?

If you think that your child has jaundice, see your doctor or midwife. This is especially important if jaundice lasts longer than 2 weeks, or doesn't start until after the first week of life, if the jaundice is worsening, or it is associated with stools that are chalky white. A blood sample will be taken and tested for levels of bilirubin.

The most common treatment for jaundice is phototherapy, in which the baby is placed under a light. This treatment helps to break the bilirubin down. Even though physiological jaundice often gets better on its own, phototherapy may be given if bilirubin levels are very high because this can damage part of the brain. A blood transfusion may be required for more serious types of jaundice.

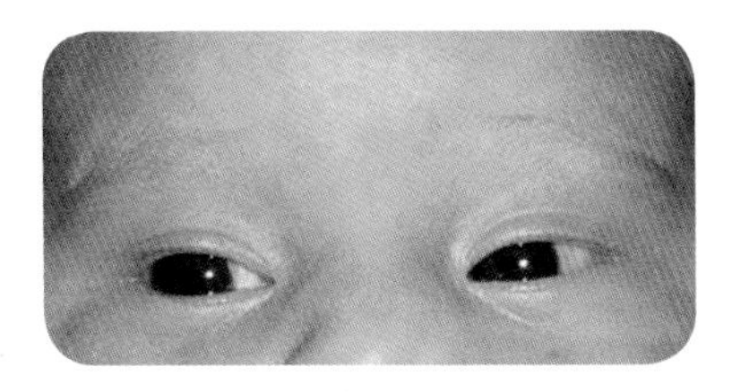

Yellowish eyes and skin This baby shows typical signs of jaundice. The yellow tinge is due to build-up of a waste product in blood.

Spots and rashes

Newborn skin is susceptible to many types of spots and rashes. Most of these blemishes are harmless and go away on their own.

WHAT ARE THE TYPES?

Four common skin blemishes affecting newborns are discussed here (see also *Birthmarks*, p90).

★ **Milia** These small, smooth white bumps, also called milk spots, affect as many as 4 or 5 out of 10 newborns. They are not present at birth, but develop a few weeks afterwards, generally appearing on the face. They are tiny cysts in the skin that form as the oil glands in the skin are still developing.

No treatment is required and they disappear spontaneously within approximately 4–6 weeks.

★ **Neonatal acne** This usually appears about 2–4 weeks after birth and is due to the effects of hormones from the mother when the baby is developing in the womb. These hormones stimulate the oil-producing glands in the baby's face.

No treatment is generally needed for neonatal acne as the spots clear up on their own by 4–6 months, without leaving scars. If they're particularly severe or not getting better, see your doctor, who may advise acne treatments suitable for use in infants.

★ **Erythema neonatorum** It is common for newborns to develop this blotchy red raised rash over the face and body. It is not known why it occurs, but it tends to get better within a few days without treatment.

★ **Heat rash** Also called prickly heat, this red, pimply rash may develop if your baby becomes overheated. It is caused by blocked sweat glands; babies are more susceptible than adults to heat rash as their glands have smaller pores. Cool your baby down by removing some of his clothing or moving him to a cooler place.

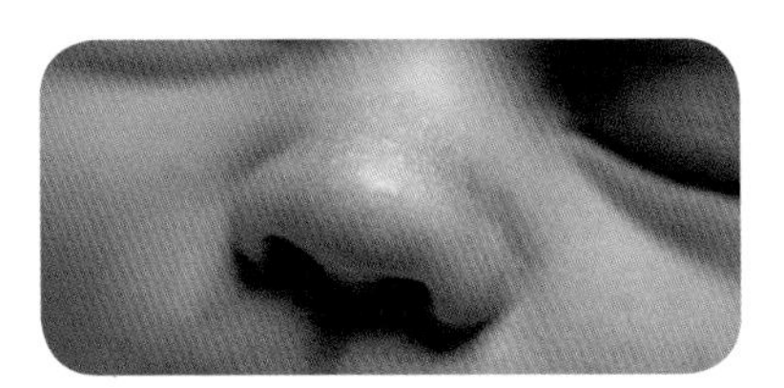

Milia These tiny white bumps, seen on the nose here, are common in young babies. They are harmless and soon disappear.

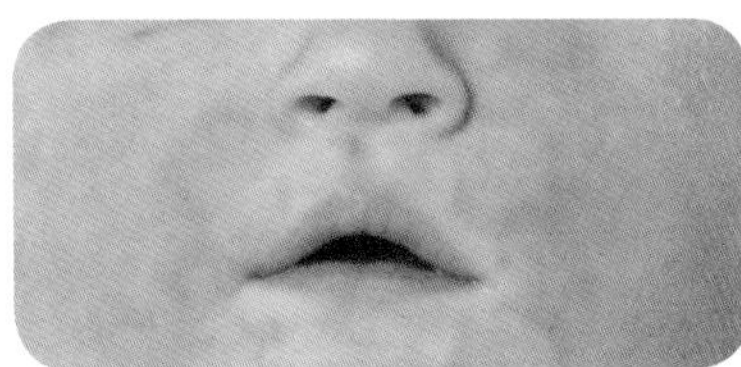

Erythema neonatorum This raised red rash, seen here on a newborn's cheeks, usually disappears in a few days.

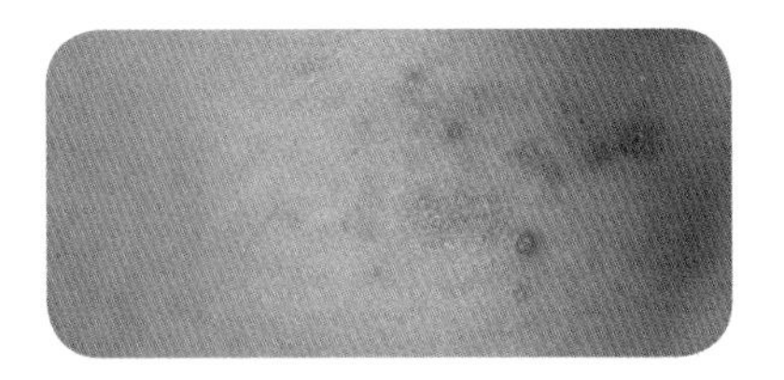

Neonatal acne This rash is similar to the spots of adolescent acne. It can appear on the cheeks, the forehead, and chin.

Heat rash The small red bumps here are due to a heat rash. They often appear in areas where clothing fits snugly.

Birthmarks

Coloured marks on the skin, known as birthmarks, can be present at birth or appear within the first few weeks of life. Some may fade with time while others are permanent.

WHAT ARE THE TYPES?

There are two main types of birthmark: those caused by malformed blood vessels in or under the skin and those caused by clusters of pigmented cells (which give skin its colour). The first type includes salmon patches, haemangiomas, and port-wine stains. The second type includes Mongolian blue spots and melanocytic naevi.

★ **Salmon patches** These are salmon pink coloured areas that occur on the eyes, forehead, and nape of neck that may get darker when the baby cries. They tend to disappear by the age of 1 year although they can persist for longer.

★ **Haemangiomas** These raised patches of discoloured skin are either strawberry haemangiomas, which are reddish, or cavernous haemangiomas, which are purple or bluish. They can be present at birth or develop within the first few weeks. They start off as a red flat area that grows quickly within a few months into a raised mark.

Parents are often very concerned about haemangiomas as they can grow to be quite large, but at approximately 18 months they begin to shrink. By the time a child is 7 years old, they have usually disappeared. As they improve on their own they are generally only treated if they are over the eye and therefore causing problems with vision, if they are in a site that causes problems with feeding or breathing, or if they bleed frequently.

★ **Mongolian blue spots** Present at birth, these spots are more common in people with dark skin. They look like a deep bluish grey area and are generally over the baby's lower back or buttocks. No treatment is required and they tend to resolve by age 4.

★ **Port-wine stain** This permanent birthmark consists of a flat, red or purple discolouration. As a child grows it may also grow and become thickened or lumpy. It can be treated using laser therapy.

★ **Congenital melanocytic naevi** These are dark pigmented moles that vary in size. Moles can become cancerous, especially if they are large, so need to be monitored for any changes. If a mole enlarges, becomes inflamed, bleeds, or itches see your doctor.

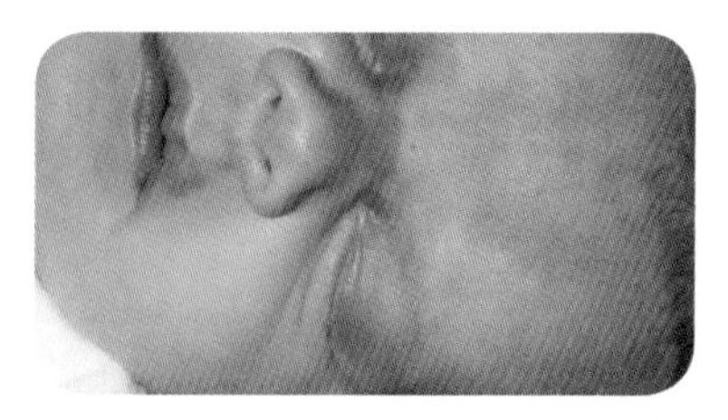

Salmon patches The pink-coloured areas on this baby's eyelids and forehead are also known as stork bites or angel's kisses.

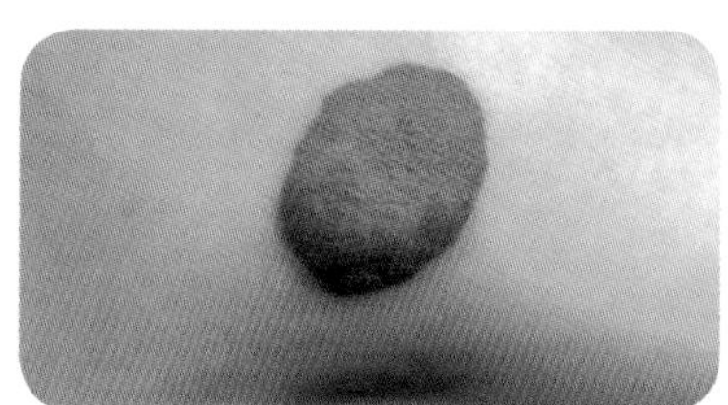

Strawberry haemangioma This birthmark resembles a strawberry – hence the name. It is caused by malformed blood vessels.

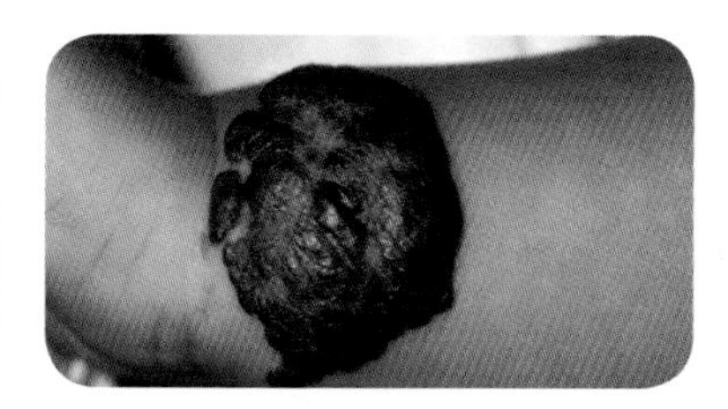

Cavernous haemangioma This is similar to a strawberry haemangioma, but is darker as malformed blood vessels are deeper.

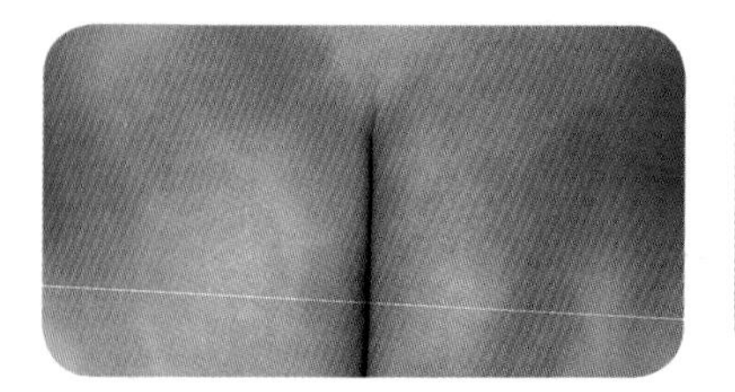

Mongolian blue spots These are deep bluish grey spots, resembling bruises, here seen on a baby's buttocks.

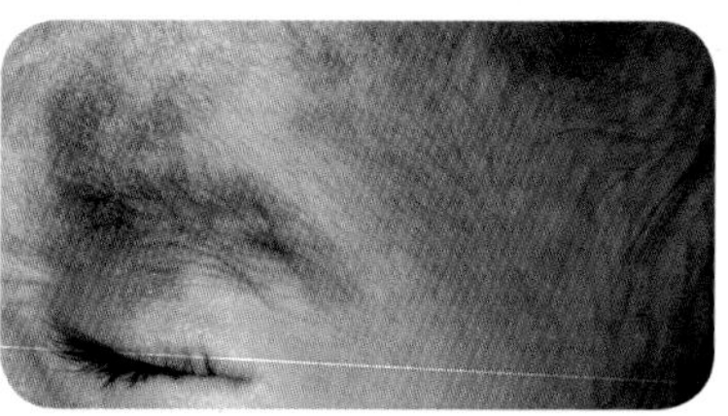

Port-wine stain As it often appears on the face, treatment of a port-wine stain may be desirable although not necessary.

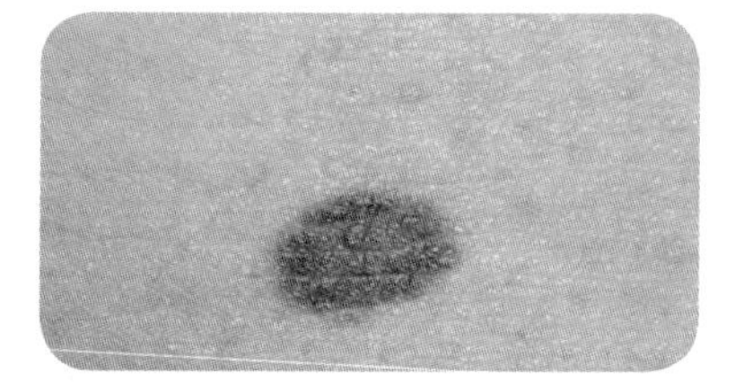

Melanocytic naevus This brown mole is a common type of birthmark, caused by a collection of pigment-producing skin cells.

Cradle cap

Also known as seborrhoeic dermatitis, cradle cap is a common skin condition that usually develops in the first few months after birth. It usually affects the scalp – hence its name – but less commonly can also affect the face, armpits, and groin.

Possible symptoms

- ★ Red, flaky, or scaly skin on the scalp
- ★ Yellow crusts or greasy patches on the scalp
- ★ Hair loss in the affected area as the greasy patches dry and flake off
- ★ Scaly, blotchy patches of skin on the face, armpits, or groin

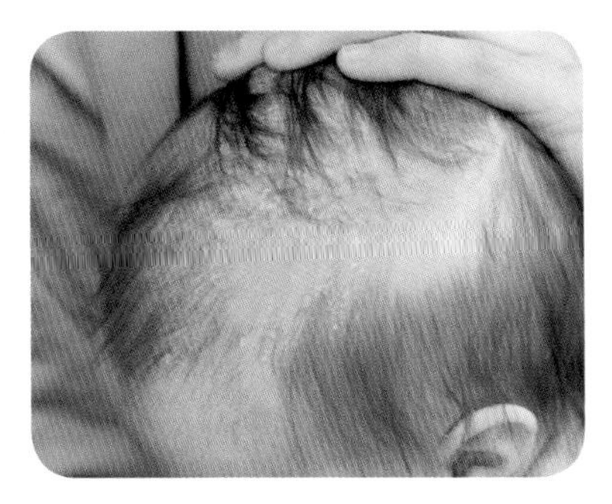

Cradle cap The scaly, yellowish, greasy patches of skin that occur in cradle cap are unsightly but harmless.

WHAT IS THE CAUSE?

The cause of cradle cap is not known, but it may be due to the effects of the mother's hormones in the womb, stimulating the sebaceous glands to become overactive and produce too much of the oily substance sebum. On the scalp, this causes dead skin cells to stick to the scalp instead of flaking off.

Cradle cap is more common in those with a family history of eczema. It is not due to poor hygiene and is not contagious. Although many parents feel cradle cap is unsightly, it does not cause any problems or pain to the baby and tends to clear up on its own, generally in a few months.

SHOULD I SEE A DOCTOR?

Try the self-help measures shown in the box below to treat cradle cap. If these don't seem to be working, see your doctor, who can prescribe an antifungal shampoo or a medicated shampoo containing coal tar or other ingredients to soothe the scalp and remove the scales. You should also see your doctor if seborrhoeic dermatitis appears on places other than the scalp. He or she may prescribe a corticosteroid cream or ointment to treat this.

What can I do to help?

Cradle cap scales can be treated by applying oil, such as olive oil, to the scalp. Alternatively, apply a moisturizer, such as emulsifying ointment, or petroleum jelly. Avoid peanut oil in case of allergy. Don't pick the scales as they can bleed; picking may also lead to sores, which can become infected.

1 **Gently rub oil or moisturiser** into the scalp to help loosen the cradle cap crusts and scales.

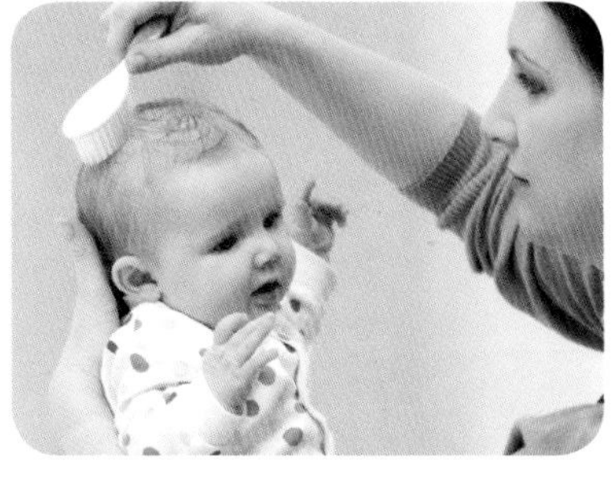

2 **Brush your baby's hair** to remove crusts after leaving the oil in for a few hours, or overnight,

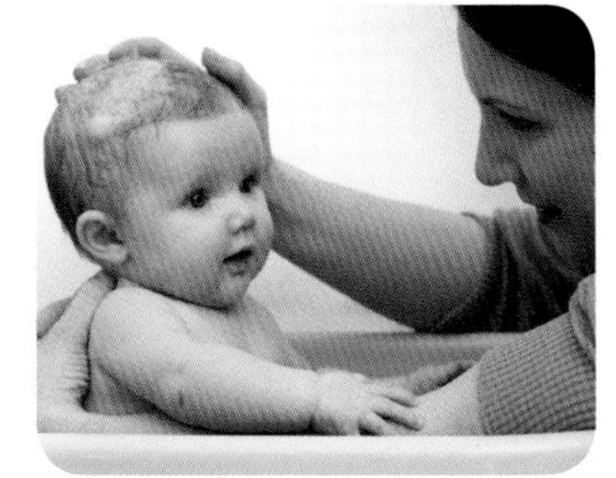

3 **Wash your baby's hair** with baby shampoo. Regular washing may help stop crusts forming.

Sticky eye

Many babies have pus or discharge coming from one or both eyes, causing the eye or eyes to become sticky. The discharge may be more obvious after the baby has been asleep when there may be some crusting around the eyes.

Possible symptoms

Blocked tear duct:

★ Watering of the eye – even when the baby is not crying

★ Sticky or glue-like discharge from the eye

Neonatal conjunctivitis:

★ Redness of the white of the eye

★ Water, bloody, or thick pus-like discharge from the eye

★ Puffy, tender [illegible]

WHAT ARE THE CAUSES?

Sticky eye in babies is often due to a blocked nasolacrimal, or tear, duct. The eyes are kept moist by tears, which then drain [illegible] the nasolacrimal duct from the eye into the nose. In about 1 in 5 babies the duct is not fully developed and free drainage of tears is blocked, causing the symptoms.

Another possible cause of sticky eye is conjunctivitis, which is an infection of the conjunctiva in the eye (the transparent membrane that covers the whites of the eyes and lines the eyelids). If this occurs during the first 28 days of life (called neonatal conjunctivitis) the bacteria causing the infection may have been picked up from the mother's birth canal during delivery.

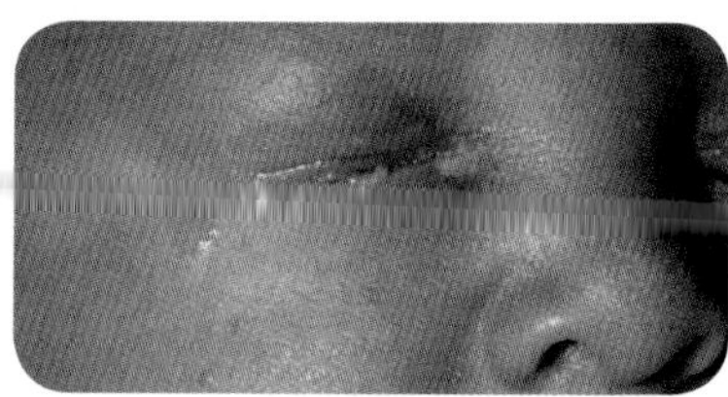

Sticky eye The yellow discharge from this baby's eye is due to a blocked tear duct.

SHOULD I SEE A DOCTOR?

If your baby is less than 28 days he should be assessed by your doctor. Even if your baby is over 28 days you may like to see your doctor to confirm the diagnosis.

A baby over 28 days diagnosed with conjunctivitis may not need any treatment; in some cases, antibiotic eye ointment or drops are prescribed. A baby less than 28 days with neonatal conjunctivitis will be referred to a specialist. If chlamydia bacteria are found to be causing the infection, prompt treatment is especially important because these bacteria can cause pneumonia or lead to blindness.

If a blocked duct is diagnosed, you can try using massage to help the duct develop (see box, left). However, if the white of the eye or the corner of the eye becomes red and painful this may be a sign of infection. See your doctor who will be able to prescribe antibiotic drops if appropriate.

What can I do to help?

If your baby has a blocked nasolacrimal duct, massage can help pooled tears to drain and help the duct develop. Wash hands first.

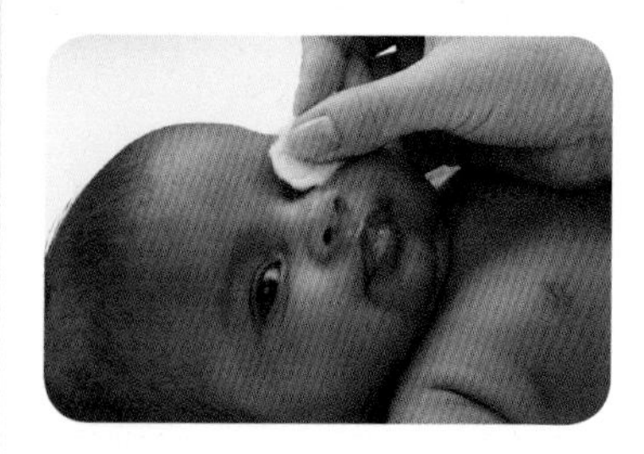

Clean the eye Gently wipe away any discharge from the eye using moist cotton wool or gauze. Preferably, use boiled, cooled water for moistening.

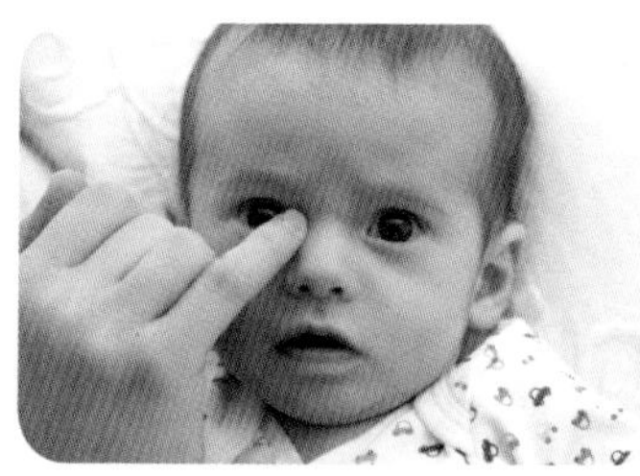

Massage the duct Apply gentle pressure to the inner corner of the outside of the nose with your finger and thumb three to four times a day.

WHAT'S THE OUTLOOK?

If neonatal conjunctivitis is treated promptly the outlook is good with many children making a full recovery. A blocked duct tends to improve with time, although you may find that symptoms worsen again temporarily during a cold as the duct becomes blocked with mucus. In most cases a blocked duct will have opened by the time the child is 1 year old. If it has not and there are still symptoms you will be referred to a specialist. Treatment involves probing the nasolacrimal duct to open it. This procedure is done under anaesthetic.

Nappy rash

Nappy rash affects most babies and toddlers in nappies at some point. It is most commonly caused by irritation of the skin from the ammonia in urine and faeces. Nappy rash can also be caused by a fungal infection.

SHOULD I SEE A DOCTOR?
If the self-help actions shown below do not help, take your child to your doctor. The doctor may prescribe a low-dose steroid anti-inflammatory cream or ointment or, if the nappy rash might be fungal, an antifungal cream or ointment. If the rash does not heal despite this treatment there may be a bacterial infection so antibiotics may be prescribed.

IS IT PREVENTABLE?
Following the tips below may also prevent your baby from developing nappy rash.

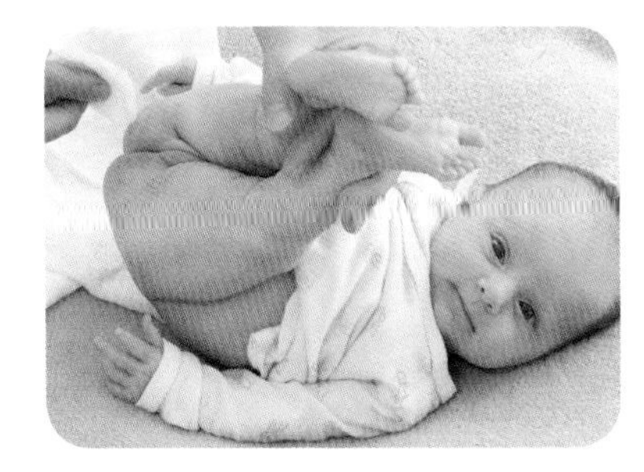

Mild rash Red, sore-looking skin is typical of nappy rash. Here, it affects only a small part of the nappy area.

Possible symptoms

Mild nappy rash:

★ Pink or red spots, which may merge into blotches, affecting a small part of the nappy area

★ Baby is well, although may cry when passing urine or faeces.

Severe nappy rash:

★ Bright red spots and cracked skin, affecting a large part of the nappy area

★ Baby may be irritable and fretful

Fungal nappy rash:

★ Inflamed skin with red spots around the edges of the rash, like satellites

★ Skin folds may be affected, unlike non-fungal rashes

What can I do to help?

The measures shown here will help treat and prevent nappy rash. Don't do up nappies too tightly and avoid using plastic pants over the nappy as this keeps moisture in.

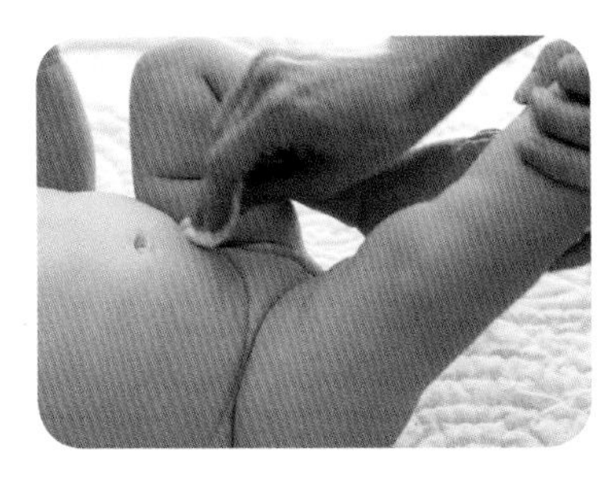

Avoid soaps Wash your baby's bottom with water; avoid all soaps as these can be irritating. If using wipes, check they do not contain alcohol which can be drying. Dry the skin thoroughly, patting instead of rubbing if the area is sore.

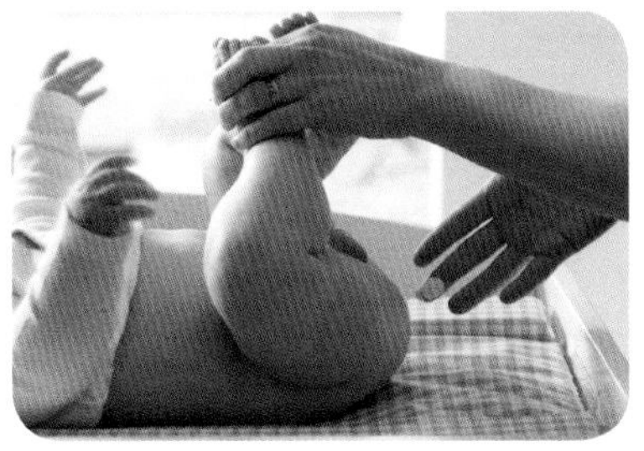

Use a barrier cream After you change the nappy, apply barrier cream, but not too much as this could stop the nappy from being absorbent – just apply a thin layer. Do not use talcum powder as this may irritate the skin further and is not necessary.

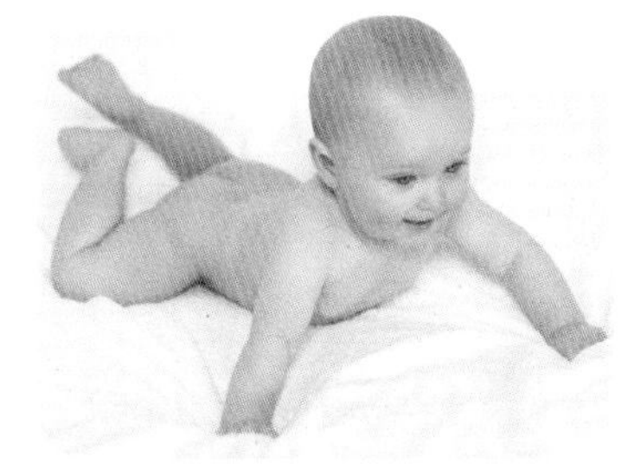

Leave your baby's nappy off Let your baby go without his nappy for as long as possible. Place him on a towel, changing it as soon as it becomes wet. If it's not possible to leave the nappy off, change it regularly and as soon as it is soiled.

Colic

While all babies cry at some point for various reasons such as tiredness or hunger, babies with colic, who are developing normally and are healthy, cry inconsolably for unknown reasons. Colic passes and most babies are better by the age of 4 months.

Possible symptoms

Intense episodes of crying, generally starting a few weeks after birth. Your baby may:

★ Cry furiously and inconsolably; little you do may have an effect

★ Arch her back or draw up her knees

★ Pass wind

★ Cry often in the evening after feeding

★ Take longer to feed or have disturbed sleep because of intermittent crying episodes

★ Be otherwise well, feeding, and gaining weight

WHAT IS THE CAUSE?

The cause of colic, or even exactly what it is, is not known. The crying of colic is not thought to be due to pain, even though the babies may look uncomfortable. It is thought that colic may be to do with trapped wind or with immaturity of the digestive system because it does disappear as the baby gets older. It may be also be caused by a temporary sensitivity to lactose.

Inconsolable crying A baby with colic cries inconsolably for no apparent reason even though she is healthy and thriving.

Colic is extremely common, and affects about 1 in 5 babies. Smoking during pregnancy increases the risk of your baby developing colic and the condition occurs more commonly in breastfed babies.

WHAT'S THE TREATMENT?

There is a range of self-help measures you can try to soothe your baby's colic (see box, opposite). If these do not help you can try medications that can be bought over the counter from your pharmacy. Try them for a week to assess your baby's response. Stop if there is no change. The medications you can try are:

★ Simeticone drops – these may reduce trapped air in the stomach.

★ Lactase drops – these help your baby digest lactose. Even if your baby responds to these drops it is unlikely she has permanent lactose intolerance.

ARE THERE ANY COMPLEMENTARY THERAPIES?

Some parents find cranial osteopathy helpful but there is little evidence for its effectiveness and it does have some risks. Cranial osteopaths believe that the process of birth puts stresses on the body, resulting in discomfort and leading to colic. They use gentle manipulation of the baby, aimed at relieving these stresses. A remedy you can try yourself is massaging your baby's tummy or "cycling" her legs (see box, opposite).

SHOULD I SEE A DOCTOR?

Although colic is thought to be harmless, it is extremely distressing for parents and carers, who may get upset and cry along with the baby or become extremely frustrated. If you feel you are not coping, do make an appointment to see your doctor. As always, see your doctor if you are concerned about the health of your baby.

IS IT PREVENTABLE?

Not smoking during pregnancy puts your baby at less risk of suffering from colic. If you didn't give up during pregnancy, give up now. Smoking around your newborn baby can affect your baby's digestive system and increase the chance of colic as well as damaging your baby's health in other ways. Smoking is, of course, also extremely damaging to your own health.

TOP TIP

It's easy to become stressed with a colicky baby. If it all gets too much put the baby in a safe place such as her cot and take a short break, or ask someone else to take over for a while.

What can I do to help?

Try using the methods shown below to soothe a colicky baby. Some babies like a quiet, dark room; others may find a background of "white noise", such as the vacuum cleaner or TV static soothing. Overstimulating a baby by continually picking her up and putting her down may aggravate crying.

If breastfeeding Don't drink too much tea, coffee, or other drinks containing caffeine. Alcohol and spicy foods can also make colic worse.

If bottle-feeding Sit your baby as upright as possible during feeding to prevent him swallowing air. Experiment with different-sized bottle teats or teat holes.

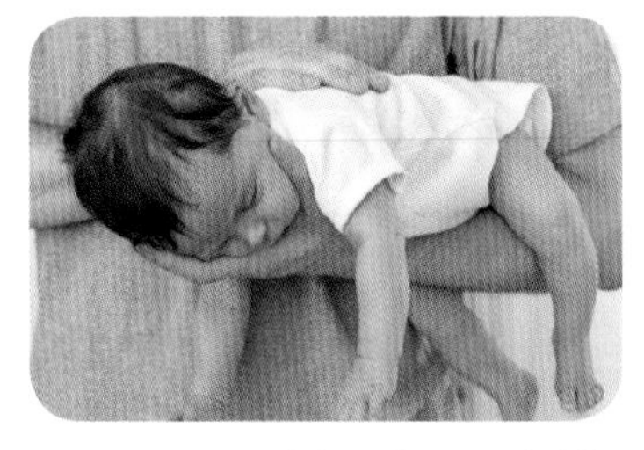

Hold your baby When she cries, hold her. Some babies like to be held on their fronts, others prefer being upright; you'll get to know what she likes. Rocking or walking while you hold her may help.

Offer a dummy Sucking often helps to soothe a colicky baby. You could try offering a dummy. If you're breastfeeding, you could also offer the breast, making sure that he latches on properly to avoid swallowing air.

Wind your baby Hold her upright as shown here, or sit her forward over your hand or on your lap. Be sure to support her head and neck. Gently pat or rub her back or tummy until she burps.

Keep her moving Babies find motion soothing so push your baby in a buggy, take her out in the car, walk while you hold her, or wear her in a sling so she can feel your motion.

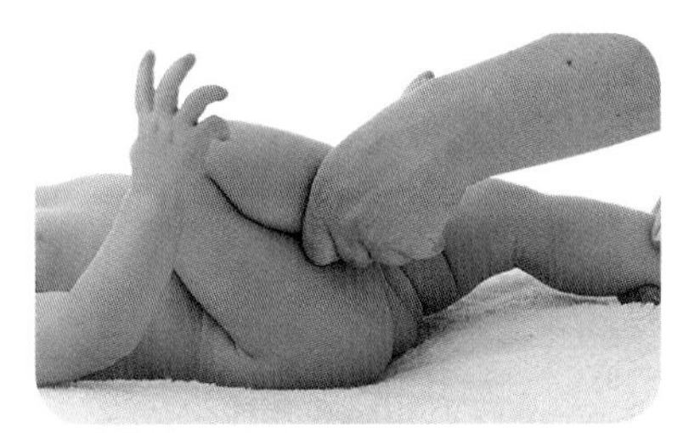

"Cycle" your baby's legs Lie your baby on her back and "cycle" her legs or bend her knees over her chest and stretch them out again. Massaging your baby's tummy in circular motions may be also be effective.

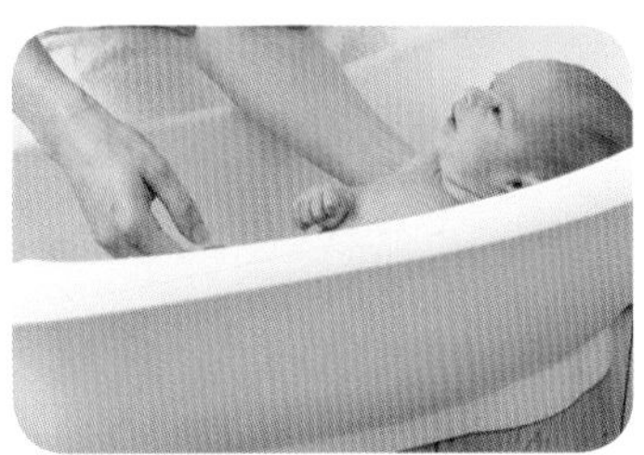

Give her a warm bath Many babies with colic seem to be helped by a warm bath. It probably relaxes them, helping to relieve pain. Try rubbing her tummy gently while she's in the bath.

Reflux

Reflux occurs when the stomach contents come back up into the oesophagus or even into the mouth. The condition, also known as gastro-oesophageal reflux, usually starts in the first 3 months of life. Most babies grow out of it.

Possible symptoms

- ★ Small amount of milk coming back up after each feed (posseting)
- ★ Persistent vomiting
- ★ Crying or apparent pain after feeding
- ★ Choking or regular cough

WHAT IS THE CAUSE?

The condition, also known as gastro-oesophageal reflux, is due to immaturity of the muscle, or sphincter, between the oesophagus and stomach. This muscle is not strong enough to stop fluids or food from the stomach coming back upwards (refluxing) when the stomach contracts as food starts to be digested

SHOULD I SEE A DOCTOR?

If your baby is bringing up small amounts of milk (posseting) after feeds this is not usually anything to worry about. However, if you are concerned or symptoms are more severe, then visit your doctor. If your baby is putting on weight you may just be given advice about positioning your baby after feeding and changing feeding patterns (see box below). If this isn't sufficient or if your baby stops gaining weight your doctor may prescribe medication to treat the reflux. There are many types of medication, but the following are often used:

★ Thickeners – if you are bottle-feeding, these can be added to a baby's normal formula. If you are breastfeeding, you can express breast milk, add the thickener, and give it in a bottle. Alternatively, some thickeners are suitable to be mixed into a paste and given before feeding. Thicker fluids are less likely to be regurgitated.

★ Antacids – these can be used to reduce the amount of acid that is being produced in the stomach.

WHAT'S THE OUTLOOK?

As the baby grows, the sphincter muscle becomes stronger. This, combined with the child being more upright (first sitting up and then standing) means that most babies will grow out of reflux by the time they are 12–18 months old.

What can I do to help?

Often, you can successfully manage reflux by feeding your baby in as upright a position as possible and keeping him upright afterwards.

It is better to breastfeed if you can, as breast milk empties faster from the stomach and breastfed babies usually take in smaller amounts at a time.

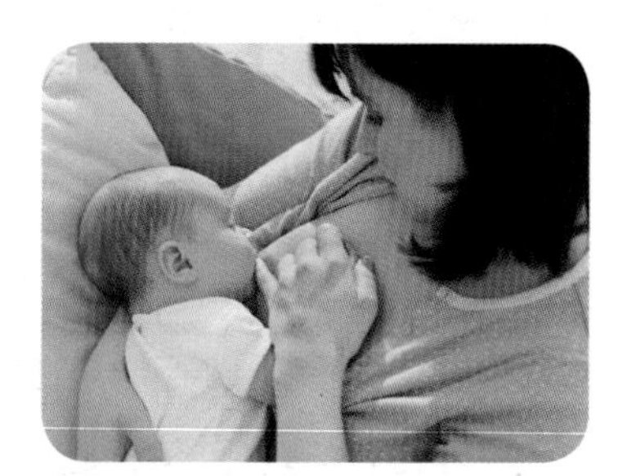

Little and often Giving your baby smaller but more frequent feeds may help to reduce reflux.

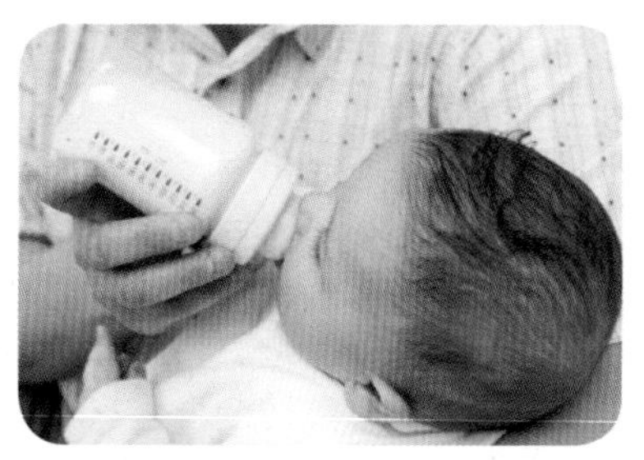

Feed in near-upright position This position helps reduce reflux by allowing gravity to keep the feed down.

Wind your baby After each feed, wind your baby and keep her in an upright position for 30 minutes or so.

Wind

Wind is air in your baby's digestive system, some of which is swallowed during feeding or crying. Wind can cause discomfort or pain and can make babies feel full so they do not feed properly. It can also cause vomiting.

Possible symptoms

★ Squirming during or after feeds, sometimes crying, often relieved by burping or winding

WHAT IS THE CAUSE?

Some babies are more windy than others. However, wind is less common in breastfed babies because they have more control over the rate of milk flow and take fewer gasps of air than bottle-fed babies.

HOW'S IT TREATED?

If the measures below haven't worked, you could try gripe water. This is a traditional remedy made from herbs, such as fennel, dill, and ginger to soothe the tummy, in a non-alcoholic base. Over-the-counter remedies containing simeticone, used for treating colic, can be helpful if your baby's wind is particularly severe.

Wind becomes less of a problem as babies grow older and can move around more to find a comfortable position.

What can I do to help?

Try the measures shown to help prevent or treat wind. When burping your baby, have a muslin or cloth close to hand as she may posset a small amount of milk. If she doesn't burp she may not have wind, but if she still appears to be in discomfort, wait a few minutes and try again.

Feed in near-upright position If bottle-feeding, keep your baby as upright as possible and tilt the bottle so that the whole bulb of the teat is filled, preventing air being swallowed. Try using different teats with varying flow rates.

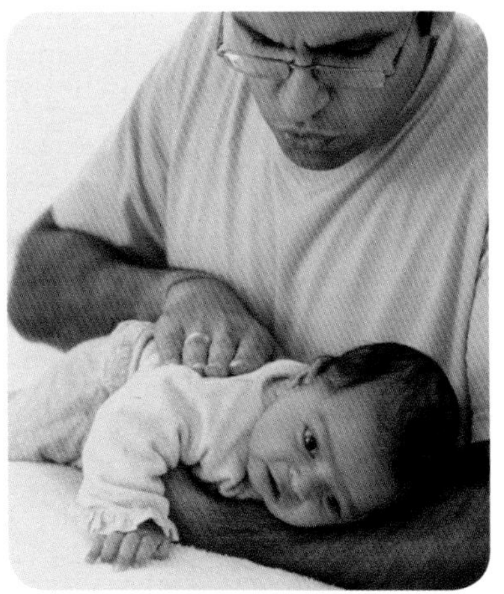

Wind your baby There are various positions you can use: sit her up on your lap, supporting her chin with your hand; hold her upright over your shoulder; or lie her on your lap. Gently rub or pat her on the back to bring up wind.

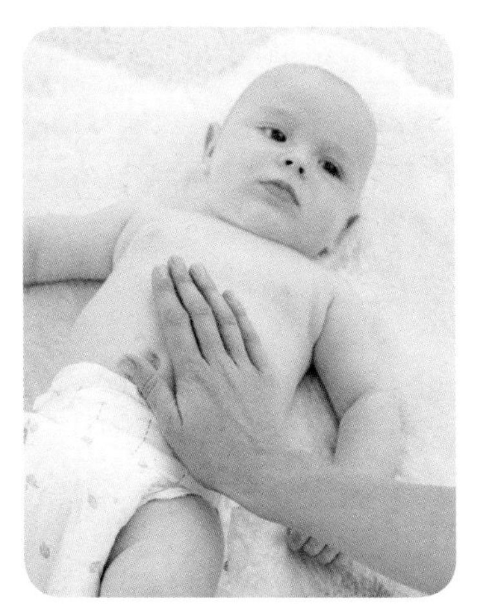

Massage your baby's tummy Lie your baby on his back and use gentle circular motions around his navel. You could also try "cycling" your baby's legs or bending his knees up to his chest and stretching them out again.

Teething

During teething, the milk teeth emerge through the gums. Many babies experience some degree of discomfort during this process.

Teething usually starts at around 6–9 months. The bottom two middle teeth generally come through first, then the top front teeth, followed by the others, with the back molars last, although they don't always follow this order. The average child has all the milk teeth by the age of 3 years.

Some babies go through teething without seeming to suffer any discomfort and the first you notice about teething is when the teeth appear. Others find it a painful experience and may have symptoms for months before a tooth emerges. The first [illegible] are usually the worst.

Possible symptoms

- ★ Red cheeks and gums
- ★ Excessive drooling
- ★ Chewing more – your baby may put everything into her mouth
- ★ Crying, or being fretful, clingy, or restless due to the pain
- ★ Decreased appetite if chewing hurts
- ★ Slightly raised temperature up to 38°C (100°F), but not above

What can I do to help?

There are plenty of things you can do to help a teething baby, as shown below. If your baby is drooling, wipe the drool off her skin to prevent a rash developing, Some parents use homeopathic remedies for teething, although there is little evidence for their effectiveness.

Cuddle your baby Holding your baby close to comfort her or distracting her by playing can help her cope.

Give healthy options to chew Cucumber, apple, or a frozen banana makes a soothing healthy snack, or try a cool drink.

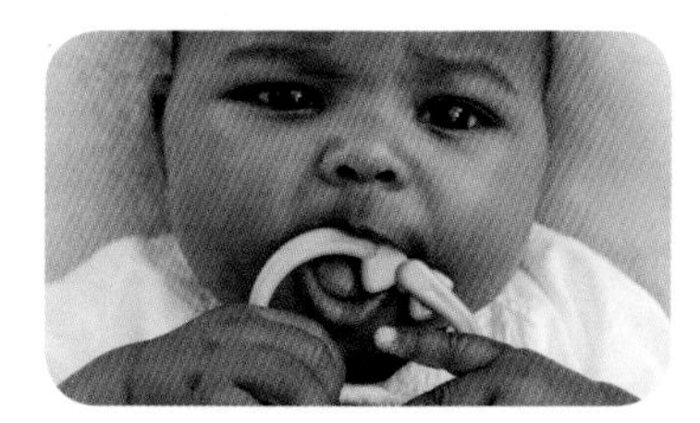

Use teething rings Some you cool in the fridge (not freezer) and help numb the gums. Or try a cooled, clean spoon.

Apply teething gel This contains local anaesthetics and often antiseptics. Check it is suitable for your child's age.

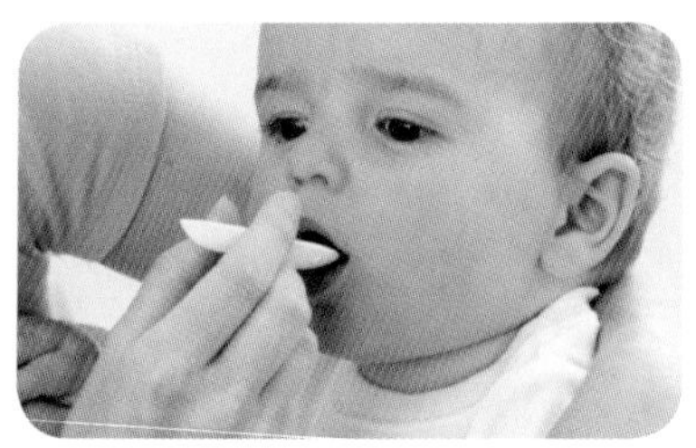

Give painkillers You can give your child paracetamol or ibuprofen to help relieve the pain of teething.

Provide soft foods Foods such as yoghurts and fruit purées may tempt your baby if his appetite is decreased.

Oral thrush

Babies can develop a yeast fungal infection in their mouths, known as oral thrush. The same fungus, *Candida albicans*, can also affect the nappy area, and lead to development of nappy rash.

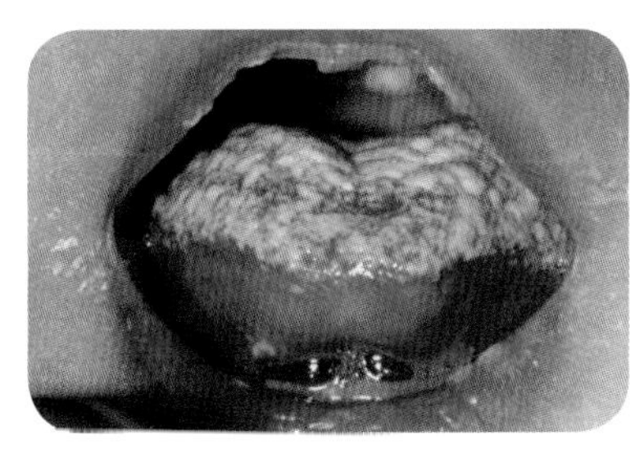

Oral thrush spots Here seen on a baby's tongue, the spots of oral thrush are often described as looking like cottage cheese.

WHAT IS THE CAUSE?

We all carry Candida in our mouths but in some babies they overgrow, or the balance between them and other bacteria changes, causing thrush. Poor hygiene is not a factor. Oral thrush is most common in babies up to 10 weeks but can affect older babies too.

SHOULD I SEE A DOCTOR?

Take your baby to the doctor who can prescribe antifungal gels or drops to put in your baby's mouth. If you are breastfeeding you will be given an antifungal ointment or cream to put on your breasts. If your baby's symptoms do not improve after a week, return to your doctor. However, if your baby stops drinking at any time, perhaps due to a sore mouth, take her to see your doctor.

If you are bottle-feeding, sterilize or replace bottle teats. You should also clean or sterilize toys and dummies.

Possible symptoms

- ★ Whitish spots or patches inside the cheeks, on the roof of the mouth (palate), gums, or tongue
- ★ Spots can be scraped off, leaving a red sore patch that may bleed
- ★ Drooling or difficulty feeding if the spots are sore

Failure to thrive

Failure to thrive is a term used to describe babies or children who are not putting on weight and growing in comparison to other children their age.

WHAT IS THE CAUSE?

There are many possible causes of failure to thrive. They include:

- ★ Not getting enough milk, for example if the baby has problems latching onto the breast or there is not enough breast milk.
- ★ Long-term (chronic) medical conditions such as heart conditions or liver disease.
- ★ Digestive system disorders such as reflux.
- ★ Any condition that affects the ability to eat, such as a cleft palate.
- ★ Hormonal disorders, such as an overactive thyroid gland.
- ★ Social reasons, such as poverty, meaning there isn't enough money for food.

SHOULD I SEE A DOCTOR?

If you're concerned that your child is not putting on weight appropriately, tell your health visitor or visit your doctor or local baby weighing clinic. Take along your baby's personal child health book which contains her growth charts. Your doctor may require at least two measurements over a period of weeks or months to assess the rate of weight gain. If your doctor feels your baby is not putting on sufficient weight you will be referred to a paediatrician.

Treatment depends on what is found. If the baby is not getting enough milk, the answer may simply be help with latching on and positioning the baby, or putting the baby to the breast more regularly to increase milk supply. Any underlying diseases will need treating. If failure to thrive is diagnosed and has a treatable cause, small babies may catch up so that they grow and develop normally.

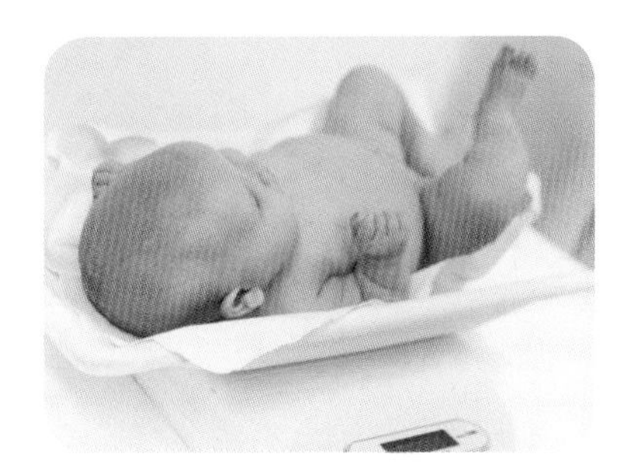

Weighing baby Your baby's weight and growth are measured regularly to identify whether she is growing as she should be.

Inguinal hernia

In an inguinal hernia, weakness in the abdominal wall causes part of the intestines to bulge out, producing a lump in the groin. It most commonly appears during a baby's first year.

Possible symptoms

- ★ Lump or bulge in the groin or the scrotum which may move in and out
- ★ The bulge may only appear during crying or when straining to pass stool

WHAT IS THE CAUSE?

Most inguinal hernias occur in boys, with up to 1 in 50 being affected, and they are more common in premature babies. In the womb the testes form in a boy's abdomen and travel down into the scrotum through a structure called the inguinal canal. If this canal does not close properly behind the testes, there is a weakness and the intestines can bulge through it.

WHAT'S THE TREATMENT?

If your child has a lump or bulge in the groin take him to the doctor. In most cases, elective surgery to repair an inguinal hernias is recommended to prevent the risk of a hernia becoming irreducible (see below).

ARE THERE COMPLICATIONS?

If an inguinal hernia is not repaired, it may become irreducible, meaning it cannot be pushed back. Symptoms of an irreducible hernia include pain (causing your baby to cry) and redness and tenderness of the lump. If your child develops these symptoms, call an ambulance because urgent surgery is needed to replace the intestines back into the abdomen and repair the defect in the tissues of the abdominal wall.

Umbilical hernia

In an umbilical hernia, part of the intestines protrudes though a weakness in the surrounding tissue causing a bulge at the navel. An umbilical hernia usually appears a few weeks after birth.

Possible symptoms

- ★ Lump or bulge at the navel
- ★ The lump may bulge out further, or may only appear when the child is crying or straining, for example during coughing or crying

WHAT IS THE CAUSE?

The navel is the site where the umbilical cord was connected. During development in the womb, there is a period when some of the intestines lie within the umbilical cord, outside the abdomen. Normally they return to the abdomen and the abdominal wall has closed by the time of birth. If the area fails to close completely there is a weak spot, which may lead to a hernia.

Umbilical hernias are common in babies: about 1 in 10 children are affected.

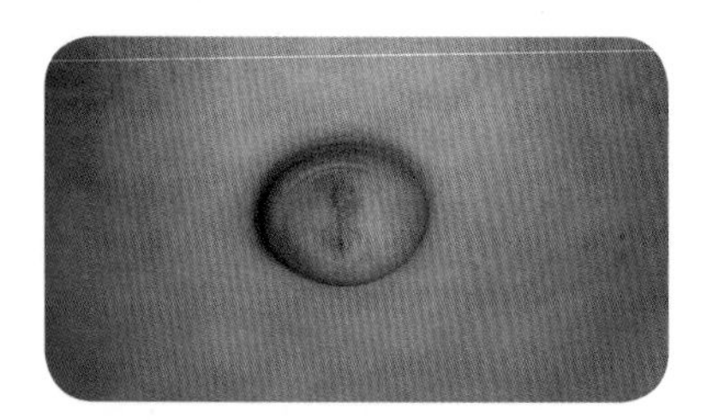

Umbilical hernia The bulge at the navel seen here is an umbilical hernia. Sometimes a hernia only appears when a child strains.

WHAT'S THE TREATMENT?

In the majority of cases no treatment is needed as the muscles seal themselves and the hernia disappears by the time the child is one year old. Some hernias persist for longer, but by the age of 4 years, 9 out of 10 hernias have disappeared. If a hernia persists after age 4, the defect in the abdominal wall can be repaired surgically. Children usually recover quickly from the operation and can resume their normal activities in a few weeks.

ARE THERE COMPLICATIONS?

Rarely, some of the intestine becomes trapped, which is known as a strangulated hernia. This complication causes pain and vomiting and the bulge becomes hard and cannot be pushed pack into the abdomen. If this happens, call an ambulance as urgent surgery is needed to replace the intestines and repair the abdominal tissues to prevent permanent damage.

Infectious diseases

The disorders covered in this section are caused by viral or bacterial infections. They are included here rather than under one of the body systems as their effects are widespread, affecting more than one part of the body. For example, the measles virus affects the skin, causing a rash, but it can also infect the nose and throat, causing stuffiness and a cough. Infections specific to particular body systems are covered in their appropriate sections.

Meningitis

Meningitis is an infection of the lining of the brain. Infection with meningococcal bacteria is very serious as they can cause septicaemia (blood poisoning), one symptom of which is a rash that does not fade when pressed (see box below).

Possible symptoms

The symptoms can occur in any order, and only some may be present:

Babies and toddlers

- ★ Decreased appetite/refusing to eat
- ★ Grunting/fast breathing
- ★ Cold hands and feet
- ★ Pale, blotchy, or blue skin
- ★ Irritability or excessive crying especially when picked up or handled (may be due to limb pain)
- ★ Floppy, listless, less alert and active than usual, and may be unresponsive
- ★ High-pitched or unusual cry or moaning
- ★ Bulging or tense fontanelle (the soft spot on a baby's head)

Older children

- ★ Severe muscle or limb pains
- ★ Irritability or confusion
- ★ Headache
- ★ Stiff neck
- ★ Dislike of bright lights (photophobia)
- ★ Diarrhoea and/or stomach cramps

All ages

- ★ Fever and vomiting
- ★ Drowsiness, lethargy, or difficulty waking up
- ★ Rash of red or purple spots that does not fade under a glass (see glass test, left). It can start as a few small spots but can extend to look like small bruises. Do NOT wait for the rash to appear before seeking medical help

WHAT ARE THE CAUSES?

In children, meningococcal bacteria are the most common cause of infection. Many people carry this bacterium harmlessly in the nose or throat; for unknown reasons, it sometimes infects the meninges and may enter the blood to cause septicaemia (blood poisoning). Meningitis and septicaemia can occur together or separately. Bacterial infection in another part of the body can also cause meningitis. Many viruses that cause other infectious diseases, such as chickenpox and influenza, can infect the meninges. Babies and young children are at especially high risk of meningitis and septicaemia.

SHOULD I SEE A DOCTOR?

If you are concerned that your child may have meningitis or septicaemia, seek urgent medical help. These conditions are emergencies that require hospital admission. Tests will be done to confirm the diagnosis. Treatment is with intravenous antibiotics and sometimes antiviral medication. The Health Protection Agency will be informed to try to prevent the infection spreading.

ARE THERE COMPLICATIONS?

Meningitis and septicaemia are serious conditions that can be fatal. Even if treated, recovery may be slow and there is a risk of various complications. Hearing loss is the most common complication of meningitis, so children who have had this will be offered hearing tests. Other complications include learning difficulties, problems with memory and concentration, vision loss, and epilepsy. There may be psychological effects from the trauma of the condition, such as anxiety, a fear of doctors, or behavioural changes such as temper tantrums.

IS IT PREVENTABLE?

Vaccines against some of the organisms that cause meningitis and septicaemia are part of the UK immunization programme. If your child has had close contact with a child who contracts bacterial meningitis she may be offered preventive antibiotics. This treatment kills the meningococcal bacteria and prevents them spreading.

The glass test

The glass test is a way of finding out whether your child has a rash that is typical of septicaemia. Check your child's entire body for the spots: they may be more difficult to see on dark skin but can be more visible on paler areas like the palms of the hands.

Checking the rash Press the side of a glass firmly against the rash. If the spots do not fade under pressure, call an ambulance.

Tetanus

Tetanus is a serious bacterial infection that can lead to kidney failure, suffocation, heart attack, or blood poisoning (septicaemia) and can be fatal if untreated. It is rare in the UK due to vaccination.

WHAT IS THE CAUSE?

Tetanus is caused by the bacterium *Clostridium tetani*, which can be found in soil and manure. It can enter the body through a cut, a fracture in which bone sticks out of the skin, or a puncture wound. The bacteria release a toxin that causes the symptoms, which appear between 4 and 21 days after exposure.

SHOULD I SEE A DOCTOR?

If your child develops any symptoms that could indicate tetanus, seek urgent medical help. Anyone with tetanus is admitted to hospital for treatment.

IS IT PREVENTABLE?

Tetanus can be prevented with the tetanus vaccine that is routinely given as part of the UK immunization programme.

Even if your child has been immunized against tetanus, you should always clean cuts, grazes, or other wounds promptly and thoroughly. If your child has not had the full course of tetanus injections or you are not sure whether he has had them and you are concerned about a wound, see your doctor. An injection of tetanus antibodies can be given to provides short-term protection against tetanus. If tetanus does develop, hospital treatment is needed.

Possible symptoms

- ★ Muscle spasms and stiffness
- ★ Difficulty breathing and swallowing (due to the muscle spasms)
- ★ Fever, headache, sore throat, diarrhoea, blood in the stool, and sweating are other possible symptoms

Wearing gloves Soil may contain tetanus bacteria. If your child likes gardening, give her gloves to guard against infection.

Scarlet fever

A bacterial infection that causes a scarlet rash, scarlet fever is no longer common in the UK due to the use of antibiotics for bacterial infections.

WHAT IS THE CAUSE?

Scarlet fever is caused by streptococcus bacteria and can follow a sore throat or, less commonly, streptococcal skin infections. It is spread by breathing in droplets from an infected person's coughs and sneezes. Symptoms appear between 1 and 4 days after infection.

SHOULD I SEE A DOCTOR?

See your doctor if you suspect scarlet fever. The illness is usually mild but can lead to complications, including pneumonia, ear infection, rheumatic fever (which can lead to heart damage), and kidney inflammation. Generally a 10-day course of antibiotics is prescribed and prevents complications. You can use paracetamol or ibuprofen to bring down a fever and should encourage your child to drink lots of fluids. Your child should be excluded from school for 5 days after starting antibiotics. She should feel better in a week, but for up to 6 weeks after the rash has faded, the skin on the body may peel.

Possible symptoms

- ★ Fever and sore throat (or skin infection)
- ★ 12–48 hours later: rash starts as red spots often on the neck or chest, then spreads over the body and becomes pinky-red and may have a rough, sandpapery texture
- ★ Flushed cheeks with pale area around mouth
- ★ Pale tongue with small red spots that may peel, leaving tongue swollen and red
- ★ Swollen lymph glands in neck
- ★ Headache

Chickenpox

Children between 2 and 8 are especially likely to catch chickenpox, although the disease can occur at any age. Usually a mild and short-lived illness in children, it causes a distinctive rash of extremely itchy spots that turn into blisters, then crust over.

WHAT IS THE CAUSE?
Chickenpox is caused by the varicella zoster virus and is spread by breathing in droplets from infected people's coughs and sneezes or by touching the blisters and is more common in the spring. It takes 10–21 days for symptoms to develop after being in contact with the virus.

Your child is infectious from 2 or 3 days before until 5 days after the rash appears. It is therefore recommended that you keep your child at home until the last spot has crusted over, which is generally about 5–7 days after the rash appears.

It is important that both children and adults with chickenpox avoid contact with pregnant women as contracting chickenpox during pregnancy can result in damage to the developing fetus as well as complications for the woman.

ARE THERE COMPLICATIONS?
In the majority of cases the illness is mild and there are no complications. However, the following can occur:

★ Skin infections are probably the most common complication of chickenpox, occurring in about 1 in 10 children. A child scratches a spot and introduces bacteria into the wound. The skin around the spot becomes red, swollen, hot, and tender to touch, often with pus or yellow crusting. The child may become more feverish. A course of antibiotics may be required.

★ Scarring can develop at the site of spots; discouraging your child from scratching may help prevent this.

★ An ear infection occurs in about 1 in 20 children.

★ Pneumonia (p.157) is a less common complication that might be suspected if a child has difficulty breathing. It may require treatment with antibiotics.

★ Extremely rarely, chickenpox can lead to meningitis (p102), encephalitis (inflammation of the brain) or myocarditis (inflammation of the heart).

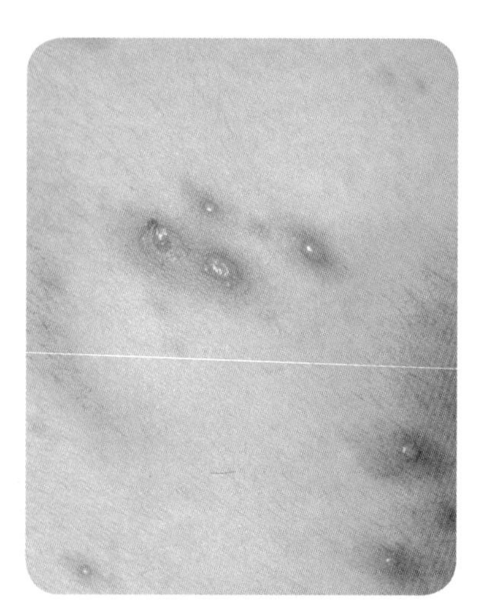

Early chickenpox rash The initial itchy red spots of a chickenpox rash soon turn into fluid-filled blisters, as seen here.

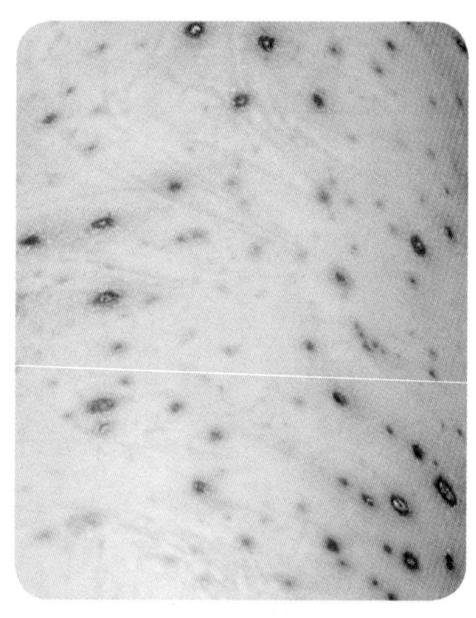

Later rash Spots that formed earlier have now crusted over, and there are new red spots, some of which have blistered.

Possible symptoms

Initially, general symptoms of any viral illness, which may include feeling unwell, decreased appetite, mild headache, or fever. A rash appears a few hours later that consists of:

★ Red, extremely itchy spots on any part of the body, including the face and inside of the mouth, that turn into small, fluid-filled blisters within about 12–24 hours and then after a few days crust over before healing

★ Crops of spots that may be at different stages: as one patch of spots develops, another patch is blistering, while another is crusting over or healing

SHOULD I SEE A DOCTOR?
Childhood chickenpox does not usually require medical care. However, you should contact the doctor if your child:

★ Becomes more unwell.

★ Develops complications such as skin infections (see above).

★ Is under one month old.

★ Has a depressed immune system (which could be due to chemotherapy or oral steroids) and has had contact with someone with chickenpox, even if there are no symptoms. Such children are at greater risk of complication, and can be given an injection of antibodies to fight the virus.

★ Affected adults should contact their doctor as they are generally more severely affected than children and are more likely to develop complications. They may be offered antiviral medications.

ARE THERE ANY COMPLEMENTARY THERAPIES?

You can apply aloe vera gel, available from pharmacies, to a chickenpox rash to help cool and soothe itching skin and speed healing. The gel can be applied as frequently as needed. Chickweed cream or ointment is also sometimes used as a natural alternative to calamine lotion. Although aloe vera and chickweed preparations may help, evidence for their effectiveness is unclear. Before using them, check with your pharmacist they are suitable for your child's age.

WHAT'S THE OUTLOOK?

Children with chickenpox usually recover completely within 7–10 days of symptoms first appearing. After an attack of chickenpox, it's very rare to have it again because the body develops immunity to the virus. However, the virus lies inactive in a part of the nervous system, and if reactivated later it causes shingles, which results in a painful rash.

What can I do to help?

There are several measures you can take to help relieve the symptoms of chickenpox. Itching can be especially distressing and it is important to treat this, not only to make your child more comfortable but also to reduce scratching and decrease the risk of infection, which can lead to scarring.

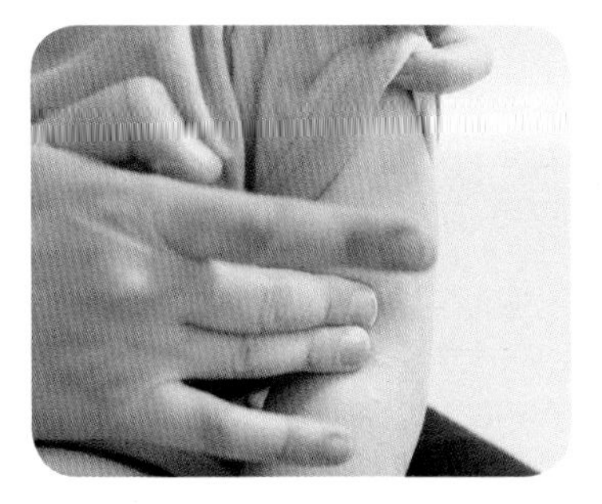

Apply calamine lotion This can be very effective in relieving itching. However, do not use calamine lotion on the face, especially near the eyes.

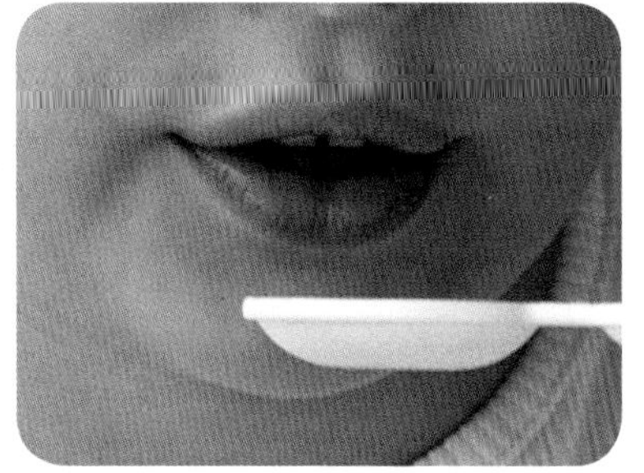

Give painkillers You can give your child paracetamol or ibuprofen to bring down a fever and relieve any aches or pains your child may have as a result of the illness.

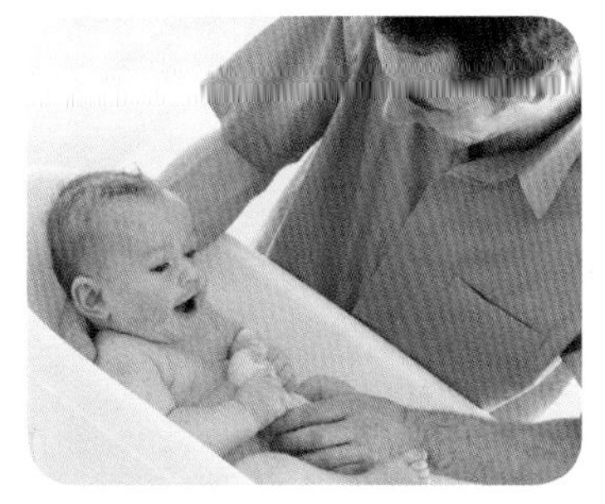

Bathe your child You can soothe your child's irritated skin by bathing her in cool water. You can add a handful of oatmeal or baking soda to the water.

Keep fingernails short Cut your child's nails regularly and encourage her not to scratch the spots, which can introduce bacteria into the skin, causing infection.

Give plenty of fluids It is important for your child to drink lots of fluids when she has a temperature in order to avoid the possibility of dehydration.

Offer sugar-free lollies These may be soothing if your child has a sore mouth. Avoid giving salty foods or foods or drinks high in acid, such as fruit juice.

Measles

Although previously thought to be eradicated, measles is now back. This viral infection can be extremely serious, even fatal. It is most common in young children under 4, but it can affect non-vaccinated people of any age.

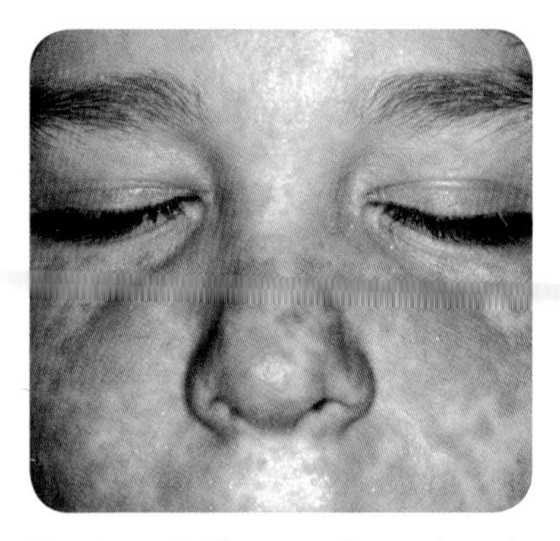

Measles rash The spots of a measles rash often join together, creating red patches. The rash spreads over the face and body.

WHAT IS THE CAUSE?

The virus that causes measles is spread by droplets of saliva from infected people's coughs and sneezes which are then breathed in by others. The virus can live outside the body for a few hours so it can also be caught from touching infected surfaces, such as door handles or toys. Symptoms appear 1–2 weeks after being exposed to the virus. The infectious period is from 2 days before the rash appears until 5 days afterwards.

SHOULD I SEE A DOCTOR?

If you think your child has measles, she should be seen by your doctor who must notify the Health Protection Agency. If the diagnosis is confirmed, you can treat your child at home (see box), but see your doctor again if your child's fever does not come down with paracetamol or ibuprofen, if your child is not eating or drinking or playing as normal, seems to be getting worse, or develops additional symptoms such as earache or vomiting. Call an ambulance if your child's breathing becomes abnormally rapid, she becomes drowsy, has a seizure, or develops a severe headache. These could indicate a serious complication, such as pneumonia, meningitis, or, rarely, encephalitis, a brain infection that can cause seizures and brain damage and can be fatal.

WHAT'S THE OUTLOOK?

Most children recover within about 10 days after symptoms appear, although a cough may persist for a short while longer. Approximately 1 in 10 children with measles needs admission to hospital because of a complication.

Once your child has had measles, she is immune to further attacks. Measles can be prevented by a vaccination. The measles vaccine is included in the MMR vaccine, which is given as part of the routine UK immunization programme.

Possible symptoms

- ★ Initially, fever, cough and cold symptoms, and red whites of the eyes (conjunctivitis)
- ★ White spots called Koplik spots may appear in the mouth, on the inside of the cheeks opposite the incisors (if these are seen the diagnosis is always measles)
- ★ A few days later, a rash of fine small red spots, which may join together, appears, typically beginning behind the ears and then spreading over the face and body
- ★ Skin may peel off after the rash disappears, usually in 3 or 4 days

What can I do to help?

There is no specific treatment for measles, but children should be excluded from school for 5 days after the onset of the rash.

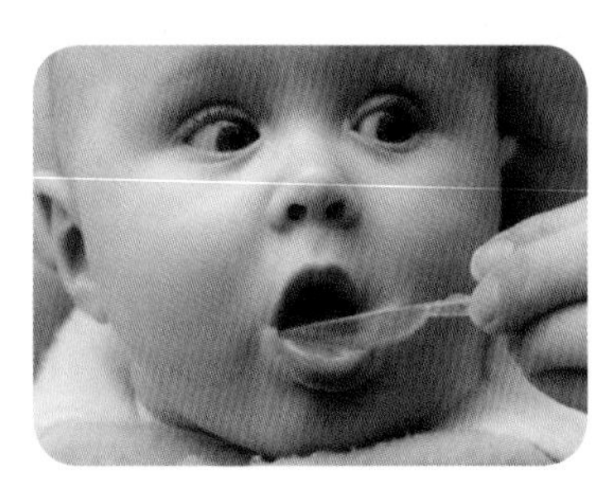

Give painkillers Paracetamol or ibuprofen can be given to bring down a fever and relieve any discomfort.

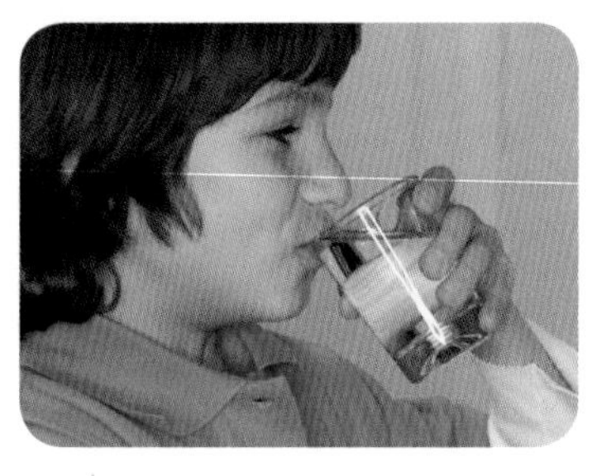

Offer plenty of fluids During a fever, fluids are lost from the body by sweating so need to be replaced.

Rubella

Also known as German measles, rubella is a viral infection that can cause a rash and swollen glands in the neck. Although often a mild condition, it can cause severe problems in an unborn baby if it is caught during pregnancy.

Possible symptoms

Prodromal or early symptoms are:

- ★ Feeling unwell
- ★ Sore throat
- ★ Runny or blocked nose, headache
- ★ Fever

The main symptoms then develop:

- ★ Swollen lymph glands in the neck, which may be painful
- ★ Pinky red rash that starts 3 or 4 days after initial symptoms, often starts behind the ears before spreading all over the body and may be itchy
- ★ Painful joints (rare in children)

WHAT IS THE CAUSE?

The rubella virus is contracted by breathing in droplets from other people's coughs and sneezes. Symptoms do not appear until 2–3 weeks after exposure to the virus.

Rubella is infectious from 7 days before until 4 days after the rash appears.

SHOULD I SEE A DOCTOR?

Rubella does not generally require medical treatment. However, rubella cases must be notified to the Health Protection Agency so if you think your child may have the condition you must inform your doctor. As always, if you are concerned that your child is unwell, do see your doctor.

ARE THERE COMPLICATIONS?

Potential complications include:

- ★ Diarrhoea and vomiting.
- ★ Ear infection.
- ★ Rarely, pneumonia, encephalitis (brain infection), myocarditis (inflammation of the heart), and problems with blood cells involved in clotting.

If a pregnant woman contracts rubella there is a risk of miscarriage or it can affect the unborn baby, potentially causing deafness, cataracts, heart problems, or brain damage. If you think your child may have rubella, keep him away from women who are pregnant or could be pregnant for at least a week after the rash develops.

WHAT'S THE OUTLOOK?

The rash and any symptoms usually disappear after a week to 10 days. Once your child has had rubella, he is unlikely to have it again. Rubella is prevented with a vaccine and has been part of the UK immunization programme for many years. It's given as part of the MMR vaccine.

Typical rubella rash The rash consists of small pink or light red spots, which may merge to form evenly coloured patches. The rash can occur all over the body.

What can I do to help?

As with measles, there is no specific treatment for rubella. However, your child will need to stay at home for 5 days after the rash appears to prevent infecting others.

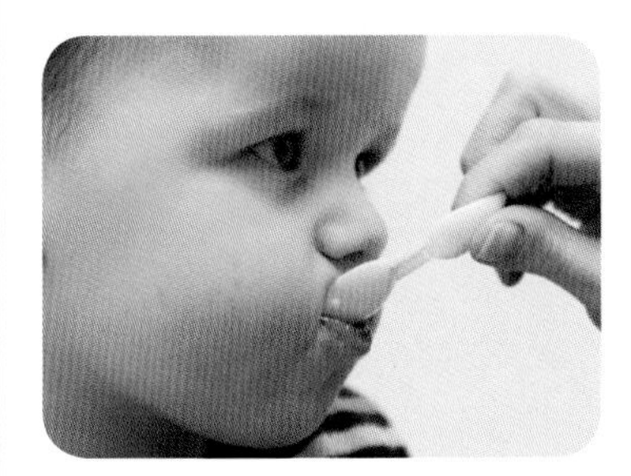

Give painkillers Paracetamol or ibuprofen will help bring down your child's fever and treat any pain.

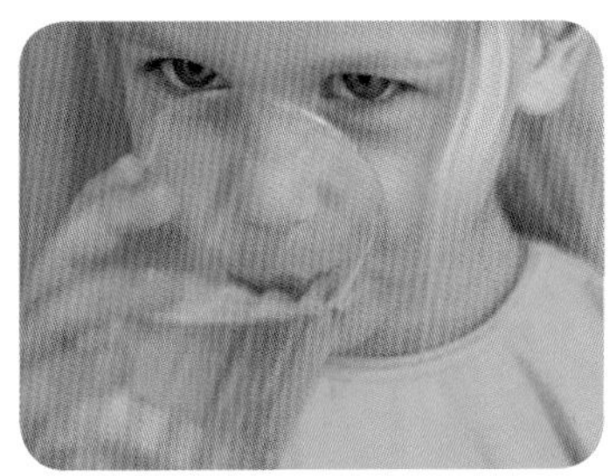

Offer plenty of fluids Your child should drink lots of fluids to prevent dehydration during illness.

Mumps

Mumps is a viral infection that causes swelling of salivary glands in the cheeks. It commonly occurs in young children although it can affect people of any age if they have not been vaccinated against it.

WHAT IS THE CAUSE?

Mumps is caused by a paramyxovirus and is caught by breathing in the virus in droplets from infected people's coughs and sneezes. Symptoms appear 2–3 weeks after being infected by the virus.

To avoid spreading the infection to others, encourage your child to cough or sneeze into a tissue, discard the tissue into a wastebin, and then wash her hands. Keep her at home for 5 days after the symptoms first appear. She should avoid contact with pregnant women who are not immune to mumps because it increases the risk of miscarriage.

SHOULD I SEE A DOCTOR?

If you think your child has mumps you should see your doctor, who will need to notify the Health Protection Agency. There is no specific treatment for mumps.

ARE THERE COMPLICATIONS?

★ Viral meningitis (inflammation of the membranes covering the brain) can occur a week after the initial infection and affects up to 1 in 10 children with mumps, who may then require hospital admission.

★ Inflammation of the pancreas occurs in approximately 1 in 20 of children; it generally causes pain in the upper tummy and may require admission to hospital.

★ Inflammation of the testes or ovaries can occur if mumps is contracted after puberty. Testicular inflammation can lead to a reduced sperm count, which in rare cases causes infertility. Infertility due to inflamed ovaries is extremely rare.

Possible symptoms

★ **Initially,** fever, headache, tiredness, or earache

★ **1–2 days later,** swelling of salivary glands on the side of the face below the ears, which may be uneven, making one side of the face look more swollen than the other

★ **Pain** or difficulty swallowing or chewing

IS IT PREVENTABLE?

Mumps can be prevented with the MMR vaccine which is routinely given as part of the UK immunization programme.

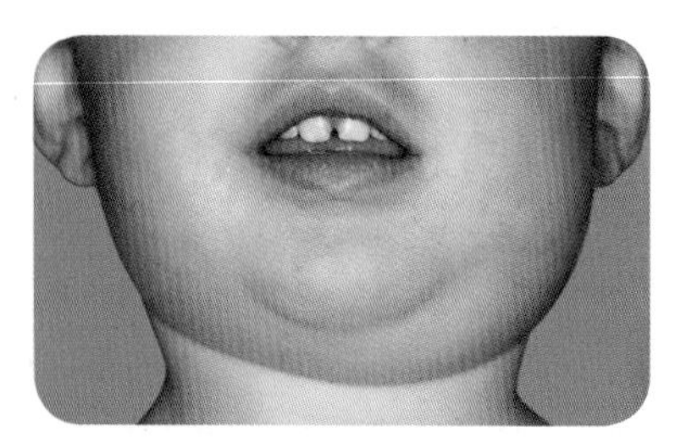

Swollen face in mumps Swelling of the salivary glands in the cheeks can give a child with mumps a hamster-like appearance.

What can I do to help?

A cold compress on the swollen glands can ease discomfort and reduce swelling. See below for other measures. Your child should not chew gum as it encourages saliva production, worsening pain.

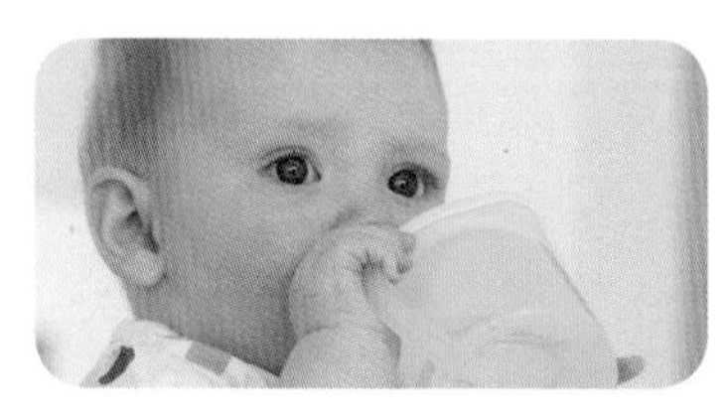

Offer plenty of fluids Give her drinks often. Avoid acidic drinks, such as fruit juice, which can make pain worse.

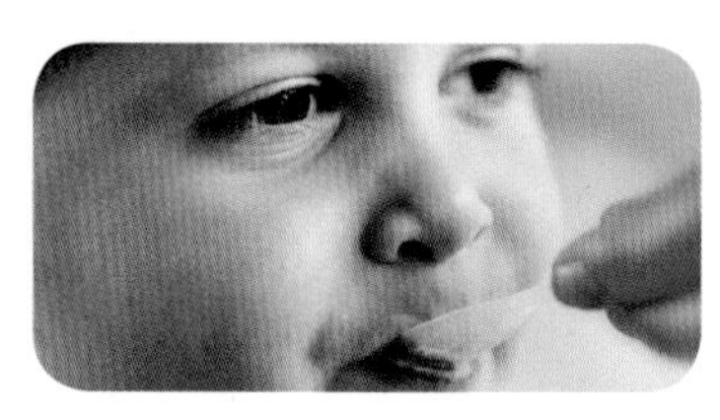

Give painkillers Paracetamol or ibuprofen help bring down any fever.

Provide soft foods Porridge, soups, mashed potatoes, or other soft foods will be easier for your child to eat if swallowing is difficult or painful.

Hand, foot, and mouth disease

This common mild viral infection, which lasts about a week, causes small ulcers to appear inside the mouth. It is *not* the same as foot and mouth disease, which affects cattle.

Hand, foot, and mouth disease is contracted by breathing in droplets containing the virus. Symptoms appear 3–6 days after exposure and usually clear up in 7–10 days.

Encourage your child to drink plenty of fluids but if she won't, take her to the doctor because there is a risk of dehydration. If spots have become infected through scratching, you should also see the doctor because antibiotics may be needed.

Your child can go back to school when she feels better, although she can still be infectious for a few weeks.

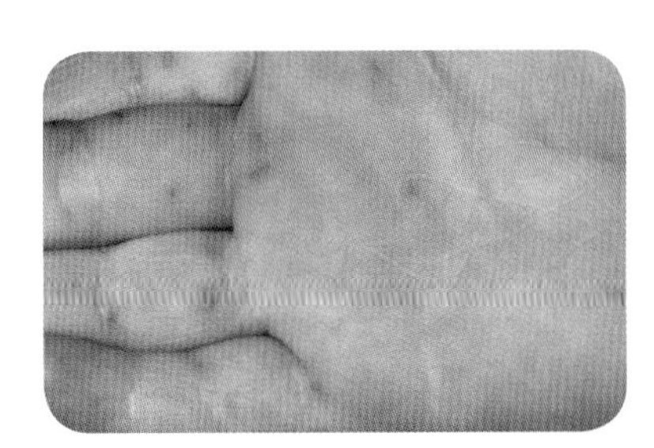

Small blisters Children with hand, foot, and mouth disease often develop small blisters on their hands and feet.

Possible symptoms

- Fever
- Feeling unwell
- Sore throat
- Red spots inside the mouth which, after 1–2 days, turn into ulcers that can be painful
- Small, red, sometimes tender spots on hands and feet, and sometimes on other areas, such as buttocks and legs, that appear 1–2 days after the mouth ulcers and may turn into small blisters (these spots occur in three-quarters of children)

What can I do to help?

The mouth ulcers can be painful so avoid giving very hot, salty, or acidic food. Sucking on an ice lolly or ice cube can help soothe your child's pain.

You could also try a teething gel or a local anaesthetic spray, but check with your pharmacist first that it is suitable for your child's age.

Encourage drinking Your child may not want to drink due to a sore mouth, but it's important to avoid dehydration.

Offer a sugar-free ice lolly Sucking on an ice lolly or ice cube helps to numb a painful mouth and also provides extra fluids.

Give painkillers Paracetamol or ibuprofen will help bring down any fever and help relieve discomfort.

Roseola infantum

This viral illness generally affects children aged 3 months to 3 years. It is caught by breathing in droplets from an infected child, and symptoms begin 5–15 days after infection.

WHAT'S THE TREATMENT?

There is no specific treatment for roseola infantum, although you can give your child paracetamol or ibuprofen to bring down a fever and should encourage him to drink plenty of fluids. Once his temperature has returned to normal and he feels better there is no need to exclude him from school.

ARE THERE COMPLICATIONS?

Roseola infantum is generally mild and most children recover from it very quickly. Rare complications, which usually only occur in children who have a suppressed immune system, include meningitis; encephalitis (an infection of the brain), and pneumonia.

Possible symptoms

- ★ Fever, lasting for about 3 days, which may start suddenly and be high
- ★ Swollen lymph glands in the neck, sore throat, or earache
- ★ After the fever subsides, a usually non-itchy rash of tiny pale pink or red spots appears, starting on the trunk (abdomen, chest and back) and then spreading to the rest of the body

Slapped cheek syndrome

Slapped cheek syndrome, also known as fifth disease or erythema infectiosum, is a viral infection that causes a distinctive red rash on both cheeks. It is generally a mild, short-lived illness.

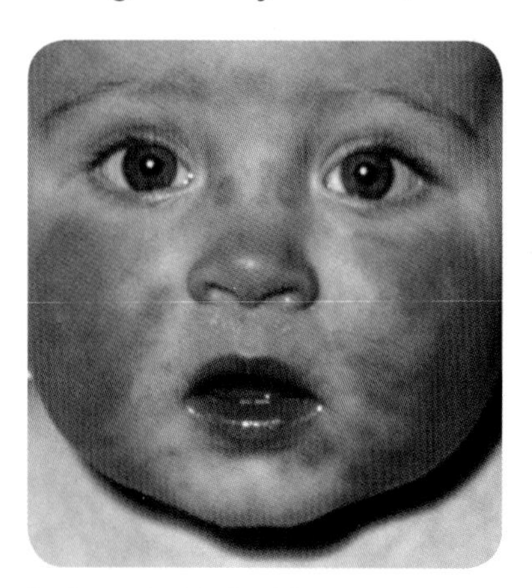

Rash on cheeks A bright red rash on both cheeks is characteristic of slapped cheek syndrome and gives the disease its name.

WHAT IS THE CAUSE?

The infection that causes slapped cheek syndrome, parvovirus B19, is spread by breathing in droplets from infected people's coughs and sneezes. The illness is extremely common, and it is thought that up to 8 in 10 adults are immune to the virus as they were exposed to it as children. Although generally a mild infection, it can cause problems if pregnant women who are not immune catch the virus.

Symptoms appear 4–14 days after infection and children are most infectious during the early stages of the illness before the rash appears.

WHAT'S THE TREATMENT?

The fever can be treated by giving paracetamol or ibuprofen, but there is no specific treatment for slapped cheek syndrome. Offer your child plenty of fluids and encourage sneezing and coughing into a tissue and good hand-hygiene.

WHAT'S THE OUTLOOK?

Once the rash appears on the body your child will generally feel better and can return to school as she is unlikely to be contagious. The rash may recur during the next few months on exposure to heat or sunlight.

Once your child has had slapped cheek syndrome, she is unlikely to have it again.

Possible symptoms

- ★ High fever, sore throat, tiredness, or feeling unwell
- ★ After 3–7 days, a bright red rash appears on both cheeks
- ★ 1–4 days later, the rash spreads over the rest of the body, and typically looks "lacy" with a raised appearance, and may be itchy or uncomfortable

Lyme disease

This bacterial infection is transmitted by tick bites. Ticks are small insects that bite humans and other mammals and live on animals such as deer. If treated early, Lyme disease is usually mild, but without treatment it can be more serious.

WHAT IS THE CAUSE?

Lyme disease is caused by infection with the bacterium *Borrelia burgdoferi*, which is carried by ticks. Although not common in the UK, there is still a risk in wooded and grassy areas where tick-carrying animals live. There has been a slight increase in the disease in the UK due to expanding deer populations and perhaps because people are taking part in more outdoor leisure activities. The disease is more common in rural areas of France, Germany, and the US.

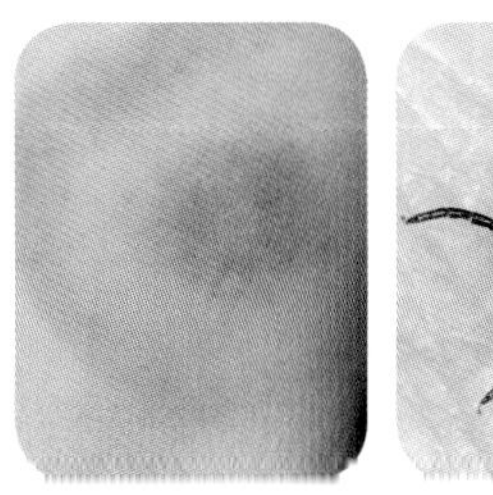

Lyme disease rash (left) The rash looks like a bull's eye. **Deer tick (right)** A tick bite can transmit Lyme disease to humans.

Possible symptoms

Early symptoms, developing 3–30 days after being bitten, include:

- ★ Rash that looks similar to a bull's eye on a dartboard, with a small red spot in the centre, surrounded by a paler area and a red outer ring
- ★ Headache, joint pains, and fatigue may accompany the rash

If the condition is not treated other symptoms can develop after weeks or months. They include:

- ★ Joint pain, stiffness, and swelling
- ★ Memory and concentration problems
- ★ Numbness in hands or feet

SHOULD I SEE A DOCTOR?

If your child develops any symptoms of Lyme disease, take him to the doctor because early treatment is essential to prevent the infection spreading to other parts of the body, such as the joints and nervous system, and causing serious problems. If your child has been in a rural area and could have been bitten by a tick, make sure to tell the doctor as this will make the diagnosis easier. The doctor can usually make the diagnosis based on your child's symptoms but in some cases blood tests are needed. Lyme disease is treated with a course of antibiotics.

WHAT'S THE OUTLOOK

With antibiotic treatment, your child will usually feel completely better within a few days, the rash will disappear within 1 or 2 weeks, and there will be no long-term consequences. Even if more serious symptoms develop, they can usually be successfully treated, although a longer course of antibiotics may be required. There is no vaccine available to protect against Lyme disease.

What can I do to help?

A tick stays attached for a few hours. Check your child's skin at the end of the day, and if you find a tick remove it gently but firmly with tweezers. Don't crush the tick. Dispose of it immediately. Clean the site of the bite, the tweezers, and your hands.

Protection from bites Children should wear long sleeves and trousers and use insect repellent. Check clothing and pet's fur for ticks at the end of the day.

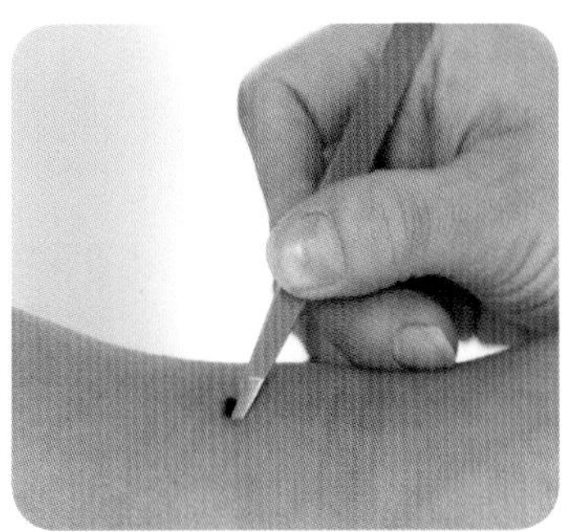

Remove an attached tick Grasp the tweezers as close to the skin as you can and pull firmly until the tick comes off. Don't twist the tweezers.

Whooping cough

Also known as pertussis, whooping cough is a bacterial lung infection that causes intense bouts of coughing that may end in a whooping sound. It is a serious illness, but is much less common than previously due to the whooping cough vaccine.

WHAT IS THE CAUSE?

Whooping cough is caused by the bacterium *Bordetella pertussis.* It is extremely infectious and is spread by breathing in droplets from an infected person's coughs and sneezes. Symptoms appear 7–10 days later.

SHOULD I SEE A DOCTOR?

If you think your child has whooping cough you should consult your doctor, who may use a swab to collect a sample of mucus from your child's throat for testing. If the diagnosis is confirmed, your doctor will have to inform the Health Protection Agency. Whooping cough is treated with antibiotics although young children may require admission to hospital for help with their breathing. Your child must stay at home for 5 days after starting antibiotics, or for 3 weeks (21 days) after the illness started if antibiotics aren't given.

ARE THERE COMPLICATIONS?

Complications are uncommon, but can include pneumonia, difficulties breathing, seizures or, very rarely, brain damage from lack of oxygen. Complications are more common in babies under 6 months old, so prompt treatment is especially important.

WHAT'S THE OUTLOOK?

Symptoms usually last for at least 2 weeks although sometimes they continue for 2–3 months even with treatment.

Whooping cough can be prevented with a vaccine that is part of the routine UK childhood immunization programme and is given at 2, 3, and 4 months and at the pre-school boosters.

Intense coughing Bouts of coughing can go on for several minutes and happen 12 or more times a day, exhausting the child.

Possible symptoms

Early symptoms lasting 1–2 weeks (similar to those of a common cold) are:

- ★ Fever
- ★ Runny or blocked nose and sneezing
- ★ Feeling unwell
- ★ Dry cough
- ★ Sore throat

Second stage symptoms, also known as the paroxysmal stage, include:

- ★ Bouts or paroxysms of intense coughing, generally about 12 bouts per day, which may produce phlegm (though young children may swallow this)
- ★ Whooping sound at the end of coughing may occur in older children
- ★ Vomiting caused by coughing
- ★ Red face after coughing
- ★ Tiredness

What can I do to help?

Eliminate irritants in the home that could trigger coughing, such as aerosol sprays or smoke from wood-burning stoves.

Let your child rest Continual coughing is extremely tiring, so let your child rest as much as possible while she recovers.

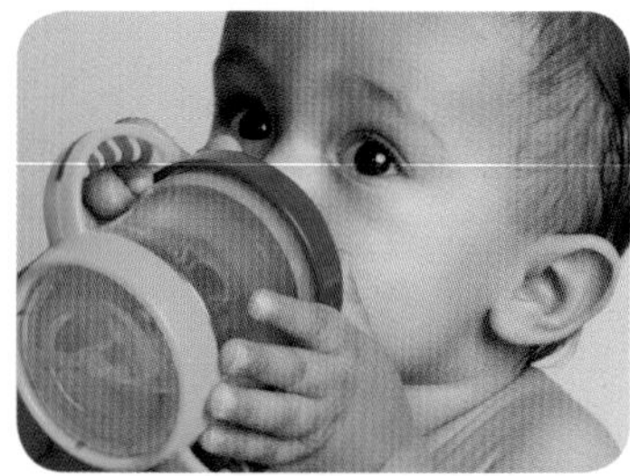

Give plenty of fluids Dehydration can be a risk, especially if a child vomits after coughing, so offer lots of fluids.

Skin disorders

Many different skin disorders can affect children. The first two conditions discussed in this section, eczema and psoriasis, tend to affect several different areas of the body. Their causes are not clear although there is probably an inherited component. The disorders discussed next are caused by infections and are generally more localized. They are grouped according to whether they are caused by bacterial, viral, fungal, or parasitic infections. The last group of conditions are due to physical injury rather than to infection.

Eczema

In this skin condition the skin becomes dry and itchy. Atopic eczema is the most common type in children, with as many as 1 in 5 developing it. Atopic refers to a sensitivity to allergens, and children with eczema may also have allergies.

WHAT IS THE CAUSE?

Although the exact cause of atopic eczema is not known, there may be an inherited component as it tends to affect children from families in which eczema, allergies, and hayfever are common.

In some children, eczema is worsened by various triggers, for example an allergy to house-dust mites or animal dander (dead skin and hair scales), or a sensitivity to laundry detergents. In approximately 1 in 10 affected children, eczema is made worse or triggered by a food allergy, commonly dairy produce or eggs.

SHOULD I SEE A DOCTOR?

Keeping your child's skin well moisturized with emollients may keep your child's eczema under control (see box, opposite) but if these are not sufficient or there are any signs of infection (see below), then see your doctor. To reduce inflammation during flare-ups, the doctor will probably prescribe a low-dose steroid cream or ointment. The steroid is usually applied at the first sign of a flare-up, until the skin looks normal again. Usually, you apply it once a day, 30 minutes after applying emollient. If skin is infected, a steroid and antibiotic may be prescribed.

If low-dose steroids don't work, the doctor may increase the dose or refer your child to a dermatologist. Alternatively creams containing other medications, oral medication, bandaging (in which wet wraps and medications are applied to the skin), or ultraviolet light therapy can be used.

You should also see your doctor if your child's symptoms seem to be triggered by certain foods – keeping a food and symptoms diary may help you to identify which ones. Do not exclude a food group without seeing your doctor first as this should be done with the guidance of a dietitian. Children need a wide variety of foods to meet their nutritional needs.

ARE THERE COMPLICATIONS?

★ Infection – the dry, cracked skin of eczema is more likely to become infected. If the skin becomes, red, hot, swollen, or has crusting, or if the eczema is not responding to treatment it may be infected.

★ Sleep problems – the itching of eczema may disturb your child's sleep, which in turn can affect mood, behaviour, and attendance at school. Keeping your child's eczema under control helps to prevent these undesirable side-effects.

★ Low self-esteem – your child may have low self-esteem or self-confidence because of the skin's appearance, or may experience bullying at school. If you are concerned about your child, speak to your doctor and the child's teachers.

Possible symptoms

Symptoms vary among children, as do severity and frequency of flare-ups. In children under 4, eczema generally starts on the face; in children over 4, it generally occurs in elbow and knee creases, wrists, and neck. Symptoms may include:

★ Red, flaky, itchy, and dry patches of skin

★ Thickened skin, which may develop painful cracks over time due to scratching

★ Raw, weepy skin where it has been scratched

★ Small raised bumps on areas of skin

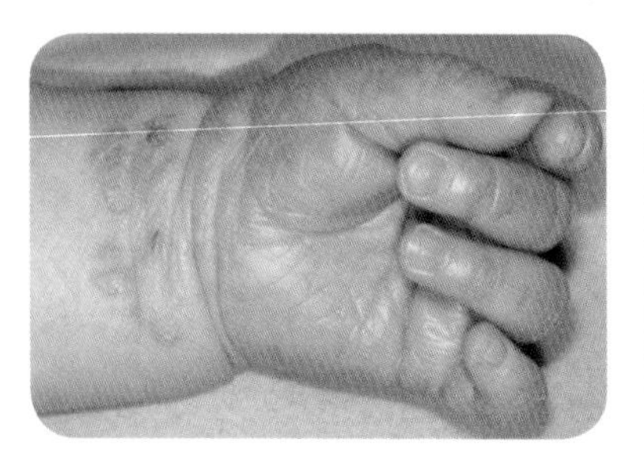

Scratched eczema rash An eczema rash sometimes consists of raised bumps, and if these are scratched, the tops may be open.

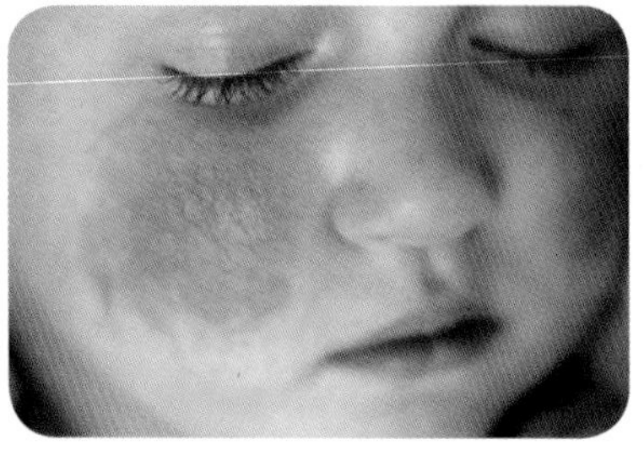

Eczema on cheeks In younger children, an eczema rash often starts on the cheeks, causing red, dry skin.

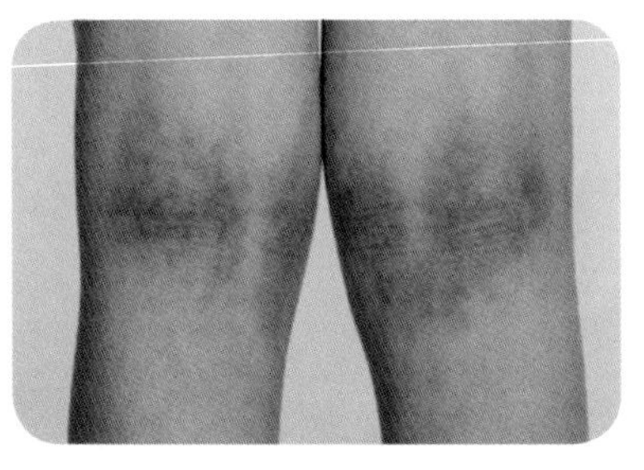

Eczema on backs of knees In older children, eczema often occurs on the backs of the knees and elbows.

ARE THERE ANY COMPLEMENTARY THERAPIES?
Many parents are anxious about using steroids or other medications for their child's eczema and turn to herbal creams or homeopathic remedies instead. While these may work in some cases there is little evidence for their efficacy, and some Chinese herbal medicines can have extremely serious side-effects.

WHAT'S THE OUTLOOK?
The course of eczema is very variable and many children improve as they grow older. In over half of children atopic eczema clears up by the time they are 11 years old.

What can I do to help?

The aim of treatment for eczema is to moisturize the skin to treat dryness. This treatment is on-going and is used to prevent flare-ups. Moisturizers (emollients) come as ointments, creams, or lotions; bath additives; and soap substitutes. They are available over the counter and on prescription.

Apply emollients Apply an emollient ointment, cream, or lotion at least 2–3 times a day, especially after bathing your child. Use enough so that your child's skin is slippery and shiny. As the skin absorbs the emollient it may look dry again. You could then apply some more.

Use soap substitutes Keeping skin clean helps prevent infection. However, soaps can be very drying to the skin and should not be used. Instead, use a soap substitute such as aqueous cream, which is just as effective as soap in cleansing the skin but does not have the same drying effect.

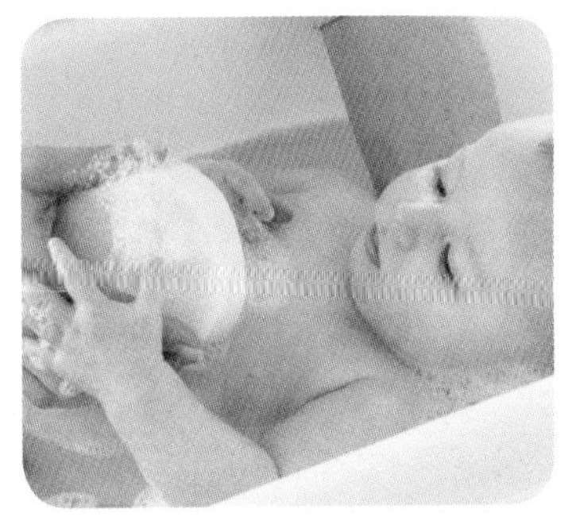

Use bath additives Children with eczema should bathe or shower once a day. Do not add bubble bath or bath oil as these are drying. Use a bath additive, which forms a waterproof barrier on the skin. After bathing, pat dry gently and apply an emollient ointment or cream.

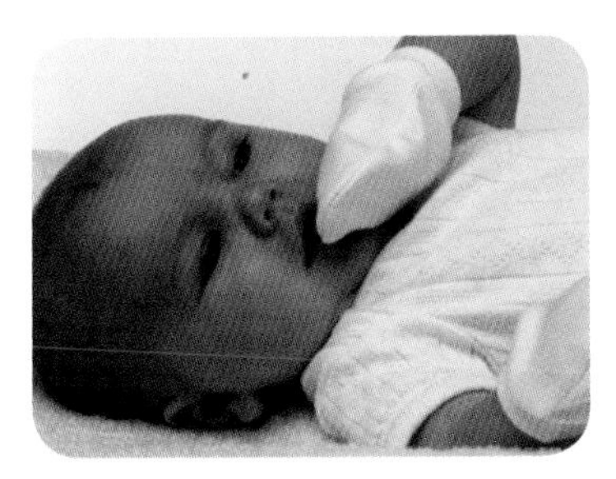

Prevent scratching Put scratch mitts or socks on your baby's hands at night, keep nails short, and dress him in loose cotton clothing. Older children may benefit from an antihistamine medicine before bed; discuss with your doctor.

Use the right amount To work out how much to use of a prescribed steroid, squeeze some cream onto your finger, from the fingertip to the first joint crease. The cream on your fingertip will treat an area twice the size of your hand with the fingers together.

Reduce house-mites If your child has an allergy to mites that triggers flare-ups, take steps to reduce them: vacuum regularly, dust furniture, air pillows, mattresses and their protective covers. Wash rugs frequently.

Psoriasis

Psoriasis affects about 1 in 50 people in the UK, causing patches of scaly skin. It is usually a chronic (long-term) condition, but it can occur temporarily in children after an infection. One in 10 people with the chronic form develops it before the age of 10.

WHAT IS THE CAUSE?

In psoriasis the process of shedding old skin cells and replacing them with new ones is much quicker than normal. Usually, skin cells take approximately 3–4 weeks to be produced, move through the layers of skin to the top layer before dying and being shed or flaking off. In psoriasis this takes only 2–6 days. It is not known exactly why psoriasis occurs, but it does run in families and is thought to be related to the immune system. It is not contagious and not related to poor hygiene.

The most common form of psoriasis in children and adults is called plaque psoriasis, in which raised, red patches of skin (plaques) develop. There is probably a trigger for the condition developing, but it has not yet been identified.

Guttate, also called raindrop or teardrop psoriasis, is a specific form of psoriasis that occurs mainly in children. It develops about 2–3 weeks after an infection, generally a throat infection caused by streptococcal bacteria. It causes a more generalized rash of small raindrop-shaped spots.

What can I do?

Moisturize your child's skin with emollients (ointments, creams, or lotions) at least two to three times a day and after a bath but as many times as possible. Dress your child in cotton clothing, and keep her nails short to prevent scratching.

Apply emollients generously Use enough so that your child's skin is slippery and shiny. As the skin absorbs the emollient it may look dry again. You could then reapply.

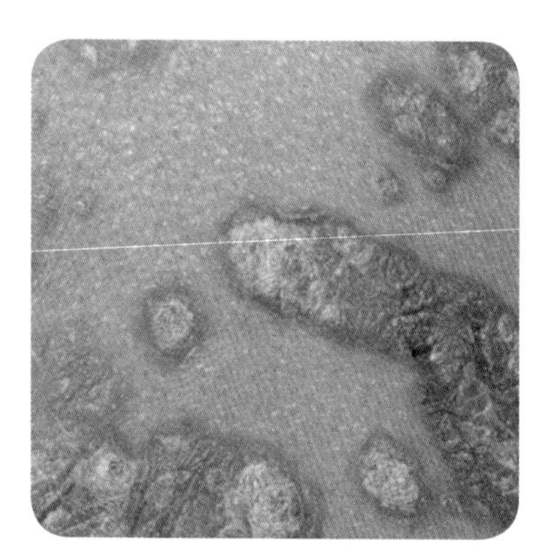

Psoriasis plaques Raised, red patches of skin (called plaques) covered with silvery scale are typical of chronic psoriasis.

Possible symptoms

Plaque psoriasis:

★ Raised, red patches (called plaques) of skin, covered with a silvery scale, with well-defined edges

★ Patches are commonly found on the backs of elbows, front of knees, scalp and lower back, but can occur anywhere, even affecting nails

★ Itching or soreness

Guttate psoriasis:

★ Rash of small salmon pink coloured spots (up to about 1cm/1/2in diameter) in the shape of teardrops

★ Spots can occur all over the body (though not the palms of hands or soles of feet)

SHOULD I SEE THE DOCTOR?

The initial treatments for psoriasis are similar to those for eczema, with the aim of keeping the skin well moisturized (see p115). For some children this is all that is needed, but if necessary your doctor can prescribe other topical treatments containing steroids, vitamin D analogues, coal tar, or dithranol. Some prescribed creams such as those containing coal tar have a strong smell and can stain clothes and bedding, so take care when applying these. If topical treatments do not work your doctor will refer your child to a dermatologist. Other therapies can include ultraviolet light therapy (phototherapy) or oral medications.

WHAT IS THE OUTLOOK?

Plaque psoriasis is likely to be lifelong, but attacks can be controlled. This is important as the appearance of the plaques can cause low self-esteem or result in bullying. Watch out for any signs of these problems due to the child's skin. In most cases, guttate psoriasis goes away after a few months, although it can become chronic.

Cellulitis

In cellulitis, bacteria that normally live harmlessly on the skin enter deeper layers of the skin, causing infection. Cellulitis needs to be treated to prevent the infection from spreading.

Possible symptoms

- ★ Heat, swelling, pain, and tenderness in affected area
- ★ Swollen glands near site of infection
- ★ Fever, feeling generally unwell, and nausea

WHAT'S THE TREATMENT?

If you are think your child has cellulitis take her to the doctor, who can usually make a diagnosis by examining the affected area. Treatment with antibiotics is required to prevent bacteria spreading and infecting a larger area. Symptoms usually go away after a few days of treatment but it is important your child finishes the course of antibiotics.

As with all infections, your child should drink plenty of fluids. You can give paracetamol or ibuprofren to help with discomfort.

IS IT PREVENTABLE?

You can reduce the risk of infection by cleaning cuts and grazes well with water and keeping them covered with a plaster or dressing to stop scratching and prevent bacteria from entering a wound. If the plaster becomes wet or dirty then change it. Children with skin conditions such as eczema in which the skin can become dry, cracked, and itchy, prompting scratching, are more susceptible to infections.

Boils

Bacteria live on our skin harmlessly most of the time, but if they enter through a wound or down a hair follicle they can cause a boil. Boils often occur in the armpits, groin, buttocks, neck, and face.

Possible symptoms

- ★ Red painful lump, becoming dome-shaped as it grows
- ★ Yellow or white spot, or head, at the centre of the boil, which contains pus
- ★ If the boil bursts, pus oozes out, generally relieving pain

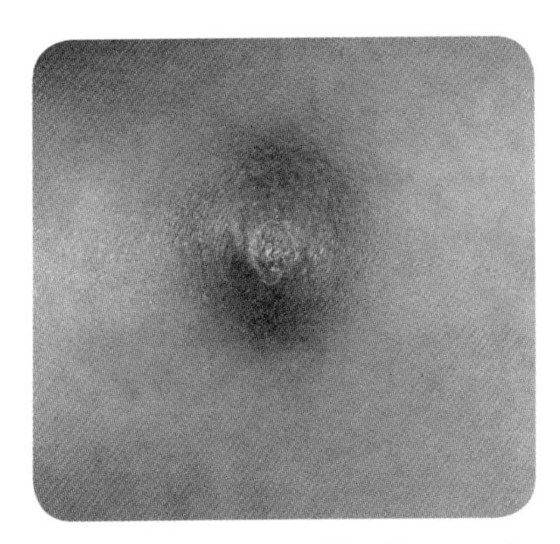

A boil As a boil grows it fills with pus, and develops a yellow or white "head". The surrounding area is red and tender to touch.

HOW CAN I TREAT A BOIL?

Many boils will burst on their own, allowing the pus to drain away. The boil then heals without the need for any medical treatment, although you can give paracetamol or ibuprofen to ease discomfort. Most boils heal without causing scarring. To help healing you can try using a hot compress: apply a clean flannel or gauze pad soaked in warm or hot water (not too hot!) for approximately 10 minutes, three or four times a day. Wash your hands after treating the boil. Do not attempt to squeeze a boil as this can spread the infection.

Good hand-washing and cleaning any scrapes or wounds thoroughly may help to prevent boils occurring.

SHOULD I SEE A DOCTOR?

If a boil is very large or painful, lasts more than 2 weeks, or occurs on the face, see your doctor. A week-long course of antibiotics may be prescribed. Alternatively, the doctor may lance the boil by inserting a small needle into it to allow the pus to drain away. You should not try to lance a boil yourself at home. This should only be done by a medical professional who will use sterile equipment. If your child suffers from boils regularly your doctor will carry out tests, such as blood tests, to check for underlying conditions such as diabetes.

Impetigo

An extremely contagious bacterial skin infection, impetigo is common in young children. It generally appears around the nose, mouth, and ears.

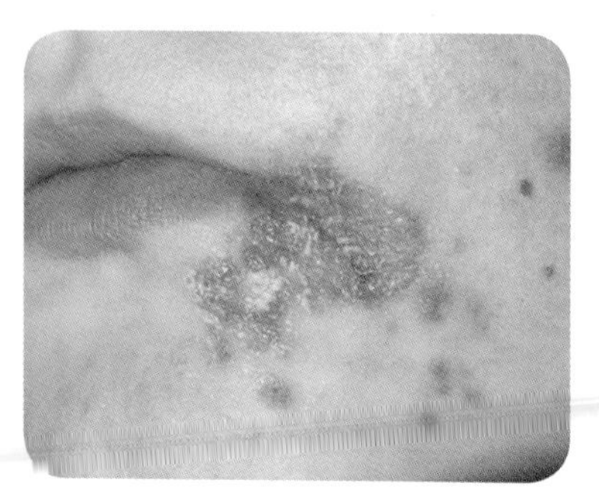

Impetigo infection Red, scabby patches of skin with honey-coloured crusts often appear around the mouth in impetigo.

WHAT IS THE CAUSE?

The bacteria that cause impetigo enter through cuts, bites or scratches so children with skin conditions that are itchy are more prone to the condition. Symptoms start 4–10 days after being exposed to the bacteria.

SHOULD I SEE A DOCTOR?

You should see your doctor if you think your child has impetigo, which is generally treated with an antibiotic cream. If left untreated it can lead to cellulitis. If there is no improvement after 7 days of treatment with an antibiotic cream your child may need a course of oral antibiotics.

Possible symptoms

- ★ **Small red blisters** form at first
- ★ **Blisters soon burst** becoming hard and scabby with a thick golden yellow brown (honey-coloured) crust
- ★ **Crusts then dry,** leaving a red mark that generally heals without causing scarring

IS IT PREVENTABLE?

Impetigo is highly contagious but keeping any wounds clean and avoiding sharing towels with infected people may help prevent the infection. Treating a skin condition such as eczema and keeping the skin well moisturized to decrease itching and therefore scratching will also help.

What can I do to help?

To treat impetigo, apply antibiotic cream as prescribed by your doctor. Preventing the spread of infection to other parts of the child's body or to other people is important. Keep your child away from school or nursery until affected areas have healed or crusted. Your child must also avoid contact with newborn babies for the same period of time as the infection can be dangerous to them.

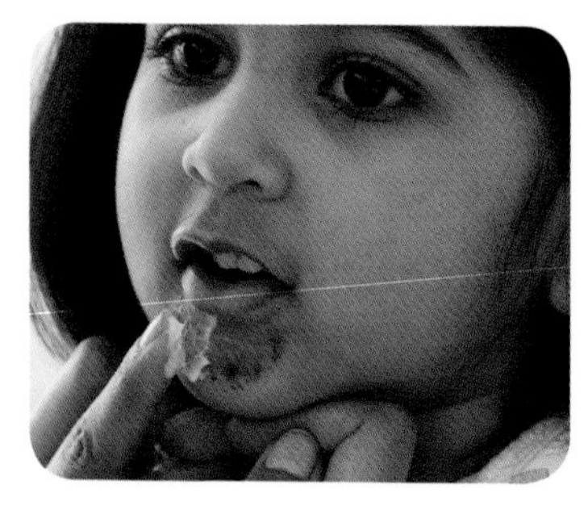

Apply antibiotic cream Apply the cream to areas affected by impetigo as directed by your doctor. Wash your hands before and after applying the cream to avoid spreading the infection.

Ensure thorough hand-washing Your child should wash his hands regularly and if he touches an affected area. Although it may be difficult, try to stop your child from touching infected skin.

Keep washcloths separate Give your child her own washcloth and towels, and keep them separate from the rest of the family's. Wash her towels, bedding and clothes at a high temperature after use.

Cold sores

Highly contagious and easily spread, cold sores are small blisters that develop on and around the lips. They are unsightly and can be painful but generally heal within 1–2 weeks without scarring.

WHAT IS THE CAUSE?

Cold sores are caused by infection with the herpes simplex virus, which spreads by direct contact, for example by kissing. Most people have been exposed to the virus but the initial infection does not usually cause symptoms. The virus stays within the body in the nervous system and can be reactivated by certain triggers, such as stress, tiredness, another infection, or environmental factors such as strong sunlight or wind.

Some people who are exposed to the virus never have a cold sore, others have one only once, while some people have recurrent cold sores that occur frequently.

WHAT'S THE TREATMENT?

Antiviral creams can prevent cold sores progressing further than the tingling stage. They can be bought over the counter or prescribed by your doctor. Some creams are not suitable for children under 12, so check with the pharmacist before buying.

Treatment with the cream should be started as soon as the tingling sensation is felt. The cream is applied to the cold sore five times a day for 5–10 days. Even if a cold sore does appear the creams can shorten the duration and severity of the attack. Wash your hands before and after applying the cream.

Possible symptoms

- ★ Tingling or itching sensation around lips a few hours before cold sore forms
- ★ Fluid-filled blisters or sores, which may be painful or itchy, then appear, often on the edges of the lips
- ★ Blisters crust over, usually within 48 hours of the initial tingling sensation and then heal

ARE THEY PREVENTABLE?

If you know that sunlight triggers your child's cold sores, apply a high protection sunblock on his lips before going out. Encourage him not to touch cold sores and, if he does, to wash his hands afterwards to avoid spreading the virus. If he's never had cold sores, he should avoid direct contact, such as kissing, with people who have them.

Molluscum contagiosum

This viral infection causes shiny, raised spots to appear on the skin. It commonly affects young children and spreads easily at nursery and school.

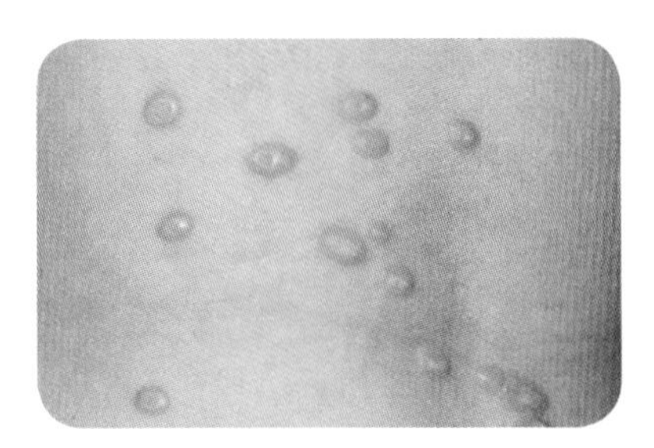

Molluscum lesions These small, raised spots are dome-shaped with a dimple in the middle. They often appear in clusters.

WHAT IS THE CAUSE?

Molluscum contagiosum is caused by a pox virus and spread by direct contact with the skin of an infected person or by sharing towels or even toys.

WHAT'S THE TREATMENT?

No treatment is usually needed as the lesions generally clear up on their own but you should see the doctor to confirm that the spots are molluscum.

It can take around 18 months or longer for the spots to heal. They do not leave scars. You don't need to exclude your child from school or swimming although she should not share towels, bedding, or clothes to help prevent spreading the infection to others. If your child is itchy encourage her not to scratch as this can spread the infection to other parts of her body.

Possible symptoms

The lesions of molluscum can be anywhere on the body and may appear in clusters. They are:

- ★ Small, firm, and dome-shaped with a dimple in the middle
- ★ Skin or pearly white in colour
- ★ Not itchy, generally

Warts and verrucas

Children often get warts, which are harmless growths on the skin. There are two main types: common warts, which can occur anywhere on the body, but more often on the hands, and verrucas which occur on the soles of the feet.

Possible symptoms

Common warts:

★ Small, firm, skin-coloured lumps with a rough surface, usually less than 1 cm in diameter

★ Occur alone or in clusters of up to 20

★ Not generally painful or itchy

Verrucas:

★ Flat, often with black dots in the centre surrounded by some hard skin

★ Can cause discomfort

★ One or many may appear at a time

WHAT IS THE CAUSE?

Warts are caused by infection with the human papillomaravirus. The virus is found within the skin cells in the wart and is passed on by direct contact, or indirectly, for example by sharing shoes, towels, or washcloths, or by walking over floors someone infected by the virus has walked over, as at swimming pools. If your child has a skin condition such as eczema that causes cracked skin, warts are more likely.

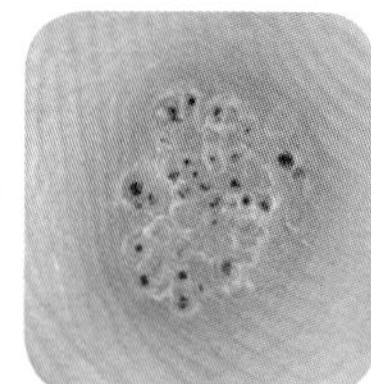

Common wart (left) This is small, raised, and skin-coloured. **Verucca (right)** This looks flat and may have black dots.

WHAT'S THE TREATMENT?

Warts and verrucas can disappear on their own although this can take a long time – sometimes years. They are also difficult to treat and none of the treatments are always effective. You may wish to try one of the various home treatments (see panel, below). If this treatment hasn't worked after about 3 months, see your doctor. A common medical treatment is cryotherapy, in which the warts are frozen off with liquid nitrogen. The procedure takes a few minutes and although it hurts, it is very quick and the pain is short-lived. After the treatment a blister or a scab may appear over the treated area before returning to normal.

ARE THEY PREVENTABLE?

Your child shouldn't share towels with anyone with warts or verrucas or shoes and socks with anyone who has a verruca and shouldn't touch other people's warts.

What can I do to help?

Try using an over-the-counter treatment containing salicylic acid. Soak the wart in warm water for 5 minutes first to soften the skin or apply after your child's bath. Wash your hands after treating the wart.

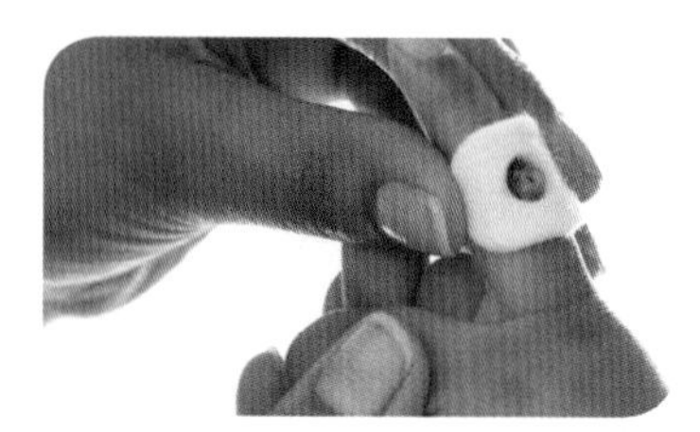

1 Protect the skin around the wart with a corn plaster or vaseline because salicylic acid is damaging to healthy skin.

2 Apply the treatment to the wart and allow to dry, then remove the protective corn plaster if used. Repeat treatment daily.

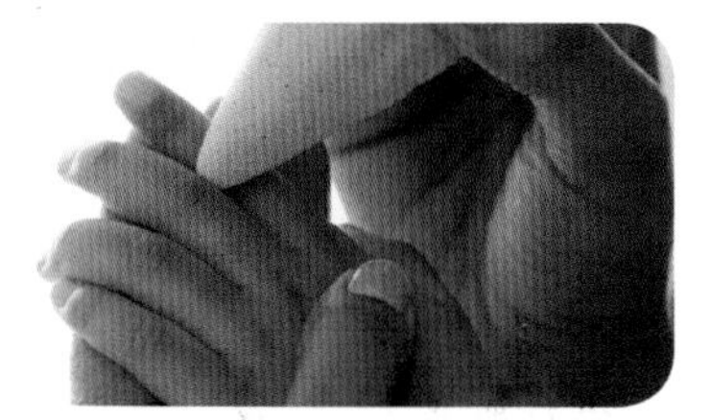

3 Once a week remove dead skin with a pumice or emery board. If the wart hasn't gone after treating for 3 months, see your doctor.

Ringworm

Ringworm doesn't refer to a worm but is a fungal infection that can affect the skin of the body and or the scalp. It's called ringworm because it produces a ring-shaped rash on the skin.

WHAT IS THE CAUSE?

Fungal skin infections are common and spread easily between people by direct contact. They can also be spread from animals and from indirect contact, from fungal spores found on towels and sheets. Scalp ringworm is particularly common in Afro-Caribbean children.

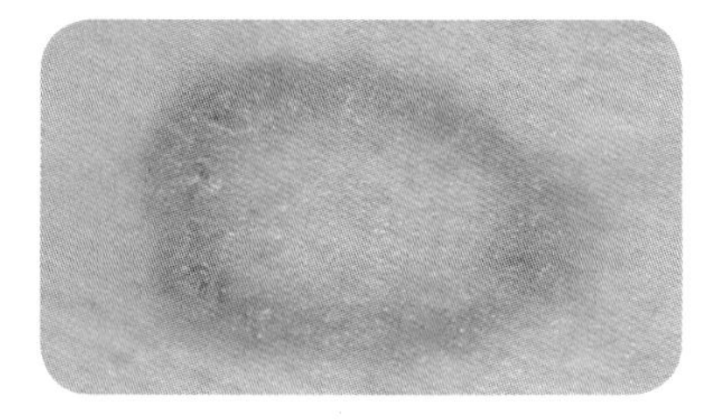

Ring-shaped rash The rash of body ringworm has a red, scaly outer rim surrounding a smoother inner area that looks almost like normal skin.

WHAT'S THE TREATMENT?

You can treat body ringworm by using antifungal creams. Some of these can be bought over the counter. Check with your pharmacist which ones are suitable for your child's age. Apply the cream as directed by the instructions on the medication. If the cream doesn't work, visit your doctor as it's possible other creams are needed or that the rash is not due to ringworm. Some other skin conditions, such as a type of eczema, produce a similar type of rash but require different treatment.

Scalp ringworm cannot be treated with creams and needs oral antifungal medication. See your doctor, who will refer your child to a dermatologist for treatment. Prescribed medication may need to be taken for anything from 4 to 12 weeks.

Any pets that could be the source of the fungal infection may need to be treated, so get advice from the vet.

Possible symptoms

Body ringworm:

- ★ Ring-shaped patches on the body, that have a red outer rim that can feel rough or scaly and raised
- ★ Itchiness, in some cases

Scalp ringworm:

- ★ Patches of scaly skin on the scalp
- ★ Hair loss within patches
- ★ Itchiness, in some cases

IS IT PREVENTABLE?

Don't share towels, flannels or bedding with someone with ringworm, or hairbrushes or hair clips/scrunchies/bands with someone with scalp ringworm. Encourage your child not to touch or scratch ringworm patches to prevent it spreading to other parts of their body or to others. While a child is being treated with oral medication for scalp ringworm, washing his hair twice a week with an antifungal shampoo will not cure the infection but may help stop it spreading to other people.

Fungal nails

Although much more common in adults, fungal nail infections can affect children. They are unsightly and should be treated as children can be teased.

Possible symptoms

- ★ Thickened discoloured nails – often yellow, green, or brown

Toenails are more often affected than fingernails, caused by infection that has spread from athlete's foot (p.122).

If you suspect a fungal nail infection, take your child to the doctor so a diagnosis can be made – other conditions such as psoriasis can also affect the nails. The doctor may take some nail clippings and send them to the laboratory to find out if a fungus is the cause. Fungal nail infections can be treated with antifungal creams and paints, which are available over the counter. These can take many months to be effective and your doctor may need to prescribe oral antifungal tables.

Good foot hygiene, treating athlete's foot, and keeping nails clean can help stop fungal nail infection from developing.

Athlete's foot

This fungal infection, which generally affects the skin between the toes, is particularly common during the summer. Although usually mild it can be extremely irritating. Good foot hygiene is important in treatment and prevention.

Possible symptoms

- ★ Red, flaky, skin between the toes that may become cracked and sore
- ★ Itchiness

WHAT IS THE CAUSE?

The fungi that cause athlete's foot are called dermatophytes, and they grow easily in the dark, moist, humid environment inside shoes. Allowing feet to become sweaty and not changing socks regularly makes infection more likely. The infection spreads easily from person to person and is often caught from walking barefoot in locker rooms or areas near swimming pools. Athlete's foot sometimes spreads to the toenails, causing fungal nails (p.121).

WHAT'S THE OUTLOOK?

Applying an antifungal cream and following good foot hygiene (see below) should bring an improvement in about a week. You may be advised to continue using the cream for 1–2 weeks after symptoms have gone to be sure that the infection is fully treated.

To prevent a recurrence of athlete's foot, your child should carry on with good hygiene measures. Wearing flip-flops or plastic sandals when in communal changing rooms may also help.

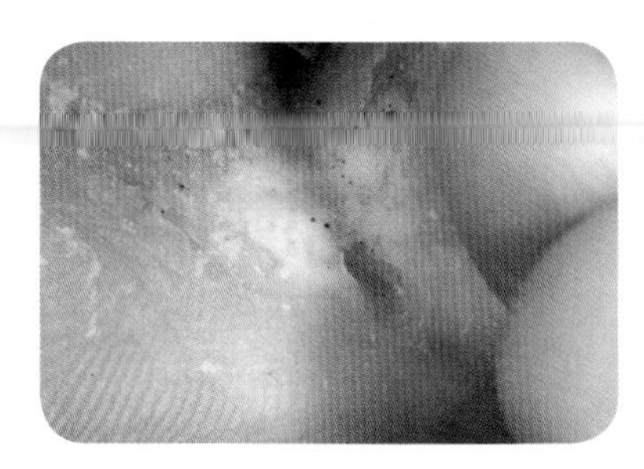

Cracked skin Athlete's foot usually affects the areas between the toes, causing sore, cracked skin that may be itchy.

What can I do to help?

You can buy antifungal creams over the counter; ask your pharmacist for advice. Keeping feet clean, changing socks daily (more often if feet are sweaty after exercise) and wearing socks with shoes and trainers are also important. Make sure your child always wears well-fitting shoes.

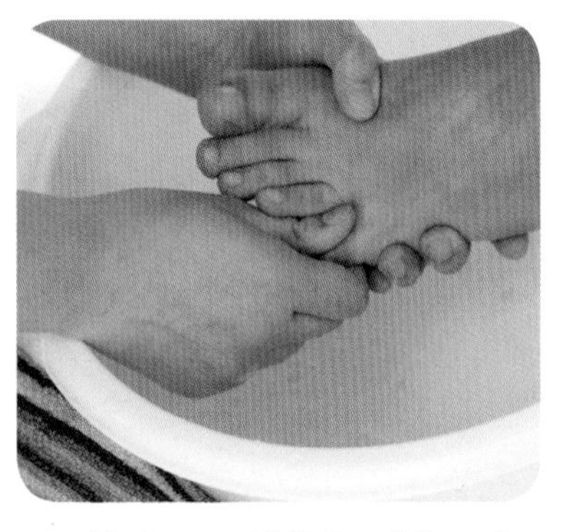

1 **Wash your child's feet daily,** paying special attention to the area between their toes (an older child can do this himself but you should supervise).

2 **Thoroughly dry your child's feet** after washing, taking extra care to dry carefully between each of the toes.

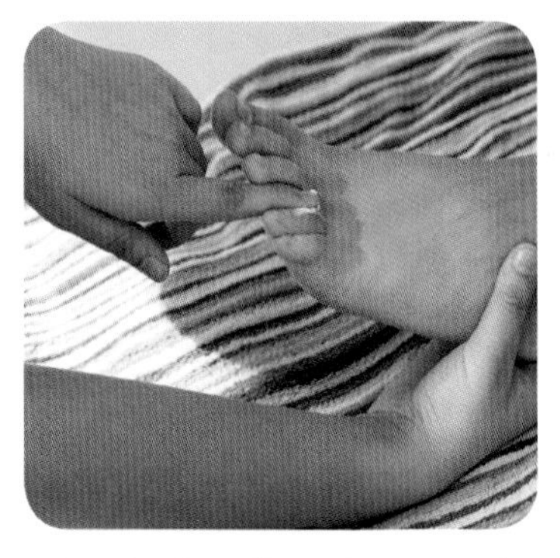

3 **Apply antifungal cream** to the affected area and nearby healthy looking skin. Wash your hands before and after applying the cream.

Pityriasis rosea

This skin rash, consisting of pink oval patches, is most common in children aged 10 or older, but it can occur in younger children.

WHAT IS THE CAUSE?

The exact cause of pityriasis rosea is not known. It is thought to be related to a virus, but it does not appear to be infectious.

WHAT'S THE TREATMENT?

You don't need to do anything as the rash generally disappears on its own within approximately 8 weeks, although it can last for 3–6 months. If the skin is itchy using a moisturiser may be soothing. It may also be helpful to avoid irritants, such as harsh soaps, and to wear loose clothes made of natural fabrics. Discourage your child from scratching affected areas.

Pytiriasis rosea rash The patches of pink skin have a scaly outer ring.

Possible symptoms

- ★ An initial "herald" patch of red skin with an outer scaly ring, approximately 2–5cm (1–2in) wide on the chest, abdomen, or back. It is not always noticed and is sometimes confused with the rash of ringworm
- ★ A few days later, smaller pink oval patches, with an outer ring of scaling, appear. They may continue to develop for about 6 weeks
- ★ Itchiness, sometimes

Pityriasis alba

In pityriasis alba, patches of lighter coloured skin develop, often on the face. It generally affects children aged 6–12 and disappears on its own.

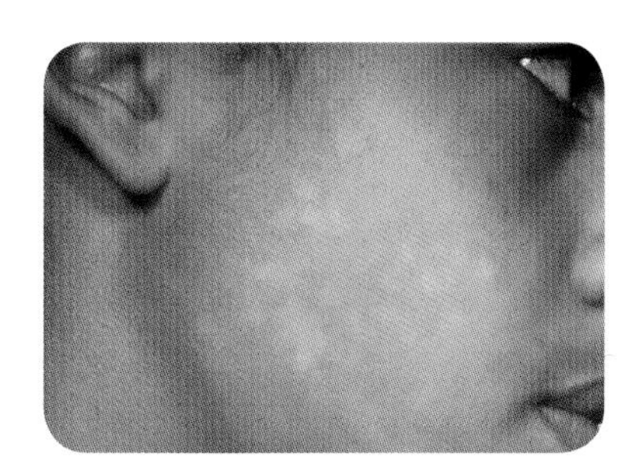

Pityriasis alba rash Lighter coloured patches of skin appear, frequently on the face. They are more obvious on dark skin.

WHAT IS THE CAUSE?

The cause of pytiriasis alba is not known, but the rash appears to become worse when the skin is dry.

WHAT'S THE TREATMENT?

No treatment is necessary as pityriasis alba will go away on its own, although this can take many months. If your child is worried about her appearance, reassure her that the skin will return to normal. Using a moisturizer may help to soothe any dryness. Some parents worry that a child with pityriasis alba has vitiligo, a lifelong condition in which areas of skin lose their pigment. Vitiligo does not usually occur before age 20 and the two conditions look quite different – in pityriasis alba there is no clear line between lighter patches and normal skin, whereas in vitiligo patches there is a very sharp line between normal skin and lighter coloured skin. However, if you are worried, see your doctor, who will be able to reassure you.

Possible symptoms

- ★ Lighter coloured patches of skin, which may be dry, and scaly
- ★ May be more noticeable in children with dark skin or in the summer when the surrounding skin becomes more tanned

Scabies

Scabies is a skin infestation by tiny mites called *Sarcopte scabei* that can't be seen by the naked eye. The mites burrow under the skin to lay their eggs, causing intense itching.

Possible symptoms

Symptoms begin between 2 and 6 weeks after infection if you haven't had the infection before, much earlier if you are re-infected.

★ **Intense itching,** often worse at night or after a warm bath

★ **Small lines** and blotches on the skin, anywhere on the body

HOW IS IT SPREAD?

Scabies mites are spread by close physical contact and can also be passed on by sharing towels and bedding as they can live for short periods without a live host.

WHAT'S THE TREATMENT?

If you think your child has scabies, visit your doctor to confirm the diagnosis as the rash is easily confused with that of other skin conditions. Scabies is treated with creams or lotions that can be prescribed or bought over the counter. Some of the treatments should not be given to young children so discuss with your doctor or pharmacist. All family members should be treated. The lotions should be applied to the entire body on two occasions 7 days apart, do not apply after a hot bath. Wash all clothes, bed linens, and towels at a temperature of at least 50°C (122°F) on the day that you apply the treatment. If certain items can't be washed, for example a teddy your child always sleeps with (although many can be washed), place in a sealed plastic bag for 72 hours, by which time any mites on it should have died. Your child can go to school after the first application of treatment.

Headlice

Headlice are wingless insects that live on the scalp and bite the skin to feed on blood. They are tiny – about 2–4mm long, or the size of a sesame seed – and so can be difficult to detect. They can make the scalp extremely itchy.

Possible symptoms

★ **Itchiness** (due to an allergy to the lice), which may cause child to scratch her head

★ **Tiny red spots on the scalp,** often behind the ears or at the back of the neck, which are common places for infestation

★ **There may be no symptoms** at all

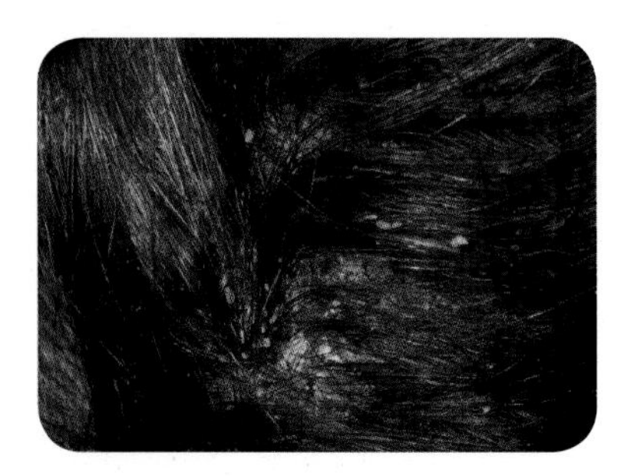

Headlice egg sacs The sacs, containing eggs, are seen here as whitish brown dots. They are firmly attached to hair shafts.

HOW ARE THEY SPREAD?

Headlice do not have wings, and therefore cannot fly; instead they spread by close contact, literally climbing from one scalp to another. So, although anyone can get headlice, they are more common in children who spend a lot of time close together, playing or working at school.

DOES MY CHILD HAVE HEADLICE?

The best method of detecting headlice is by wetcombing, in which you work through the hair section by section with a fine-toothed nit comb (available from a pharmacy), checking for lice with each stroke. This technique is also used as a method of treating headlice and is described in the panel opposite.

Working through the hair gradually is a slow process but it is important to be thorough to detect any lice. Depending on the hair, its length, and thickness, it can take up to an hour or so to work through the whole head. Seeing a live louse on the comb means that your child has headlice. Seeing the whitish-brown egg sacs (nits), or empty egg sacs, which look like shiny white dots, does not necessarily mean your child is currently infested. These can stick to the hair shaft even after lice have been treated. If you do not see any lice and your child has an itchy scalp, take her to the doctor because various skin conditions can cause this symptom.

You may decide to carry out detection combing regularly to check if your child has headlice. If you do find them then check other family members and inform the school, although your child does not need to stay at home. Only treat family members if lice are found. The lice can only live on humans so there is no need to wash bedding or clothing.

WHAT'S THE TREATMENT?

There are various different treatments although none is guaranteed and they do not protect against re-infection with headlice. If you are using over-the-counter treatments check with the pharmacist that they are suitable for use in children.

★ Insecticides – these can be water- or alcohol-based and contain a substance that kills the lice. Water-based products are safer (as alcohol is flammable) and may be less irritating to the skin (see panel below for how to apply them).

★ Dimeticone – this is not an insecticide but a product based on silicone that is thought to kill lice by stopping them from getting rid of water. It is odourless and is applied as with insecticides but only needs to be left on the scalp for 8 hours before washing off. A second application is needed after 7 days.

★ Wetcombing – this is the same technique as used for detecting headlice, whereby the comb reveals any lice, but for treating lice you need to wetcomb every 4 days until the lice are gone (see box below).

ARE THEY PREVENTABLE?

Having headlice is not a sign of poor hygiene: they do not prefer dirty hair. To help avoid catching them, your child should not share hairbrushes or combs with an affected person. Tying back long hair may also help reduce the likelihood of contact with another child. The only real method to prevent spread of headlice is to regularly check your family's hair as described above and treat headlice if you find them.

What can I do to help?

The methods for treating headlice are wetcombing (also used for detection) and lotions that kill lice (insecticides or dimeticone). Wetcombing removes lice but not the eggs so you need to repeat it until you have had three separate sessions, each 4 days apart, where no lice have been seen.

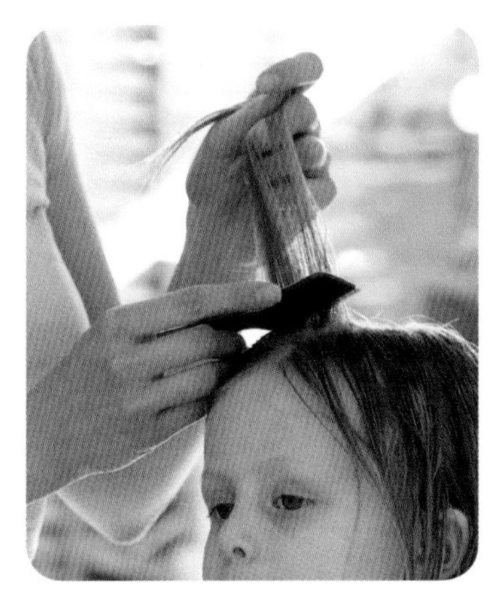

1 **For wetcombing** first wash your child's hair, put on plenty of conditioner, and leave it in. Comb out any tangles. Separate hair into small sections, then work through each section with a nit comb. Comb the hair through from scalp to ends with each stroke.

2 **Check for lice on the comb** with each stroke. Once you have worked through all the hair in small sections, rinse off the conditioner. Each session can take up to an hour or so to do properly. Wash the nit comb in boiling water after you have finished.

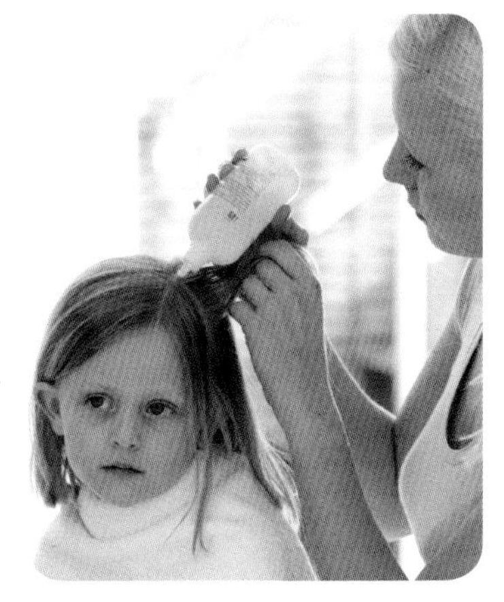

Lice-killing lotions These are usually applied to dry hair. You may need to section the hair so that you can saturate the roots. You generally leave the lotion on for 8–12 hours before shampooing. Apply a second application in 7 days to kill any lice that have hatched from eggs.

Insect bites and stings

Most insect bites and stings are mild and get better in 2 or 3 days. However, some children can have a serious allergic reaction to a sting (or, rarely, a bite) called anaphylactic shock. In the UK, it's rare to catch a disease, such as malaria, from insects.

Possible symptoms

- ★ **Small red lump with a small hole** (the puncture wound or bite) if your child has been bitten
- ★ **Redness and swelling around the sting** if your child has been stung
- ★ **Pain and sometimes itchiness** (often intense with a bite)
- ★ **If your child is allergic** to the bite or sting, the reaction may be more severe, with a raised pink or red area around the lump or swelling around a sting; urticaria (right); or in very severe cases, anaphylactic shock (p.218)

WHAT ARE THE CAUSES?

Insect bites can be caused by various insects, such as midges, fleas, bed bugs, and mosquitoes. In the UK, insect stings are most commonly from bees and wasps. When an insect punctures the skin the saliva causes skin irritation. A stinging insect injects venom (poison) into the skin as a defence mechanism.

SHOULD I SEE A DOCTOR?

Call an ambulance if your child develops any of the following symptoms, which are indications of anaphylactic shock: wheezing or difficulty breathing, a blotchy rash over a wide area of the body, dizziness, nausea, or a swollen face or mouth. If your child has had a severe allergic reaction the doctor may prescribe a syringe containing adrenaline for you to use in case he is stung or bitten again (see p.218).

Also see your doctor if a bite or sting doesn't start to improve within 48 hours or there are signs of infection, such as increased redness and soreness, swollen glands, or flu-like symptoms.

ARE THEY PREVENTABLE?

★ Wearing trousers and long-sleeved tops, especially at dusk and dawn (when insects are most active) reduce the amount of skin exposed to biting insects.

★ Use insect repellent – repellents that contain the substance DEET are considered to be most effective but before buying a repellent check whether it is suitable for children and the correct amount to use.

★ If you are travelling to an area with a high risk of malaria, check with your doctor's surgery or travel clinic about medication to prevent malaria; when you are in a malarial area, use mosquito nets over beds and follow the other precautions for avoiding insect bites as even if you are taking medication, it is better to avoid being bitten.

★ Do not disturb insect nests.

★ Keep any food and drink outside covered as insects are attracted to them, particularly to sweet items.

★ Avoid perfumed soaps, shampoos, or other strong-smelling products as these attract insects.

★ Teach your child to walk away slowly and calmly if a bee or wasp approaches and not to wave his arms around. These insects sting as a defence reaction so movement can provoke them.

What can I do to help?

For both bites and stings, you can use an over-the-counter antihistamine cream or apply a cold flannel to soothe itching; paracetamol can help with any discomfort. The stinger of a bee needs to be removed before any other treatment. Keep your child's nails short to reduce the risk of infection from scratching.

1 **Scrape away a bee sting** with a credit card or your fingernail. Do not use tweezers as you may squeeze more venom into your child.

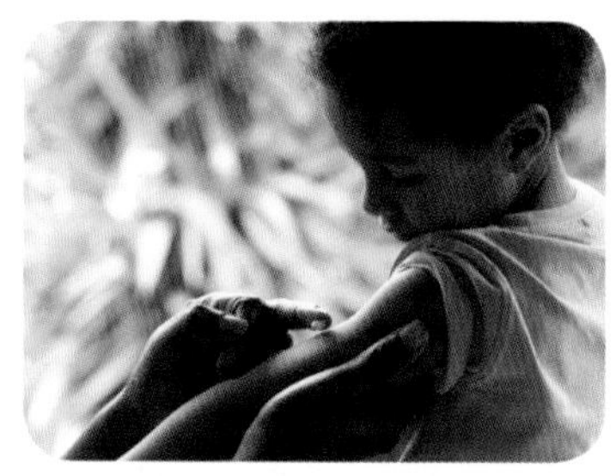

2 **Apply antihistamine cream** if needed after you've washed and dried the area. Discourage your child from scratching to prevent infection.

Urticaria

Also called hives, urticaria is an itchy skin rash that occurs when a particular trigger causes a reaction in the body. It can be accompanied by a serious condition called angioedema that causes swelling.

Possible symptoms

Urticaria:

★ Pink or red raised areas (weals) that vary in size

★ Intense itchiness, in most cases

★ Each weal lasts a few hours; as weals fade, others appear in different areas

Angioedema:

★ Swelling of the face or mouth

★ Difficulty breathing

WHAT ARE THE CAUSES?

Urticaria does not always have an identifiable cause but often it is due to an allergic reaction, for example to certain foods or to insect stings. It can also be a reaction to irritants from nettles, to medications, or even to changes in environment such as heat or cold. The rash is generally short-lived, lasting about a day; rarely it can become chronic (long-lasting). The symptoms are due to release of the chemical histamine from cells. It causes fluid to leak out of blood vessels in skin. In some people with urticaria, there is leakage of fluid in deeper tissues, a condition called angioedema, which can be serious.

WHAT'S THE TREATMENT?

If urticaria is mild no treatment may be needed. You can treat the symptoms as for insect bites and stings with antihistamine creams (see box, opposite). Oral antihistamines are available from your pharmacy or on prescription and can be used to block the histamine that is causing the condition. Check with your pharmacist whether the medication is appropriate for your child's age. Try to avoid exposing your child to any identifiable triggers.

If your child develops symptoms of angioedema, seek urgent medical attention.

Cuts and grazes

Active developing children will fall and hurt themselves, and cuts and grazes are very common! A cut is a split in the skin, while a graze, or abrasion, means layers of skin are scraped off. Most minor cuts and grazes heal without scarring.

Possible symptoms

★ Bleeding and pain, followed by a scab that falls off a few days later

HOW DO I TREAT A CUT OR GRAZE?

★ First, a cuddle goes a long way to making a cut or graze feel better!

★ Wash a cut or graze thoroughly. You do not need to wash with an antiseptic.

★ If there is bleeding, apply some pressure with a clean pad or dressing to stop it.

★ Cover with a plaster or dressing to keep clean and dry.

★ Change the plaster if it gets dirty or wet (you can use waterproof plasters to help prevent this).

SHOULD I SEE A DOCTOR?

You should seek medical advice if the wound won't stop bleeding (see also First aid: Serious Bleeding, p.216), appears very deep, if you can't clean it, if the wound won't close with a plaster or if a cut is in a place you wouldn't want a scar such as on the face. Some cuts need medical treatment such as skin closure strips, tissue glue, or stitches. Dirty wounds have a higher risk of tetanus so be sure that your child is fully immunized against it.

If you have treated a cut or graze and subsequently you notice worsening redness, swelling, or pus then see your doctor as there could be an infection.

ARE THEY PREVENTABLE?

You can't stop every cut or graze as children like to run around and explore, but they should avoid unnecessary risks by wearing cycle helmets and other protective equipment such as knee pads for activities such as skateboarding. Keep your first aid kit stocked up so that you can treat cuts and grazes as appropriate.

Bruising

Bruises are due to bleeding from very tiny blood vessels that burst or are damaged after being hit, for example in a fall. They can happen in the skin or deeper in your body, for example in your organs.

Possible symptoms

★ **Pain or tenderness** at first

★ **Purple or red skin,** which may change colour, such as to brown, yellow, or green

All children get bruises on their skin at some point, and these are generally minor and heal on their own. An ice pack may limit the bleeding in a bruise (see right) and you can give ibuprofen or paracetamol for pain. The homeopathic or herbal remedy of arnica, which is available as a tablet or in the form of cream, is often used to treat bruises, although the evidence for its effectiveness is controversial.

See your doctor if your child has had a blow or fall and you are concerned about the possibility of internal bruising. Internal bruising does not cause discoloured skin, but your child may complain of pain and you might see swelling. If your child gets frequent bruises without any cause then visit your doctor.

Cold compress Apply a cold compress, such as a bag of frozen peas wrapped in a tea towel, to the bruise for about 20 minutes. This may help limit bleeding.

Splinter

Children are continually exploring and touching everything and frequently get splinters. These are often wood but can be glass, metal, or plastic.

Possible symptoms

★ **Pain or tenderness**

★ **Visible splinter** or a line under the skin

★ **Sometimes, a small red dot,** which is the entry site of the splinter

Remove a splinter With tweezers, grasp it as close to the skin as possible and draw out in a straight line, at the same angle it went in.

HOW DO I REMOVE A SPLINTER?

You should attempt to remove splinters to prevent an infection developing. Wash your hands before you start.

★ You may be able to remove the splinter by simply squeezing either side and the bottom to encourage the splinter to come out.

★ Sterilize a pair of tweezers by immersing in boiling water, and if you can see the end of the splinter gently pull it out (see left).

★ If you can't see the end of the splinter then you could try to scrape the skin from the top of the splinter, so that you can grasp it with the tweezers.

★ Once the splinter is out wash the area.

★ If you can't get the splinter out, the body will naturally try to extrude it over time but watch out for signs of infection: redness, swelling, heat, and tenderness. If these symptoms develop (whether the splinter is left in or was removed) take your child to see your doctor.

ARE THEY PREVENTABLE?

Your child should wear shoes when she is outside and be careful when touching rough surfaces. If you break a glass, make sure you vacuum up all the tiny pieces.

Blister

A blister is a fluid-filled swelling in the skin. Blisters often develop as a result of friction, for example from ill-fitting shoes or the handle of a new sports racquet. They may also develop after a burn.

Possible symptoms

- ★ Swelling on the surface of the skin that looks like it's filled with fluid
- ★ May be tender or painless

Blisters form on damaged skin as a way of cushioning and therefore protecting undamaged skin underneath. They can be tender or painless and are generally filled with a clear fluid (serum) though they can be filled with blood.

Most blisters heal on their own without scarring. You can apply a plaster to the blister, or use a cushioned dressing if it is painful because of being rubbed. The skin under the blister is healing and is protected from infection by the blister itself so do not pop it or peel off any skin if it bursts itself. Just keep it clean and dry. If a blister becomes infected the surrounding skin may redden and it will become painful and may fill with pus. This may need treating with antibiotics so visit your doctor.

To prevent friction blisters have your child's feet measured regularly and her shoes fitted by a professional. If going on a long walk your child should wear shoes that have been broken in (worn before) and should always wear socks with shoes.

To prevent blisters due to sunburn, follow the self-help measures on p.130.

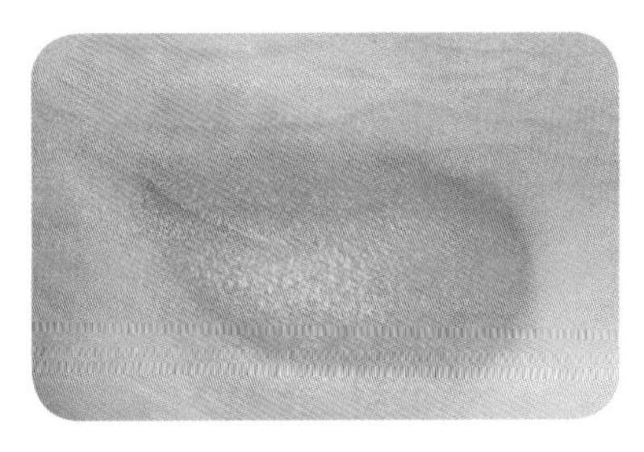

A blister Blisters are usually filled with clear fluid and so are normally skin-coloured. They are sometimes tender.

Minor burns

Burns and scalds that damage just superficial layers of the skin can be treated at home. More severe burns (p.216) require medical attention.

Possible symptoms

- ★ Reddened skin
- ★ Pain in the burned area
- ★ Later, blisters and peeling skin

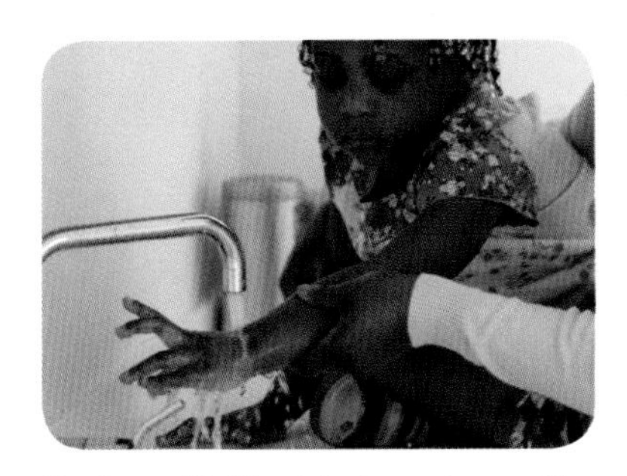

Cool the skin Flood the burned area with lukewarm or cool water, such as by placing under a running tap, for at least 10 minutes.

HOW DO I TREAT A BURN?

Minor, superficial burns and scalds can be treated at home.

★ Stop the burning process by removing the heat; in general people do this by moving away: for example, moving a hand off the iron.

★ Cool the skin with lukewarm or cold water for at least 10 minutes.

★ Do not cover with something fluffy such as cotton wool, or sticky like a plaster.

★ Do not use ice or iced water which can cause more damage to the skin.

★ Do not apply butter, eggs or any other type of greasy substance to the burn.

★ If a blister forms, do not burst it.

★ You can give paracetamol or ibuprofen for any pain.

★ Seek medical help if a burn is large, deep or affects the face, or if signs of infection develop: redness, swelling, or pus.

ARE THEY PREVENTABLE?

Keep hot fluids and chemicals out of the reach of children, and teach them that the hob is hot and should not be touched.

Sunburn

Children's skin is easily burned by the ultraviolet rays of the sun. Sunburn damages the skin and can increase the risk of skin cancer later in life.

Sunscreens

To protect your child's skin, it's important to use a high-SPF (sun protection factor) sunscreen.

Choose a sunscreen with an SPF of 15 or higher that protects against both UVA and UVB rays (called broad-spectrum sunscreen). Apply a generous layer 30 minutes before your child goes out and reapply regularly and after your child has been swimming.

WHAT IS THE CAUSE?

A suntan is the body's natural defence mechanism against the effects of the sun. The skin produces more of the pigment melanin when exposed to sun, making the skin go dark. This is why darker skin burns less easily in the sun. However, even having dark skin containing lots of melanin does not protect a person from the long-term effects of sun exposure such as cancer. Conversely, pale skin is at increased risk of sunburn.

HOW DO I TREAT SUNBURN?

Prevention is the best cure for sunburn but if your child does develop sunburn then bring her into the shade and keep her cool. Encourage her to drink plenty of fluids. You can apply a moisturizing cream or aftersun cream to moisturize and cool the skin and give paracetamol or ibuprofen for pain. If the skin peels, you can continue using moisturizer until the skin heals. If a burn is severe, you think it has become infected, or you are concerned seek medical advice.

Possible symptoms

Symptoms may not appear until a few hours after being burned.

- ★ Red, painful skin that feels warm or hot, even when in the shade
- ★ Skin may peel after a few days
- ★ Blistering may occur in more severe sunburn
- ★ Skin may turn back to its original pale colour or may fade into a tan, as the burn heals

What can I do to help?

Your child should stay out of the sun when it is at its hottest between 11am and 3pm, and when in the sun, she should cover up and use sunscreen.

To avoid heat exhaustion (p.217), encourage children not to wear themselves out playing in the heat and sun, and also to have rest periods.

Cover up In the sun, your child should wear clothes with sleeves and a hat with a large brim that shadows the face.

Protect skin and eyes Apply sunscreen generously and regularly. Your child should also wear sunglasses in bright sunlight.

Replace fluids It's essential to drink plenty of fluids when it's hot to replace those lost through sweating.

Eye, ear, nose, and throat disorders

The eyes, ears, and nose are all sense organs. They are grouped together here with the throat because anatomically the ears, nose, and throat are closely connected: the Eustachian tube, which maintains equal pressure on either side of the eardrum, connects the middle ear to the back of the nose and the throat. This means that problems in one area can affect the others, which is why there are specialists in ear, nose, and throat (ENT) disorders. The common cold, a viral infection of the nose and throat, is included in *Respiratory system disorders*.

Squint

In a child with a squint, when one eye looks forward the other eye looks in a different direction. Approximately 1 in 20 children have a squint.

Squint affecting the right eye In this case, the eye looks inward instead of straight ahead to match the left eye.

WHAT CAUSES IT?

A squint is caused by an imbalance of the eye muscles that control the direction of eye movements. It is not always known why a squint occurs, although squints can run in families. Short- or long-sightedness can cause a squint.

SHOULD I SEE A DOCTOR?

Squints are extremely common in babies but should settle by the time the baby is 3 months old. If you notice that your baby's or child's eyes still look in different directions, or do not move together after this age, then visit your doctor. He can refer you to a paediatric eye clinic for assessment.

Sometimes it may look like a child or baby is squinting because of the shape of their face or eyes, but in fact there is not a squint. This is called pseudosquint and is not a cause for concern. However, if you're worried, take your child to the doctor.

It is important that a squint is detected and treated early to prevent problems with vision in the future. If the eyes do not look in the same direction the brain receives two separate images, which would result in double vision so the brain suppresses the image from the weaker eye. If a squint is not corrected the weaker eye will become lazy and give poor vision (a condition called amblyobia) so the child will not have binocular vision – this requires that both eyes work together to allow us to perceive depth. Amblyobia cannot be corrected by wearing glasses. However, if amblyobia occurs it can still be treated as long as this is done before the age of 6 or 7 when a child's vision is still developing. After this age it becomes irreversible.

WHAT'S THE TREATMENT?

Tests depend on the age of the child and may involve shining a light into the eyes and asking the child to look at different objects.

Possible symptoms

- ★ Eye looks inwards, outwards, upwards or downwards when the other eye is looking straight ahead
- ★ Can be constant or only seen at certain times (intermittent) and if they are minor can be difficult to spot
- ★ Eyes may not move together when following an object

Drops may be put into the eyes so they can be examined further.

Treatment depends on the cause of the squint and includes wearing glasses to correct long- or short-sightedness, an eye patch (see box, below), eye exercises, and occasionally eyedrops to blur the good eye and force the other to work. If these are not effective injecting botulinum toxin (Botox) into an eye muscle under anaesthetic or eye surgery may be offered.

What can I do to help?

If an eye patch is recommended it is worn over the good eye, forcing the affected eye to work and catch up. The length of time your child needs to wear a patch varies.

Putting on an eye patch The patch has an adhesive back. You need to use a new eye patch every time.

Wearing glasses If your child is short- or long-sighted she'll need to wear glasses over her eye patch.

Vision problems

There are three main types of vision problems, which are also known as refractive errors: long-sightedness (hypermetropia), short-sightedness (myopia), and astigmatism. All of these can cause some degree of blurred vision.

WHAT ARE THE CAUSES?

To see clearly, light rays that enter the eye must be focused onto the retina, the light-sensitive membrane at the back of the eye. In short-sightedness vision is clear for close objects but distance vision is blurred. Here, the eyeball is generally too long or the cornea is curved too much so light rays are focused in front of the retina instead of on it, causing blurred vision. Short-sighedness often runs in families. In long-sightedness vision is clear for distant objects but close vision is blurred. Here, the eyeball is too short or the cornea is too flat so light rays are focused behind the retina. Many babies are born with mild long-sightedness that improves as they get older. In astigmatism, the front of the eye is not a smooth curve but is slightly irregular, so that not all parts of an object are in focus at the same time. It may be partly genetic.

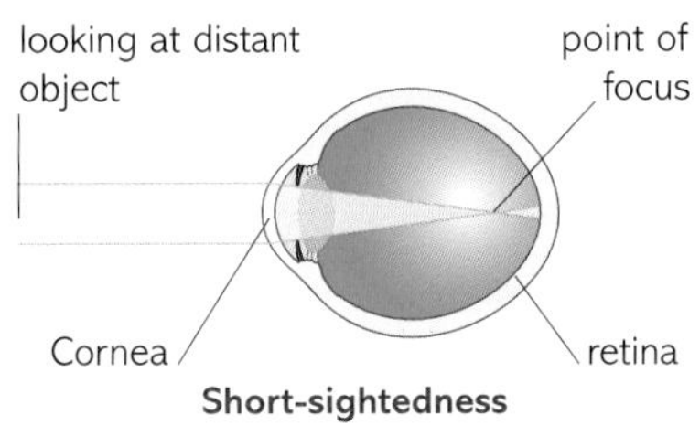

Short-sightedness

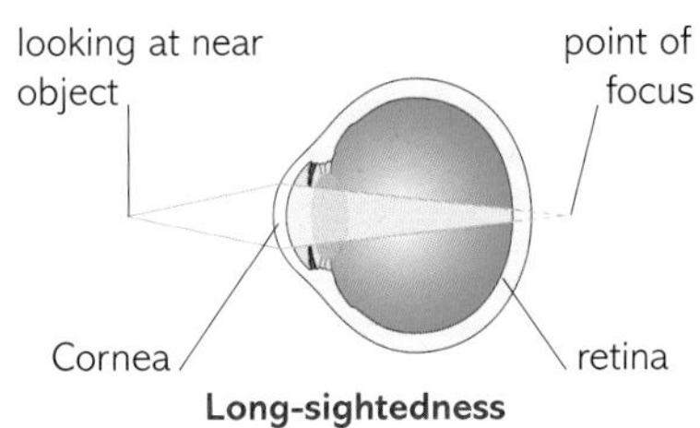

Long-sightedness

Focusing problems Light rays must be focused onto the retina to enable sharp vision. In short-sightedness, they are focused in front of the retina, while in long-sightedness, they are focused behind it.

SHOULD I SEE A DOCTOR/ OPTOMETRIST?

Your child's eyes will be looked at birth and at the 6–8 week check. Thereafter, if your child's eyesight is normal it is recommended that you have her vision checked every 2 years. If your child is found to have a vision problem you may be recommended to have her vision checked more regularly. In the UK, children under 16 (or under 19 and in full-time education) are entitled to free eye care with an optometrist.

Even if your child has had her 2-yearly checks, visit your doctor or optometrist if you are concerned about her eyes. Children aren't always aware they can't see properly: a child may think it is normal to be able to see her school books but not the board. Your child's teacher may notice the problem.

WHAT'S THE TREATMENT?

Vision problems are treated by wearing glasses. The shape of the lens in the glasses bends the light to compensate for the error in focusing the image. Children can wear contact lenses, but have to be able to insert and remove them themselves so they are generally not suitable for young children. Laser eye surgery is not suitable for children as their eyes are still growing and changing shape. In the UK, children under 16 (or under 19 and in full-time education) are entitled to vouchers to help with the cost of glasses or contact lenses.

Possible symptoms

Signs that your child may have a problem with vision include:

- ★ Sitting very close to the board
- ★ Always frowning or straining to see
- ★ Complaining of headaches or tired eyes

What can I do?

If your child has to wear glasses, show her how to clean them and teach her that it's important not to let anyone else wear them. In case she gets teased at nursery or school for wearing glasses, you'll need to be prepared to give her some emotional support so that she can deal with it.

Choosing glasses Help your child to choose glasses that she likes – she'll be more likely to wear them when she needs to.

Conjunctivitis

Conjunctivitis is inflammation of the conjunctiva, the transparent membrane that covers the white part of the eye and the inner eyelids. Depending on the cause, it can affect one or both eyes.

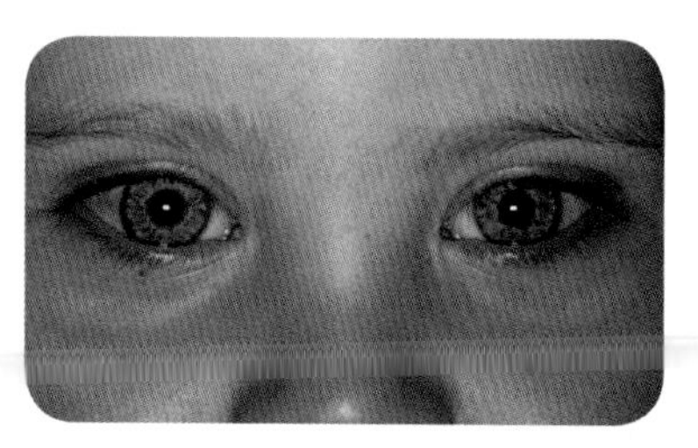

Conjunctivitis Red, watery eyes are typical of all types of conjunctivitis, whether due to infection, allergy, or an irritant.

WHAT ARE THE TYPES?

Conjunctivitis can be caused by an infection, an allergy, or an irritant, such as chlorine in the eye.

★ **Infective conjunctivitis** Various types of bacteria and viruses can infect the eyes, causing conjunctivitis.

Babies sometimes develop bacterial conjunctivitis as a result of infection from the mother as they pass through the birth canal (see Sticky eye, p.92).

Possible symptoms

Infective conjunctivitis:

★ Red eye that may water or be sore or itchy

★ Sticky yellow or green discharge from eye; may be more obvious in morning when eyelashes appear stuck together

★ Often starts in one eye before spreading to the other

Allergic conjunctivitis:

★ Red, watery, itchy eyes

★ Swollen eyelids that may be sore or uncomfortable

Irritant conjunctivitis:

★ Red, watery, itchy eye or eyes

What can I do to help?

If your child has infective conjunctivitis, you can make her eyes feel more comfortable and relieve itchiness by using lubricating eye drops that can be bought over the counter. Infective conjunctivitis is easily spread from one eye to another and from person to person, so good hand hygiene is vital.

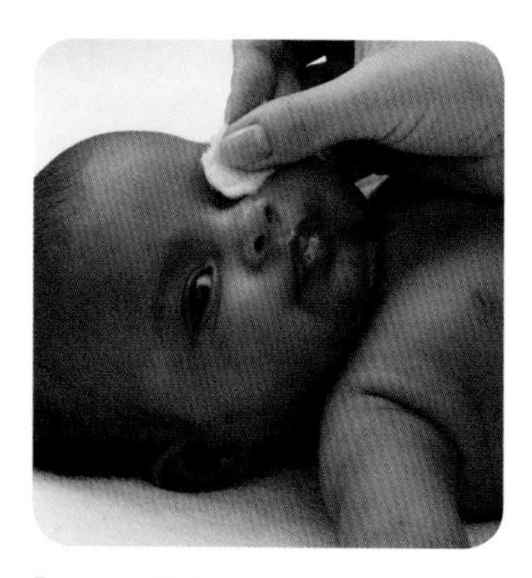

Remove discharge Use moistened cotton wool or gauze to remove sticky discharge, especially in the morning. Use a separate piece for each eye.

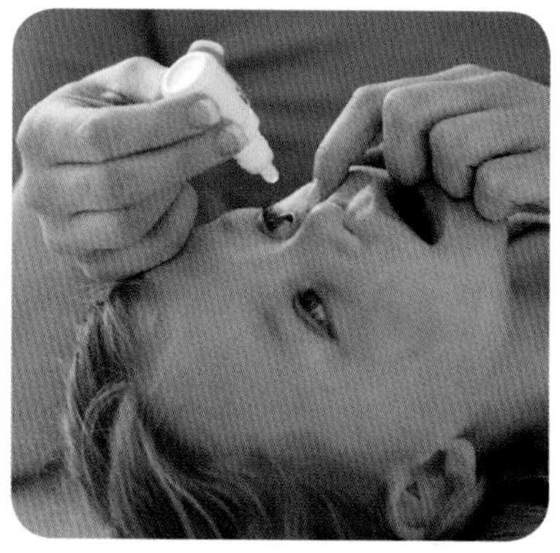

Insert lubricating eye drops Have your child lie down with her head face up on your lap. Pull down the lower eyelid and squeeze a drop into the area.

Hand hygiene Your child should wash his hands if he touches his eyes (but encourage him not to). He should not share towels, washcloths, or pillows.

In older children infective conjunctivitis is most often caused by a virus, although occasionally bacteria are responsible. It is caught by being in close contact with another person and is very contagious. The Health Protection Agency has stated that children do not need to be excluded from school if they have infective conjunctivitis. Despite this, some schools and nurseries will insist your child stays at home.

Most cases of infectious conjunctivitis are mild and do not require medical treatment as they get better within a few days. If the conjunctivitis lasts longer than this or is very severe, see your doctor. There are no particular symptoms that help the doctor tell whether the cause is viral or bacterial, so a small sample of pus or mucus may be taken from the eye and sent to a laboratory to be tested. If the cause is found to be bacteria, the doctor may prescribe antibiotic eye drops or ointment.

If your child's eyes become very painful, or if he develops sensitivity to light (photophobia) or changes in vision seek medical advice urgently as there could be a more serious eye problem.

★ **Allergic conjunctivitis** This is caused by an allergen, such as pollen, and can occur in conjunction with allergic rhinitis (p.144). Depending on the allergen, it may appear seasonally or all year round (perennially). For example, if your child has an allergy to pollen, the conjunctivitis may only occur in the spring and summer months or if the allergy is to house-dust mites or animal dander (flakes of dead skin), symptoms may be present all year round. Allergic conjunctivitis is not contagious.

If at all possible, help your child to avoid the allergen that is causing the problem. For example, if it is pollen encourage your child to wear sunglasses (preferably wrap-around ones) when he is outdoors, or if it is animal dander, he should avoid animals! Encourage your child not to rub his eyes as this may cause further irritation and inflammation. A cold wet flannel applied to the eyelids can be soothing. Antihistamine or other anti-inflammatory eye drops can be bought over the counter or are available on prescription. You can also buy special wipes to get rid of any debris such as pollen in the eyelashes to prevent further irritation. See your doctor if allergic conjunctivitis is especially troublesome. Oral antihistamines can be used as a preventive measure.

★ **Irritant conjunctivitis** This type of conjunctivitis is caused by any irritant that gets in the eye. The irritant could be a chemical such as chlorine, shampoo, or soap, or a foreign object such as an eyelash or a piece of grit in the eye.

Try to find ways to help your child avoid the irritant; for example, if he finds chlorine in swimming pools irritating to the eyes, wearing goggles may help. Your child should avoid rubbing his eyes as this can irritate the eyes further and increase inflammation. Irritant conjunctivitis is not contagious.

Chalazion

A chalazion is a small swelling in the eyelid that is due to a blockage of a gland in the area. It does not usually cause problems unless it gets infected.

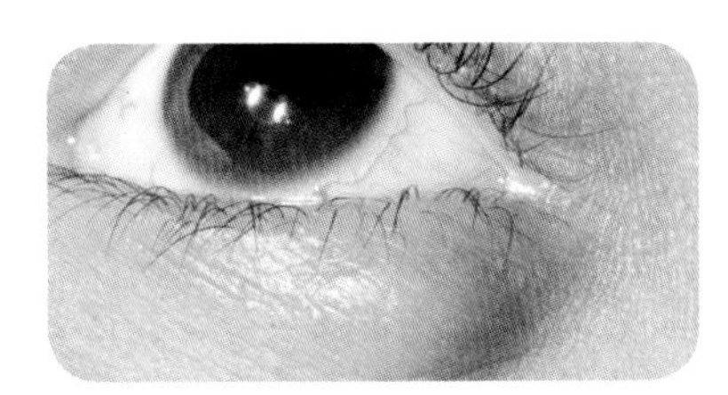

Chalazion This small lump underneath the lower eyelid is a chalazion. It is caused by a blocked gland inside the lid.

HOW CAN I TREAT A CHALAZION?

Often no treatment is needed for a chalazion and it will go away on its own, although this can take a few months. If the chalazion is causing your child discomfort, applying a hot compress to the area may help: soak a clean flannel or cotton pad in hot water and place it over the affected eye. The water should not be boiling; it should be hot but comfortable when applied to your child's eye.

Possible symptoms

- ★ Small lump in the eyelid
- ★ Eye or eyelid may feel irritated or uncomfortable
- ★ Lump may turn red, feel hot or tender, and swell if infected

SHOULD I SEE A DOCTOR?

If you think that a chalazion has become infected see your doctor, who can prescribe antibiotic eye ointment. A chalazion that does not go away or is causing problems (such as interfering with vision) can be removed with a minor operative procedure.

Stye

A stye is an infection of the follicle (root) of an eyelash, which causes the follicle to swell and fill with pus. Styes are common in children, although they can occur at any age.

WHAT IS THE CAUSE?

Styes are most commonly caused by staphylococcal bacteria. If a child doesn't wash his hands properly, these bacteria can easily be carried from the nose to the eye. Infection may be more likely if tiny glands at the base of the follicles, called sebaceous glands, become blocked.

SHOULD I SEE A DOCTOR?

Many styes get better on their own in about a week without the need for medical treatment. If a stye doesn't appear to be improving or is severe, take your child to the doctor, who can prescribe an antibiotic eye ointment to treat the infection. A child who suffers from recurrent styes should also be seen by a doctor as they can be a sign of other skin conditions.

IS IT PREVENTABLE?

Good general hygiene, including frequent hand-washing and not sharing towels and flannels, helps to prevent styes. Your child should avoid touching or rubbing his eyes, especially with unwashed hands. To clean the eyelids, use cotton wool soaked in cooled, boiled water, wipe across the eyelid and discard the cotton wool; repeat on the other eye. You can use a dilute soap wash of baby shampoo and water and rub along the eyelashes and eyelids (with eyes closed).

Possible symptoms

- ★ Firm, red, painful lump on edge of eyelid
- ★ Red, swollen eyelid around lump
- ★ Small yellow spot or "head" of pus may be visible at centre of lump

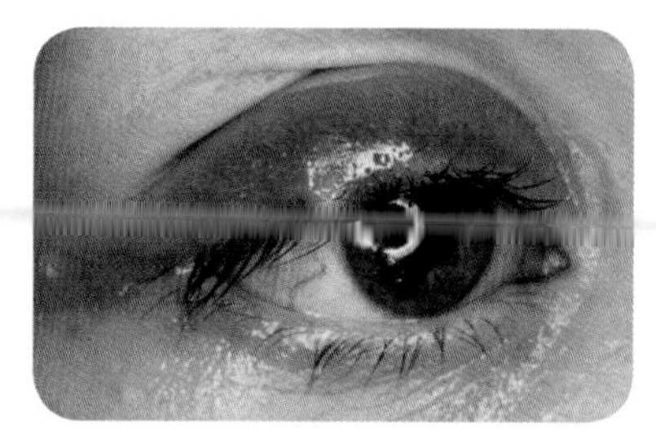

Stye on upper eyelid The stye has a "head" of yellow pus and the surrounding eyelid is very red and swollen.

What can I do to help?

You can help the healing process by applying a hot compress to the stye 3 or 4 times a day for 15–20 minutes at a time. Do NOT pull the eyelash out. Although this will allow the pus to drain faster it can lead to eyelashes ingrowing, which can cause further problems.

Apply hot compress Place a clean flannel or cotton pad soaked in hot water over the eye. The water should be hot but comfortable to apply.

Give painkillers If the stye is causing your child any discomfort or pain, you can give her either paracetamol or ibuprofen to help relieve this.

Ensure proper hand-washing To avoid spreading infection, your child should wash her hands if she touches the stye (but encourage her not to).

Foreign bodies

A foreign body is an object in the body that is not usually found there. Children are naturally curious and may put an object where it doesn't belong and may not always tell you they have done so.

Possible symptoms

Foreign body in eye:

- ★ Sensation of something in the eye
- ★ Pain in the eye
- ★ Redness and watering of eye

Foreign body in ear:

- ★ Decreased hearing, or, if there is a live insect in the ear, a buzzing sound
- ★ Ear pain
- ★ Offensive smelling discharge from one ear, if the foreign body leads to infection

Foreign body in nose:

- ★ Child may complain that one nostril feels blocked or is painful
- ★ Offensive-smelling discharge from one nostril, if the foreign body leads to infection

WHAT ARE THE TYPES?
The most common places for a foreign body in children are the ear, nose, or eye. Objects in the ear or nose may be put there by a child voluntarily whereas an object in the eye is usually accidental.

★ **Foreign body in ear** Various objects can fit inside the ear canal, such as small nuts or seeds, toys, the end of cotton buds (which shouldn't be used to clean ears), and even insects. An older child may tell you if they have put something in their ears, or if they think something has flown in, but a younger child may not.

Do NOT attempt to remove the object yourself: doing so can cause damage to the ear and eardrum as you may push the object further into the ear instead of removing it. Do not put water in the ear to attempt to get the object out, as the object may swell, causing more pain and making it more difficult to be removed. Instead, take your child to the doctor who will refer you to the local ear, nose, and throat (ENT) department for the object to be removed.

★ **Foreign body in nose** Toddlers and young children very commonly put things inside their noses, such as beads, buttons, small toys (such as marbles), nuts and seeds, sweets, peas, or pieces of corn. As with a foreign body in the ear, an older child may tell you if she has got something stuck in her nose, but a younger child may not.

Do NOT try to remove a foreign body from the nose as you may push it further in or cause damage to tissues. Instead, take your child to the doctor who will refer you to the local ENT department so that the object can be removed.

Foreign body in eye Foreign bodies in the eye are common, but usually they are not put there intentionally. Rather, sand, grit, or another object enters by accident. If your child has something in her eye, tell her not to rub the eye as this may cause more damage. You can try to flush it out with water, but if the eye is still irritated after this, see your doctor as the surface of the eye may have been scratched and antibiotic eyedrops may be required (see box, below).

Sometimes, an object can penetrate the surface of the eye and can't be seen. If your child complains that something went in her eye even though you can't see anything and the eye is irritated, see your doctor urgently.

What can I do to help?

You can try to remove a foreign object from the eye by flushing the eye with water or saline eyedrops. Antibiotic eyedrops are sometimes needed if the object scratches the eye's surface.

Pour water into eye Position your child's head over the sink and gently pull down the lower eyelid. Gently pour clean water (not hot) into the eye.

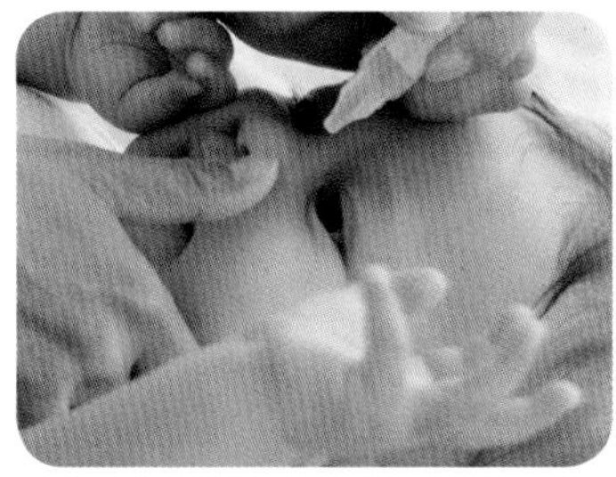

Inserting antibiotic eyedrops To insert the eyedrops, ask your child to look up, pull the lower eyelid down, and drop the medication into her eye.

Inflamed ear canal

Inflammation of the outer ear canal, the tube between the eardrum and the visible outer ear, can occur at any age. Also known as otitis externa, it is more common in those who swim regularly.

WHAT IS THE CAUSE?

Inflammation can be caused by infection with bacteria or fungi or can result from an allergy, for example to a particular shampoo. It can also occur if eczema or another skin condition irritates the ear, prompting the child to scratch it, leading to infection. In swimmers, irritation by chlorinated or sea water or pooling of water in the ear makes infection more likely.

SHOULD I SEE A DOCTOR?

Take your child to the doctor who will look in his ears. An inflamed outer ear canal is generally treated with a short course of steroid anti-inflammatory eardrops or spray, which may also contain an antibiotic or antifungal medication. It usually clears up within 7–10 days of starting treatment.

IS IT PREVENTABLE?

★ If your child is susceptible to an inflammation, keeping his ears dry may help prevent it. He should wear ear plugs or tight-fitting cap when swimming and a shower cap when taking a bath or shower.
★ Do not clean your child's ear canal with cotton buds or insert anything into it in an attempt to remove wax. It is not necessary to do this and it may scratch and irritate the ear further, increasing the risk of infection, and it can also damage the eardrum. Earwax naturally works its way out and should only be removed once it is on the visible part of the outer ear.

Possible symptoms

Your child may not have all of the following symptoms.

- ★ Pain or itching in the ear
- ★ Red or peeling skin in the ear
- ★ Discharge from the ear
- ★ Discomfort on opening the mouth, for example when chewing
- ★ Swollen glands in the neck

What can I do to help?

To insert eardrops or spray, lie your child down on her side with the affected ear facing upward. Gently remove any earwax from the visible outer ear only; do not attempt to remove wax from inside the ear and do not insert items like cotton buds. You can give painkillers for discomfort.

1 **Warm the eardrops** or spray by rolling the bottle between your hands to make it comfortable for your child when you put the drops in.

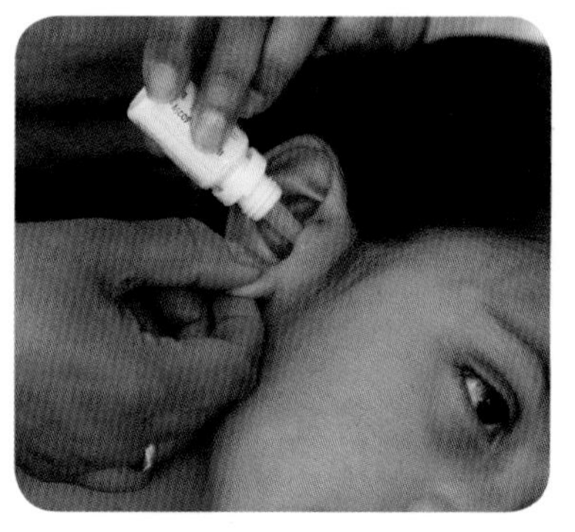

2 **Hold the bottle** so that its tip is just above the entrance to the ear canal, then squeeze to insert the prescribed number of drops or sprays.

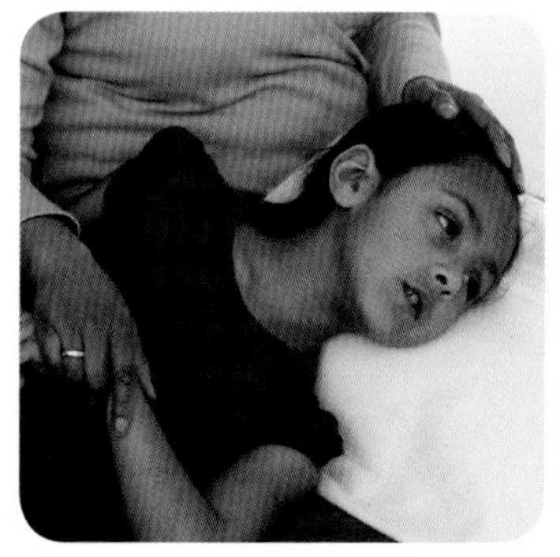

3 **Your child should remain** lying down for approximately 5 minutes to prevent the ear drops coming out of her ear.

Middle-ear infection

Infection of the middle ear, which is located between the eardrum and inner ear, is a common cause of earache in children. Also known as otitis media, the infection may be acute (short-lived) or longer lasting or recurrent (chronic).

WHAT IS THE CAUSE?

Middle-ear infection generally occurs when an infection causing a cold spreads upwards through the Eustachian tubes, which connect the ears to the throat. The Eustachian tubes normally allow air into the middle ear, but during a cold they become blocked with mucus. Mucus then builds up in the middle ear and can become infected. Both viruses and bacteria can cause middle-ear infection.

Children are more likely than adults to develop middle-ear infection because their Eustachian tubes are shorter and more horizontal than those in adults, so it is easier for an infection to spread along them. Also enlarged tonsils or adenoids, more common in children, can block the Eustachian tubes.

SHOULD I SEE A DOCTOR?

Middle-ear infections usually get better on their own within 2–3 days. If you are concerned that your child is not improving, if she is very young, or if she is very unwell see your doctor, who will examine her ears, and, if the eardrum looks infected, may prescribe oral antibiotics, although these will not be effective for viral infection.

If your child has had a perforated eardrum, you should see your doctor approximately 6 weeks after the infection has cleared up. This is to check that the eardrum has healed; if the perforation is still present you will be referred to an ENT department as treatment may be needed to repair the perforation.

What can I do to help?

The majority of middle-ear infections get better on their own, but they can be painful (although they don't always cause earache). You can make your child more comfortable by giving painkillers.

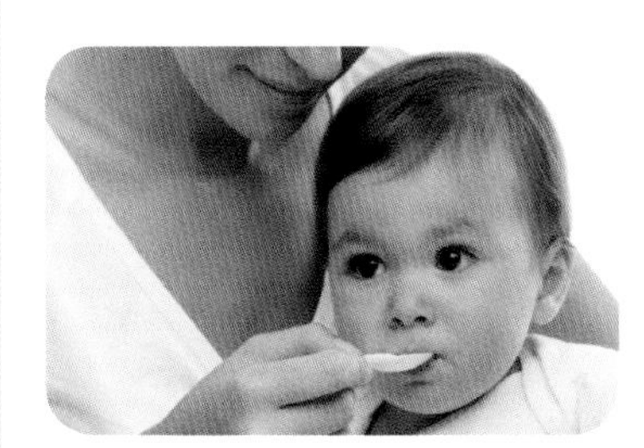

Give painkillers Paracetamol or ibuprofen will help reduce earache and also bring down your child's fever.

Encourage drinking Give your child plenty of water to drink in order to prevent dehydration.

Possible symptoms

- ★ Fever and other symptoms of an infection – tiredness, decreased appetite, feeling unwell
- ★ Earache (doesn't always occur and can also indicate other problems, such as teething or an inflamed ear canal)
- ★ Pulling at one ear (can also indicate other problems, such as teething)
- ★ Decreased hearing (temporary – during the infection)
- ★ Discharge from ear that often relieves pain (due to the eardrum perforating)

If your child has very regular recurrent episodes of middle-ear infection or if an acute episode does not clear up she may be advised to have a longer course of antibiotics in an attempt to clear the infection. Specialists may also recommend the insertion of grommets (see p.141) in children with recurrent middle-ear infection.

ARE THERE COMPLICATIONS?

As the infection clears up some fluid or mucus may remain in the middle ear, causing decreased hearing. Generally this clears up within a few days, although if it remains it can lead to glue ear.

IS IT PREVENTABLE?

Most children get ear infections at some point and it is generally not possible to prevent them. However, breastfed children appear to have fewer ear infections, as do children who live in a smoke-free home. So, breastfeed your children if possible and if you smoke, stop, both for your own health and that of your child! Babies who do not use dummies may get fewer ear infections, but dummies appear to protect against sudden infant death syndrome. However, stopping dummies when a child is 6–12 months old, when the highest risk period for sudden infant death syndrome has passed, may help prevent ear infections.

Build-up of earwax

Earwax serves a useful purpose and does not usually need to be removed. However, in some people it can build up, causing discomfort and decreased hearing, and requires treatment.

Possible symptoms

- ★ Decreased hearing
- ★ Ear pain
- ★ Ringing in the ears (tinnitus)
- ★ Spinning sensation (vertigo)

WHAT IS THE CAUSE?

Earwax is a substance that protects the skin of the external ear canal as well as cleaning it and keeping it lubricated. It is antibacterial and helps to prevent infections. Without earwax the skin in your ear canal would be dry and cracked and likely to get infected. So earwax serves a purpose and in most people does not need to be removed – it falls out of the ear in small pieces on its own. However, some people produce too much earwax and it can build up. This is more likely to occur if your child has repeated ear infections or learning difficulties although why this occurs is not clear.

WHAT CAN I DO?

Do not attempt to remove earwax by inserting cotton wool buds or any other objects into the ear. Such attempts may only push the wax further in. You should only clean wax that has come out onto the external ear itself. Eardrops available over the counter can be used to soften the wax (for how to insert eardrops, see p.138).

SHOULD I SEE A DOCTOR?

If using eardrops is not effective, see your doctor who will be able to remove the wax by irrigation (syringing), where warm water is inserted into the ear to flush out the wax.

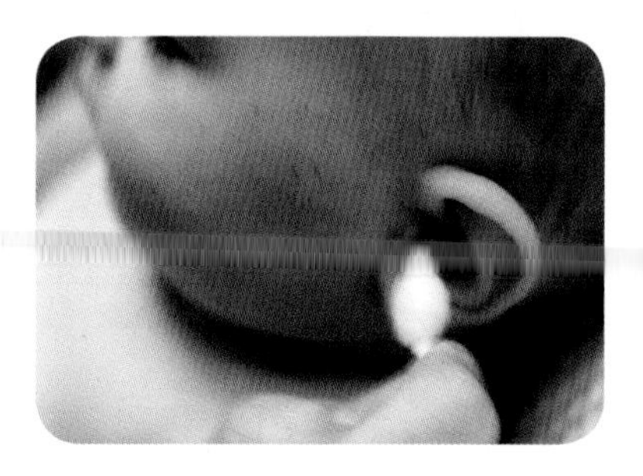

Cleaning off earwax Only clean off wax that is on the external part of the ear. Do not insert anything into the ear.

Glue ear

In glue ear, also called otitis media with effusion, there is a build-up of a sticky fluid in the middle ear, hence the name glue ear.

Possible symptoms

- ★ Difficulty hearing far away or quiet speech, when there is background noise, or when concentrating on something else such as television.
- ★ Irritability or naughtiness due to frustration at not hearing or speech delay (p196)
- ★ Ear pain, less commonly
- ★ Episodes of fever and increased pain due to frequent ear infections (glue ear increases the likelihood of infection)

WHAT IS THE CAUSE?

The middle ear, which is the space behind the eardrum, contains three small bones that vibrate and transmit sound into the inner ear. The build-up of fluid that occurs in glue ear means that these bones cannot move as normal so that hearing decreases and sounds become muffled.

Glue ear is not due to water getting in the ear from swimming or washing. The exact cause is not known but it may be due to a problem with the Eustachian tube that prevents it from draining fluid away from the middle ear. Although fluid can persist in the middle ear after an episode of middle-ear infection (p.139) this does not always lead to glue ear, and glue ear can occur in the absence of an ear infection previously. Glue ear is very common in children between the ages of 2 and 6.

SHOULD I SEE A DOCTOR?

Often no treatment is required and in half of cases the fluid in the ear drains away and hearing returns to normal within 3 months. However, do visit your doctor if you are concerned about your child's hearing so that she can be assessed and other causes of hearing loss can be excluded or treated. Your doctor will do this by looking at the eardrum using an instrument called an otoscope. If the glue ear is severe or not improving after 3 months, you will be referred to an ENT specialist for further hearing tests and examination. Even in this case treatment is not always given as 9 in 10 cases will get better after a year.

WHAT'S THE TREATMENT?

There are a number of different treatment options for glue ear:

★ Hearing aids – these can be used as an alternative to surgery to improve hearing while waiting for the glue ear to improve.

★ Autoinflation – here the child is given a special balloon to blow up with his nose. This may help open the Eustachian tube. It is difficult for young children to perform and has to be done regularly so is more suitable for older children.

★ Adenoidectomy – if the adenoids are obstructing the Eustachian tube they may be removed.

★ Grommet insertion – a small tube is inserted into the eardrum, which allows fluid to drain from the middle ear. Hearing generally improves immediately; in fact children may say everything sounds too loud! As the ear and the eardrum grow, the grommets fall out, generally after 9–12 months and the hole in the eardrum where the grommet was heals up. Occasionally grommets have to be re-inserted.

IS IT PREVENTABLE?

Although the exact cause of glue ear is not known, there is evidence that, as in middle-ear infection (p.139), children who are breastfed and not exposed to cigarette smoke are at lower risk.

What can I do to help?

If your child has glue ear, speak clearly and loudly to her without shouting and try to decrease background noise while you are speaking, for example by turning off the television.

Speak directly face-to-face Get down to your child's level so that she can see you as well as hear you. Be sure that you have her full attention before you start speaking to her.

Make sure he can hear Sitting near the front of the class helps your child to hear the teacher better. Tell the teacher about your child's hearing problem so she can make sure he is able to hear.

Looking after grommets

If your child has grommets (see text, left), take note of the following points:

★ **For the first 1–2 weeks** after surgery your child should avoid getting water in the ears so should wear earplugs in the bath or shower and should not go swimming.

★ **Ear discharge** occurs in some children after the operation, often during or after a cold. This can be treated with antibiotics from your doctor, generally antibiotic eardrops (see p.138 for how to insert them).

★ **Occasionally the grommets** can get infected; this is treated with antibiotics. If antibiotics don't work, the grommets may be removed.

★ **Wash the outside** of the ears as normal but try to avoid getting soapy water in the ears. Some surgeons recommend using cotton wool balls with vaseline to stop soapy water entering the ear when bathing.

★ **Swimming** – this is usually fine with grommets after the first 1–2 weeks but diving or deep underwater swimming should be avoided.

★ **It is safe to fly** with grommets; in fact your child should have no ear pain as the tube helps to equalize pressure in the ears.

Wearing earplugs If your child has grommets, you may be advised that he wear earplugs when swimming.

Barotrauma

Ear pain caused by unequal air pressure on either side of the eardrum is known as barotrauma. It commonly occurs during flying, usually during descent of the airplane.

Possible symptoms

- ★ Ear pain
- ★ Feeling of fullness in the ear
- ★ Pain is relieved if the eardrum perforates

WHAT IS THE CAUSE?

The middle ear is the space behind the eardrum that is normally filled with air. The Eustachian tube connects this space to the back of the nose and throat and lets air in to maintain equal pressure on either side of the eardrum. When a plane descends, the air pressure increases as the plane nears the ground, pushing the eardrum inwards. Sometimes the Eustachian tubes cannot respond fast enough and ear pain results, and sometimes the eardrum may perforate.

Children are more likely to get pain in the ears when flying because their Eustachian tubes are narrower than in adults and the tubes may be blocked by large adenoids. If you or your child has a cold or ear infection it is more difficult for the pressure in the ears to equalize, which increases the chance of the eardrum perforating.

WHAT'S THE OUTLOOK?

In many cases the pain improves after the ears "pop", which means the Eustachian tubes have opened, or on landing. If the eardrum perforates, it generally heals within 6 weeks. Until then, there may be some hearing loss, and the risk of developing an ear infection is increased. If you think your child has a perforated eardrum, he should avoid getting his ears wet while it heals, so he should wear a showercap or ear plugs when in the bath. If your child needs to fly with a perforated eardrum it should not cause any further problems as the perforation will allow the pressure to equalize on both sides of the eardrum. If you think your child's eardrum has perforated, see a doctor after 6–8 weeks to check that the eardrum has healed.

What can I do to help?

If your child has painful ears when flying give a sugar-free sweet to suck on, or teach him to use one of the other techniques shown below. They all help to open the Eustachian tubes, which connect the middle ear with the back of the throat, and so equalize pressure on either side of the eardrum.

Give him a sweet Sucking, chewing or swallowing can help open the Eustachian tube, so give your child a sugar-free sweet. For babies, try breastfeeding or giving a drink.

Encourage yawning Yawning is a simple method that can be effective in opening the Eustachian tubes. Your child will hear a pop when the tubes open. The discomfort and feeling of fullness in the ears then disappear.

Teach the Valsalva manoeuvre Ask her to breath in and then pinch her nostrils together and keep her mouth closed while trying to breathe out. Probably only an older child can do this.

Nosebleed

Nosebleeds are common in children and generally due to bleeding from blood vessels on the lower part of the septum (wall dividing the nostrils). These blood vessels are delicate and bleed easily. Most children grow out of nosebleeds by adolescence.

Possible symptoms

★ Bleeding from the nose, which can come from one or both nostrils

WHAT IS THE CAUSE?

Some children are more prone to nosebleeds than others although children who pick their noses or who have allergic rhinitis (p.144) and use nasal sprays may be more likely to have them. Nosebleeds can also occur after an injury.

SHOULD I SEE A DOCTOR?

If your child develops a nosebleed straight after an injury such as falling over or getting a football in the face, take her to the doctor as the nose may have been broken.

Most other nosebleeds can be treated at home (see box, below). If your child is getting very regular nosebleeds – one per week or more – or they are very severe, you should take her to your doctor who will refer you to an ENT specialist. Treatments for nosebleeds include applying antiseptic cream to the septum, surgery, and a technique called cauterization that involves applying heat or another agent to the blood vessels that are causing the problem in order to seal them.

IS IT PREVENTABLE?

Encouraging your child not to pick her nose can help prevent nosebleeds. Applying some vaseline to the inside of the nose may also help, although there has been little research about its effectiveness. Some people are more prone to nosebleeds in very dry environments. Using a humidifier, or placing a wet towel over a chair near a radiator helps humidify the air and may prevent nosebleeds.

After a nosebleed has stopped, your child should not blow her nose for 12 hours, as this may dislodge a blood clot and start the nosebleed again. She should also avoid strenuous exercise or rough-and-tumble games for 12 hours.

What can I do to help?

To stop a nosebleed, apply pressure for 10 minutes. If bleeding hasn't stopped after this time, repeat for another 10 minutes. You can apply an ice pack to the cheeks at the same time. If the bleeding does not stop after 20 minutes, seek medical help.

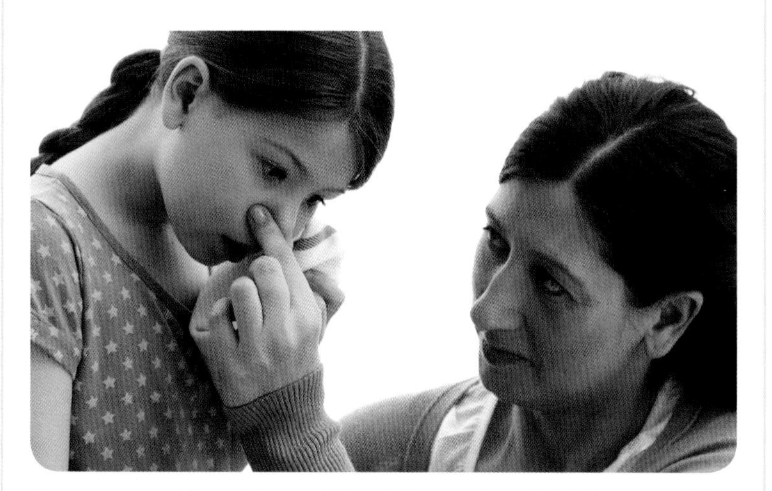

Stopping a nosebleed Ask your child to sit down and lean slightly forwards with her mouth open. Firmly pinch the nose, just above the nostrils. Placing an ice pack on the face while you do this can also help. Don't let her lie down or tip her head back as blood can run down the back of the nose into the throat and cause choking.

TOP TIP

When you are applying pressure to stop a nosebleed, use a watch or a clock to time yourself. Ten minutes can feel like a very long time if you are anxious that your child is bleeding.

Allergic rhinitis

Allergic rhinitis is inflammation of the membranes lining the nose, caused by an allergen – something to which you are allergic. Allergic rhinitis may be seasonal, occurring for a few months a year, or it may be perennial, occurring all year round.

WHAT IS THE CAUSE?

Whether allergic rhinitis is seasonal or perennial depends on the particular allergens that trigger symptoms. Seasonal allergic rhinitis, also known as hayfever, is commonly caused by tree, grass, and weed pollens. Perennial allergic rhinitis is most commonly caused by house-dust mites or animal dander (flakes of dead skin) from pets. Symptoms are due to the chemical histamine, which is released from cells during an allergic reaction.

Sneezing and runny nose If your child suffers from allergic rhinitis, he's likely to sneeze a lot and have a runny nose.

Allergic rhinitis may exist on its own or may occur in association with allergic conjunctivitis (see photo, right and p.134). Rhinitis can also be non-allergic, in which the inflammation is caused by other triggers such as a change in temperature; for example, many people get runny noses in the cold.

SHOULD I SEE A DOCTOR?

Some treatments for symptoms of allergic rhinitis are available over the counter – check with your pharmacist which are suitable for your child's age. If these don't help, see your doctor, who can prescribe steroids or antihistamines that are stronger than those available over the counter.

If it isn't clear what is causing the symptoms, your child may be referred to a paediatrician for skin-prick testing. This procedure involves exposing your child to various common allergens, such as animal dander, pollens, or house-dust mites by placing a solution of these substances on the arm or leg and introducing them by pricking the skin. If your child is allergic to a substance the skin around the pricked area will become red, itchy, and swollen. Alternatively, blood tests can be used to identify allergens.

WHAT'S THE OUTLOOK?

In many children, hayfever or perennial rhinitis improves as they get older. If it continues to be severe then immunotherapy could be considered. This is a specialist treatment to treat allergy by exposing the person to gradually increasing doses of the allergen (initially only extremely tiny doses are given) so that tolerance builds up.

Possible symptoms

Symptoms occur quite soon after being exposed to the allergen, so you may notice that your child has symptoms after petting an animal or playing outside in the garden.

- ★ Sneezing
- ★ Runny or blocked nose
- ★ Itchy nose
- ★ Tiredness, irritability, or problems with school performance if severe symptoms interfere with sleep
- ★ In children with asthma, symptoms may become worse when they have hayfever

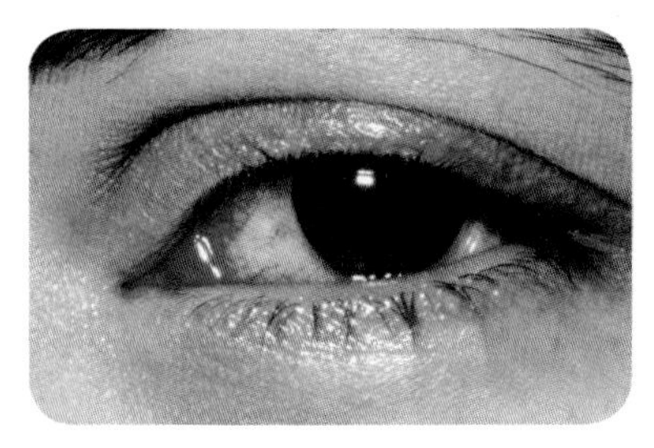

Red eyes Many children with hayfever also have red or itchy eyes (see Conjunctivitis, p.134) as the eyes can be sensitive to the same allergens that cause hayfever.

TOP TIP

Don't smoke in the home or around your child. Cigarette smoke irritates the airways, nose, and eyes and so can make symptoms worse.

What can I do to help?

Make a diary about your child's symptoms and where he has been/what he has done each day to help identify allergens (or skin-prick or blood tests can be used). Once the trigger has been identified, avoiding it may prevent symptoms, although for some allergens this is very difficult. Some medications are available over the counter but check they are suitable for your child's age. Nasal sprays contain steroids or antihistamines. Oral antihistamines are also available.

Protect eyes from pollen If your child is allergic to pollen and often suffers from allergic conjunctivitis, give him wrap-around sunglasses to wear to help prevent pollen entering the eyes.

Use house-dust mite protectors Mites live in beds and soft furnishings, so if your child is allergic to them, cover mattresses, pillows, and duvets with protectors, and wash bedding at high temperatures.

Reduce house-dust mites Wooden or tiled floors are preferable. Vacuum often and damp dust (this picks up dust as opposed to moving it around). Wash any rugs, and even soft toys, regularly.

Give oral antihistamines These medications work quickly as they block histamines, the chemicals released during an allergic reaction that are responsible for symptoms.

Use nasal spray After gently blowing his nose, your child should tilt his head slightly forwards, insert the tip of the spray into a nostril, and spray as he breathes in. Repeat in other nostril. Don't blow the nose after.

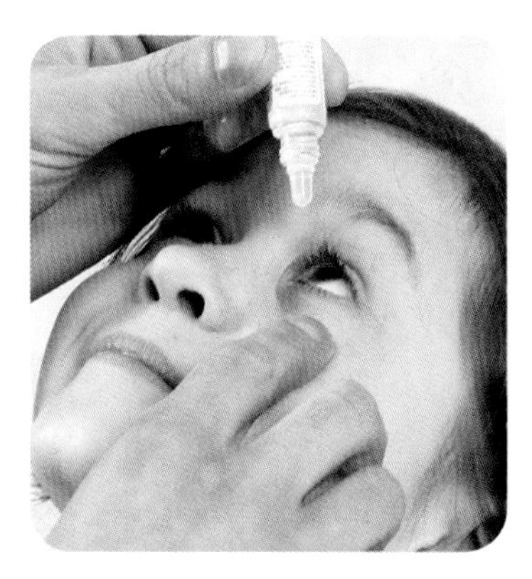

Insert eyedrops Eyedrops can be used to relieve itchy eyes. Hold the child's lower lid down and drop the liquid into the pocket created by doing this or into the inner corner of the eye.

Enlarged adenoids

The adenoids, which are at the back of the nose, are part of the body's infection-fighting system. They can become enlarged in young children.

The adenoids may become enlarged after recurrent colds and sore throats. This can cause problems by blocking the back of the nose and also the Eustachian tube, which connects the back of the nose to the ears. Often no treatment is needed as the symptoms are mild, although they can worsen if your child also has a cold. As your child grows and develops, the adenoids generally shrink so symptoms improve. If your child's symptoms are severe, for example if they are affecting sleep, if recurrent infections are causing him to miss a lot of school, or he has glue ear due to large adenoids, surgery to remove the adenoids may be recommended.

Possible symptoms

- ★ Noisy breathing
- ★ Mouth breathing, which leads to dry, cracked lips and dry mouth
- ★ Bad breath (from infected adenoids and/or a dry mouth)
- ★ Snoring and sleep apnoea
- ★ Ear infections as the Eustachian tube may be blocked

Epiglottitis

Epiglottitis is a serious condition that can cause difficulties with breathing due to swelling of the epiglottis, the structure that covers the trachea (windpipe) during swallowing to prevent food from entering the lungs.

Possible symptoms

- ★ Fever
- ★ Sore throat
- ★ Drooling – the throat is so painful the child may not swallow saliva
- ★ Hoarse voice
- ★ Noisy breathing
- ★ Difficulty breathing

WHAT IS THE CAUSE?

Epiglottitis is caused by an infection, most commonly with the bacterium *Haemophilus influenza* type b (Hib) and can sometimes be a complication of croup (p.155). It is less common than previously due to the vaccine against Hib. It can affect people of any age although it is more common in children between the ages of 2 and 7.

SHOULD I SEE A DOCTOR?

Epiglottitis is a medical emergency so call an ambulance. At the hospital your child will be given oxygen to improve breathing. This is given in a highly concentrated form by means of a face or nose mask or tubes inserted into the nose. In severe cases, a child may need to be put on a ventilator, a machine that acts like artificial lungs and takes over the task of breathing. Antibiotics are usually given into a vein (intravenously) to treat the infection.

Provided a child is treated promptly in hospital, he should make a full recovery from epiglottitis.

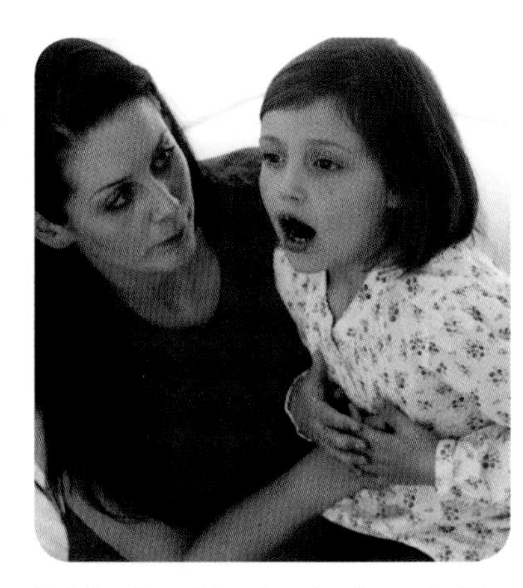

Helping breathing Leaning forward with mouth open will help your child breathe more easily as you wait for an ambulance.

IS IT PREVENTABLE?

Hib, the most common cause of epiglottitis, is preventable with a vaccine that is part of the routine immunization programme in the UK. If your child has had close contact with someone who has epiglottitis and he has not been vaccinated he may be offered antibiotics to stop him developing it.

Throat infection

An infection of the throat (pharynx) can involve mainly the tonsils, structures at the back of the throat that help fight infection – this is called tonsillitis. If the tonsils are not involved, the infection is known as pharyngitis.

What can I do to help?

Most throat infections get better on their own within a few days. Your main concerns are to ease your child's sore throat and to give her foods that she will be able to swallow easily.

Encourage your child to drink Plenty of water is needed to replace fluids lost through having a raised temperature.

Provide soft foods Soft foods or soups may be easier to swallow when your child's throat is sore.

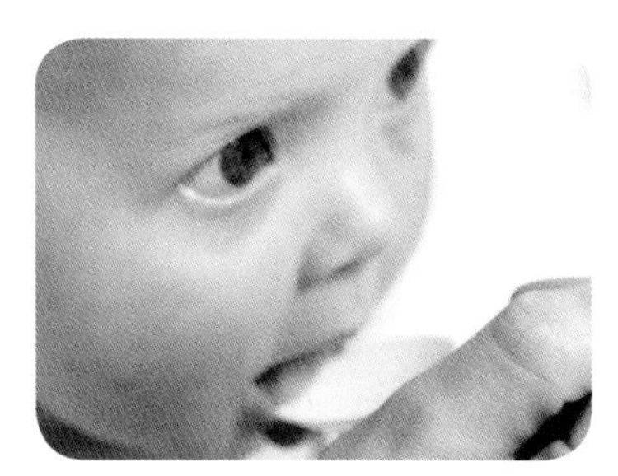

Give painkillers You can give your child paracetamol or ibuprofen, if required, to ease the pain of a sore throat and to bring down a fever.

Offer an ice lolly Lollies, ideally sugar-free ones, and cold drinks may soothe pain. A local anaesthetic spray might help, but check it suits your child's age.

Possible symptoms

- ★ Sore, inflamed throat
- ★ Pain on swallowing
- ★ Pain in the ears (referred from the throat)
- ★ Fever
- ★ Swollen lymph glands in the neck, which may be painful
- ★ Headache
- ★ Hoarse or lost voice
- ★ In tonsillitis, enlarged tonsils, which may have white/yellow patches on them
- ★ Decreased appetite, which may be due to feeling unwell or sore throat
- ★ Young children may also have stomach pain due to swollen lymph glands in the abdomen

WHAT ARE THE CAUSES?

Throat infections are generally caused by a virus. However, they can also be due to a bacterium, the most common being streptococcus, and these throat infections are sometimes called strep throat. Infection can by caught by breathing in droplets from the coughs and sneezes of an infected person, or in the case of bacterial infection, by direct contact with an infected person.

SHOULD I SEE A DOCTOR?

If your child appears very unwell, or if the symptoms are long-lasting, see your doctor who may prescribe antibiotics in case bacteria are the cause of the infection. It is not possible to tell by looking at the throat whether the infection is viral or bacterial.

A tonsillectomy can be performed to remove the tonsils if your child has regular episodes of tonsillitis – at least 5 per year – that affect her life, for example if she is missing lots of school due to the illness. Tonsillectomy may be recommended if enlarged tonsils are causing other problems such as obstructive sleep apnoea (p.148).

Obstructive sleep apnoea

Apnoea is a pause in breathing. In obstructive sleep apnoea (OSA), pauses occur during sleep as a result of a blockage in the upper airways. The pause causes the child to wake slightly so that breathing starts again, but sleep has been disturbed.

Possible symptoms

- ★ Snoring
- ★ Mouth breathing at night
- ★ Episodes of pauses in breathing or snoring, which may be followed by gasping
- ★ Tiredness in the daytime, sleepiness or irritability, or difficulty concentrating at school due to disturbed sleep

WHAT IS THE CAUSE?

In children, obstructive sleep apnoea can be caused by large tonsils or adenoids blocking the passage of air into the lungs. A child who is overweight is at increased risk. Obstructive sleep apnoea can be temporary, for example when the tonsils or adenoids are enlarged due to a cold, or it can be longer term if the tonsils or adenoids remain enlarged as a result of recurrent colds or sore throats. Sleep apnoea affects about 1 in 50 children, most commonly those aged between 2 and 7.

SHOULD I SEE A DOCTOR?

If your child has symptoms of obstructive sleep apnoea that last more than a few days or that occur without a cough or cold, see your doctor, as obstructive sleep apnoea can have serious consequences for a child's growth and development. To make a diagnosis, your doctor will refer your child for a sleep study. Your child will be admitted to hospital for one night (you will be able to go too) and monitored during sleep. If obstructive sleep apnoea is detected, there are various treatment options, depending on the cause. Enlarged tonsils and/or adenoids can be surgically removed, and if your child is overweight you may be given advice to help him lose weight. For children who cannot undergo surgery and those in whom surgery has not cured the problem, continual positive airway pressure (CPAP) may be suggested: this involves the child wearing a special breathing mask at night.

Daytime sleepiness Falling asleep during the day, tiredness, and attention problems are common symptoms of obstructive sleep apnoea and can cause problems at school.

What can I do?

If your child is overweight, losing weight through a programme of exercise and diet can help make the symptoms of obstructive sleep apnoea less severe.

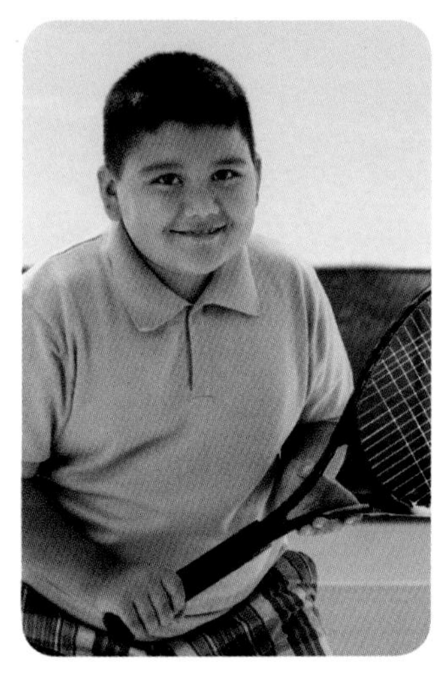

Encourage exercise Your child will be more likely to exercise regularly if he finds an activity he enjoys. Also make sure he has a healthy diet.

Respiratory system disorders

The respiratory system is divided into an upper and a lower part. The upper respiratory tract consists of the nose, throat, sinuses, and windpipe (trachea). The lower respiratory tract includes the lungs and the airways leading to the lungs (bronchi and smaller bronchioles). Most of the disorders included in this section are caused by infection, and these are arranged in order from the upper respiratory tract downwards to the lungs. There is also an article on asthma, an increasingly common problem whose cause is unclear, followed by one on viral-induced wheezes, which can cause symptoms similar to those of asthma. See also *Eye, ear, nose, and throat disorders*, pp.131–148.

Asthma

About 1 in 10 children have asthma, which causes recurrent episodes of breathlessness and/or wheezing. Asthma is usually a mild or moderate condition, although in cases that are more severe it can be life-threatening if not promptly treated.

WHAT IS THE CAUSE?

The symptoms of asthma are caused by narrowing of the small airways in the lungs (bronchioles), so that less air can get into the lungs. This happens as a result of inflammation and swelling of the airways and an increase in their mucus production. Contraction of the muscles in the walls of the airways also causes narrowing. These muscles are naturally twitchy, so contraction is triggered easily.

Individual attacks can be triggered by substances that are breathed in, such as pollen, house-dust mites, or cigarette smoke. Viral infections and some medications can also be triggers, as can hayfever and other forms of allergic rhinitis and reflux.

The cause of asthma is not known, but it does run in families so there may be a genetic factor involved. It is more common in boys than girls. Your child is more likely to develop asthma if either parent has it, or if there is a family history of allergies such as hayfever or eczema. It is also more common in children who were born prematurely, or whose mothers smoked during pregnancy. Children who are breastfed may be less prone to asthma.

Asthma attack A child having an asthma attack becomes short of breath, and she may wheeze and have a tight feeling in her chest.

SHOULD I SEE A DOCTOR?

If you think that your child may have asthma take her to the doctor. If she shows any of the symptoms of a severe asthma attack (see right) call an ambulance or take her to the nearest accident and emergency department immediately.

HOW'S IT DIAGNOSED?

It is difficult to diagnose asthma in young children as many have episodes of wheezing for other reasons, for example when they have a virus. So, wheezing when she has a cold does not necessarily mean that your child has asthma.

Your doctor will ask about your child's medical history and will examine her chest. If she is over 5 years old, she may be asked to breathe into a peak-flow meter, which measures how much air she can breathe out of her lungs. This is called the peak expiratory flow rate (PEFR). You may be asked to keep a diary of readings. Your doctor may give your child a trial on a bronchodilator medication (see right) and ask you to monitor her PEFR before and after each dose. If the rate improves after she has been given the medicine then she probably has asthma. However, these medicines are not always effective in young children.

Possible symptoms

Mild asthma:

★ Wheezing

★ Shortness of breath

★ Tight chest

★ Coughing that is often worse at night or on exercise

Severe asthma attac:

★ Very rapid breathing

★ Rapid pulse

★ Difficulty talking

★ Laboured breathing – muscles in between and under the ribs drawing in and nostrils flaring with each breath

★ Bluish lips and fingers and/or fingernails

★ Exhaustion and drowsiness if the attack continues

WHAT'S THE TREATMENT?

Asthma is usually treated with medication that your child takes using an inhaler. There are various different types of inhaler and your child may find one particular type easier to use. Different coloured inhalers are used for different medications. These medications are either relievers, given only when symptoms occur, or preventers, used to prevent symptoms occurring.

★ Short-acting bronchodilators are a commonly used asthma treatment. These are relievers, and work by relaxing muscles in the airways, opening them up and making it easier to breathe.

★ Longer-acting bronchodilators relax the airways in the same way as the short-acting bronchodilators, but their effects last longer.

★ Inhaled steroids are preventer medications, and these are thought to work by reducing the amount of inflammation in the airways. After your child has used a steroid inhaler (usually twice a day), it's a good idea to encourage her to wash her mouth out with a mouthwash to prevent oral thrush from developing.

★ If these inhaled treatments do not control your child's asthma, leukotriene receptor antagonists, oral steroids, or other oral medications will be tried.

Treatment of asthma goes up in steps, starting with a reliever inhaler and adding to or changing the medication as required, depending on whether or not your child's asthma is under control. Signs that it is not under control include having symptoms more than twice a week; needing to use a reliever inhaler more than twice a week; and waking up more than once a week from asthma symptoms. Your child will be seen regularly by the doctor to make sure that she is receiving the most appropriate treatment for controlling her asthma.

What can I do to help?

You'll need to learn how inhalers work and about the various types. A spacer can make an inhaler easier to use. It is placed between the inhaler and mouth or, for a young child, the mouth and nose.

Measure the flow Your child may be asked to blow into a special device (peak-flow meter) to help diagnose or monitor asthma.

Avoid allergens If you know of specific triggers for your child's asthma, such as house-dust mites, take steps to remove them, by vacuuming daily for example.

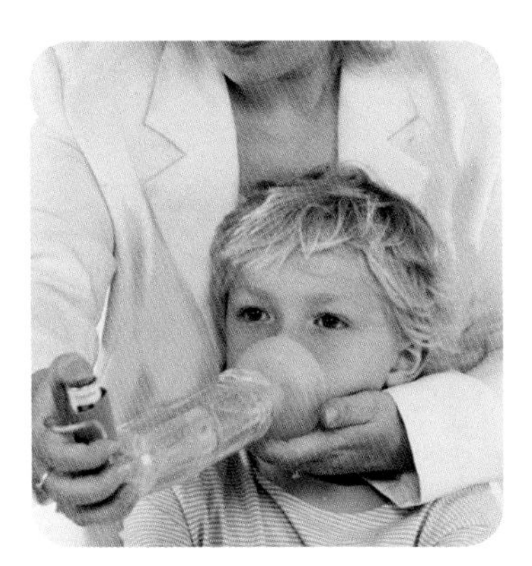

Use a spacer After you've pressed the inhaler your child breathes in and out into the spacer 5–10 times. If a second dose is needed, wait a few seconds first.

Help with an inhaler An older child will soon learn how to use his spacer and inhaler himself, but to start with, he'll need supervision.

ARE THERE ANY COMPLEMENTARY THERAPIES?

Various complementary therapies have been suggested to treat asthma, such as herbal medicine or acupuncture, although there is little evidence to suggest that these are effective. A particular breathing technique called the Buteyko technique may help. This focuses on breathing in through your nose, holding your breath, and relaxation. The technique is suitable only for older children, as young children may find it difficult to manage.

ARE ASTHMA ATTACKS PREVENTABLE?

The common triggers for asthma are the same as those for hayfever and other types of allergic rhinitis, such as house-dust mites and pollen. If these trigger your child's asthma, follow the tips for avoiding them on p.145. If hayfever does occur, treating it with medications such as oral antihistamines may help, as can treatment for reflux if this is a trigger. Other triggers, such as infections or pollution, are less easily avoidable, but you can make sure you do not smoke around your child (and preferably not at all).

If your child's symptoms are brought on by exercise this may mean that her asthma is poorly controlled and her treatment plan will need to be reviewed. If poor control is not the problem, she will be given advice about specific ways to use her inhalers before, during, and after exercising. There are also breathing techniques, such as the Buteyko technique described above, that can help her manage her asthma.

WHAT'S THE OUTLOOK?

Up to three-quarters of children with asthma grow out of it as they get older. Children who have mild asthma and those who develop it at a younger age are more likely to grow out of it.

Viral-induced wheeze

About a quarter of children aged under 5 develop a wheeze when they have a viral infection, such as a cold. However, this is not the same as asthma, and does not mean that your child will develop asthma.

WHAT IS THE CAUSE?

A viral-induced wheeze may occur because children under the age of 5 tend to have smaller air passages. Parents often worry that if their child wheezes it means that he has asthma, but if the wheezing subsides once the viral infection has cleared up, this is highly unlikely. A child with asthma will still have symptoms even when he doesn't have a viral infection and in addition he will usually have a family history of asthma or allergy.

SHOULD I SEE A DOCTOR?

If your child is wheezing and you are concerned, take him to the doctor. He will do an examination and ask about your child's medical history in order to make a diagnosis. Often no treatment is needed if your child is otherwise well. In some cases, bronchodilators given through an inhaler are prescribed. These drugs, which are also used to treat asthma, open up the airways and make it easier for your child to breathe. Sometimes oral steroids are also prescribed.

Possible symptoms

- ★ Wheezing
- ★ Cough, which may bring up phlegm (mucus), although young children often swallow phlegm
- ★ Shortness of breath

If wheezing is severe, your child may need help with breathing and he may be admitted to hospital where oxygen can be given through tubes inserted into his nose.

WHAT'S THE OUTLOOK?

Most children with viral-induced wheeze grow out of the condition as they get older. A few go on to develop asthma.

Common cold

The common cold is a viral infection of the nose, throat, and sinuses (the upper respiratory tract). It is extremely common, especially in children, with the average child having up to eight colds a year.

Good habits Encourage your child to cough or sneeze into a tissue, throw the tissue into a bin, then wash his hands.

WHAT IS THE CAUSE?

Viruses are spread by breathing in droplets from infected people's coughs and sneezes or by droplets containing the virus landing on a surface that a child then touches before transferring the virus to his mouth. Children most commonly catch colds from other children and are more likely to have them during the autumn and winter months.

ARE THERE COMPLICATIONS?

If a cold virus spreads to the lungs, a child may develop pneumonia, bronchitis, or bronchiolitis. Middle-ear infection, which can be caused by viruses or bacteria, is another possible complication.

Possible symptoms

- ★ Fever
- ★ Runny or blocked nose
- ★ Discharge that is clear or thick, and yellow or green
- ★ Sneezing
- ★ Irritation in the nose or facial pain
- ★ Coughing
- ★ Sore throat
- ★ Hoarse or croaky voice
- ★ Loss of appetite and feeling unwell

SHOULD I SEE A DOCTOR?

If your baby is less than 3 months old, you should seek medical advice at the first sign of a cold. Otherwise, you do not need to see the doctor unless your child appears very unwell, his symptoms last for more than

2 weeks, or you are concerned that he has developed any complications. Antibiotics are not effective against colds because they are caused by viruses and antibiotics are only effective against bacteria.

ARE THERE ANY COMPLEMENTARY THERAPIES?

Natural remedies used to treat or prevent a cold include vitamin C, echinacea (a type of herb that grows in North America), zinc, and garlic, although there is little evidence that any of these is effective.

WHAT'S THE OUTLOOK?

The symptoms get worse over the first few days before improving. Older children tend to feel better within a week, but young children can take up to 2 weeks to recover. A cough that develops as part of a cold can last for several weeks even though the child feels otherwise well again.

TOP TIP

Do not give cold remedies to children under 6. In children over 6 do not give decongestants for more than 5 days as they may make the congestion worse.

What can I do to help?

There is no specific treatment for the common cold – the best course of action is to relieve the symptoms while the body fights the virus. However, you can make your child feel more comfortable by following the measures here. Don't forget to keep offering plenty of fluids to avoid dehydration.

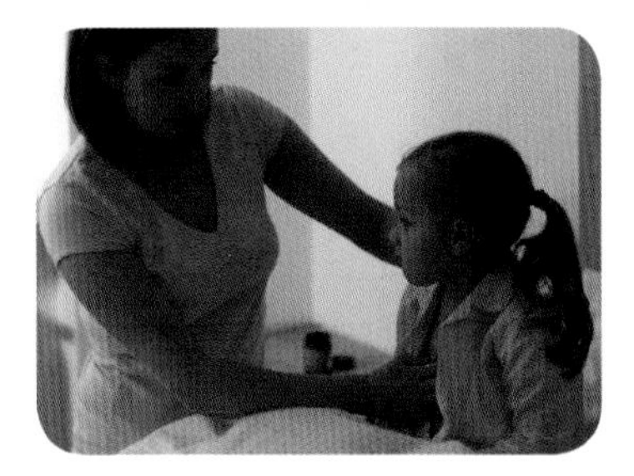

Ease congestion Apply a vapour rub onto your child's back or chest, or add some to a bowl of water and place it near a warm radiator.

Give painkillers You can give paracetamol or ibuprofen for any fever or discomfort. You should not give over-the-counter cold remedies to a child under 6.

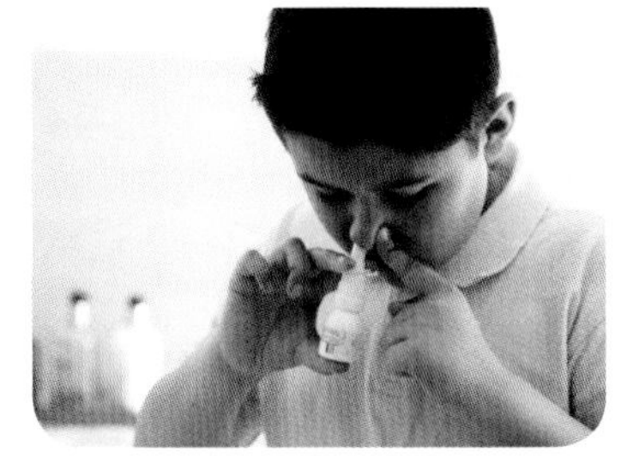

Loosen mucus A nasal saline spray can loosen any mucus in the nose so it can be blown out. Spray into one nostril at a time, holding the other nostril closed.

Steam the airways Close windows and doors in the bathroom and run the shower to fill the room with steam. Sit with your child for 15 minutes. This should loosen mucus and help breathing.

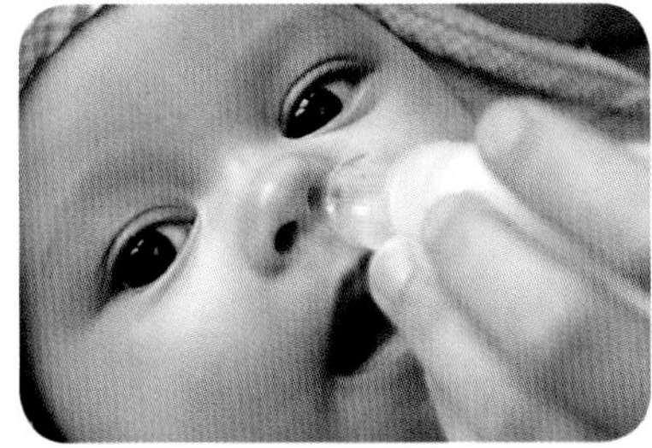

Unblock your baby To relieve congestion in an infant you can use a suction device. This has a bulb that you squeeze to create suction and a soft rubber tip that goes into the baby's nostril.

Give soothing drinks Add a little honey and lemon juice to warm water to make a drink that soothes a cough or sore throat. (Not for children under 1.) Brush your child's teeth after drinking.

Influenza

Also called flu, influenza is a seasonal viral illness that is common in the winter months. Flu viruses change, or mutate, constantly. So even if your child has had flu, she can still get it again because she won't be immune to new strains.

WHAT IS THE CAUSE?

The flu virus is spread in droplets from infected people's coughs and sneezes. The droplets can be breathed in or can land [illegible] your child if she puts the toy in her mouth or touches the toy and then puts her hand to her mouth.

Symptoms develop 1–4 days after being infected. Your child is infectious from about one day before symptoms begin until about a week after; in young children the infectious period can be up to 2 weeks.

Flu sometimes occurs in epidemics (when many people are affected within a short period of time). These happen because of the viruses' ability to mutate, allowing them to spread rapidly among people who are not resistant to the new strains.

ARE THERE COMPLICATIONS?

The most common complication of flu is pneumonia caused by a bacteria that can be treated with antibiotics. Other rare complications are middle-ear infection and tonsillitis.

SHOULD I SEE A DOCTOR?

You do not need to see your doctor if you think your child has flu unless she is very unwell, symptoms do not improve after a week, she has a chronic (long-term) condition that affects her heart or lungs, or you are concerned that she may have developed pneumonia. Symptoms of pneumonia include rapid, noisy breathing and a cough that brings up phlegm, although you don't always see this in younger children as they are likely to swallow it.

In some situations, for example if your child is very unwell, your doctor may advise an antiviral medication for the treatment of flu. This does not get rid of the flu virus, but shortens the length of the illness and may help prevent complications.

IS IT PREVENTABLE?

Flu is an infectious condition but the spread may be prevented with good hygiene, so encourage your child to cough or sneeze into a tissue, throw it into a bin, then wash her hands. You should wash your hands, too. There is a seasonal flu vaccine produced each year. If your child has a chronic condition, such as asthma, heart disease, or diabetes, she will be offered the vaccination each year. Protection takes a few weeks to develop, so it is usually recommended that vaccination is done in September or October before the flu season starts.

WHAT'S THE OUTLOOK?

Symptoms tend to worsen over the first few days of the illness before improving within about a week, although some children may continue to feel tired or unwell for a few weeks.

Possible symptoms

- ★ Fever
- ★ Loss of appetite
- ★ Feeling unwell
- ★ Tiredness
- ★ Headache
- ★ Muscle and joint aches and pains
- ★ Runny or blocked nose
- ★ Cough
- ★ Diarrhoea

What can I do to help?

You can usually treat flu at home. Your child should not go back to school or nursery until symptoms have gone.

Give plenty of fluids Make sure your child drinks lots of fluids to prevent her from becoming dehydrated. An unweaned baby can have extra milk.

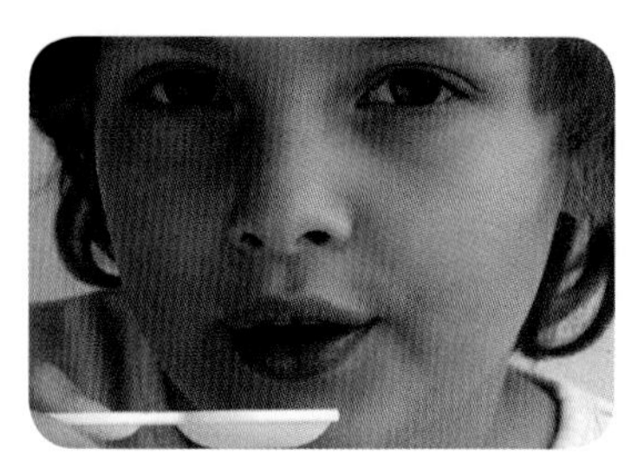

Relieve symptoms Paracetamol and ibuprofen help relieve the aches and pains that flu often causes, and will help bring down your child's fever.

Croup

A barking cough characterizes this viral infection of the voice box (larynx) and windpipe (trachea). It mainly affects children aged 6 months to 3 years.

WHAT IS THE CAUSE?

The most common cause of croup is the parainfluenza virus. Children catch it by breathing in droplets from affected people's coughs and sneezes, or by touching an infected surface and then their mouths.

SHOULD I SEE A DOCTOR?

If you think your child has croup you can take her to your doctor to confirm this and to rule out any other conditions. Do NOT attempt to look at your child's throat yourself as this can cause a spasm of the airways and make any breathing difficulties worse. If your child is having breathing problems, your doctor may recommend a steroid to calm down any inflammation. In serious cases, oxygen or ventilation treatment may be given in hospital. If your child develops any symptoms of severe croup (see right) always seek urgent medical assistance.

IS IT PREVENTABLE?

There is not much you can do to prevent your child getting croup. However, you can help to prevent her from spreading it to others. Teach her to cough and sneeze into a tissue, throw the tissue into a bin, and then wash her hands.

WHAT'S THE OUTLOOK?

Most children recover from croup within a few days, although the cough may persist for a few weeks even when the child is better. Children can get croup more than once.

Possible symptoms

Croup starts with fever and a runny nose. One to 4 days later the following symptoms develop:

★ Barking cough that is often worse at night

★ Raspy noise on breathing in (stridor), that is often worse when the child is distressed

★ Hoarse voice

If severe croup develops, there may be:

★ Laboured breathing muscles in between and under the ribs drawing in, and nostrils flaring with each breath

★ Blue lips or fingers

★ High fever

★ Drooling and difficulty swallowing

★ Exhaustion and drowsiness as a result of working hard to breathe

What can I do to help?

Croup can get worse if a child becomes anxious and starts crying, so sit your child upright in your lap, cuddle her, and try to keep her calm. You can read her a book to help take her mind off her irritating cough, or let her watch a favourite programme – this might help her to relax.

Give plenty of fluids Offer your child frequent drinks of water to avoid dehydration. Drinking also soothes the throat, which coughing can irritate.

Relieve discomfort You can give your child liquid paracetamol or ibuprofen to help relieve the discomfort caused by the barking cough.

Humidify the bathroom Close the window and doors, then run the shower or hot taps and let your child breathe in the moist air to help her breathing.

Bronchitis

Inflammation of the main airways that branch from the windpipe (bronchi) is known as bronchitis. The airways produce excess mucus causing coughing, and they may narrow, causing difficulties breathing.

Possible symptoms

Symptoms are similar to those of pneumonia but less severe. They include:

- ★ Fever
- ★ Cough, which may bring up white or yellowish-green phlegm (young children may swallow any phlegm produced)
- ★ Wheezing
- ★ Fast breathing or shortness of breath
- ★ Sometimes, a runny nose

WHAT IS THE CAUSE?

Bronchitis is most often caused by a viral infection that has spread to the airways from an upper respiratory tract infection, such as a common cold or influenza. It is sometimes caused by a bacterial infection, and can also be [illegible] airways caused by inhaling certain substances such as cigarette smoke.

SHOULD I SEE A DOCTOR?

If your child is eating, drinking, and behaving normally, you may not need to see your doctor. However, if his symptoms seem severe or if they persist for more than a few days you should make an appointment at the surgery. Seek medical assistance immediately if your child's breathing becomes very rapid, if he is struggling to breathe, or if his lips or fingers turn blue.

The doctor will examine your child to rule out a more serious infection such as pneumonia or bronchiolitis. He may prescribe antibiotics if he thinks the infection might be bacterial (remember that many cases of bronchitis are viral and antibiotics will not be effective) or he might prescribe a bronchodilator drug to help open up the airways and make breathing easier; this is usually given to your child via an inhaler.

IS IT PREVENTABLE?

To prevent the infection from spreading, encourage your child to cough or sneeze into a tissue, throw it in the bin, and then wash his hands. Studies show that children whose parents smoke are more likely to develop bronchitis so if you do smoke consider stopping, not just for the sake of your own health but also that of your child.

WHAT'S THE OUTLOOK?

Bronchitis usually gets better on its own within a few days. The cough can persist for a few weeks although the child feels better and well in himself; this usually resolves on its own, too.

What can I do to help?

Humidifying the air helps relieve congestion and fluids can ease coughing. Some children benefit from a cough mixture but check with your pharmacist what's suitable for a young child.

Treat the symptoms Give paracetamol or ibuprofen to reduce a fever and to ease discomfort caused by coughing.

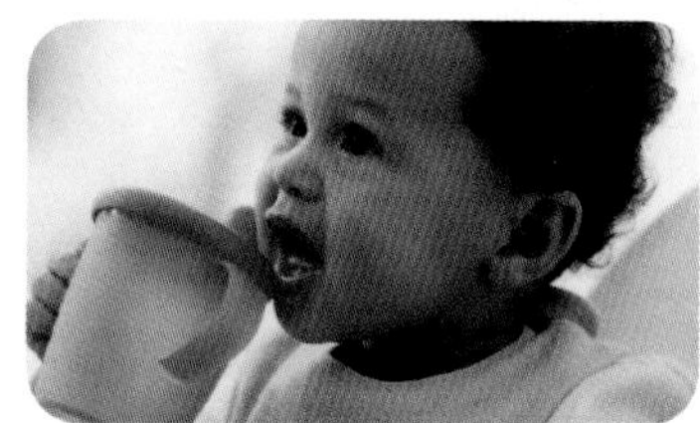

Give plenty of fluids These help prevent dehydration and make phlegm watery so that it is easier to cough up.

Breathing at night Drape a wet towel over a chair placed close to a warm radiator to humidify the air.

Give soothing drinks Add a little honey and lemon juice to warm water. (Not for children under 1.)

Pneumonia

Pneumonia is a type of chest infection in which the air sacs in the lungs (alveoli) become infected and fill with fluid, resulting in a cough and difficulty breathing. Prompt treatment is important.

WHAT IS THE CAUSE?

Pneumonia can be caused by various bacteria, viruses, and other organisms such as fungi. Often, the illness starts 2 or 3 days after an upper respiratory tract infection, such as a common cold or influenza. People of any age can develop pneumonia, although babies and young children are at higher risk. Children who also have another lung condition, such as asthma or cystic fibrosis, are especially vulnerable. Pneumonia is more common in children whose parents smoke.

Pneumonia is caught by breathing in droplets containing the organism from other people's coughs and sneezes, or by touching surfaces on which infected droplets have landed. The time between catching the infection and showing symptoms depends on the organism causing the pneumonia.

SHOULD I SEE A DOCTOR?

Call an ambulance if your child's breathing is laboured (see right), or if his lips are blue. Otherwise, if you suspect pneumonia, take your child to the doctor, who will listen to his chest and may order a chest X-ray. Antibiotics are usually prescribed. Most children can be treated at home. If your child is having difficulty breathing or is very unwell he may be admitted to hospital for antibiotics and help with breathing, for example by giving extra oxygen via tubes inserted into the nose.

IS IT PREVENTABLE?

Encourage your child to cover his mouth and nose when he sneezes or coughs, to blow his nose into a tissue, throw the tissue into a bin, and wash his hands. As part of their immunization schedule, children are offered vaccination against a bacterium that commonly causes pneumonia.

WHAT'S THE OUTLOOK?

Most children make a full recovery within a few weeks. If your child is not recovering, see your doctor who will investigate whether or not there is an underlying cause for the pneumonia, such as cystic fibrosis.

Possible symptoms

- ★ Fever
- ★ Cough, which may produce phlegm (young children may swallow this)
- ★ Rapid, noisy breathing
- ★ Loss of appetite
- ★ Feeling unwell
- ★ Laboured breathing – muscles in between and under the ribs drawing in, and nostrils flaring with each breath
- ★ Vomiting
- ★ Chest pain on coughing or taking deep breaths

What can I do to help?

If your child is being treated for pneumonia at home, make sure that he finishes the prescribed course of antibiotics. Don't give over-the-counter cough and cold medicines to children under 6.

Give plenty of fluids Your child needs lots of fluids to prevent dehydration. An unweaned baby just needs milk.

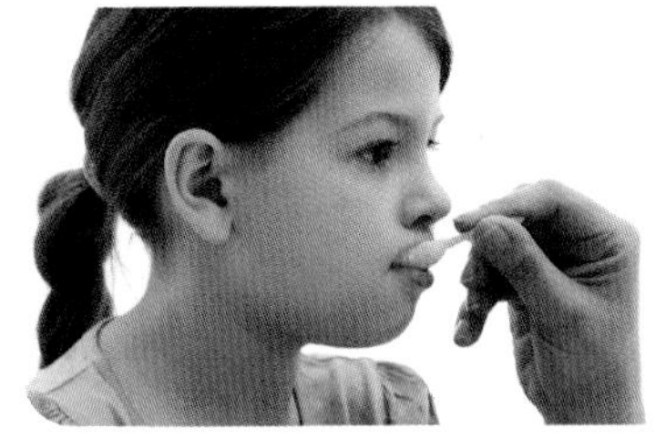

Relieve the symptoms Paracetamol or ibuprofen will help bring down your child's fever and relieve discomfort.

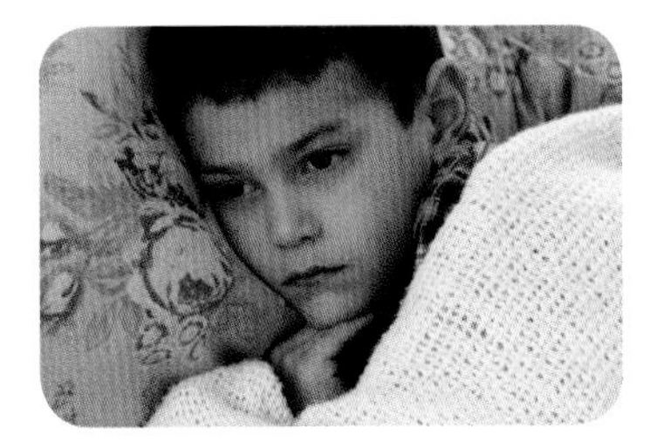

Encourage rest Make sure your child rests to speed recovery. He may be more comfortable propped up on pillows.

Bronchiolitis

In bronchiolitis, the small airways in the lungs (bronchioles) become infected and swollen, which can cause difficulties breathing. It is usually a mild illness and most commonly affects babies.

Possible symptoms

- ★ Fever
- ★ Blocked or runny nose
- ★ Coughing
- ★ Noisy or fast breathing
- ★ Difficulties feeding or reduced feeding
- ★ Laboured breathing – muscles in between and under the ribs drawing in, and nostrils flaring with each breath

WHAT IS THE CAUSE?

Bronchiolitis is most often caused by a virus called the respiratory syncytial virus (RSV), which is also a common cause of colds. It occurs more frequently in the winter months, between November and March.
[illegible]
bronchiolitis by the time they are 1 year old, with most being affected at between 6 and 9 months. Babies who have already have a lung or heart problem, such as congenital heart disease or lung disease due to prematurity, are more susceptible.

The viruses that cause bronchiolitis are spread as a result of breathing in droplets containing the virus from coughs or sneezes, or when the droplets land on a surface, such as a toy, which your child then touches or puts in her mouth.

SHOULD I SEE A DOCTOR?

Bronchiolitis is usually mild and gets better on its own. See your doctor if your child is having difficulties feeding or if you are concerned. Call an ambulance or take your child to the nearest accident and emergency [illegible] if her breathing is laboured (see right), she is getting exhausted or difficult to rouse, or if her lips or fingers turn blue.

About 3 in 100 children require treatment in hospital, either to support their breathing, for example with oxygen, or to help with feeding, which may be done through a special tube while the child recovers.

IS IT PREVENTABLE?

To prevent the infection spreading, your child should cover her nose and mouth with a tissue when coughing, throw the tissue in a bin, and then wash her hands. You may also wish to clean her toys to remove germs.

WHAT'S THE OUTLOOK?

The symptoms of bronchiolitis tend to get worse over the first 3 days or so before improving. Symptoms usually last about 2 weeks, but in some children they continue longer. A minority of children wheeze or cough on and off for a few years, often when they have another cold.

What can I do to help?

Most children with bronchiolitis can be looked after at home. However, you should keep a close eye on your child and be prepared to seek medical help if symptoms get worse.

Give plenty of fluids Give your baby extra water while she has bronchiolitis to prevent dehydration.

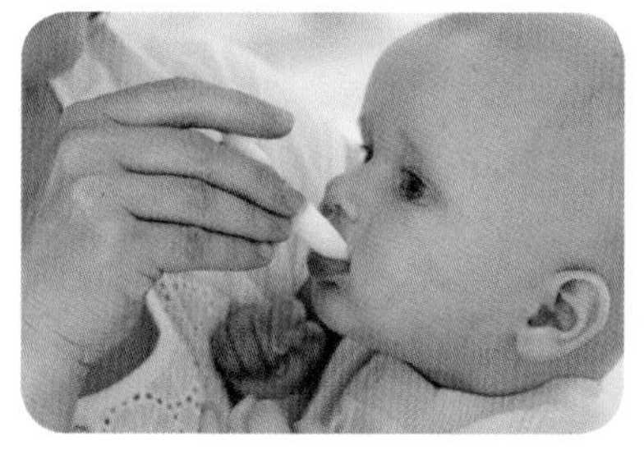

Treat the symptoms It's easiest to give ibuprofen or paracetamol to your baby while holding her in your lap.

Watch your child Keep a close eye on your child (this may involve checking at night) to see if symptoms are worsening.

Digestive system disorders

The digestive system consists of the digestive tract – the mouth, throat, oesophagus, stomach, small intestines, large intestines (colon and rectum), and anus – as well as the liver, gall bladder, and pancreas. As food moves through the digestive tract during the digestive process it is broken down so that nutrients can be absorbed into the blood; waste products are excreted as faeces. The liver, gall bladder, and pancreas have many roles, including aiding digestion by secreting juices that help to break down food.

This section begins with problems affecting the mouth and teeth, then discusses general adverse reactions to food followed by infections of the digestive tract. Conditions causing abdominal pain come next, followed by two common problems with bowel movements, constipation and toddler's diarrhoea.

Tooth decay

In tooth decay, or dental caries, the enamel of a tooth is broken down. If not treated, nerves at the centre of a tooth may become exposed, giving your child toothache. Tooth decay is preventable with careful dental hygiene and a healthy diet.

TOP TIP

Fluoride helps strengthen enamel. Use a toothpaste with at least 1000ppm of fluoride; and after age 3, one with between 1350 and 1500ppm.

WHAT IS THE CAUSE?

Bacteria in your mouth break down food, producing acid. This acid, along with food and bacteria, sticks to your teeth as plaque. [illegible] plaque dissolves and destroys tooth enamel.

SHOULD I SEE A DENTIST?

It's important that your child has dental check-ups every 6 months to keep problems at bay – but if he does have toothache see a dentist straight away. Take your baby along, too, even before he has teeth. He can sit in your lap while the dentist looks in his mouth so that he gets used to seeing him.

IS IT PREVENTABLE?

You can prevent tooth decay by making sure your child's teeth are properly cleaned, taking him to the dentist every 6 months, and ensuring he eats a healthy diet. Apart from limiting sweet foods, such as cake, you should restrict squash, fruit juice, and fizzy drinks (even those without sugar). Give juice or squash in a cup rather than a bottle.

See the dentist Visits to the dentist can begin when the first tooth appears. Children are entitled to free NHS dental care.

What can I do to help?

Start brushing as soon as your child's first tooth appears. Brush twice daily so that a life long habit is formed. Try not to let your child eat or swallow toothpaste – excess fluoride can stain teeth.

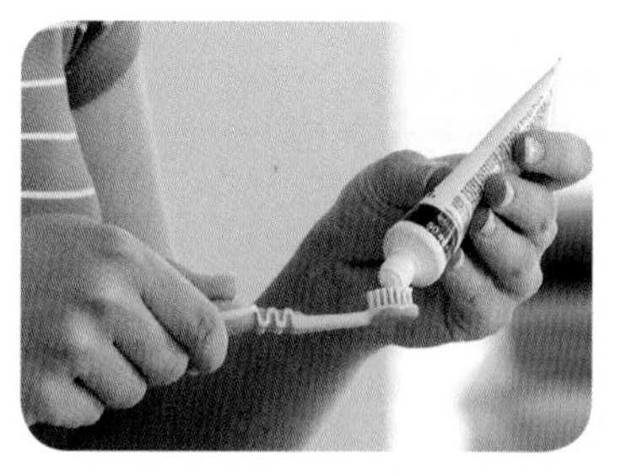

Choose the right toothbrush Pick one with a small head and soft bristles. Use a smear of toothpaste for a child under 2; a pea-sized amount for an older child.

Help with brushing Work your way around your child's mouth to clean all her teeth. Children need help and supervision until around age 7.

Encourage independence An older child can take responsibility for his own toothbrushing. Using a timer is a good way to help him do a thorough job.

Limit sugar Keep sugary snacks or drinks (including juice) between meals to a minimum. Offer healthy snacks, such as raw vegetables, instead.

Gum disease

Inflamed gums that bleed easily are a sign of early gum disease, known as gingivitis. It is reversible with good dental hygiene but – if ignored – can progress to more serious gum disease.

WHAT IS THE CAUSE?

Gingivitis can occur if plaque, a sticky deposit of food debris, bacteria, and acid, is not removed by regular toothbrushing and accumulates between the teeth. Plaque turns into a hard material called calculus that irritates the gums. Gum irritation and the bacteria in plaque are responsible for the development of gingivitis, but some people are more susceptible than others.

WHAT'S THE TREATMENT?

In most cases, gingivitis clears up when the teeth and gums are kept clean and healthy. It's important that your child practises good oral hygiene, brushing regularly and correctly (see Tooth decay, opposite). You should also make sure that he visits the dentist for check-ups every 6 months. Such measures will prevent gingivitis from developing in the first place.

Possible symptoms

★ Swollen, red, sometimes painful gums (healthy gums are pink)

★ Easy bleeding of gums, especially during brushing

SHOULD I SEE A DENTIST?

If you're worried that your child's gums are not improving, see your dentist. It is important that gingivitis is not allowed to progress to a more serious form of gum disease, called periodontal disease, which affects the tissues that support the teeth and can lead to loss of teeth.

Dental abscess

If tooth decay isn't treated, a dental abscess may develop. This is a collection of pus around the root of a tooth due to bacterial infection. Urgent treatment from a dentist is needed.

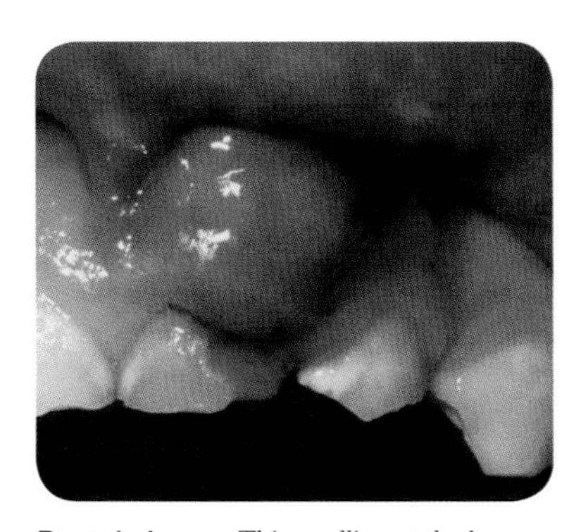

Dental abscess This swelling at the base of a tooth is filled with pus as a result of bacterial infection that has spread from a cavity through the centre of the tooth.

WHAT IS THE CAUSE?

If a child has tooth decay, the enamel of the tooth is broken down and bacteria in the mouth can infect the soft tissues at the centre of the tooth (the pulp) and spread down to the bone surrounding the root.

SHOULD I SEE A DENTIST?

If you think your child may have a dental abscess, seek dental help urgently. Your dentist will probably release the pus in the abscess by drilling into the tooth to remove the infected pulp. The cavity in the middle of the tooth is then filled (a procedure called root canal treatment). If a milk tooth is affected, it may be removed. Your dentist or doctor may also prescribe a course of antibiotics to treat the infection. You can give painkillers such as paracetamol or ibuprofen to relieve discomfort.

Possible symptoms

★ Severe, throbbing pain in the tooth; this can spread to the side of the face or ears

★ Red swelling around base of tooth

★ Fever

★ Difficulty opening the mouth or swallowing

★ Sensitivity of the tooth to heat, cold or even pressure such as when chewing

★ Swollen face if the infection spreads into the facial tissues

IS IT PREVENTABLE?

Dental abscesses can be prevented by good dental hygiene (see Tooth decay, opposite).

Mouth ulcers

Ulcers are open sores that can occur in the mouth, inside the cheeks or lips, or on the tongue.

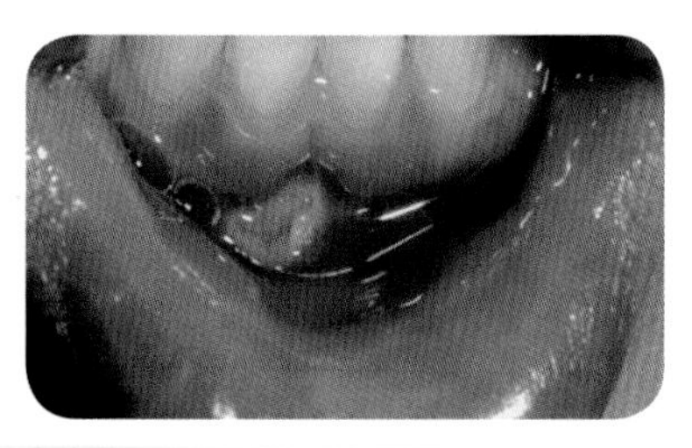

[illegible] lower jaw is seen here at the base the gums. It has a hollowed-out, greyish centre.

WHAT ARE THE CAUSES?
The most common type of mouth ulcer is known as an aphthous ulcer. The reasons these ulcers occur are not known. Mouth ulcers can occur as part of various infections, such as hand, foot, and mouth disease, and sometimes develop as a result of injury, for example from a toothbrush.

Some children have recurrent ulcers [illegible] usually aphthous ulcers, they can occasionally be due to an underlying disease.

Possible symptoms

- ★ A single ulcer or a cluster of ulcers, each of which looks like an open sore; usually with a greyish-coloured centre
- ★ Painful mouth, which may may make your child reluctant to eat

SHOULD I SEE A DOCTOR?
If your child's ulcers are severe and prevent her from eating and drinking, or she has ulcers that have persisted for more than a week, or she has recurrent ulcers, take her to see your doctor.

What can I do to help?

Most ulcers improve on their own within a week. Meanwhile, avoid giving your child acidic food or drinks, such as citrus fruit juice, or salty, spicy, or vinegary foods, all of which may irritate the ulcers. Cool drinks are often soothing. Other measures that may help are given below.

Provide a straw If liquid irritates the ulcers, give your child a straw to drink through so the liquid bypasses them.

Make soft foods Your child will find it easier to eat soft foods, such as mashed potato. Avoid hard foods, such as crackers.

Apply numbing gel Use an over-the-counter teething or local anaesthetic mouth gel suitable for your child's age.

Give painkillers You can give your child ibuprofen or paracetamol to ease discomfort and irritation.

Food intolerance

Children who have a food intolerance are unable to digest a particular food and have unpleasant symptoms if they eat the food. Food intolerance is not the same as food allergy because it does not involve a reaction by the immune system.

Possible symptoms

- ★ Nausea
- ★ Abdominal pain and/or bloating
- ★ Diarrhoea (a slight change in the stool does not usually signal food intolerance)

WHAT IS THE CAUSE?

With a food intolerance, the body lacks a specific enzyme needed to break down particular foods. The most common type of intolerance experienced by babies and children involves lactose, a substance found in dairy products, such as milk. Babies have high levels of the enzyme lactase, which breaks down lactose. But sometimes the level of this enzyme is too low, or after age 2, falls too much, causing symptoms of intolerance when dairy produce is consumed. Children can sometimes develop lactose intolerance after having a tummy bug but this is only temporary. Some children who have coeliac disease also suffer from lactose intolerance. The condition is more common in Asian, African, Mediterranean, and Native American populations.

Symptoms of a food intolerance are related to how much of the food is eaten, so your child may be able to eat a small amount of the offending food without any symptoms, but a larger amount may cause problems.

SHOULD I SEE A DOCTOR?

Don't restrict your child's diet by cutting out any food groups without first consulting your doctor, as children need a balanced and varied diet. Your child should always be examined by the doctor because food intolerance symptoms are non-specific and may be due to various other causes.

There is a test for lactose intolerance but many other food intolerances are difficult to test for. Your doctor may suggest eliminating a particular food from your child's diet to see if symptoms improve, then reintroducing it. Treatment is to avoid the trigger food. If your child is diagnosed with a food intolerance you may be referred to a paediatric dietitian to discuss a healthy and appropriate diet for your child.

Abdominal symptoms If your child has a food intolerance, she may suffer from abdominal pain and sometimes bloating hours or days after eating a particular food.

What can I do to help?

Because symptoms do not start immediately after eating a trigger food, it can be difficult to pinpoint the cause. A food diary may help. Once the problem food is identified, you can adjust your child's diet.

Keep a food diary Write down everything your child eats each day and whether he has had any symptoms, to establish which food is responsible.

Use substitutes Children with lactose intolerance can have soya yogurts, cheese, and milk. Lactose-free formula can be prescribed for babies.

Food allergy

Unlike a food intolerance, the symptoms of a food allergy occur quickly after eating the food and, in severe cases, the allergy may cause a very serious and even life-threatening reaction known as anaphylactic shock.

WHAT ARE THE CAUSES?

A food allergy occurs when the immune system mistakes a foodstuff for something harmful and attacks it. This reaction causes the body to release histamine and other chemicals that cause the symptoms of an allergic reaction. Even a tiny amount of the food can prompt a reaction.

Food allergies are more common in children with asthma and/or eczema, or where there is a family history of these conditions or food allergies. Common allergy-inducing foods include milk and other dairy products, fish, nuts, eggs, tomatoes, and citrus fruits.

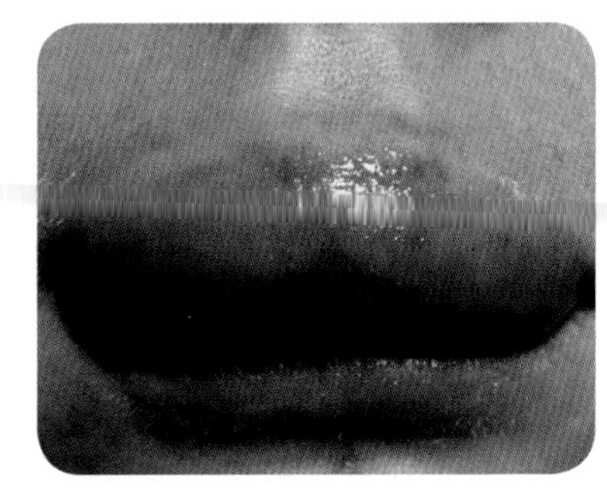

Swollen lips An allergic reaction to a food may cause the lips and mouth to swell up soon after eating the food.

SHOULD I SEE A DOCTOR?

If a severe reaction occurs (see Possible symptoms, right), call an ambulance or take your child to the nearest accident and emergency department. Otherwise, if you suspect a food allergy take your child to your doctor. Do not cut out foods from your child's diet without seeing your doctor first.

Your doctor may refer your child for allergy tests, such as skin-prick tests, in which small amounts of common allergens are introduced into the skin by means of small pricks. If your child is allergic to any of the substances he will come out in a red rash around the site. You may be referred to a dietitian to discuss your child's diet so that he can continue to meet his nutritional needs while avoiding trigger foods. If your child is at risk of severe allergic reactions, the doctor may prescribe an autoinjection adrenaline syringe for use in an emergency.

Some children outgrow their allergies so you may be advised to try the food again at some point in the future.

Possible symptoms

The symptoms of an allergic reaction can be very varied and some are not specific to food allergy. They include:

- ★ Skin rashes, such as urticaria, or a worsening of eczema
- ★ Nausea, which may lead to vomiting
- ★ Diarrhoea
- ★ Bloating
- ★ Runny nose
- ★ Red, itchy, watery eyes

A more severe reaction may cause:

- ★ Itching and/or swelling of the mouth, lips, tongue, and throat
- ★ Wheezing or shortness of breath
- ★ Difficulty breathing; faintness, drowsiness, or loss of consciousness (signs of anaphylactic shock)

What can I do to help?

Call an ambulance if your child suffers a severe reaction, such as swelling, and use an injector if you have one (see p.218). There are steps you can take to avoid or ease food allergy symptoms.

Avoid triggers Read ingredients and allergy information on foodstuffs carefully to be certain that they do not contain anything your child is allergic to.

Give antihistamines These can help mild allergic symptoms such as a skin rash. If asthma worsens during a reaction, a salbutamol inhaler may help.

Irritable bowel syndrome

Children can be affected by irritable bowel syndrome (IBS), which causes bouts of abdominal pain, bloating, and other abdominal symptoms.

WHAT IS THE CAUSE?

The cause of irritable bowel syndrome is not known, although the symptoms can be managed. Some common triggers include stress and anxiety, eating big meals, or eating spicy or very fatty foods.

Abdominal pain Irritable bowel syndrome often causes abdominal pain and discomfort. Having a bowel movement may bring relief.

Irregular bowel habits It is common for children with irritable bowel to suffer from diarrhoea or constipation, or both.

SHOULD I SEE A DOCTOR?

Do not exclude any foods without first consulting your doctor. Children need a balanced and varied diet. Take your child to your doctor to be assessed, as it is also important to rule out other conditions. Your doctor will ask questions about symptoms, examine him, and may order blood tests. He may refer you to a paediatric dietician to make sure all your child's nutritional requirements are met. There are various medications that can be prescribed for the treatment of irritable bowel syndrome.

You can try to identify situations or foods that may cause symptoms. For example, find out if anything might be causing your child anxiety and take steps to resolve it.

ARE THERE ANY COMPLEMENTARY THERAPIES?

Peppermint tea may help relieve the symptoms of irritable bowel syndrome.

WHAT'S THE OUTLOOK?

Symptoms of irritable bowel syndrome can fluctuate. Sometimes they go away for a long time and then suddenly recur for no apparent reason.

KEY FACT

People often think of irritable bowel syndrome as being an adult problem, but it affects up to 1 in every 5 children, boys and girls equally.

Possible symptoms

- ★ Abdominal pain, often cramping in nature, which may be relieved by passing a stool
- ★ Bloating of the abdomen
- ★ Needing to pass wind a lot
- ★ Diarrhoea and/or constipation
- ★ Mucus in the stool

What can I do?

It may be helpful to make a food and symptom diary to see if there is a pattern or particular food that triggers your child's symptoms.

Keep a food diary Write down everything your child eats each day and whether or not he has had any irritable bowel symptoms.

Coeliac disease

People with coeliac disease are sensitive to gluten, a protein found in wheat, rye, and barley. Eating these foods leads to symptoms such as abdominal pain and bowel upsets. They may also react to a similar protein found in oats.

WHAT IS THE CAUSE?

It is not known why coeliac disease occurs, although it can run in families and is more common in people who also have type 1 diabetes. The condition is not an allergy to gluten, but an autoimmune disease in which the body mistakenly attacks itself. In coeliac disease when gluten enters the digestive system, the immune system attacks it and causes inflammation of the lining of the intestine. This means that food cannot be absorbed properly, resulting in the symptoms of the disease.

Coeliac disease affects about 1 in 100 people and can occur at any age, although the symptoms may vary among different age groups and from one person to the next. The symptoms do not start before gluten is introduced into the diet when a child is weaned.

SHOULD I SEE A DOCTOR?

Coeliac disease can be diagnosed by blood tests, so if you are worried that your child has symptoms, see your doctor. If the tests are positive your child will be referred to a paediatrician to have a small sample of tissue (biopsy) taken from her intestines to look for characteristic changes in the

Possible symptoms

- ★ Pale, smelly, oily, stools that are difficult to flush away
- ★ Diarrhoea
- ★ Bloated stomach
- ★ Thin, wasted arms and legs
- ★ Failure to grow or put on weight as expected
- ★ Shortness of breath or tiredness due to anaemia (as the body can't absorb the nutrients needed to make red blood cells)
- ★ Itchy blister-like rash on elbows and knees

What can I do to help?

Your child needs to avoid all foods made from wheat, barley, and rye, and possibly oats. Produce commonly made from these grains includes breads, cereals, pasta, cakes, and biscuits. Fruit, vegetables, meat, poultry, fish, eggs, and most dairy products are fine for your child to eat.

Check labels Gluten can be hidden in some foods, such as tinned soups, ready-made meals, pies, or prepared sauces, so check ingredients carefully.

Find alternatives Your child can eat rice, corn, maize, potatoes, and soya, and you can use these products to make gluten-free versions of everyday foods, such as bread.

Choose gluten-free Many gluten-free foods, such as pasta, pizza bases, cereals, bread, and biscuits are available from shops or on prescription.

intestinal wall that occur in coeliac disease. It is important not to cut gluten out of your child's diet before the tests and biopsies are carried out, as the results of blood tests are not conclusive. Also, it's not a good idea to restrict a child's diet unless really necessary. If your child is diagnosed with coeliac disease, blood tests may be performed to check for anaemia and assess levels of other vitamins and minerals. The treatment for coeliac disease is to avoid gluten, as this stops the symptoms. You may be referred to a dietitian for advice about your child's diet. Children with coeliac disease are also eligible for the annual flu jab and may be advised to take other nutritional supplements by their doctor.

WHAT'S THE OUTLOOK?

A gluten-free diet reverses the damage to the intestines and stops the symptoms of coeliac disease. Your child will need to follow this diet for the rest of her life to prevent the symptoms returning.

TOP TIP

Tell your child's teachers about her condition and inform friends' parents if she is invited to eat at their homes or to attend birthday parties.

Travel sickness

Feeling sick when travelling by car, sea, or air is common in children. Although unpleasant, it generally disappears when the journey is over.

Travel sickness is thought to be due to a mismatch between information supplied to the brain from the eyes and the balance system in the inner ear. For example, your child's eyes tell her brain that she is moving really fast in a car, while her ears tell her brain that she is sitting still.

Some medications for motion sickness are available on prescription only, others can be bought over the counter, but check with your pharmacist about their suitability for your child's age before giving them. Generally, antihistamines are used.

Possible symptoms

- ★ Nausea
- ★ Vomiting
- ★ Feeling unwell

What can I do to help?

Avoid giving children a large meal before travelling. Put a travel-sick child in the front seat of a car (check air bags are disabled). Choose seats in the middle of a boat or over the wing of an airplane.

Give tips Suggest your child looks straight ahead or closes her eyes. Open a window for fresh air.

Try natural remedies Eating a ginger biscuit, sucking on a peppermint sweet, or wearing acupressure bands may be helpful.

Avoid dehydration If your child does vomit, encourage her to keep drinking, sipping small amounts of fluids regularly.

Hepatitis

In children, the most common cause of hepatitis (inflammation of the liver) is a viral infection. Several strains can cause the disease.

Possible symptoms

- ★ Fever
- ★ Nausea and vomiting
- ★ Jaundice (yellow discoloration of the skin and eyes)
- ★ Dark urine and pale stools

WHAT ARE THE CAUSES?

The hepatitis A virus is the most likely strain to cause hepatitis in children. It can be contracted by drinking water or eating food that has been contaminated with infected faeces and occurs more commonly in countries where sanitation is poor. A vaccination against hepatitis A may be recommended if you are travelling to these parts of the world.

Hepatitis B is far less common in the UK. It can infect babies during birth if the mother carries the virus but as women are tested for it during pregnancy and their babies vaccinated if necessary, this is rare.

SHOULD I SEE A DOCTOR?

If your child has symptoms of hepatitis, seek medical advice urgently. There is no specific treatment for hepatitis A, but if symptoms are severe, your child may be admitted to hospital. If your child is recovering at home, he should rest and will need to be given plenty of fluids.

WHAT'S THE OUTLOOK?

Children who contract hepatitis A usually [illegible] They are then immune to future attacks. Children with hepatitis B may remain carriers of the virus throughout life and can infect others.

Gastroenteritis

Bouts of gastroenteritis – an infection of the stomach and intestines – are extremely common in children. The illness is generally caused by a virus, often rotavirus, but can be due to a bacterial infection. Most children feel better in a few days.

Possible symptoms

- ★ Fever
- ★ Abdominal pain, often cramping
- ★ Nausea and vomiting
- ★ Diarrhoea

If dehydration occurs, there may be:

- ★ Dark, concentrated urine passed in small amounts, or no urine
- ★ Tiredness
- ★ Dry lips and mouth
- ★ Sunken fontanelle (soft spot on the top of the head) in babies
- ★ Sunken eyes
- ★ Reduced amount of tears if crying
- ★ Cold hands and feet, and drowsiness when severely dehydrated

Tiredness Gastroenteritis can make your child feel very tired, especially if he's deydrated. Make sure he drinks lots of fluids.

WHAT ARE THE CAUSES?

Viruses can be picked up by touching an infected person who hasn't washed their hands properly after going to the toilet, or by touching an object an infected person has touched, then transferring the virus or bacteria to the mouth. Some viruses are spread by breathing in droplets from other people's coughs and sneezes. Bacteria that cause gastroenteritis can also be picked up in contaminated food or drinking water.

Babies who are breastfed are less likely to develop gastroenteritis than babies who are bottle-fed.

SHOULD I SEE A DOCTOR?

Seek medical advice if your child is less than 6 months old, is unable to tolerate even small amounts of fluid, or is showing signs of dehydration. If there is blood in the stool or vomit, if pain is severe, or if you feel symptoms are worsening, or not improving after a few days, you should also see your doctor, who may send some stool to the laboratory for testing. If your child is very unwell he may need intravenous fluids to treat dehydration.

ARE THERE COMPLICATIONS?

Some children develop lactose intolerance (see Food intolerance, p.163) after an episode of gastroenteritis. This is usually temporary and occurs as the lining of the intestine is damaged by the infection. If your child has symptoms of lactose intolerance, such as diarrhoea, abdominal bloating, or pain when dairy foods are introduced into the diet after an episode of gastroenteritis, stop giving dairy products for a few days to give the intestine time to heal, then try reintroducing them.

A rarer complication is haemolytic uraemic syndrome, which is caused by infection with a type of *E.Coli* bacteria that can be caught from undercooked meat. It causes bloody diarrhoea and can lead to anaemia and kidney failure. Treatment is usually given in hospital, and most children recover fully.

WHAT'S THE OUTLOOK?

Most children who contract gastroenteritis improve within a few days.

TOP TIP

Giving oral rehydration solution, which can be bought over the counter, helps replace salts lost by vomiting and diarrhoea, and may be preferable to giving water only.

What can I do to help?

The only treatment usually needed is to prevent dehydration. Your child must be excluded from school or nursery, and avoid contact with other children until 48 hours after the last episode of diarrhoea.

Give plenty of fluids If she can't keep them down, give smaller amounts more often – every 5 minutes or so.

Breastfeed your baby Keep offering your breast to make sure she gets small amounts of milk regularly.

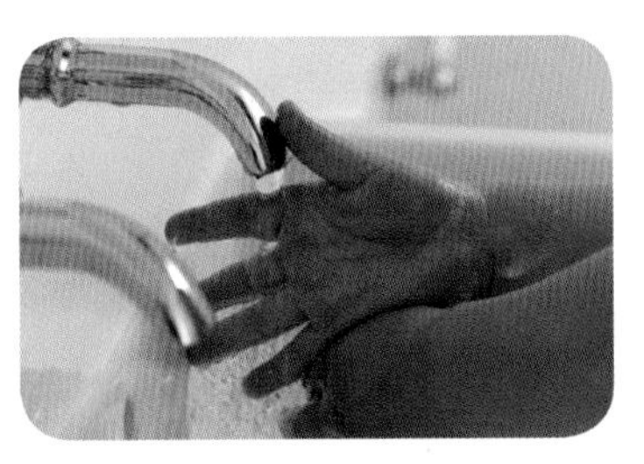

Be hygienic Wash your and your child's hands well after going to the toilet or touching animals, and before eating.

Don't share Use separate washcloths, towels, cutlery, and glasses, and don't let your child help prepare or serve food.

Observe kitchen hygiene To help prevent gastroenteritis, follow good hygiene in the kitchen, such as using separate chopping boards for raw and ready-to-eat foods.

Giardiasis

A digestive tract infection that causes diarrhoea, giardiasis is most common in countries with poor sanitation. It does also occur in developed countries, most often affecting young children.

WHAT IS THE CAUSE?

Giardiasis is caused by a tiny parasite called *Giardia lamblia*, which can live for long periods outside the body. The parasites can be spread by poor hand-washing after going to the toilet and then touching other people or handling or serving food to them. The parasites can also be caught by drinking contaminated water. Many infected children have no symptoms. If symptoms do occur, they usually don't appear until 1–2 weeks after infection occurred.

SHOULD I SEE A DOCTOR?

If you think your child could have giardiasis you should see your doctor. Stool samples can be sent to the laboratory for testing to find the parasite. More than one stool sample may be needed as the giardia cysts are not present in every stool motion.

WHAT'S THE TREATMENT?

Giardiasis is treated with an antibiotic called metronidazole. Your doctor may also advise treating all family members. Make sure that your child drinks enough fluids to prevent her from becoming dehydrated.

IS IT PREVENTABLE?

To prevent your child from spreading the infection, she should not share towels, cutlery or glassware or prepare or serve food to others. Teach her to wash her hands thoroughly after going to the toilet.

Possible symptoms

- ★ Fever
- ★ Nausea
- ★ Abdominal pain
- ★ Watery diarrhoea
- ★ Burping

You should keep her home from nursery or school until there has been no diarrhoea for at least 48 hours.

To prevent your child from contracting giardiasis when travelling to countries where it is prevalent, make sure that she drinks only bottled or boiled (not tap) water. Peel all fruits and vegetables before giving them to her, don't let her have ice cubes in drinks, and practise good hand hygiene.

WHAT'S THE OUTLOOK?

If treated with appropriate antibiotics, most children recover quickly from giardiasis.

Threadworms

Infection of the intestines with threadworms is common in children. These tiny worms (a few millimetres long) lay eggs around the anus, which causes intense itching.

WHAT IS THE CAUSE?

Threadworms are caught by swallowing eggs laid by female worms. This can happen if your child touches the hands of an infected person whose hands are contaminated with eggs, and then transfers the eggs to her mouth. The eggs can also be swallowed in contaminated food or drink. Once ingested, the eggs hatch into worms in the intestines and live for about 5–6 weeks. The female worms lay eggs around the anus (back passage) causing itching. Your child scratches (often at night), so has the eggs under her fingernails and on her hands. When she touches her mouth, she swallows the eggs and the cycle starts again. If your child touches someone else, that person could catch the infection. The eggs can live outside the body for up to 2 weeks on clothes, bedding, toys, or surfaces, so can easily be transferred to the mouth. Threadworms can also be spread by sharing cutlery, glassware or toothbrushes.

Possible symptoms

- ★ Itchy anus, especially at night
- ★ Itchy vagina
- ★ Disturbed sleep as a result of itching

HOW DO I CHECK FOR THREADWORMS?

You may suspect your child has threadworms if she has an itchy bottom. If you look, you may see the small thread-like worms in the stool. You could look for the worms on your child's anus at night. Part the buttocks and look at the anus with a torch: you may see the worms coming out. If you do, don't be alarmed. See your pharmacist, who can recommend an over-the-counter medication. Prescription medications are also available if you prefer to see your doctor first.

SHOULD I SEE A DOCTOR?

If you can't see any worms but your child has symptoms that suggest threadworms, or you would like confirmation of your findings, take your child to the doctor. The doctor may take a swab from the skin of the anus to send to the lab to see if the eggs are present. Alternatively, the doctor might ask you to press some clear sticky tape to your child's anus first thing in the morning before she goes to the toilet or washes; the tape can then be examined in the laboratory.

WHAT'S THE TREATMENT?

The medication most commonly used for treating threadworms is mebendazole, which is suitable for use in children older than 6 months. It can be bought over the counter or prescribed by your doctor and is available in chewable tablet form or as a liquid. One dose kills all the adult worms in a few days but not the eggs, which can live for 2 weeks outside the body. Therefore, the medication needs to be combined with hygiene measures (see below) to eliminate the eggs and prevent re-infection of your child and other members of the family. A second dose of the medication may be needed 2 weeks after the first one as re-infection is common.

What can I do to help?

To get rid of threadworms and prevent re-infection, you need to combine over-the-counter medication with the introduction of hygienic measures. Your child needs to wear underwear at night and you should wash her hands and bottom first thing in the morning.

Give medication All family members, even those with no symptoms, must take the medication. Do not take it if you are pregnant or breastfeeding.

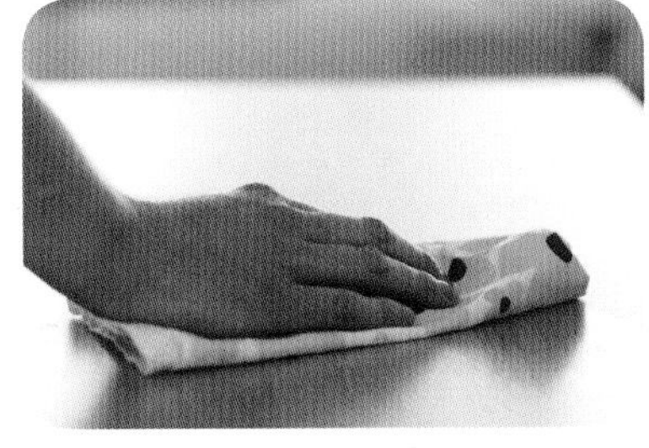

Damp dust Clean the house thoroughly. Every day, use a damp cloth to dust – dusting with a dry cloth just spreads dust, and potentially worm eggs, around.

Wash hands Your child should wash her hands and scrub under her fingernails every time she uses the toilet. You should do this if you are changing nappies.

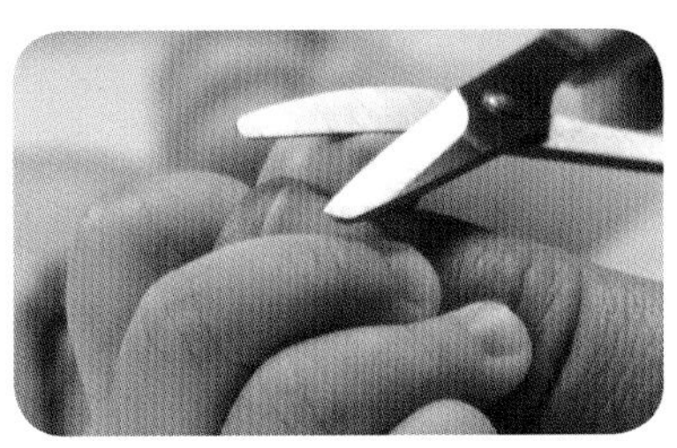

Cut nails To help prevent your child scratching and getting eggs under her fingernails, keep them short. Discourage nail-biting and thumb-sucking.

Wash household items You should wash all towels, nightclothes, and bedding. Your child can help you to wash her toys to get rid of any eggs.

Appendicitis

The appendix is a small finger-like organ that hangs down from the large intestine. If it becomes infected and inflamed (appendicitis) it needs to be removed immediately. Appendicitis can occur at any age but is rare in children under 2.

WHAT IS THE CAUSE?

The cause of appendicitis is often not known, but it can occur if the opening of the appendix into the large intestine becomes blocked, by a hard piece of stool, for example. This allows bacteria to multiply easily, causing infection.

Swollen glands in the abdomen

Swelling of lymph glands in the abdomen is known as mesenteric adenitis and it can cause symptoms similar to those of appendicitis.

Symptoms include pain in the centre of the abdomen, nausea and vomiting, diarrhoea, and fever. Mesenteric adenitis will get better on its own but you should take your child to the doctor in case the symptoms are due to appendicitis.

Your child may be referred to a paediatrician or surgeon, or you may be advised to wait and watch your child carefully. If the symptoms improve no action is needed; if they worsen you may be referred. Mesenteric adenitis improves within a few days without specific treatment; you can give painkillers such as paracetamol or ibuprofen.

ARE THERE COMPLICATIONS?

If appendicitis is not treated urgently, there's a risk that the appendix could burst and lead to infection of the inner lining of the abdomen (peritonitis). This is a very serious and potentially life-threatening condition.

SHOULD I SEE A DOCTOR?

If your child has constant abdominal pain that is getting worse, contact your doctor immediately. Do not give him anything to eat and drink before seeing the doctor. If your child has had constant pain for more than six hours or has symptoms of peritonitis, call an ambulance.

Abdominal pain and fever can be due to other conditions, such as a urinary tract infection or swollen lymph glands in the abdomen (see box, left), which often happens after a viral infection, such as a cold. Your doctor will therefore need to assess your child carefully to confirm the diagnosis and exclude other possibilities.

The doctor will examine your child's abdomen for signs of pain and tenderness and may arrange for blood and urine tests to look for infection. If the doctor feels that it would be dangerous to wait for the results of these tests, or has been able to confirm the diagnosis without further tests, your child will be admitted to hospital straight away for an operation to remove the appendix (appendectomy).

The operation to remove an appendix is usually carried out by key-hole surgery, in which several small incisions are made in the abdomen. In some cases, traditional surgery, which involves making a larger incision, may be carried out.

Possible symptoms

- **Abdominal pain** starting around the navel then moving to the lower right hand side that comes on quite quickly and gets worse over a few hours
- Low-grade fever
- Nausea or vomiting
- Lack of appetite

If appendicitis is untreated and the appendix bursts (peritonitis):

- Pain across entire abdomen
- High fever (up to 40°C/104°F)

WHAT'S THE OUTLOOK?

Your child is likely to be in hospital for 2 to 3 days, possibly longer if there are any complications. He should be able to return to school in about a week and should suffer no long-term ill-effects.

Comfort your child If your child has abdominal pain that you think could be appendicitis, medical attention is essential. While waiting, comfort and reassure her.

Abdominal migraine

Children, often those between the ages of 5 and 9, sometimes get a form of migraine that causes abdominal pain rather than a headache.

Possible symptoms

- ★ Bouts of abdominal pain, in the middle of or all over the abdomen, that last between 1 hour and 3 days
- ★ Nausea and vomiting
- ★ Pale or flushed skin
- ★ Wanting to lie down and sleep in a darkened room

WHAT IS THE CAUSE?

The cause of abdominal migraine is not known, but there may be inherited factors: often other family members suffer from migraine headaches. Certain triggers may bring on abdominal migraine, such as foods, additives, exercise or stress. Symptoms are similar to those of migraine headaches, so more debilitating than normal tummy ache.

SHOULD I SEE A DOCTOR?

It is important to visit your doctor so that other causes of abdominal pain can be ruled out. Medications can be prescribed but often they are not necessary and your doctor may suggest that you try self-help measures first (see below). If your child has very regular or severe abdominal migraines attacks that prevent him from going to school or participating in his usual activities, your doctor may prescribe medication to control or prevent attacks.

What can I do to help?

The best way to deal with abdominal migraines is to pinpoint the triggers and then avoid them. Keeping a food/symptom diary is a good way of identifying what the triggers might be.

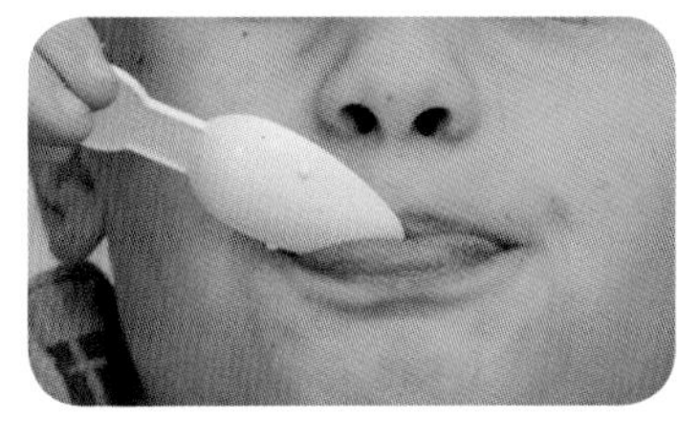

Relieve the pain Paracetamol or ibuprofen can be effective in treating abdominal pain.

Keep a food diary Note down foods, activities and symptoms daily to help find triggers for your child's migraine.

Darken her room During a migraine your child may like to lie down in a darkened room. She may feel better after a sleep.

Relieve stress Talking to your child and/or her teacher about problems may help to relieve stress and avoid migraines.

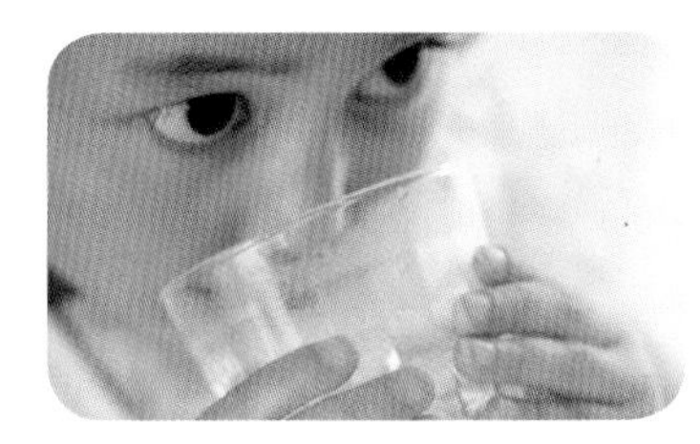

Give plenty of fluids Drinking enough fluids and eating healthily can help prevent bouts of abdominal migraine.

Recurrent abdominal pain

Most children have a tummy ache at some point for one reason or another, but 1 in 10 may have recurrent tummy aches. These tend to improve with age.

SHOULD I SEE A DOCTOR?

Take your child to see your doctor so that she can be assessed and other causes of abdominal pain can be treated or excluded. In the majority of children, a cause is never found. If this is the case, then your doctor will be able to reassure you that there is nothing else going on.

WHAT CAN I DO?

You may wish to keep a symptom or pain diary in which you and your child write down when she had pain and what was going on that day or what she ate, and see if patterns may emerge. When your child gets abdominal pain you can try painkillers such as paracetamol or ibuprofen, and/or a warm bath or hot water bottle (not too hot!).

Talk to your child Stress or anxiety can sometimes trigger abdominal pain so try to find out if anything is worrying your child; speak to her teachers, too.

Possible symptoms

- ★ Generalized abdominal pain that comes and goes
- ★ At least three episodes of pain within 3 months
- ★ Pain severe enough to disrupt normal activities

TOP TIP

Even if no cause can be found for your child's pain, remember that the pain she experiences is real and must never be dismissed.

Constipation

Bowel habits vary among children: some pass stool twice a day, others twice a week. Both are normal. A child is constipated if she starts to pass stool much less often than usual, and the stools are hard, dry, and difficult to pass.

WHAT ARE THE CAUSES?

There are many causes of constipation, including insufficient fibre in the diet, not drinking enough water, or holding in stool when needing to go to the toilet (some children don't want to go at school or nursery, for example). A common cycle is that children get constipated and stool is painful or difficult to pass. The next time they need to go, instead of relaxing the muscles of the back passage (anus) to allow the stool to pass, they tighten them so they don't have to go straight away. The amount of stool then builds up and becomes hard, so that it is even more difficult and painful to pass, and the cycle perpetuates itself.

Possible symptoms

- ★ Dry hard stools that look like pellets or rabbit droppings
- ★ Straining when passing stool
- ★ Stomach ache
- ★ Pain when passing stool
- ★ Avoiding going to the toilet to pass stool
- ★ Overflow diarrhoea if constipation is severe, as watery stool passes around the hard faeces in the rectum

SHOULD I SEE A DOCTOR?
Constipation often only lasts a few days and clears up either with no treatment or with basic self-help measures (see below). If your child's constipation doesn't improve after a few days, or if you are concerned, then see your doctor, who will be able to prescribe laxatives. Those used for children often work by increasing the amount of water in the stool to make it softer.

Laxatives may be liquids or in powder form, in which case they are mixed with water to make a drink. Although laxatives are available over the counter, some are not appropriate for children, so see your doctor before giving your child any laxatives.

Another treatment option is called toilet training. Here children learn to relax the correct muscles and to tense others as they pass a stool. The results of research into whether this works are not clear but it may help in combination with other treatments.

IS IT PREVENTABLE?
The measures for treating constipation will also prevent your child from becoming constipated. These include eating a diet rich in fibre, drinking plenty of water, getting enough exercise, and sitting regularly on the toilet to pass stools.

What can I do to help?

Constipation should be treated promptly to try to prevent the cycle of painful stools leading to not wanting to go to the toilet. Fibre rich foods and lots of water are very important. To help your child relax while on the toilet, give her something special to enjoy such as her favourite book.

Give water Drinking plenty of water is one of the most important ways of treating and preventing constipation.

Encourage fibre-rich foods Give brown bread, wholegrain cereals and pasta, and lots of fruit and vegetables (preferably raw).

Teach toilet techniques Sit your child on the toilet at regular times. Sitting with thighs horizontal or higher helps straighten the anal canal so stools pass more easily.

Keep a diary Write down what your child eats and when he goes to the toilet, exercises, or has a drink of water. Give rewards when he does something that helps constipation.

Keep him moving Make sure that your child is active and gets plenty of exercise. Physical activity prevents the intestines from becoming sluggish.

Toddler's diarrhoea

Persistent diarrhoea in children is most commonly due to toddler's diarrhoea. It generally affects children aged between 1 and 5.

Possible symptoms

- ★ Loose or poorly formed stools that may be more smelly than usual
- ★ Pieces of food, such as corn, peas or carrots seen in stool

WHAT IS THE CAUSE?

The cause of toddler's diarrhoea is not clear. However, the condition does not lead to malabsorption of food and your child will still be getting all the nutrients she needs from her diet.

SHOULD I SEE A DOCTOR?

You may wish to see your doctor to exclude other causes of diarrhoea but in toddler's diarrhoea children are generally well, have no fever, are eating and drinking, active, and growing as normal.

What can I do to help?

Often, no treatment is needed and symptoms improve with age. Making a food diary can help identify foods that might be causing diarrhoea, but don't exclude foods without seeing your doctor first as children need a varied and balanced diet. Making the changes below can help.

Keep a food diary Write down what your child eats and whether or not she has diarrhoea to see if a pattern related to certain foods emerges.

Give water Give your child mainly water, restricting fruit juice or squash, which are high in sugar and can pull more water into the stool, leading to diarrhoea.

Avoid a low-fat diet A low-fat diet can cause diarrhoea. Give under 2s full-fat milk and over 2s semi-skimmed milk, and give normal yogurts and cheeses.

Increase fibre Try increasing how much fibre your child eats. Foods such as wholemeal bread help absorb water in the bowel, making stools less watery.

Change nappies Be sure to change your child's nappy frequently and clean her bottom carefully after each change to prevent nappy rash from developing.

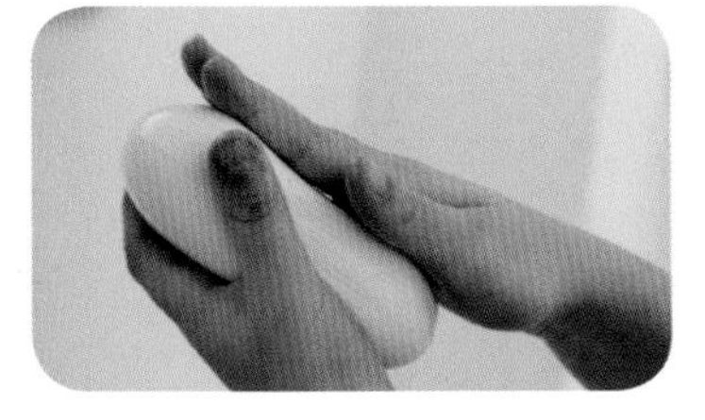

Teach hand hygiene Show your child how to wipe properly and to wash her hands after using the toilet to prevent infection that could worsen diarrhoea.

Urinary and genital disorders

The urinary system is responsible for filtering out waste products from blood and excreting them as urine. Filtration of blood takes place in the kidneys, and urine then passes down two tubes called ureters to the bladder. Urine leaves the body through the urethra, a passageway that in males runs through the penis, and in females exits in front of the vaginal opening.

This section includes two important urinary problems in children: urinary tract infections and bladder control problems (not being dry during the day and/or night). The other articles are about genital problems. In boys, these may affect the testes or penis; in girls, inflammation or infection of the vulva (external genitals) or the vagina are common problems.

Urinary tract infections

Infections of the urinary tract are caused by bacteria. They are more common in girls because the urethra, the tube that carries urine out of the body, is shorter than in boys, so bacteria don't have to travel so far to reach the bladder.

Possible symptoms

In young children (under 2 or 3), general symptoms of being unwell:

★ Fever

★ Vomiting

★ Decreased appetite

★ Failure to thrive (gain weight)

In older children, general symptoms as above and also:

★ [illegible] frequency of passing urine

★ Burning or stinging when passing urine

★ Blood in the urine (may be noticeable in nappy of a younger child)

★ Pain in lower abdomen or lower back

★ Offensive-smelling urine

Collecting a urine sample

If your doctor has asked you to collect a urine sample so that it can be tested for infection, you can try various methods, depending on the age of your child.

★ **Toilet-trained children** Ask your child to start urinating and then pass the collection bottle into the stream of urine to "catch" a midstream sample without the bottle touching your child.

★ **Potty-trained children** Clean the potty with hot water, allow your child to urinate into it, then pour the urine into the sample container.

★ **Younger children** You can try taking a younger child's nappy off and following him around to catch a sample. If this doesn't work, you could use a urine collection pad, which you insert into a nappy. Once the pad is wet, you suck up a urine sample with a syringe then transfer this to a bottle. Alternatively, urine can be collected in an adhesive collection bag stuck to the genital region. Urine collection pads and bags have a risk of contamination from bacteria on the skin.

WHAT ARE THE TYPES?

Infection of the bladder and/or urethra is the most common type of urinary tract infection in children. [illegible] can spread further up the urinary tract to affect the kidneys. This is potentially more serious as it can lead to scarring of the kidneys, but is relatively rare in children.

WHAT ARE THE CAUSES?

It is not always clear why a child develops a urinary tract infection. In girls, it may be caused by wiping their bottoms from back to front after a bowel movement as this lets bacteria pass from the anus to the urethra. (The distance between the anus and the urethra is shorter in girls than it is in boys.) Children who are constipated are more prone to urinary tract infections as a full rectum can put pressure on the bladder, preventing it from emptying properly and allowing bacteria to multiply in stagnant urine. Children who "hold on" to their urine

What can I do to help?

Drinking lots of liquids helps flush out bacteria from the urinary tract and also replaces fluids lost through fever or vomiting.

Give fluids Encourage your child to drink plenty of fluids to speed recovery and prevent dehydration.

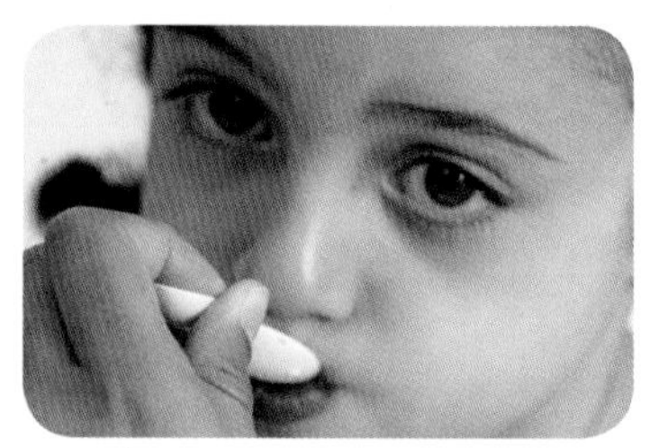

Treat symptoms You can give your child paracetamol or ibuprofen for pain and to bring down a fever.

even if they need to urinate are also more likely to develop urinary tract infections for the same reason.

Children with vesicoureteral reflux are at increased risk of infection. In this condition, urine flows back up (refluxes) the ureters to the kidneys as a result of a fault in a valve between the bladder and the ureters.

SHOULD I SEE A DOCTOR?

If your child has symptoms of a urinary tract infection, she should be seen by a doctor. Treatment will depend on his age.

If your baby is under 3 months old and your doctor suspects a urinary tract infection from the symptoms, he will be sent to hospital so that urine testing can be carried out quickly and, if infection is confirmed, he can be started on intravenous antibiotics straight away.

For children older than 3 months, the doctor will test a urine sample for infection. He or she may collect a sample or may ask you to do this at home (see box, opposite). The doctor will dip a test stick into the urine sample and, if there are signs of a possible infection, a sample will be sent to a laboratory to identify the type of bacteria causing the infection. The doctor may wait for the results before starting your child on antibiotics. However, if your child is very unwell the doctor may decide to start him on antibiotics straight away, then when the results are available change them, if necessary, to a type that targets the specific bacteria found.

Depending on your child's age, the type of bacteria found to be causing the infection, and whether he has had recurrent infections, he may be referred for further tests, such as an ultrasound scan or other imaging test, either during the infection or a few weeks after it has cleared up. Most children recover very quickly from urinary tract infections, although some have repeated (recurrent) infections.

IS IT PREVENTABLE?

Teach your daughter to wipe from front to back after using the toilet. This can be difficult for children so they may need repeated explanations and demonstrations.

Wiping correctly Teach your child how to wipe from front to back to prevent transferring bacteria from the anus to the urethra.

Boys should also clean around their foreskins, but you should not attempt to clean under the foreskin. If your child is constipated, seek medical advice to treat the constipation. Encourage your child to drink plenty of water and to go to the toilet to pass urine regularly, not to hold it in.

Balanitis

Inflammation of the head (glans) of the penis, known as balanitis, can occur at any age. The foreskin may be inflamed at the same time.

Possible symptoms

- ★ Swollen, red, sore head of penis
- ★ Itchiness
- ★ Rash
- ★ Discharge
- ★ Offensive smell

WHAT IS THE CAUSE?

Balanitis can be due to a skin condition affecting the glans, such as eczema or psoriasis, or to an infection, commonly by fungi (candida) or bacteria. It can also occur as a reaction to an irritant, such as a harsh soap. The condition is more common in young boys before the foreskin can be retracted and in boys with phimosis, in which scarring prevents retraction (see p.181), as sweat and urine can accumulate under the foreskin causing irritation. It is also more common in uncircumcised boys.

WHAT CAN I DO?

Avoid using soap to wash your son's genital area. Instead, use just water. Wash the genitals daily and be sure to dry the penis thoroughly. Dress him in cotton underwear. Sometimes children benefit from bathing in salt water when they have balanitis; add about 4 tablespoons to a full bath.

SHOULD I SEE A DOCTOR?

If your son's balanitis does not clear up with the self-help measures described above, take him to the doctor. If the inflammation is caused by infection, the doctor can prescribe an antifungal or antibiotic cream. Alternatively, if it is due to a skin condition or an allergy, it may be treated with a mild steroid cream. A steroid may be used in conjunction with an antifungal or antibiotic cream. If your son has had recurrent bouts of balanitis and has phimosis, circumcision may be advised.

Bladder control problems

As they get older, children gain bladder control and generally are dry in the day first, then at night. If a child is not dry during the day by age 4 or is bed-wetting after age 7, seek medical advice.

WHAT ARE THE CAUSES?

Daytime wetting can be due to an overactive bladder, in which small amounts of urine are released before the bladder has filled. Children who hold their urine in, perhaps because they do not want to go at school, are also more likely to wet in the day.

Bed-wetting may occur because a child sleeps very deeply and the part of the nervous system that tells him to wake up and go to the toilet is immature. It can also occur because the body does not yet produce enough antidiuretic hormone, which reduces urine production at night. If a child's parents wetted the bed after age 7 the child is also more likely to do so.

A child who starts wetting again after having been dry in the day or night could have an underlying medical condition or could be suffering from stress or anxiety.

SHOULD I SEE A DOCTOR?

See your doctor if your child:

★ Is still wetting regularly in the daytime after the age of 4.

★ Has previously been dry in the day or night for at least 6 months and has started wetting again.

★ Is still regularly bed-wetting (more than twice a week) after the age of 7, despite self-help measures.

The doctor will examine your child and treat any problems, such as an infection. If no physical cause for wetting is found, try the self-help measures shown below. If these are unsuccessful, you could try using an enuresis alarm. This device wakes your child when the sheets become wet, so that he can either go to the toilet or hold on. With time, your child will become aware of the sensation without the noise of the alarm. Medication is also available but this is generally only given for short periods, for example to cover holidays or school trips.

WHAT'S THE OUTLOOK?

Bed-wetting is common in children but not so common in adults, so most children do grow out of it as they get older.

What can I do to help?

You can take various measures to help a child who is bed-wetting. First of all, do not blame your child, get angry, or punish him for wetting the bed, as this can make him stressed and anxious and more likely to keep doing it. Give praise for staying dry and make sure he can get to the toilet easily.

Monitor drinking Give your child plenty to drink, preferably water, during the day but restrict fluids in the evening and avoid caffeinated drinks (tea, coffee, cola, hot chocolate) which can cause wakefulness as well as night wetting.

Ease toilet access Make sure that your child can get out of bed and access the toilet easily. You could leave a night light on by his bed and perhaps near the toilet. If your child sleeps in a bunk bed, he should sleep on the bottom bunk.

Praise and reward Children often respond to praise and rewards. You could try to encourage bladder control by giving your child a small present or treat after she's been dry for a certain number of nights.

Foreskin problems

The foreskin is the fold of skin that covers the penis (when not erect). Several conditions affecting the foreskin may be of concern to parents.

WHAT ARE THE TYPES?

Parents often worry that their son's foreskin cannot be pulled back (retracted), but in fact this is perfectly normal and rarely needs treatment. Conditions that do need treating are a tight foreskin (phimosis) and a foreskin that has become struck in a retracted position (paraphimosis).

★ **Non-retractile foreskin** In the majority of newborn boys, the foreskin is attached to the head (glans) of the penis and cannot be pulled back. As boys develop, the foreskin separates from the glans. At 6 months, 3 in 4 boys have a non-retractile foreskin, by 1 year, this reduces to 6 in 10, and to 1 in 10 at 4 years. By puberty only 1 in 100 boys still have a non-retractile foreskin.

Until the foreskin becomes retractile, it may balloon slightly when a child passes urine. You should not try to pull the foreskin back for cleaning as forcing it back can cause scarring. It is normal for smegma, a yellowy-white material, to collect under the foreskin, and you don't need to do anything about this. Treatments for a persistently non-retractile foreskin include steroid ointments, although as the foreskin may continue to separate until puberty, often no treatment is needed.

★ **Phimosis** A tight foreskin can occur if scar tissue constricts the opening for urination at its tip. The scarring can be a result of forcibly retracting the foreskin, and can also occur if there is recurrent infection of the head of the penis. Phimosis causes ballooning of the foreskin on urination and increases the risk of infection because urine and sweat collect under the foreskin. The condition can be treated with steroid creams. In some cases, circumcision may be recommended.

★ **Paraphimosis** If the foreskin becomes stuck in the retracted position, the head of the penis swells up, making it more difficult to return the foreskin to its normal position. It is painful and requires urgent medical treatment – take your child to your doctor immediately. Your son will be sedated and the foreskin returned to its normal position.

IMPORTANT

Don't attempt to pull back a boy's foreskin forcibly; you're likely to injure tissues causing bleeding and leading to the formation of scar tissue.

Undescended testes

When in the womb, boys' testes develop within their abdomens; moving down into the scrotum towards the end of pregnancy. One or both testes sometimes fail to descend before birth.

HOW IS IT DIAGNOSED?

Undescended testes do not cause any symptoms but a doctor will not be able to feel them in the scrotum. During your baby's newborn and 6–8 week checks, your doctor will check the scrotum to see if the testes are in the correct place. If a testis cannot be felt, your doctor will attempt to feel it in the groin or abdomen. If it is cold, or the doctor has cold hands, the testis may simply have been pulled up out of the scrotum, as this reflex is well developed in babies and children. If the examination is repeated on another occasion, the doctor may be able to feel the testis in the scrotum. If he or she cannot feel a testis, the doctor will ask you to bring your baby back for another examination when he is about 3 months old, as many boys' testes descend into the scrotum at around this time.

WHAT'S THE TREATMENT?

If one or both testes cannot be felt on examination at 3 months, your doctor will refer you to a specialist. Treatment is recommended to prevent problems with fertility and because boys with undescended testes are at a greater risk of developing testicular cancer. The treatment generally involves surgery to bring the testis down into the scrotum.

Hydrocele

Newborn babies are sometimes born with a hydrocele. This is a collection of fluid within the scrotum, the sac that encloses the testes.

Possible symptoms

- ★ Swelling in the scrotum that feels like a fluid-filled balloon
- ★ Generally painless

WHAT IS THE CAUSE?

As boys develop in the womb the testes are formed within the abdomen and then travel down a passageway into the scrotum before birth. The passageway normally closes after the testes have descended but, if it remains open, fluid can build up, causing a hydrocele. These generally only affect one side of the scrotum. They may be associated with an inguinal hernia.

SHOULD I SEE A DOCTOR?

Many hydroceles improve with time, and often no treatment is required. If your son's hydrocele has not disappeared by the age of 1 or it is very large and causing discomfort, it can be surgically removed. Hydroceles have no long-term effects and fertility is not affected.

Vaginal problems

Inflammation of the external genitals (vulva) and the vagina is a common problem in young girls. It is also known as vulvovaginitis.

Possible symptoms

- ★ Soreness or itching of the genitals
- ★ Stinging or pain when urinating
- ★ Vaginal discharge

What can I do?

Dress your child in loose-fitting clothes; don't let her wear leotards, tights, or other tight clothes for long periods.

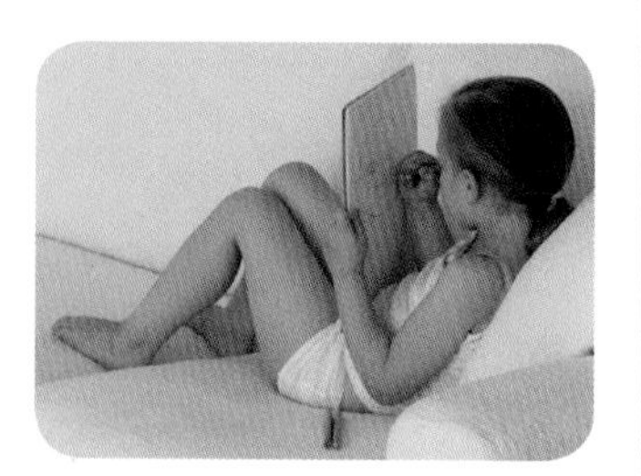

Let the air in Give your child loose cotton pants to wear. She should avoid wearing knickers at night.

WHAT IS THE CAUSE?

Inflammation of the vulva and vagina is often caused by infection with bacteria. Young children frequently don't wipe themselves properly – from back to front – after going to the toilet. In young girls, as the anus is very close to the vulva and vagina, bacteria from stool around the anus are easily carried to the vaginal area. Before puberty, young girls have less oestrogen and do not have much fat in the lips of the vagina (labia) or pubic hair to protect the vulva and vagina, making infection more likely. Occasionally, children insert something into the vagina, which can cause an infection.

Vulvovaginitis can also be caused by irritants, such as soaps or bubble baths, or a persistent threadworm infection.

WHAT'S THE TREATMENT?

Inflammation can often be improved if your daughter washes with water or a soap substitute, avoids bubble baths, and wears loose-fitting clothes (see left). However, if symptoms persist or are severe, take your child to the doctor who may prescribe an antibiotic cream. Correct wiping after using the toilet will help prevent recurrences.

TOP TIP

To prevent irritation and possible infection of the vulva and vagina, rinse the vaginal area well with clear water and a hand held sprayer when a bath is finished.

Nervous system and hormonal disorders

The nervous system consists of the brain and spinal cord and all the nerves that travel throughout the body. Disorders affecting this system can be serious and the articles in this group emphasize the importance of recognizing symptoms that require medical attention. For example, headaches are normally short-lived and often a result of muscle tension, but in some cases they may indicate a serious underlying disorder, such as inflammation of tissues around the brain.

Hormones are chemicals that control a large number of body functions. If too much or too little of a hormone is produced or cells are unable to react to a hormone, effects on the body can be widespread. For example, in diabetes mellitus there is either a problem in the production of the hormone insulin, produced by the pancreas, or the body is resistant to its effects, meaning that cells cannot absorb glucose, which they need for energy.

Headache

Children often get headaches and in most cases, they are not a cause for concern. However, you need to know when a headache could be a symptom of something more serious.

WHAT ARE THE CAUSES?
Headaches often accompany an infectious illness such as a cold or sinusitis and these get better when the illness improves. If your child has recurrent headaches not related to illness, these may be migraines (see opposite) or tension headaches. Rarely, a headache is a symptom of a serious underlying condition, such as a brain tumour, pressure inside the head due to a head injury, or meningitis.

Tension headaches can have various causes including stress or anxiety, poor posture leading to tightness of the neck and head muscles, noise, tiredness, caffeine (often from hot chocolate or cola), certain foods, hunger, and dehydration. Visual problems, such as short sight or astigmatism, can also lead to headaches, caused by tightness in the muscles in the face and scalp as a result of frowning or screwing up the face to see.

SHOULD I SEE A DOCTOR?
If your child has symptoms that could indicate a serious disorder (see right), seek medical help at once. Otherwise, if your child gets regular headaches, see your doctor to make sure there is no underlying cause and see an optician for an eye test.

WHAT'S THE OUTLOOK?
With good management, tension headaches can be kept to a minimum. Headaches caused by vision problems should disappear once these are treated.

Possible symptoms

Tension headache:

- ★ Feeling of pressure or tightness, generally on both sides of the head
- ★ No nausea and vomiting, and pain not made worse by physical activity – unlike migraine

The following may indicate a headache due to a serious underlying disorder:

- ★ Headache wakes child up or is worse in the morning
- ★ Headache is worse on lying flat, straining (such as during a bowel movement), coughing, or sneezing
- ★ Fever, neck stiffness, and rash
- ★ Double vision
- ★ Change in personality or confusion
- ★ Difficulty waking child up
- ★ Persistent vomiting

What can I do to help?

Giving painkillers should relieve the pain of most headaches. If your child gets regular headaches, you may want to keep a food, activity, and symptom diary to help identify what triggers them.

Relieve pain You can treat your child's headache with painkillers such as paracetamol or ibuprofen.

Give plenty of fluids Drinking enough fluids and eating regularly can help to prevent tension-type headaches.

Talk about worries Encourage your child to let you know of any worries or stresses she has that you could help with.

Migraine

Up to 1 in 10 children suffers from migraines, which are a type of recurrent headache. They can have a significant effect on a child's life, by causing frequent absence from school, for example.

The cause of migraines is unknown, but triggers include certain foods, such as chocolate or cheese, food additives, exercise, stress, strong smells, and tiredness. Migraine attacks can last from 30 minutes to 48 hours. Painkillers can help but if they don't, your doctor can prescribe other medication. He or she may also prescribe medicines to help with nausea or vomiting during a migraine. If your child gets regular or severe migraines, which stop her doing normal activities such as going to school, enjoying hobbies, or seeing friends, your doctor can prescribe medication to prevent attacks. About half of children with migraines stop having them by the time they reach puberty.

Possible symptoms

- ★ Warning signs (aura) before the attack, such as seeing zig-zag lines or getting pins and needles
- ★ Bad headache, felt on one or both sides of the head, which may throb
- ★ Sharp pain that may be severe enough to stop the child from doing normal activities
- ★ Nausea and/or vomiting
- ★ Dislike of light and/or noise

What can I do to help?

You can try to prevent attacks by avoiding triggers. If there are signs that an attack is imminent, encourage your child to lie down and rest to prevent a migraine from developing.

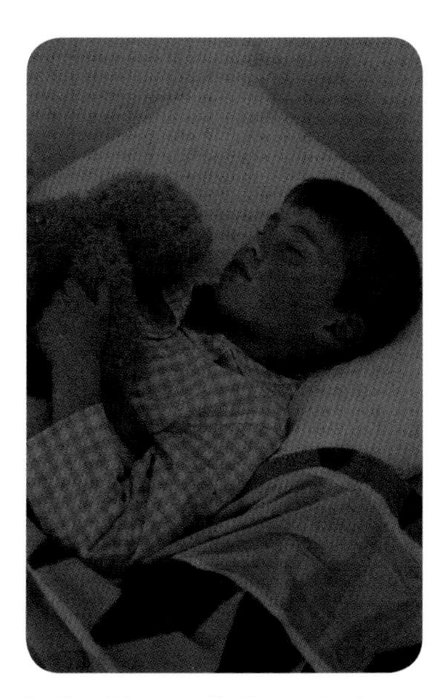

Darken his room During a migraine your child may like to lie down in a dark, quiet room. A sleep can help.

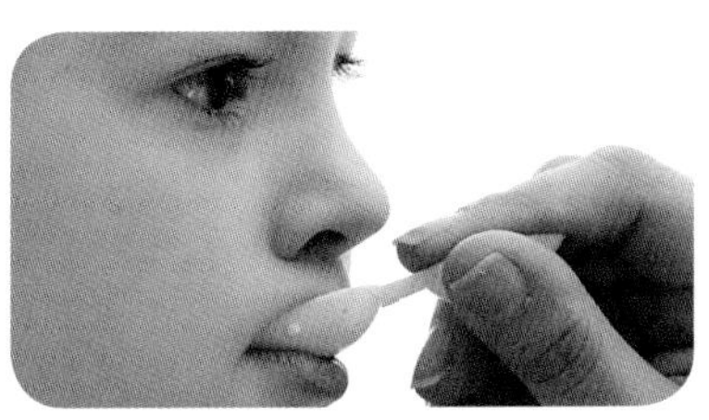

Relieve pain Paracetamol or ibuprofen is often effective in relieving the pain and discomfort of a migraine attack.

Discuss worries Talking to your child and/or his teachers about any problems may help relieve stress and avoid migraines.

Keep a diary You could make a food/activity and symptom diary to try to find any triggers for your child's migraine.

Give plenty of fluids Drinking enough fluids and eating regularly and healthily can help to prevent migraines.

Head injury

Bumps and blows to the head are extremely common in children who are very active and may have little fear or sense of danger. Although most head injuries are minor, you need to be aware of signs that could indicate something more serious.

WHAT ARE THE CAUSES?

There are many situations in which children can sustain head injuries: falling out of bed or a cot, tripping on stairs, or even when playing in the playground, for [illegible]

SHOULD I SEE A DOCTOR?

Fortunately, the brain is very well-protected within the bones of the skull, so most head injuries are minor and do not require treatment, but if you are concerned seek medical advice. A more severe head injury can cause bleeding within the skull, which could lead to brain damage. Call an ambulance or take your child to the nearest accident and emergency department if she has any danger signs of a potentially serious head injury (see right). If your child goes to hospital, she may have a brain scan; treatment will depend on the type of injury.

What can I do to help?

Call an ambulance if you suspect a serious head injury (see right). For a minor injury, you can let your child rest but observe her for the next 48 hours to check that her symptoms do not worsen.

Encourage rest Your child may be tired from crying or from distress.

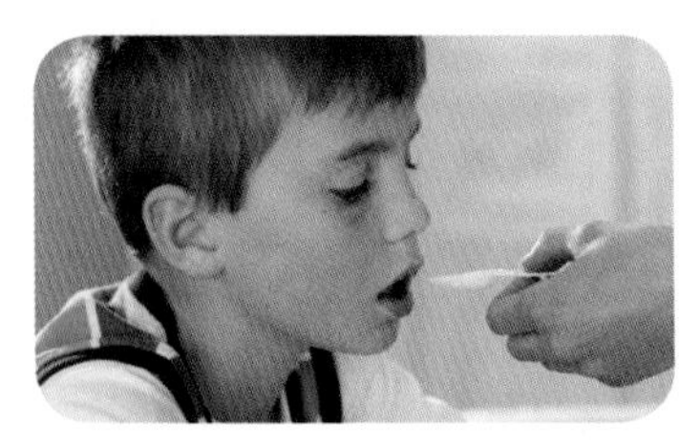

Relieve pain You can give paracetamol or ibuprofen to treat any pain.

Keep watch Wake your child an hour or so after she has gone to sleep and at intervals during the night. If she becomes increasingly drowsy and harder to wake or develops any of the other danger signs (see right), take her to hospital or call an ambulance.

Possible symptoms

Minor head injury:

- ★ Bruise on the head
- ★ Bump or lump on the head, which may be tender
- ★ Nausea
- ★ Headache, which is generally mild
- ★ Dizziness, which is generally mild

Danger signs of a potentially serious head injury:

- ★ Vomiting on two or more occasions
- ★ Headache that is severe, or lasts longer than six hours after the injury
- ★ Loss of consciousness, for a short or longer period of time (a child who cries immediately after hitting her head has not lost consciousness)
- ★ Abnormal drowsiness, or sleepiness that persists hours after the injury
- ★ Severe dizziness
- ★ Pupils of unequal size
- ★ Bloody or yellowish/straw-coloured fluid coming from the nose or ears
- ★ Confusion or memory difficulties
- ★ Blurred or double vision
- ★ Slurred speech
- ★ Changes in hearing
- ★ Seizure

IS IT PREVENTABLE?

Many head injuries occur as accidents during normal play, but you can help to prevent them by following sensible safety precautions. Your child should wear a properly fitting cycle helmet every time she cycles. You should also childproof your home, for example by installing stairgates at the top and bottom of stairs and making sure that windows have locks to prevent children from climbing out of them. Only allow your child to use swings and slides appropriate to her age group.

Febrile convulsions

Febrile convulsions are seizures that sometimes occur in children who have a high fever due to an infection. They most commonly affect children aged between 6 months and 6 years and often occur during the first day of the illness.

Possible symptoms:

- ★ Stiffening of the body
- ★ Loss of consciousness
- ★ Twitching of arms and legs
- ★ Passing urine and/or faeces
- ★ Foaming at the mouth
- ★ Bitten tongue
- ★ After the seizure, drowsiness; child may sleep for about an hour

WHAT ARE THE CAUSES?

The cause of febrile convulsions is not clear. Although they occur with a high fever, they may not be caused by the fever as keeping a child's temperature down does not prevent them. They do run in families, however, so if you or your partner had febrile convulsions as a child it is more likely that your child may have them. This is not the same as having epilepsy, in which recurrent seizures occur without a fever, nor does having febrile convulsions mean that your child will develop epilepsy.

In most cases, febrile convulsions last less than 15 minutes and do not recur during the child's infection. If a seizure lasts longer than 15 minutes and it recurs several times during the infection it can indicate a more serious illness.

SHOULD I SEE A DOCTOR?

If the seizure lasts less than 5 minutes and your child recovers fully within a few minutes, no treatment is needed for the convulsion itself. Treatment may be needed for the infection that is causing the fever however, so seek medical advice.

Call an ambulance or take your child to the nearest accident and emergency department if this is the first time your child has had a seizure, a seizure lasts longer than 5 minutes, or you are worried that your child is not recovering normally after a seizure.

In hospital, if your child is still having a seizure, medication can be given to stop it. Children with a first febrile convulsion are often seen by a paediatrician, who can teach the parents about the seizures and what to do when they occur. Parents are sometimes given the medication used to prevent seizures for use at home in case their child has a seizure lasting for more than 5 minutes. In cases where the seizures last longer than 5 minutes, the cause of the child's illness will be investigated. Tests may include blood and urine tests to look for an source of the infection, and sometimes an EEG (electroencephalogram), which looks at the brain's activity. Treatment given will depend on what is found.

WHAT'S THE OUTLOOK?

Of the children who have had a febrile convulsion, about a third will have another febrile convulsion with another fever-inducing illness in the future. Recurrence is more likely if the first febrile convulsion occurred when your child was less than 18 months old, the seizure was prolonged, or you have a family history of febrile convulsions or epilepsy. Only 1 in 10 children who have had a febrile convulsion will have three or more in the future. Febrile convulsions do not cause any serious damage to the child and the risk of long-term complications is very low. A small minority go on to develop epilepsy.

What can I do to help?

While your child is having a seizure, do not try to restrain her or stop the jerking movements, and do not try to put anything in her mouth. You can take measures to bring down a fever, but there is no proof that this prevents febrile convulsions.

1 Stay with your child. Remove from the area objects that might hurt her. She may be safest on the floor with cushions on either side.

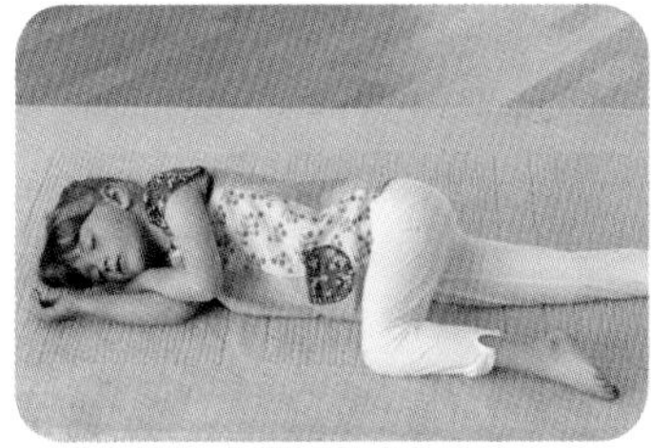

2 When the seizure has finished place your child in the recovery position (see p.212) to prevent choking when she is unconscious.

Diabetes mellitus

In diabetes mellitus (type 1), levels of sugar (glucose) in the blood are too high due to an autoimmune condition in which the body attacks its own tissues. Children usually have type 1 diabetes, although type 2, related to obesity, is on the increase.

Possible symptoms

- ★ Constant thirst
- ★ Passing urine very frequently
- ★ Tiredness
- ★ Weight loss (although appetite may increase)

WHAT ARE THE CAUSES?

When we eat, glucose is released into the bloodstream and then used by cells in the body for energy. In diabetes mellitus, cells in the pancreas are destroyed and they stop making the hormone insulin, which is necessary for the body cells to use and store glucose. In type 2 diabetes, the pancreas still produces insulin, but either it cannot produce enough, or the insulin it produces doesn't work properly. The effects of both types of diabetes is the same: because cells are not taking in glucose they cannot produce energy, and there is a build-up of glucose in the blood. This is then excreted in frequent, large volumes of urine, causing your child to be thirsty. The cause of type 1 diabetes is not yet known, although there is probably a genetic factor among others, such as viral infections. Type 2 diabetes is related to lifestyle factors, such as poor diet and lack of exercise, which lead to obesity.

Feeling thirsty A common symptom of diabetes is increased thirst, making your child want to drink all the time.

SHOULD I SEE A DOCTOR?

If you are concerned that your child has diabetes, seek medical advice from your doctor, who can test for glucose levels in your child's blood. If your child is diagnosed with diabetes, he may be admitted to hospital for a few days so the condition and its treatment can be explained. A hospital usually has its own paediatric diabetic team consisting of a paediatrician who may have a particular interest in diabetes, a specialist nurse, a dietician, and often a child psychologist. A diagnosis of diabetes will have a significant impact on the lives of both your child and the whole family.

WHAT'S THE TREATMENT?

Type 1 diabetes is treated using injections of insulin, with the aim of keeping blood sugar levels as normal as possible.

There are different types of insulins: short-acting insulins need to be given frequently throughout the day (for example, three or four times a day), while longer-acting insulins may only need to be given once a day. The amount of insulin required will change according to various factors, such as what your child eats, whether he is unwell (for example, with a cold), and how much exercise he is taking. If his blood sugar level goes too high it can make your child unwell. If blood sugar becomes too low, it can cause symptoms such as shaking, sweating, and dizziness, which, if not treated, can be life-threatening. High blood sugar levels are treated with insulin, low blood sugar levels are treated with glucose – for example by eating something sugary, or with other medication.

Type 2 diabetes is controlled through eating a healthy diet, regular exercise, and sometimes oral medication.

WHAT'S THE OUTLOOK?

Type 1 diabetes is a life-long condition that is controlled using insulin. Type 2 diabetes may improve with weight reduction. Keeping blood glucose levels as normal as possible prevents long-term complications that can affect organs such as the kidneys or eyes, or the nervous system.

Importance of exercise Eating healthily and exercising can keep your child's weight healthy, decreasing the risk of type 2 diabetes.

What can I do to help?

If your child is diagnosed with diabetes, you or your child (depending on his age) will have to take a sample of his blood, which can be done using an automatic pricking device, to test his sugar levels at various intervals throughout the day. You'll need to inform your child's school or nursery, as he may need to have injections while there and may need permission to have snacks in class. Anyone who cares for your child – grandparents, babysitters, friends' parents – need to be informed.

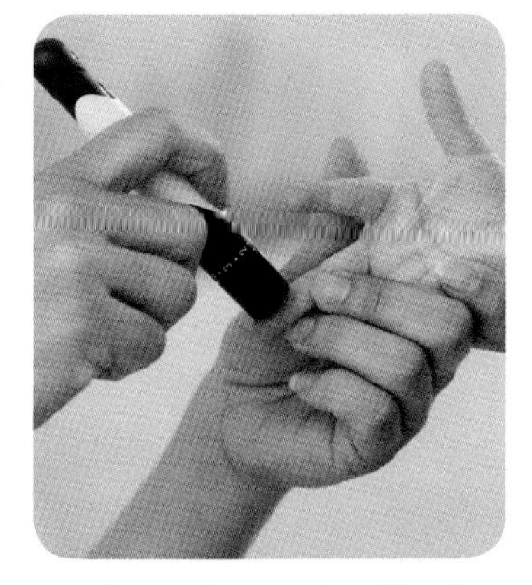

1 **To obtain a sample** of blood, prick the side of your child's finger, then squeeze the finger gently until a blob of blood appears.

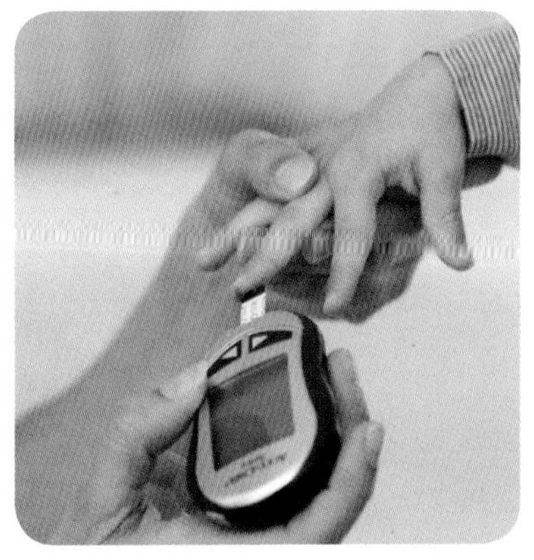

2 **Insert a test paper** into the testing machine, then hold your child's finger so blood transfers onto it. The blood sugar level appears on the screen.

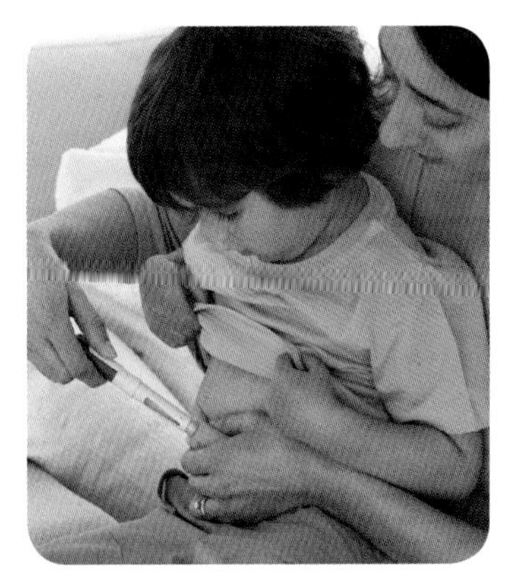

3 **Inject the insulin** using an insulin pen – you will be taught how to decide how much, using the blood sugar readings you have taken.

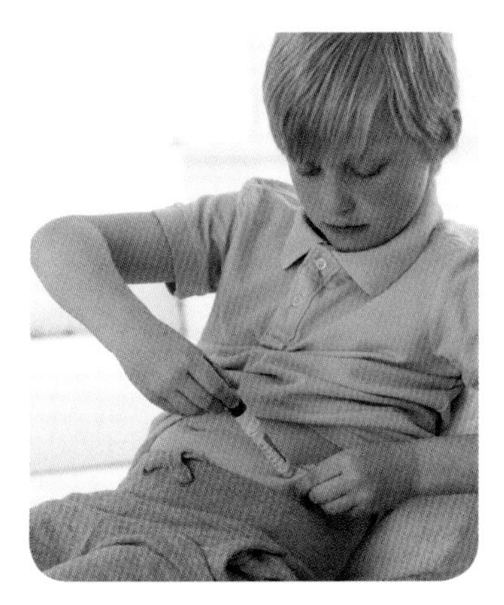

Giving his own injection An older child can take a blood sample and test it, then give his own injection, although he will still need supervision.

Boost glucose levels If your child has any symptoms of low blood sugar, such as sweating, shaking or dizziness, she should eat something sweet straight away.

Provide a healthy diet A child with diabetes needs a healthy diet, consisting of carbohydrates, fats, and proteins, with lots of fruit, vegetables, and fluids.

Short stature

The term short stature describes a child who is shorter than average, taking into account age, gender, and ethnicity. It is not a disease and may not even be a symptom of a disease.

WHAT ARE THE CAUSES?

In the developing world, the most common cause of short stature is malnutrition. In developed countries, short stature often runs in the family: two short parents are likely to have a [illegible]. Such children are growing at an appropriate rate and start puberty at the appropriate time. Short stature can also be caused by a long-term disorder such as inflammatory bowel disease, by hormone disorders such as growth hormone deficiency (rare), or by genetic conditions such as Down's syndrome. Some children have short stature initially, but grow quickly during puberty (constitutional growth delay).

SHOULD I SEE A DOCTOR?

If you are concerned about your child's height, visit your doctor. Her height and weight may be measured over a period of time. Blood tests and X-rays may be performed to assess her bone age and to try to find a cause for the short stature.

KEY FACT

To predict how tall your child will be, add both parents' heights (in centimetres or inches) then add 13cm (5in) for boys and subtract it for girls. Divide by 2 to get your result.

Treatment may be offered depending on whether a cause is found.

WHAT CAN I DO?

Short stature can cause problems with self-confidence and can lead to bullying, so encourage your child to talk about any problems she may be having.

Precocious puberty

During puberty, various physical and emotional changes take place as the body becomes capable of reproduction. In precocious puberty, these changes take place abnormally early.

Possible symptoms

- ★ Pubic hair development
- ★ Underarm hair development
- ★ Growth spurt
- ★ Body odour or acne
- ★ Growth of testes and penis in boys
- ★ Breast development in girls

WHAT ARE THE CAUSES?

Hormones in the brain stimulate the ovaries in girls and the testes in boys to produce oestrogen and testosterone. These hormones then cause the physical changes that occur in puberty, such as growth of pubic and underarm hair.

The average age for a girl to start puberty is around age 10 to 11 years, and the first signs are generally breast changes. The average for a boy to start puberty is around 12 to 13 years, with the testes enlarging in size. These ages are approximate as children from different ethnic backgrounds may start puberty at different ages. Afro-Caribbean girls, for example, enter puberty earlier than Caucasian girls. In many cases, the cause of precocious puberty is unknown, but it can be due to a disorder that affects hormone production. If your child is obese, she may enter puberty earlier than the average age.

SHOULD I SEE A DOCTOR?

If your child is a girl younger than 8 or a boy younger than 9 and has signs of puberty (see Possible symptoms, right) then take her or him to your doctor for an assessment. Blood tests may be carried out. Some girls develop breasts and some children develop pubic hair without having any other signs of precocious puberty. This may not require any treatment. If a cause for the precocious puberty is found, it may be treated, otherwise treatment is usually only given if it is thought that early puberty is going to cause problems in later life – for example, if it is predicted that it would mean the child will be short. Treatment involves medication to block the hormones that are causing puberty.

Developmental and behavioural conditions

The conditions in this section include minor behavioural problems such as difficulties going to sleep, habits such as nail biting, and common anxieties and fears such as separation anxiety. These often respond to self-help measures and many children do grow out of them. Another problem is failure to reach the expected stages in speech development, and in this case parents need to be aware when it may be advisable to seek medical advice. Similarly, stuttering can be a normal part of acquiring language but if it persists may need treatment.

Tics are involuntary muscle contractions that don't usually need treatment in young children as they often disappear with time. Children with dyspraxia (problems coordinating movements) and dyslexia (reading and writing difficulties) often benefit from professional help. The last two conditions discussed here – ADHD (attention deficit hyperactivity disorder) and autistic spectrum disorders – affect many aspects of development and behaviour. Various types of therapy and sometimes medication can help.

Sleep problems

Children under 6 are most likely to have sleep problems, although older children can have them, too. These problems are not usually serious and most of them are temporary.

WHAT ARE THE TYPES?

The most common sleep problem in young children, and one that parents struggle most to cope with, is not sleeping. The problem may be either not going to sleep, or else waking up during the night or very early in the morning. In older children, the main problems are nightmares, night terrors and, less commonly, sleepwalking.

★ **Not sleeping** While new parents expect a new baby to wake regularly through the night, they hope that he will soon settle down and start sleeping in a more regular pattern. Often this takes longer than expected but, by the age of 2, many children have developed a good sleep routine. After this age, any of the following can be considered a sleep problem:

Feeling frightened Your child may wake up frightened if she has a nightmare. Let her tell you about it if she wants to and reassure her there's nothing to be scared of.

★ Taking more than 30 minutes to get to sleep
★ Refusing to sleep unless a parent is nearby or only sleeping when in parents' bed
★ Waking three or four times in the night
★ Staying awake for more than 20 minutes at a time when waking up at night
★ Children who have difficulties getting to sleep or staying asleep may also have tantrums around bedtime.

If your child normally sleeps through the night but doesn't when he is teething or unwell, this is not a sleep problem.

There are several things you can do to help your child develop a better sleep routine (see box, opposite). If problems continue, talk to your doctor or health visitor, who can give you advice or may be able to refer you to a local children's sleep specialist or clinic.

★ **Nightmares** Most children (and adults) have occasional nightmares – scary vivid dreams from which they may wake in distress and needing comfort. Usually these need no treatment but they may be a sign of anxiety or stress, so do check if your child is worrying about anything.

★ **Night terrors** A child with night terrors starts screaming as if terrified, generally about an hour or so after going to sleep. Although the child's eyes may be open, he is not awake, even if sitting or standing up. The child does not appear to recognize his parents or carers and generally can't be comforted. If woken, he may be confused.

Night terrors can be rather distressing to observe but there is little you can do apart from being with your child. You do not need to wake him. After about 20 minutes, the night terror subsides and he will go back into a normal sleep. He will not remember the night terror in the morning. Night terrors are most common in children between the ages of 4 and 12, and they usually outgrow them in time.

Early riser Many children wake up early in the morning and will not go back to sleep, wanting you to play with them instead.

★ **Sleepwalking** A child who sleepwalks gets out of bed while still fast asleep and walks around or performs an activity, such as getting dressed or going to the toilet. Although the child's eyes will be open, he is not awake. Sleepwalking can occur at any age, and may be more frequent if a child is tired, stressed, or anxious.

Children may grow out of sleepwalking but in the meantime make sure that your child is safe when he sleepwalks. This may involve checking that doors and windows are locked at night and that there is a stairgate at the top of any stairs. If you do see your child sleepwalking, you don't need to wake him up, instead gently guide him back to bed.

What can I do to help?

One of the most important ways to help a child who either won't go to sleep or wakes in the night is to establish a regular bedtime routine. You can also try behavioural sleep training techniques, which can be very successful. Ask for advice about these from your doctor or health visitor.

Encourage exercise Make sure that your child gets some exercise during the day, out in the fresh air if possible, so that she is physically tired at night.

Run a calming bath A quiet, soothing bath before your child goes to bed should help him settle down and make it easier for him to go to sleep.

Read a bedtime story A regular story before bed will make your child aware that it is winding-down time. Avoid active games before bed.

Block out light If your child is an early riser, lined curtains or black-out blinds can help prevent him from being woken up by the morning light.

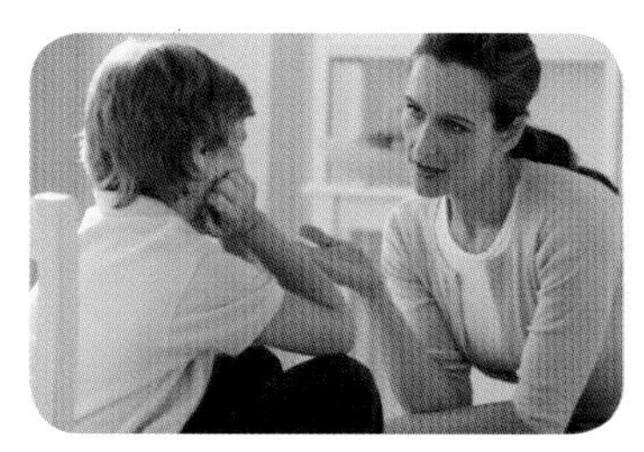

Talk about anxieties A child who is having trouble sleeping may be worried about something. Talk to your child to see if anything is bothering him; you could also talk to his teachers.

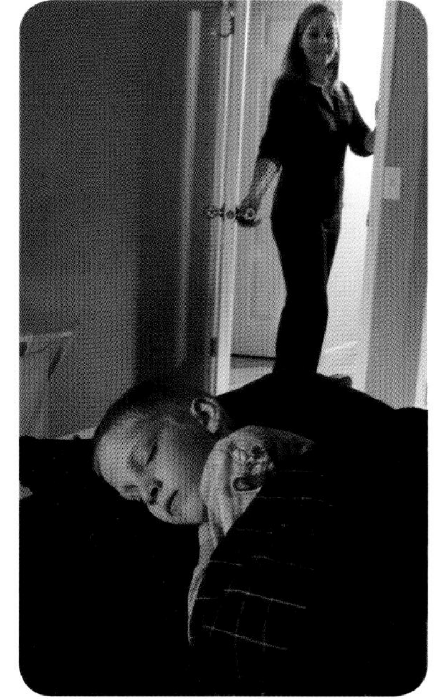

Withdraw gradually This technique is used for children who will only sleep with a parent in the room. Start in your normal position on day 1, and each night gradually start further away as your child goes to sleep.

Leave her distracting toys If your child always wakes up early in the morning, put some toys in her cot or bed (make sure they're safe) for her to play with quietly until it is time to get up.

Bad habits

Repetitive habits are common in children and may be a way of relieving anxiety or boredom, or can occur if a child is angry or frustrated. Most of these habits are not harmful and will be outgrown.

WHAT ARE THE TYPES?
Repetitive behaviour can take lots of different forms. Some of the most common bad habits are discussed below.

Head banging This is common and usually occurs between the ages of 6 months and 4 years: the child repetitively bangs her head, for example against the mattress or side of her cot or bed. Up to 1 in 5 children head bang at some point. Although extremely distressing to watch, babies and children will not cause any damage to themselves by head banging – if it hurts them, they will stop. Instead, it is thought that children head bang as a way of relaxing or soothing themselves. They often do it before going to sleep, or if they are in pain, as with teething, for example. Head banging can be associated with other developmental conditions, but is not of concern if it is the only symptom and if, for the remainder of the day, your child is happy, appears healthy, and is developing appropriately. A calming night routine may be of some benefit. Rest assured that your child will grow out of head banging.

★ **Breath-holding attacks** About 3 in 100 children have breath-holding attacks, in which, after crying, they hold their breath. An affected child may turn red or blue and may lose consciousness for a short period. The cause of these attacks is not known, but they may be triggered by anger or pain, for example if a child falls over and hurts herself, or they may occur after a fright. The tendency to have breath-holding attacks runs in families.

If your child has a breath-holding attack try to stay calm: remember that your child will start breathing again on her own. You may be able to identify when an attack is likely to happen and take action to prevent it. For example, if your child has attacks when she is frustrated, if you can anticipate this and distract her by changing activities, you may be able to prevent one.

Breath-holding attacks usually improve on their own; however, if your child's attacks are becoming more frequent or if there is any shaking during the period of unconsciousness, see your doctor.

Nail biting A child may bite her nails as way of dealing with anxiety. It can be a difficult habit to break.

What can I do?

A child who head bangs does not generally cause any damage, but if you are worried then you might like to place cushioning around his cot or bed to protect him.

Soft padding You could pad the cot or bed if your child is a head banger, but be sure padding is secure so your child doesn't get caught up in it. Check your child's cot or bed regularly to make sure that the motion has not caused any screws or fixings to become loose.

★ **Hair pulling** Children with this habit twist and pull on their hair, usually on their heads although in severe cases they can pull out eyelashes and eyebrow hairs.

If hair pulling starts before the age of 5, it is usually mild and improves on its own within a few months. It can lead to bald patches but these grow back after the behaviour stops. It is thought that young children pull hair as a method of relaxing or soothing themselves so it may start, for example, with the stress of starting a new school. Do not tell your child off for hair pulling; just ignore it and try to keep your child calm, perhaps by introducing a relaxing bedtime routine. Hair pulling may be associated with thumb sucking. If this is the case, then stopping the thumb sucking may stop the hair pulling. See your doctor if hair pulling is severe or if it doesn't stop within a few months.

★ **Nail biting** Children, as well as adults, usually bite their nails to relieve stress or boredom. The nails or cuticles can be bitten, and fingers can become sore and prone to infection. Try to stop the habit, but don't draw attention to it by telling your child off. Instead praise her when she doesn't bite her nails. See if you can find any triggers for nail biting – for example, does she only bite her nails when anxious? If so, then finding other ways of relieving anxiety may help stop the nail biting. Some children are not really aware that they are biting their nails; in this case, using a bitter-tasting nail polish may help. If you think your child may have an infection in her fingers, see your doctor.

★ **Thumb sucking** Many babies and young children suck their thumbs or fingers for comfort. It is not harmful as long as it stops before the baby teeth are lost. If it continues, it can lead to buck teeth in adulthood. If your child hasn't stopped on her own by the time the milk teeth have fallen out, you might try a reward system, such as a star chart, to encourage her. Some children may suck almost without realizing it so putting a plaster on the finger may remind them.

Thumb sucking Young children often find it comforting to suck their thumbs when they are going to sleep.

Anxiety and fears

It is normal for children to experience anxiety and fears; indeed they can be a safeguard. They are only a problem when they impact on your child's life, such as if worries about school lead to refusal to attend.

Anxious child Comfort your child and talk to her with calm reassurance when she's afraid of something.

WHAT ARE THE CAUSES?

Separation anxiety is common in babies and toddlers, who become distressed when their parents or carers leave because they are afraid they won't come back. Other common fears in children include being scared of the dark, thunder, or some other specific thing or situation. Most children grow out of these fears as they get older.

WHAT CAN I DO?

To help a child with separation anxiety, reassure her you will come back if you have to leave her (to go to work, for example) then say goodbye and go. Remember that it's unlikely that she will cry for more than a few minutes. Be consistent. If you tell her when you will be back, make sure you are back when you said you would be.

Never belittle or disregard a child's fears. Instead, take them seriously and try to help her to deal with them. Simply recognizing and talking about a fear can help. Your child should not necessarily avoid triggers as this could reinforce her fears. If, for example, she is scared of cats then don't avoid all animals but support her in her experiences of them. In some cases she may not be ready to deal with the feared situation, so don't force her.

WHAT IS THE OUTLOOK?

Most children grow out of anxieties and fears. However, if these do not fade, if they are stopping your child from doing normal activities, or if you are at all concerned about her, see your doctor.

Possible symptoms

- ★ Becoming clingy
- ★ Difficulties getting to sleep
- ★ Tummy aches
- ★ Feeling sick
- ★ Getting sweaty or clammy
- ★ Rapid breathing or pulse rate
- ★ Wanting to avoid the cause of anxiety

Speech delay

Delay in speaking may occur because a child is physically unable to produce words or because he cannot understand or process speech. Children develop speech at different rates, but certain language skills are expected, depending on age.

WHAT ARE THE CAUSES?

Speech delay may be caused by a physical condition affecting the mouth or palate or by decreased hearing (commonly due to glue ear). It can also occur because a child's parents do not speak enough around him or, possibly, because a child is being brought up bilingually. A child who does not communicate – even non-verbally – for example by making signs or taking you by the hand to show you want he wants, may have autistic spectrum disorder.

SHOULD I SEE A DOCTOR?

The symptoms listed (see right) are only some of the indications of possible speech delay. If you have any concerns about your child's speech development, then see your doctor or health visitor. Your child will be referred for a hearing test and often to a speech and language therapist for assessment. The therapist will assess what your child can say as well as what he is able to understand, and may then be able to treat your child.

Possible symptoms

- ★ By 1 year: does not communicate with physical gestures such as waving or shaking his head; does not understand simple instructions; no babbling
- ★ By 2 years: does not imitate actions or words; cannot point to pictures in a book when asked; cannot join two words together (for example, "all done"); has vocabulary of fewer than about 20 words
- ★ By 3 years: cannot be understood by others at least 50 per cent of the time; cannot speak in short phrases; cannot follow instructions
- ★ By 4 years: not yet almost 100 per cent understandable
- ★ By 5 years: still stutters frequently when attempting to produce a sound

What can I do to help?

The best way to help your child's speech develop is to talk to him as much as possible. Speak clearly, use gestures to reinforce meaning, and songs and rhymes to make learning fun. Reading regularly to your child is also important to help development of vocabulary and language.

Pronounce words If your child speaks but with errors, for example saying "wawa" for "water", repeat the word correctly, saying "water". Then answer her: "Yes, Mummy will get some water."

Use words and pictures One way to encourage your child to speak is to point to pictures in a book and ask him to tell you what he sees. Or you could ask him to tell you about what's on the page.

Name objects Help your child to recognize words by asking him to name what he can see in the street when out for a walk. You could also point to things and ask him to tell you what they are.

Stuttering

A disruption to the flow of speech is known as stuttering or stammering. Many young children stutter as part of normal speech development, but if stuttering persists beyond the age of 5, speech therapy may be needed.

WHAT IS THE CAUSE?

Many children between the ages of 2 and 5 stutter over words as they acquire language because they are not yet physically able to form the sounds. This usually stops by the age of 5. The cause of persistent stuttering is not known, but it often runs in families. The degree of severity is variable.

SHOULD I SEE A DOCTOR?

If your child has not stopped stuttering by the age of 5, or if stuttering is accompanied by tics at a younger age, then visit your doctor. Your child may be referred to a speech and language therapist for assessment and help.

WHAT CAN I DO?

If your child has a stutter, slow down your own speech when you are talking to him and give him plenty of time and space to talk. Avoid interrupting your child when he stutters, telling him to hurry up, or anticipating what he is trying to say.

Maintain eye contact with your child when you are having a conversation. Even if you are upset or frustrated by his stuttering, try not to show it. If your child feels anxious about speaking, his symptoms may get worse. Don't forget to praise your child when he speaks fluently.

Possible symptoms

- ★ **Repetition:** this can be of sounds, consonants, vowels, words, or phrases; for example "I, I, I, I, I, I, don't want to", "I d,d,d,d,d,don't want to", "I don't want, don't want, don't want to"
- ★ **Blocks:** these are pauses in speech where the child is silent; he may seem to be struggling to get his words out; for example, "That's mm….ine!"
- ★ **Prolongation or stretching of words or parts of words:** for example, "Caaaaaaaaan I come?"

Tics

A tic is a repetitive, involuntary, quick muscle contraction with no purpose. Tics in children are usually transient, lasting for only a few months.

WHAT ARE THE TYPES?

Tics may be either motor tics, in which the contractions produce a movement, or vocal tics in which a sound is produced. Common motor tics are blinking, jerking the head, shrugging the shoulders, and twitching of facial muscles. Vocal tics include coughing, grunting, sniffing, and clearing the throat.

About 1 in 10 children between the ages of 6 and 9 are affected by transient tics at some point. Such tics are often more pronounced when a child is tired or under stress. Less common are chronic tics, which persist for at least a year. An even more troublesome tic disorder is Tourette's syndrome, in which there are many vocal and motor tics and, in a very few children, outbursts of uncontrollable cursing.

SHOULD I SEE A DOCTOR?

If your child has a tic that occurs very regularly, or is becoming more severe or frequent, or is changing, see your doctor. Tics can be treated with medication if they are severe although the medication can have side-effects.

WHAT CAN I DO?

If your child suffers from a tic, he may feel embarrassed about it, have low self-esteem or be bullied at school, so encourage him to talk to you about his feelings.

Don't ask your child to stop the tic. The action is involuntary, and he has no control over it. If you draw attention to the tic, he may become stressed about it, which may make it worse. Instead, reassure your child that it is fine to have a tic and that it will probably go away in time.

WHAT'S THE OUTLOOK?

Most tics disappear on their own. In about half of children with Tourette's syndrome, the tics improve greatly during the teenage and early adult years, although they do not disappear completely.

Dyspraxia

In this type of learning difficulty, children have difficulties coordinating their movements. Children with dyspraxia are often described as clumsy.

The cause of dyspraxia is not known but it is thought to be related to the nerves that connect the muscles to the brain. Children with dyspraxia are of normal intelligence. The condition affects up to 1 in 30 children, more commonly boys, with varying severity. Dyspraxia can occur with dyslexia.

If you are worried that your child may have dyspraxia take her to the doctor, who will be able to refer you to a paediatrician, psychologist, or specialist therapist. There are various ways to treat dyspraxia, such as occupational therapy to help your child with daily activities such as dressing, and language therapy to help with speech and communication.

"Clumsy" child Children with dyspraxia often fall over and bump into things, so they are often thought of as clumsy.

Possible symptoms

Young children:

★ Walking, crawling, or speaking later than peers

★ Speech may be hard to understand

School-age children:

★ Difficulties with movements and co-ordination – for example, difficulties kicking a ball, or getting dressed

★ Problems with fine motor control such as tying shoelaces or drawing

★ Difficulties concentrating

★ Difficulties learning new skills

★ Fidgeting or always swinging arms or legs

Soiling

A child who does not use the toilet when passing stool may soil her underwear instead. Soiling is normal in babies and young children but, by the age of 4, most children will be using the toilet or potty.

WHAT ARE THE CAUSES?

Soiling can be the result of long-standing constipation developing into overflow diarrhoea, in which watery stools leak out around hard faeces. Soiling can also be due to the child not going to the toilet regularly or holding it in – for example, if she doesn't want to go at school and then can't wait.

If your child previously had control over her bowels, but starts to pass stool in inappropriate places, such as at the dinner table when she normally would go to the toilet, or if she starts to smear her faeces around, there may be some emotional issues to address.

SHOULD I SEE A DOCTOR?

If your child is soiling after the age of 4, or starts soiling after previously having had control of her bowels, see your doctor. The doctor will examine your child and if he feels the cause of the soiling is overflow diarrhoea, you will be given treatment for this. You may also be given advice about how to encourage better bowel habits and ways to prevent constipation. If this is not thought to be the cause, your child may be referred to a paediatrician.

WHAT CAN I DO?

★ Encourage your child to open her bowels regularly; she should sit on the toilet for 5 minutes after meals and before bed. Praise her when she passes a stool in the toilet.

★ Look for any possible sources of anxiety, such as problems at school, and alleviate them as far as possible. Just talking about worries may be helpful.

★ Give your child a healthy diet that is rich in fibre, consisting of plenty of fresh fruit and vegetables, as well as encouraging her to drink lots of fluids to help keep her bowels regular and prevent constipation.

Dyslexia

Dyslexia is a specific learning difficulty in which a child has problems with reading and writing. Children with dyslexia are of normal intelligence.

WHAT IS THE CAUSE?

When you hear a word spoken out loud you hear the whole word, not the components or sounds that make up the word. To read or write, however, you need to think of how the sounds that make up a word are spelt, which letters are needed, and what they look like on the page. It is thought that children with dyslexia have difficulties with this because of problems relating to the brain's language areas. Dyslexia is the most common type of learning difficulty; it affects up to 1 in 12 schoolchildren. It tends to run in families and is more common in boys. It can occur with dyspraxia (see left).

SHOULD I SEE A DOCTOR?

If you are concerned that your child may have dyslexia speak to her teacher and your doctor, as the earlier a child can obtain treatment, the better. Your doctor will first need to exclude other conditions that may lead to problems with reading and writing. For example, if your child has poor hearing she may not hear the sounds that make up a word. Your child may be referred for further assessment to an educational psychologist.

WHAT'S THE TREATMENT

This includes having extra help and support at school during lessons. There are specific techniques that can help your child process sounds within words, which may then help with reading and writing skills.

WHAT'S THE OUTLOOK?

With treatment, most children go on to develop good reading and writing skills.

Possible symptoms

Infants and young children:

★ Speaking later than normal

★ Muddling up or confusing words in a sentence

★ Little interest in clapping or rhythm games

School-age children:

★ Difficulties learning the names of letters and the sounds letters make

★ Difficulties copying words or letters, for example from the whiteboard

★ Difficulties spelling, often spelling words inconsistently

★ Difficulties understanding how words are constructed or with rhyming words

★ Slow at reading

★ Low self-esteem and behaviour problems

What can I do to help?

You can help your child improve her reading skills by reading with her and encouraging her to read. You may have to go over the same words many times to help her learn. Your child may be embarrassed about needing extra help or become frustrated with herself, so offer emotional support.

Help with reading Set a regular time for reading with your child and talk about it together afterwards.

Use a computer Older children may benefit from using a word processor or computer when doing written work.

Talk to your child Your child may find school very stressful; encourage him to talk to you about his feelings.

ADHD

Children with ADHD (attention deficit hyperactivity disorder) have short attention spans, are easily distracted, and may be overactive and impulsive. The condition can have an extremely harmful effect on their schooling and development.

WHAT ARE THE CAUSES?

The exact cause of ADHD is not known but various factors make it more likely to develop, including genetic predisposition, exposure to cigarettes or alcohol while in the womb, and brain injury. The condition affects about 1 to 2 in every 100 children, and is about four times more common in boys than girls.

SHOULD I SEE A DOCTOR?

All children have a lot of energy and at some point may show some of the symptoms associated with ADHD. If your child has all of the symptoms, or their symptoms are affecting their school performance or social life, then see your doctor. He will refer your child to a paediatrician or a child psychiatrist or psychologist. If your child is diagnosed with ADHD, various treatment options will be discussed with you.

Be sure to speak to your child's school and teacher, as he may be eligible for an assessment by an educational psychologist or extra help in lessons.

TOP TIP

Raising a child with ADHD can be exhausting. If you feel at your wits' end, take a break or seek support. By looking after yourself, you'll be a better parent!

WHAT'S THE TREATMENT?

Treatment for ADHD generally involves a combination of medication and therapy.

★ Medication – this can improve concentration and reduce impulsiveness for a short period. It can be useful in school, for example, so that your child can learn. Your doctors may advise some medication-free periods, for example during the school holidays, to help assess how your child's symptoms are changing over time.

★ Therapy – there are different types of therapy, ranging from traditional talking therapies to behavioural therapies in which

Full of energy Many children with ADHD are hyperactive: they are full of energy, and constantly moving and busy, much more so than a normally active child.

Possible symptoms

Symptoms can occur at any age but often become evident around the time of starting school. There is a wide range of symptoms, but they fall into three general groups:

Inattentiveness:

★ Cannot listen to or obey instructions

★ Easily distracted or unable to concentrate

★ Does not finish tasks or switches activities constantly

★ Loses things

★ Forgets things or instructions

★ Makes careless mistakes, such as in school work

Hyperactivity:

★ Fidgets constantly

★ Talks a lot; finds it difficult to enjoy quiet activities

★ Unable to sit down and concentrate – always running or moving even when expected to sit still, such as when eating at the table

Impulsiveness:

★ Unable to wait for a turn

★ Interrupts others

★ Breaks rules

★ Acts without thinking about the consequences, so may have limited sense of danger

Acting on impulse Children with ADHD will carry out actions without thinking, sometimes upsetting other children.

you and your child are taught methods to control the child's behaviour. Simple methods, such as rewarding good behaviour, can be effective.

★ Diet – some parents find that their child's symptoms are improved by changing what they eat. Do not cut out foods without first speaking to your doctor or dietician as it is important for children to have a wide and varied diet to meet their nutritional needs.

★ Supplements – talk to your doctor before giving your child any supplements. Some parents have found that supplements of omega-3 or certain minerals such as zinc can be effective. However, the evidence regarding these supplements is controversial.

WHAT'S THE OUTLOOK?

There is no cure for ADHD, and the disorder cannot be prevented, but with treatment most symptoms can be controlled. Although up to half of children with ADHD do continue to experience some problems as adults, many adjust to their disorder and lead productive lives.

What can I do to help?

The treatment for your child may involve several techniques for modifying his behaviour, including therapy, reward systems, and exercise. Some parents find that when their child consumes food additives or colouring or sugary foods, symptoms worsen, so modifying diet may also be beneficial.

Support him in therapy sessions You may be asked to attend therapy sessions with your child where he may, for example, be encouraged to make a drawing and then talk about it or to perform a task, such as doing a jigsaw, that helps concentration and attention.

Give rewards Using a simple reward system, such as a star chart, can help to encourage good behaviour.

Keep a diary You could make a food and symptom diary to see if you can find a trigger for your child's symptoms, so that it can be avoided.

Plan regular exercise Frequent, structured exercise or sport is an excellent coping strategy for children with ADHD as it focuses their excess energy and allows them to expend it appropriately.

Autistic spectrum disorders

Autistic spectrum disorders are a range of conditions that affect how a child can communicate and interact with other people. The term "spectrum" is used because the severity of the symptoms can vary between individuals.

Possible symptoms

- ★ Delayed speech or no speech development
- ★ Speech may sound strange – for example, monotonous
- ★ Poor eye contact
- ★ Happier playing alone than with other children
- ★ Not wanting to be cuddled or comforted even when hurt
- ★ Difficulty in understanding other people's feelings
- ★ Difficulties managing own emotions, for example may have angry outbursts
- ★ Repetitive playing with the same toys
- ★ Limited imaginative play
- ★ Repetitive movements, such as flapping
- ★ Extreme sensitivity to sound or touch

WHAT ARE THE TYPES?

Asperger's syndrome and autism are known as autistic spectrum disorders. Asperger's syndrome is at the mildest end of the spectrum and children who have it are of average or above-average intelligence, often with good language skills, although they still have problems with social interaction. Children with autism find it difficult to communicate and interact with others, and they may have learning difficulties.

Repetitive play Many children like to line up toys or other objects, but doing this excessively could signal a problem.

WHAT ARE THE CAUSES?

The cause of autistic spectrum disorders is not known. The measles, mumps, and rubella vaccine is not linked with autism. About 1 in 100 children have an autistic spectrum disorder and boys are more commonly affected than girls.

SHOULD I SEE A DOCTOR?

If you are concerned that your child may have an autistic spectrum disorder, take her to the doctor who will refer her for further assessment, most often by a paediatrician and/or child psychologist.

Treatments focus on improving communication, social interaction, and other skills, such as developing imaginative play. Parents stay closely involved. Therapy generally includes interacting with other children without the disorder. It may also involve developing a routine to be followed, but your child will still be exposed to new environments so that she can develop new skills. Depending on the severity of the condition, your child may require extra support at school or she may need to attend a school for children with similar conditions. Small class sizes are beneficial. Medication can be given to treat specific symptoms, such as aggression or agitation.

There are various complementary treatments for autism but before starting any you should check with your doctor regarding their safety. Specific diets are sometimes suggested but do not change your child's diet or cut out any food groups without first speaking to your doctor.

WHAT'S THE OUTLOOK?

People with Asperger's syndrome are usually able to lead fully independent and productive lives. With treatment, autistic children generally improve, and as adults many are able to lead productive lives, but they will probably need continuing support.

Help with communication A speech and language therapist may encourage you to use a sign language, such as Makaton. Here, parent and child are using the sign for book.

Glossary of other medical conditions

This section includes some of the less common and serious disorders affecting children: some are present from birth (congenital disorders), while others develop later. Most require medical treatment.

Bone infection

This usually occurs when an infection spreads from another site, such as an infected insect bite or wound. It is more common in children aged between 3 and 14 years, although it can affect people of any age. Usually, it is the long bones of the arms or legs that are affected. Bone infection causes fever and pain in the limb, which can be severe, and is sometimes made worse when the limb is touched. Your child may be reluctant to move the limb. The skin over the infected bone may be swollen and red, and may feel hot to the touch.

A child with bone infection needs urgent treatment in hospital. He will be given antibiotics, and occasionally surgery is needed to remove the infected area of bone. If a child hasn't moved a limb for a period of time due to the infection, he may need physiotherapy to help get the limb moving properly again. With prompt treatment, children generally make a good recovery.

Cerebral palsy

Cerebral palsy is a specific problem with muscle control caused by damage to the brain that occurred during pregnancy or birth, or soon after birth. It can lead to abnormalities affecting movement, posture, speech, hearing, and vision. It affects about 1 in every 400 children in the UK.

The symptoms vary according to the part of the brain that is damaged and can take a few months to appear. They commonly include difficulties with walking and problems with coordination and balance. In some cases cerebral palsy is associated with other conditions, such as epilepsy. Children with cerebral palsy usually have a normal range of intelligence. There is no cure, but physiotherapy, occupational therapy, and speech and language therapy are used to treat symptoms.

Cleft lip and palate

This birth defect occurs in about 1 in 600 babies. A cleft lip is a gap in the upper lip which varies in severity from a small notch to a wide gap that runs from the lip to the nose. A cleft palate is a separation in the roof of the mouth (palate). Clefts of the lip and palate can occur separately or together or in combination with other birth defects, and can affect one side of the mouth or both.

The cause of clefts is unknown, but they can run in families and are more likely if the mother smokes, drinks alcohol, or does not take folic acid during pregnancy. A small cleft lip may cause few difficulties, but more severe defects may cause difficulty feeding; speech, language, and dental problems; and sucsceptiblity to ear infections.

Newborns are assessed for cleft lip and palate during their routine check. Treatment involves surgery; your child will be assigned a specialist cleft team that includes doctors, nurses, orthodontists, speech and language therapists, and psychologists. The prognosis depends on how severe the condition is, but most children with only a cleft lip have little scarring and get on well after surgery.

Club foot

About 1 in 1,000 babies is born with club foot, a deformity of the foot and ankle. It is more common in boys than girls and can affect one or both feet. There are two types. In the first, the ankle may be twisted and the foot turns inwards and points down; if both feet are affected the soles touch each other. In the second, the foot turns outwards and upwards. Newborns are assessed for club foot during the routine newborn check. Treatment depends on the severity. In mild cases, it may simply involve doing exercises. If it is more severe, the foot may be gradually manipulated into the correct position and held in place using a series of plaster casts. Surgery can also be used. In most cases, manipulation or surgery successfully corrects club foot.

Congenital heart disease

Any defect in the structure of the heart that is present at birth comes under the heading congenital heart disease. About 1 in every 140 children is born with congenital heart disease, and there are many different types. The most common is a hole in the wall (septum) between the two lower chambers (ventricles) of your baby's heart, known as ventricular septal defect. Another example is failure of a blood vessel called the ductus arteriosus (which allows your baby's circulation to bypass the lungs before birth) to close after your baby is born.

Symptoms of congenital heart disease vary in severity and depend on the specific type of heart defect. They may include blue lips and tongue (cyanosis), heart murmurs, and difficulties breathing and feeding. Your child's heart will be examined before you leave hospital after delivery and again at the 6–8 week check. The treatment and prognosis will depend on the particular type of heart defect. Most ventricular septal defects heal on their own without treatment; other types of heart defect may require surgical treatment.

Cystic fibrosis

Cystic fibrosis is the most common genetic condition in the UK, with more than 8,000 children and adults affected. It is caused by a defect in a gene that controls the amount of salt and water in cells. If not enough water can enter your baby's cells then body fluids turn into thick mucus, which can block up the airways and other tubes in the body. The gene that causes cystic fibrosis is recessive. This means that for a child to have the condition both parents must be carrying the gene. The parents may not know that they carry the gene because you can be a carrier without having symptoms.

Cystic fibrosis affects various organs, such as the lungs and pancreas, causing problems that may include recurrent chest infections, poor growth, and problems with nutrition. There is no cure for cystic fibrosis although treatments such as antibiotics for chest infections, chest physiotherapy, and other medications can help the symptoms. A healthy diet and exercise are also helpful. Research is continuing into the gene that causes this condition.

Developmental dysplasia of the hip

Sometimes known as congenital dislocation of the hip, this is a condition in which the hip joint fails to develop properly so that the head of the thigh bone (femur) does not fit snugly into its socket, making the joint unstable. Hip dysplasia occurs in about 1 in 1,000 babies, and is more common in first-born children, girls, babies who were in a breech presentation in the womb, and those with affected relatives. It most often affects the left hip.

Developmental hip dysplasia is usually present at birth and is tested for by doctors as part of the newborn check and again at the 6–8 week check. If it is not diagnosed at birth, it may not be suspected until your child limps when he starts to walk. The treatment depends on when the condition was diagnosed. Babies under 6 months old generally wear a pelvic harness to hold the hips in the correct position for about 3 months. If the harness is not effective or if your child is older than 6 months when the condition is diagnosed, surgery may be offered.

Down's syndrome

This genetic condition affects about 1 in every 1,000 children in the UK, both girls and boys. People affected by Down's syndrome have three copies of a specific chromosome – chromosome 21 – instead of the usual two copies. The chance of having a baby with Down's syndrome increases with increasing maternal age.

Down's syndrome children usually have characteristic facial features that may include upward-slanting eyes, a flat face and flat back of the head, small mouth with a protruding tongue, and a flattened bridge of the nose. The physical, mental, and social development of children with Down's syndrome is slower than that of other children, although the degree of severity of learning difficulties can vary. Children with Down's syndrome may also have associated problems, such as heart defects, hearing and sight problems, and low thyroid hormone levels, and they are at increased risk of developing conditions such as leukaemia and Alzheimer's disease.

Pregnant women are offered a screening test for Down's syndrome, which generally consists of an ultrasound scan at 12 weeks and a blood test. Depending on the result, a more definitive test called chorionic villus sampling may be offered, in which the genes of the fetus are examined. There is no specific treatment for Down's syndrome but children can be helped by various therapists such as those specializing in speech and language therapy.

Encephalitis

In this rare condition, the brain becomes inflamed, generally as a result of a viral infection. The herpes simplex virus is most commonly responsible, although the viruses that cause measles, rubella (German measles), and chickenpox can also cause encephalitis. In mild cases, symptoms include fever and headache, and resemble those of a mild flu-like illness. These symptoms may improve on their own without any treatment, and you may not even notice them in your child. In more severe cases, symptoms include stiff neck, vomiting, severe headache, confusion, seizures, and drowsiness or coma.

When treated promptly in hospital using antiviral medications such as aciclovir, your child is likely to make a full recovery. Complications can include brain damage, which can cause problems such as learning difficulties, epilepsy, or a change in personality. Vaccinating your child with the MMR virus will protect him from encephalitis caused by the measles virus.

Epilepsy

Children with epilepsy have recurrent episodes of abnormal electrical brain activity that causes seizures or a change in consciousness. The cause of epilepsy is often not known, although it can occur if there has been some damage to the brain for example after an infection or injury.

There are several types of epilepsy. In a common type, seizures are preceded by unusual or irritable behaviour, after which your child will fall to the floor unconscious. During the seizure, there are jerking movements of her body, and she may drool or be incontinent, followed by a period of confusion or drowsiness. Do not restrain your child or attempt to put anything in her mouth during a seizure. Instead, keep her safe by removing any objects in the way and only move her if she is at risk – in the bath, for example. Put her in the recovery position (see p.212) until she regains consciousness.

In another type of epilepsy, absence seizures occur, in which a child stops what she is doing and stares into space, unaware of anything around her, for 10–15 minutes.

Epilepsy is usually treated with medication and can generally be controlled. Most affected children do not have any other disabilities and can go to a mainstream school and participate in most sports.

Fragile X syndrome

This genetic abnormality is the most common inherited cause of learning difficulties among children. A faulty gene on the X chromosome means that a protein required for brain development is either not produced or is produced in insufficient quantities. Boys are usually more severely affected than girls as they have only one X chromosome whereas girls have two and so the non-faulty copy is used to produce the protein. Symptoms include delay in achieving developmental milestones, learning difficulties, and behavioural problems such as hyperactivity. Your child may also have characteristic facial features including long ears, a large jaw, and large testes in boys at puberty. There is no specific treatment for fragile X syndrome, but your child may be helped by therapies such as speech and language therapy and occupational therapy. Support in school will be needed. Some medications can help with behavioural problems.

Glomerulonephritis

The kidneys contain thousands of microscopic structures called glomeruli, which act as filters, allowing the kidneys to clean the blood and control the amount of water in the body. In glomerulonephritis the glomeruli become inflamed so the kidneys do not function properly, allowing waste products, salt, and water to build up in the body. The cause of glomerulonephritis is often unknown, but in children it may occur a few weeks after a throat or skin infection caused by a specific type of strepotococcal bacteria. Nowadays this is a less common cause than it was previously due to the use of antibiotics.

Symptoms are not always present, but may include blood-stained urine, tiredness, vomiting, hiccups, swelling (caused by the accumulation of fluid in tissues), high blood pressure, or seizures. Treatment depends on the cause of the glomerulonephritis but may include restriction of fluids, diuretic medication (to help rid your child's body of excess fluid), a low-salt and protein diet, steroids, and other medications. The condition may be reversible and short-lived, but it can develop into chronic (long-term) kidney failure, which is treated with dialysis or a kidney transplant.

Haemophilia

This is an inherited genetic disorder that affects blood-clotting. There are various types of haemophilia in which different components required to clot blood (clotting factors) are either partially or completely missing. The symptoms and their severity can vary, depending on how severe the deficiency is, but include bruising easily, prolonged bleeding after minor injury, and bleeding into joints or the brain. There is no cure, although if your child is affected he will be given injections of the clotting factor that he is missing. Depending on the severity of the condition, the injections are either given only after an injury or on a regular basis to prevent abnormal bleeding.

Henoch–Schönlein purpura

In Henoch–Schönlein purpura the immune system produces an antibody called IgA, which attacks blood vessels, causing them to become inflamed. It is more common in boys and may develop soon after an upper respiratory tract infection.

Symptoms include a rash of purple spots, typically on the buttocks and lower legs, that does not go away under pressure; joint swelling and pain; and abdominal pain. There is no specific treatment for Henoch-Schönlein purpura and it usually gets better on its own in about 6 weeks. Anti-inflammatory painkillers such as ibuprofen may help with joint pain. If your child has had Henoch-Schönlein purpura he will be monitored by doctors even when he is better in order to check the function of his kidneys, because the condition can lead to glomerulonephritis (see above).

Hypospadias

This is a congenital disorder affecting about 1 in 300 baby boys. In hypospadias the opening of the urethra, the tube through which urine passes out of the body, is on the underside of the child's penis rather than at the tip. Usually, it is on the head (glans) of the penis, although it can be on the shaft. The foreskin is gathered at the back of the penis and the penis may be bent when erect. Boys with hypospadias should not be circumcised because the foreskin can be used to make the urethral opening at the tip of the penis and to straighten out the penis. This corrective surgery is likely to be carried out when your child is between 6 months and 1 year old.

Hypothyroidism

The thyroid gland is located in the neck and produces hormones that help to control the body's metabolic rate as well as having various roles in your child's physical and mental development. In hypothyroidism the thyroid gland is underactive, so that not enough thyroid hormones are produced. It can be present from birth or it can develop later in life. All babies in the UK are tested for hypothyroidism a few days after birth so that if it is identified it can be treated before symptoms develop. Symptoms include lack of energy, slow growth, and learning difficulties. If hypothyroidism is diagnosed, your child will be given thyroxine, the main hormone produced by the thyroid gland. It usually needs to be continued for life.

Intestinal obstruction

If the intestines become blocked (obstructed) their contents, which may be digested food or faeces, are unable to pass through. Causes of intestinal obstruction in children include a congenital defect, twisting of the bowel, a hernia (a weakness in the abdominal wall), and the bowel telescoping in on itself (intussusception). Intestinal obstruction leads to bloating of the abdomen, constipation, pain, and vomiting. Urgent treatment in hospital is needed. Depending on the cause of the obstruction, surgery may be required.

Iron-deficiency anaemia

This is the most common type of anaemia in children. Anaemia means there is a lack of haemoglobin, the part of red blood cells that transports oxygen from the lungs to other body cells. Iron is needed to produce haemoglobin and if it is deficient cells that normally get oxygen from red blood cells may not receive enough to function. Iron-deficiency anaemia can be caused by inadequate iron in the diet. It is common in premature babies who do not have sufficient stores of iron before birth to cope with a diet of milk for the first few months (milk does not contain much iron). It also occurs in older children who may not be eating enough foods high in iron content.

The symptoms of anaemia vary in severity, but include fatigue, pale skin, and shortness of breath on exercising. If you are concerned that your child may have anaemia take her to your doctor. Blood tests can determine whether anaemia is present and identify the cause. If iron-deficiency anaemia is found your child may be given iron supplements. These are also given to premature babies to prevent anaemia. To increase the iron in your child's diet give her lots of green leafy vegetables and protein and fortified breakfast cereals. As children get older they tend to eat a more varied diet so their iron needs are met and anaemia is less likely.

Irritable hip

Irritable hip mainly affects children, usually those of primary school age, and is twice as common in boys as it is in girls. The membrane that lines the hip joint becomes inflamed, leading to pain in the hip, or in the groin, knee, or thigh. Movement of the hip is also usually restricted, which can cause difficulty standing and walking, or a limp. Irritable hip can develop after a viral infection or following an injury, such as from a fall, but often the cause is not known. If your child has irritable hip she'll need complete rest, so that the hip is not moved. Rest can be at home or in hospital, where your child's leg can be put in traction to keep it still. Symptoms improve within 1–2 weeks, and complications are rare.

Joint infection

Infection of a joint (also called septic arthritis) can be caused by infection that has spread through the bloodstream from another site, such as an infected wound, or from infected tissues nearby, for example from an infected bone near the joint. It can occur at any age, but most affected children are under 3. The hip joint is the most common site of infection in children.

An infected joint becomes inflamed and fluid collects inside it. The joint feels hot and is swollen and painful, so your child may be reluctant to move it. A fever may develop. Seek medical help immediately if you think your child could have a joint infection. She will be treated in hospital with antibiotics, and fluid may be drained from the joint. Physiotherapy may be required after treatment to keep the joint flexible. If joint infection is treated quickly, children generally make a good recovery.

Juvenile idiopathic arthritis

In arthritis, joints become inflamed and painful. Juvenile idiopathic arthritis is an umbrella term for several types of chronic (long-standing) arthritis that occur in children. It affects 1–2 in every 1,000 children. In the most common form, known as oligo-articular arthritis, four or fewer joints are affected. In other types more joints are affected, and in some types there are accompanying symptoms such as fever.

Treatments used to help relieve pain and swelling include painkillers, anti-inflammatory medications, and steroids. In some cases medications that can slow down progression of the disease may be given. Affected children are also offered physiotherapy to keep the joints mobile and strong, as well as occupational therapy. Regular exercise, such as swimming or running, can be helpful.

The outlook for children with juvenile idiopathic arthritis depends on the type. Eight out of 10 children with oligo-articular arthritis recover completely after 15 years. Some of the other types may be lifelong, but treatment can usually keep symptoms under control, and most children are able to lead normal, active lives.

Kawasaki disease

This rare disease, the cause of which is unknown, usually affects children under 5, and is most common in babies aged 9–12 months. It more often affects children from North Asia. Kawasaki disease causes a high temperature that usually lasts for more than 5 days and does not respond to medication as well as various other symptoms that may include red eyes (conjunctivitis), a blotchy red rash over the body, swelling or peeling skin on the hands or feet, swollen lymph glands in the neck, and a red throat or tongue with dry lips.

If your child is diagnosed with Kawasaki disease she will be treated in hospital with aspirin and intravenous immunoglobulin (antibodies) with the aim of preventing complications that can affect the blood vessels and heart. With prompt treatment (within 10 days of the symptoms starting) children usually make a full recovery.

Leukaemia

Leukaemia is a type of cancer in which the bone marrow produces large numbers of abnormal white blood cells. These cells are not able to perform effectively the usual role of white blood cells, which is to defend the body against infection. In addition, they upset the balance of other types of blood cell, so that there are fewer red blood cells and platelets (cells that help blood clot).

The most common type of leukaemia in children is acute lymphoblastic leukaemia. The exact cause is unknown, but genetic and environmental factors are thought to be involved. It is most common in children aged between 1 and 4, affecting boys more often than girls. Symptoms include tiredness and shortness of breath due to anaemia (lack of haemoglobin, the oxygen-carrying part of red blood cells); bruising easily; bleeding; and swollen lymph glands. Initially these symptoms may seem similar to those of a viral infection [illegible] Treatment involves chemotherapy; 8 out of 10 children are cured.

Nephrotic syndrome

The kidneys filter out waste products from the blood to be excreted as urine, while keeping in blood cells and protein. In nephrotic syndrome the kidneys become leaky, with at least 25 times more protein than usual being lost from the blood. The low blood protein level allows water to seep into other tissues, causing swelling (oedema).

Nephrotic syndrome is an uncommon disorder that can affect people of any age; in children it usually occurs between the ages of 2 and 5, with boys being affected more often than girls. Symptoms include swelling, commonly around the eyes; weight gain (due to accumulation of excess fluid); tiredness; and passing a smaller amount of urine, which may be frothy. It is diagnosed by measuring the amount of protein in a urine sample collected from your child over a 24-hour period. If your child has nephrotic syndrome he will be treated in hospital with steroids. His fluid intake may be restricted and he'll be given diuretic drugs to help his kidneys produce urine and to get rid of excess fluid from his body. Nephrotic syndrome in children does not usually cause any long-term kidney damage.

Muscular dystrophy

Progressive weakness and wasting of muscle are the main features of muscular dystrophy. There are several different types but the most common and most serious is Duchenne muscular dystrophy, which is a genetic condition that only affects boys.

In Duchenne muscular dystrophy the leg muscles usually become weak first. This may cause late walking or difficulties standing up from lying down – children may use their hands to climb up their legs to stand up. Unfortunately there is no cure; although physiotherapy can help your child maintain mobility for as long as possible, the muscle weakness is progressive and gradually affects an increasing number of muscles. Affected children usually have to use a wheelchair by age 10 or 11 and the condition becomes life-threatening on average by age 20 to 30.

Perthes' disease

This condition affects the head of the thigh bone (femur) where it meets the pelvis. The blood supply to this area becomes insufficient so the bone softens; as the blood supply recovers the bone reforms and hardens again but may do so in a deformed shape. Perthes' disease is rare but tends to affect children aged between 4 and 8, and is more common in boys. Symptoms include a limp or pain in the hip, groin, or knee. Treatment depends on the severity of the condition and can involve bed rest, placing the leg in a plaster cast or splints, or surgery.

Phenylketonuria

Phenylalanine is an amino acid found in many protein-containing foods, and is normally broken down by an enzyme and used by the body. Phenylketonuria is a rare, inherited condition in which levels of this enzyme are low so that phenylalanine can't be broken down, resulting in abnormally high levels in the body. This can cause irreversible brain damage, in turn leading to learning difficulties. Phenylketonuria can be treated if it is diagnosed early, before any significant brain damage occurs. Babies in the UK are tested for it as part of the heel-prick test, which is carried out a few days after birth. Treatment involves following a diet that is low in phenylalanine to prevent levels rising in the blood. This means avoiding giving your child many protein-rich foods; a diet containing artificial protein may be recommended.

Pyloric stenosis

In pyloric stenosis the outlet from the stomach into the intestines is narrowed so that not enough food can enter the intestines while the rest is vomited back up. It affects about 1 in 500 babies, usually under 2 months old, and is more common in boys. Symptoms include projectile vomiting (forcefully produced vomit that lands some distance away), constant hunger, and weight loss. Dehydration may occur due to the vomiting. The narrowing can be diagnosed with ultrasound scanning and is treated with surgery.

Sickle cell anaemia

In this inherited form of anaemia, red blood cells become sickle shaped and are destroyed more easily than normal. This results in low levels of oxygen-carrying haemoglobin in the blood. In addition, the sickle-shaped cells can block narrow blood vessels. Sickle cell anaemia is caused by a faulty gene and is more common in people of African or Afro-Caribbean origin. If a child inherits two copies of the faulty gene he will have sickle cell anaemia; if he inherits only one copy, he has sickle cell trait. Children with sickle cell trait usually do not have symptoms but can pass the condition on to their children if their partner is also a carrier of the faulty gene.

Children with sickle cell anaemia have symptoms common to other anaemias, such as tiredness and shortness of breath on exertion. However, your child may also have episodes of jaundice (yellow skin and whites of eyes) and sickle cell crises, when sickle-shaped cells block narrow blood vessels, causing pain, often in the bones or abdomen. Treatment includes avoiding triggers that can cause a crisis, such as dehydration; vitamin supplements; painkillers for crises; and regular antibiotics to prevent infections.

Testicular torsion

The testes hang down in the scrotum, supported by a cord-like structure called the spermatic cord. In testicular torsion, this becomes twisted. As a result, the blood supply to the testes is cut off, causing pain. Testicular torsion can occur at any age, but it is more common in very young children and around the time of puberty and can occur after an injury to the scrotum.

The symptoms of testicular torsion are sudden onset of severe pain in the testis, which may appear higher than normal in the scrotum. The scrotum may then become swollen. Other symptoms include nausea and vomiting. If you think your son may have torsion of a testis call an ambulance, as the condition needs to be treated urgently (within a few hours) in order to try and save the testis. The treatment involves surgery to untwist the testicle. If it is carried out promptly the testis may continue to work as normal

Turner's syndrome

Turner's syndrome affects about 1 in every 2,500 girls. It is a genetic disorder in which one of the X chromosomes is missing (girls normally have two X chromosomes).

Girls with Turner's syndrome are short in height, and their ovaries do not develop so they may not develop breasts or start their periods in puberty, and they may be infertile. Some girls with Turner's syndrome are not diagnosed until their periods fail to start at puberty. Other symptoms can include a thick or wide neck and widely spaced nipples. There may also be problems with the kidneys, bones, heart, ears, and thyroid glands. Intelligence is not usually affected.

There is no specific treatment for Turner's syndrome although girls will have regular check-ups for any complications. Short stature can be treated with growth hormone, and oestrogen and progesterone hormone replacement can be given to encourage sexual development and periods.

Wilms' tumour

This rare form of kidney cancer usually develops in children under 4. It generally affects only one kidney. Symptoms include swelling of the abdomen, which can be painful, and blood in the urine (it may look red or pink). It is diagnosed using scans, such as ultrasound or CT scans. Treatment can involve surgery, chemotherapy, and radiotherapy, and most children are cured.

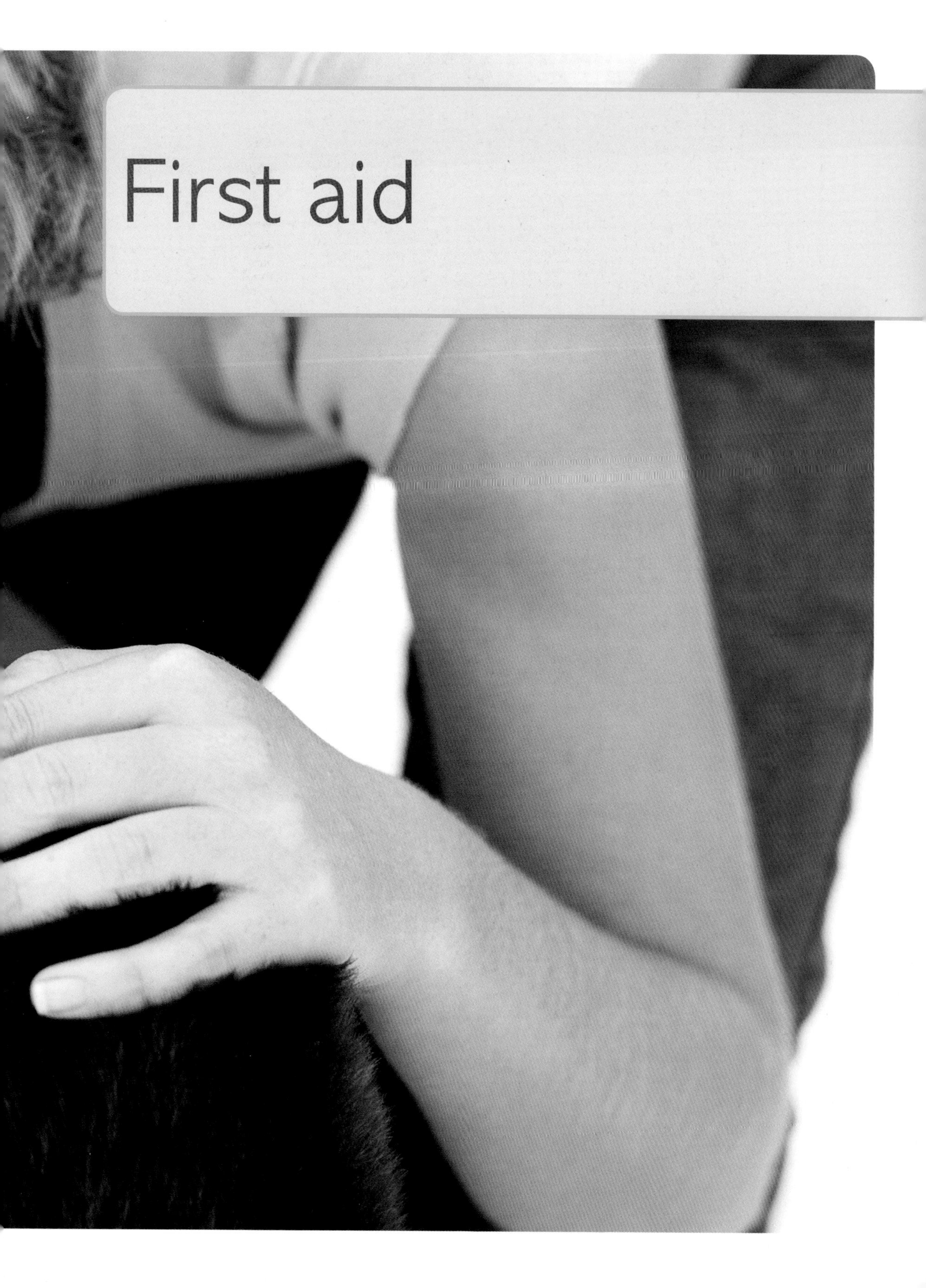

First aid

Unconscious baby

Act quickly if a baby (under 1 year) is unconscious, as he may not be breathing and his heart may stop. Open his airway, check breathing and if necessary, begin cardiopulmonary resuscitation (CPR) – chest compressions and rescue breaths.

Emergency action

★ **Check for response** Tap his foot; call his name. If no response, he's unconscious.

★ **Get help** Ask someone to call an ambulance. If you're alone, give CPR for one minute, then call an ambulance.

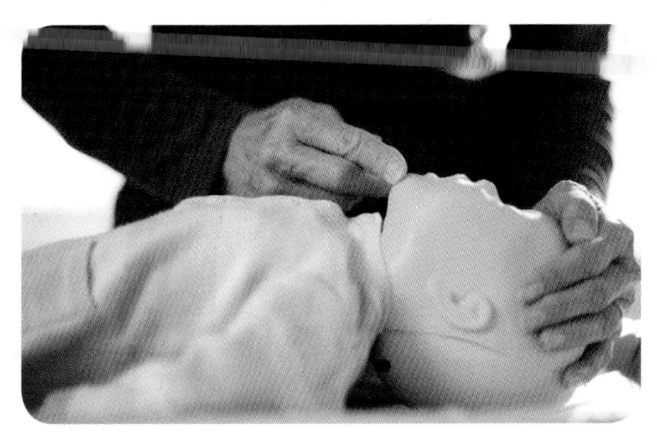

1 **Open the airway** If the baby is unconscious and on his back, his tongue could fall back and block the air passages to his lungs. First, lay him on a firm surface. Put one hand on his forehead and tilt his head back slightly. Place one finger of your other hand on the chin and lift it.

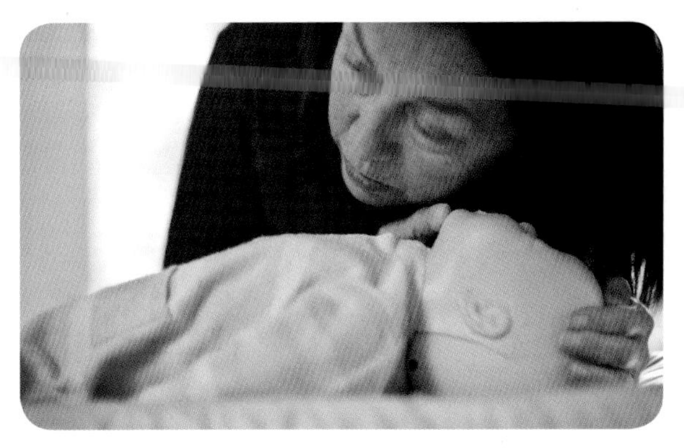

2 **Check breathing for 10 seconds** Lean over your baby so that your ear is near his mouth, then look along his chest. Listen for breathing sounds and feel for breaths against your face. Look at his chest for signs of movement. If he is breathing, see below. If he is not breathing, go to the next step.

Recovery position for a breathing baby

If your baby is unconscious but breathing, hold him in the recovery position while you wait for help. Cradle him in your arms so that his head is lower than his body. Support his head with your hand. In this position, his tongue can't fall back and block his air passages and he can't choke if he vomits. Call an ambulance and monitor your baby's breathing until it arrives.

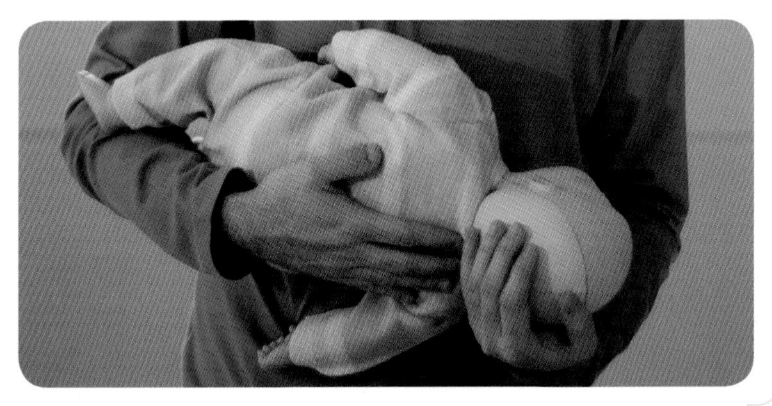

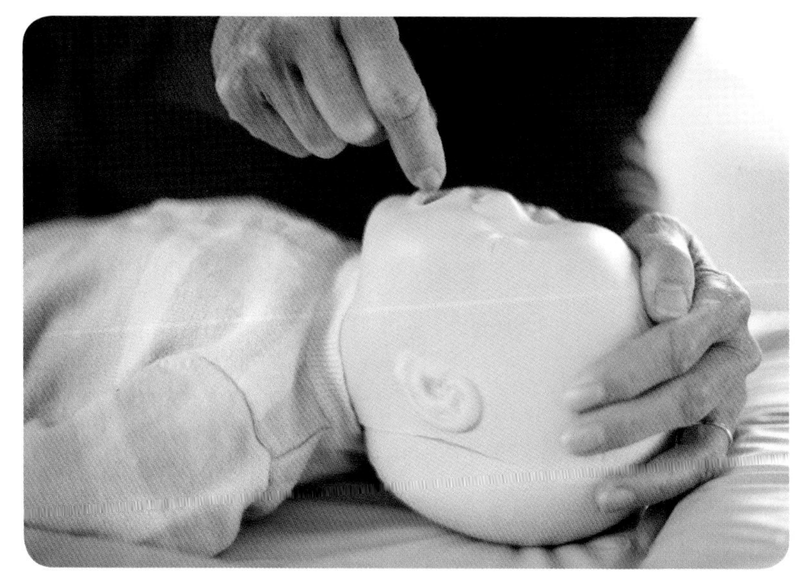

3 **Clear the airway** Make sure the airway is open. Check your baby's mouth to see if there is an obvious obstruction over his mouth or nose. If you can see anything pick it out – but don't put your finger into the mouth to look for obstructions.

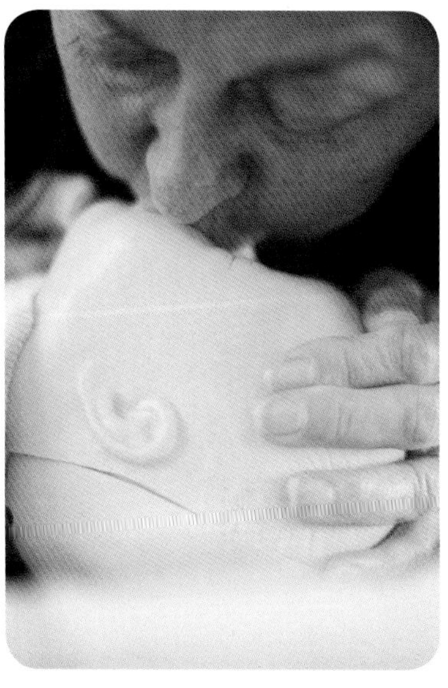

4 **Start with five rescue breaths** Take a breath, seal your mouth over the mouth *and* nose, then blow gently for a second. Repeat FIVE times.

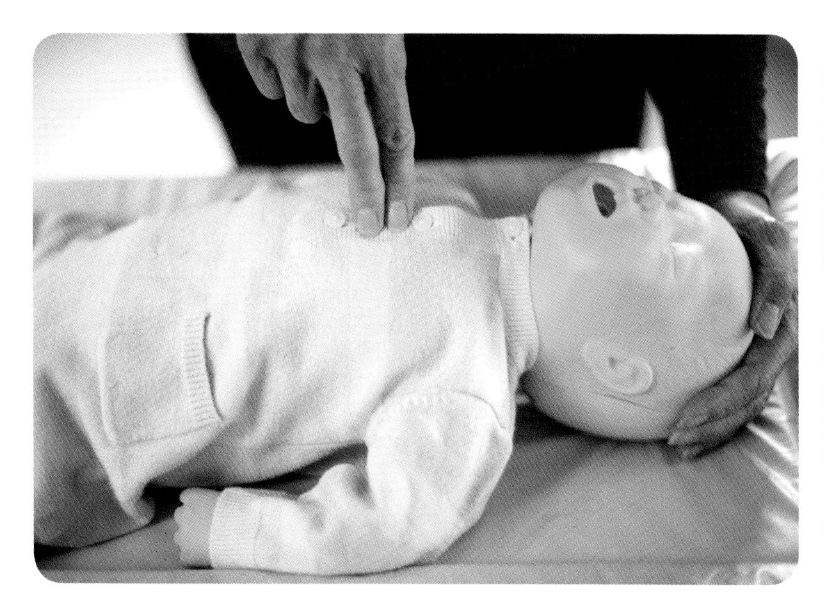

5 **Give 30 chest compressions** Place two fingertips of one hand on the centre of the baby's chest, keeping your other fingers tucked away. Press down vertically to about one-third of the depth of the chest, then release the pressure but don't move your fingers. Let the chest come back up to its normal position. Repeat to give 30 compressions.

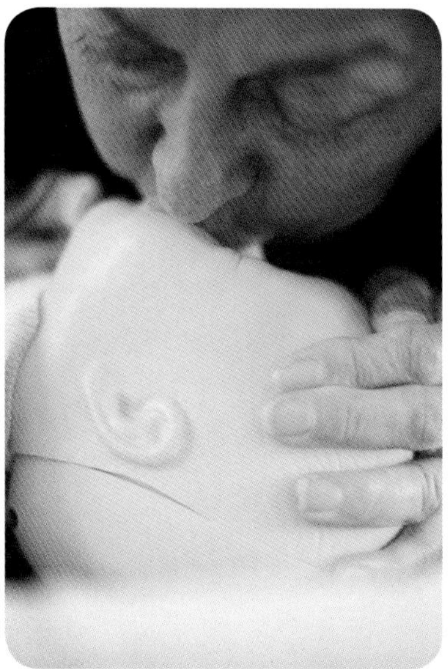

6 **Give two rescue breaths and repeat 30 chest compressions** Continue giving 30 compressions then two rescue breaths until help arrives or your baby starts breathing again.

Unconscious child

You must act quickly if your child (over 12 months) is unconscious as her tongue may fall back and block the air passages, preventing breathing. If necessary, begin CPR – chest compressions and rescue breaths.

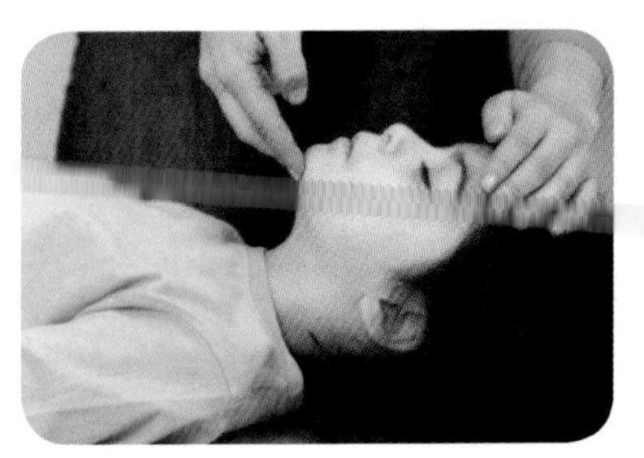

1 Open the airway Put one hand on your child's forehead to tilt her head back slightly. Place two fingers of your other hand on the chin and lift it.

2 Check breathing Lean over your child so that your ear is near her mouth and look along her chest. Listen for breathing sounds and feel for breaths against your face for 10 seconds. Look at her chest for signs of movement.

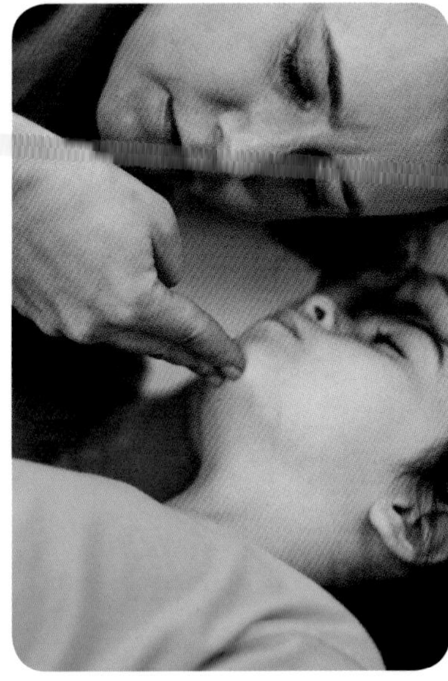

Emergency action

★ **Check for response** Tap the child's shoulder calling her name. Never shake a child. If there is no response, the child is unconscious.

★ **Get help** Ask someone to call an ambulance while you attend to the child.

★ **If you are alone** Give CPR for one minute before you call the ambulance.

Recovery position for a breathing child

If your child is breathing, lay her on her side with her head tilted back and her lower leg and spine aligned. Bend her lower arm and upper leg so that they are at right angles to her body, preventing her falling forwards. Support her head with her upper hand. In this position her tongue can't fall back and block her air passages and she can't choke if she vomits. Call an ambulance.

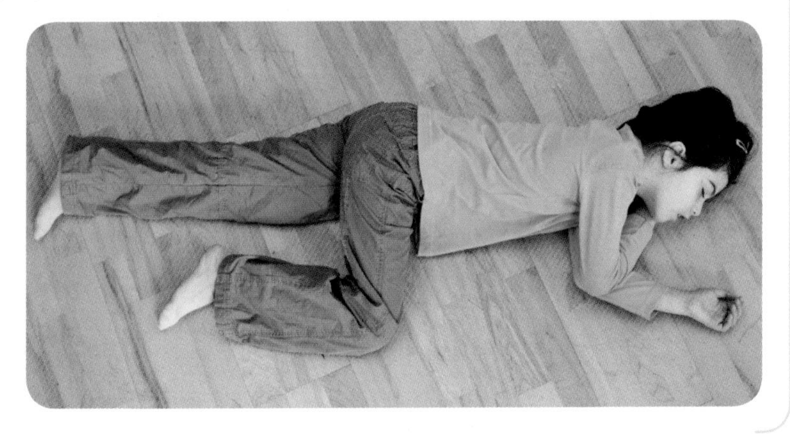

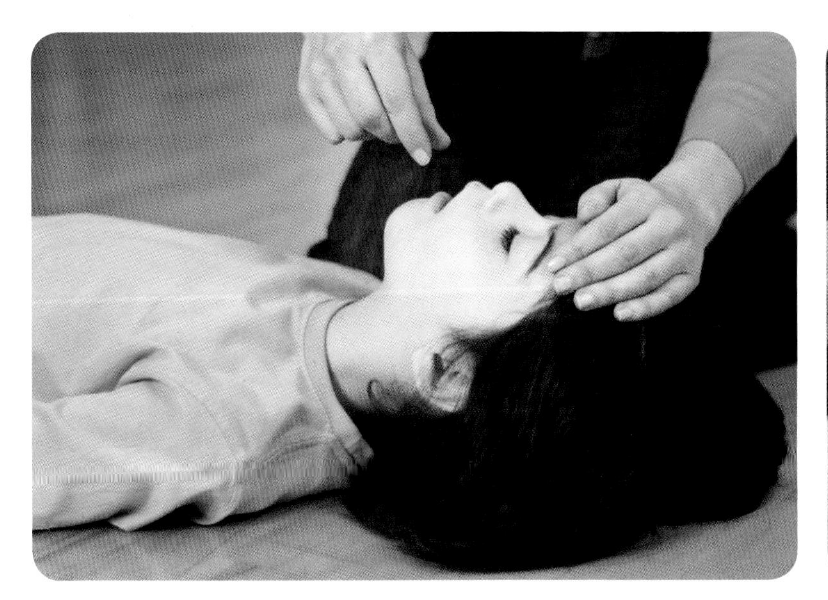

3 **Clear the airway** If she is not breathing, make sure that the airway is open by tilting her head and lifting the chin again. Check her mouth to see if there is an obvious obstruction over her mouth or nose. If you can see anything lift it out, but don't put your finger into the mouth to look for obstructions.

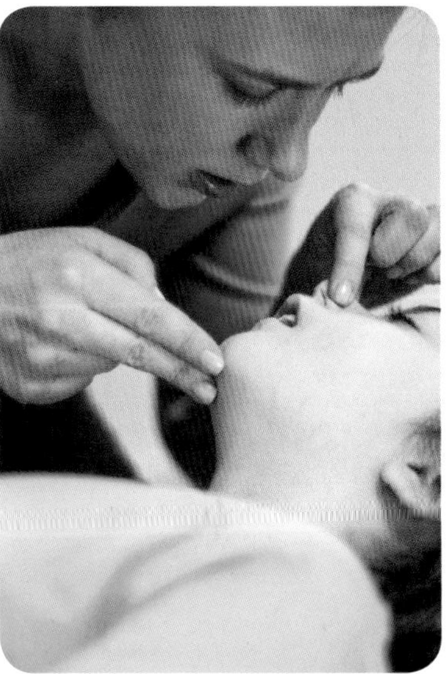

4 **Start with five rescue breaths** Take a normal breath. Pinch her nose, seal your mouth over hers, and blow gently for about a second – watch to see if the chest rises. Remove your mouth and let the chest fall again. Repeat FIVE times. If the chest does not rise, try adjusting the head position and try again.

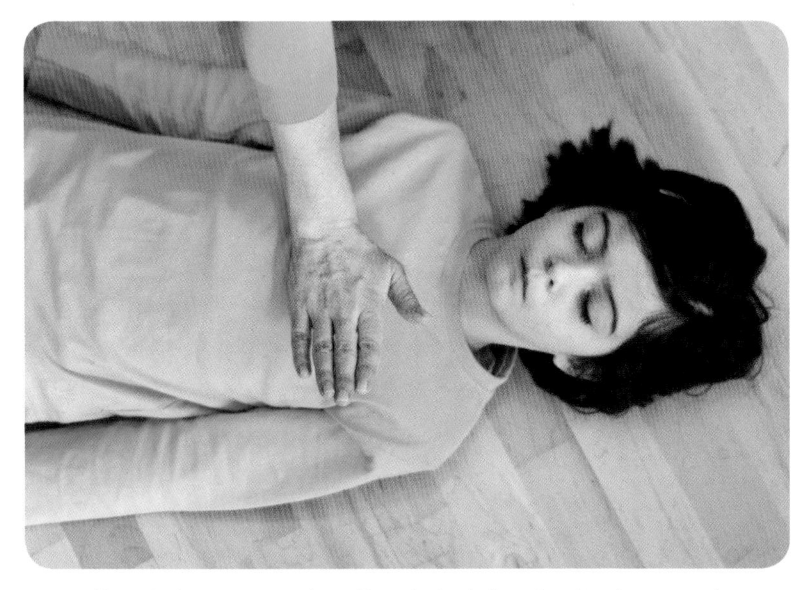

5 **Give 30 chest compressions** Place the heel of one hand on the centre of your child's chest. Keep your other fingers raised so there is no risk of them pressing on the child's ribs. Press down vertically to about one-third of the depth of the chest, then release the pressure but don't move your fingers. Let the chest come back up to its normal position. Repeat to give 30 compressions.

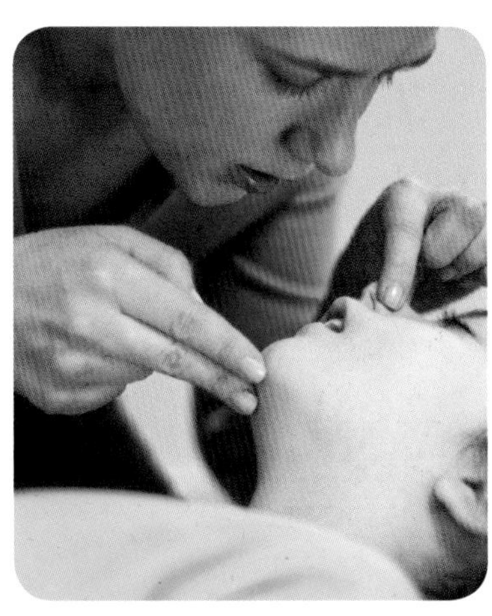

6 **Give two rescue breaths and repeat 30 chest compressions** Continue giving 30 compressions then two rescue breaths until help arrives or your child starts breathing again.

Choking baby

Babies are especially at risk of choking when eating, but they also often put objects in their mouths. If your baby begins to choke, let him cough, but act as described here if he is having difficulties breathing.

1 **Give five back blows** Start by letting your baby cough to try to clear the blockage. If he can't cry, cough, or breathe, lay him face down along your arm – support his head with your hand. Give five back blows between the shoulder blades with the heel of your other hand. Turn the baby over, so that he is lying face up along your other arm and look inside his mouth. Remove obvious obstructions.

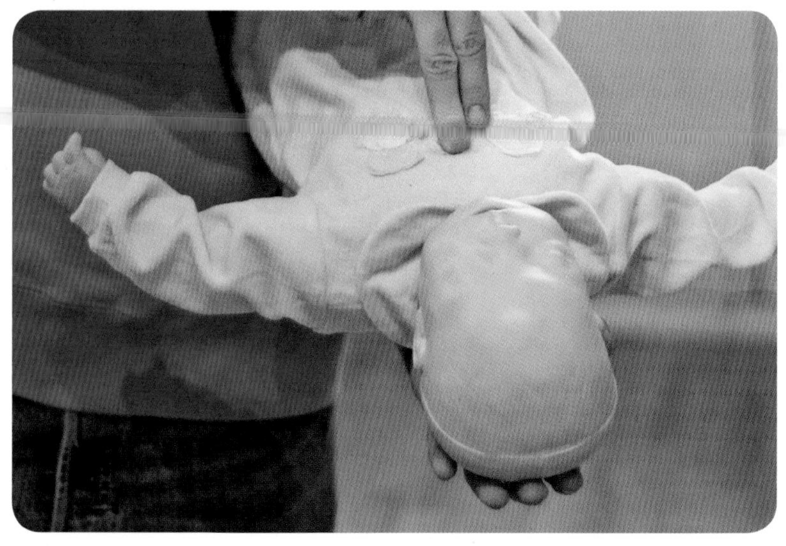

2 **Give five chest thrusts** If the airway is still blocked, try chest thrusts. Keep your baby face up along your arm with his head low – support his head in your hand. Put two fingers on the baby's breastbone, just below the line between his nipples. Push sharply inwards and upwards towards the head up to five times. Check his mouth again.

REMEMBER

Make sure small objects are kept out of your baby's reach. Always use a high chair when he is eating, and never leave him alone with food.

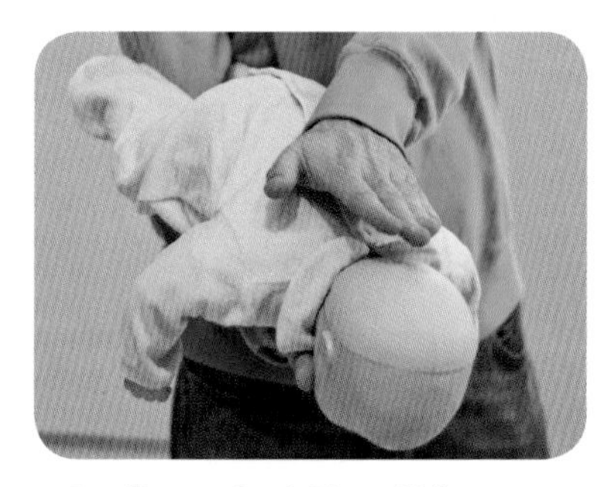

3 **Repeat back blows** If the obstruction has still not cleared, turn the baby over onto your other arm again, and repeat the five back blows. Turn him face up and check his mouth.

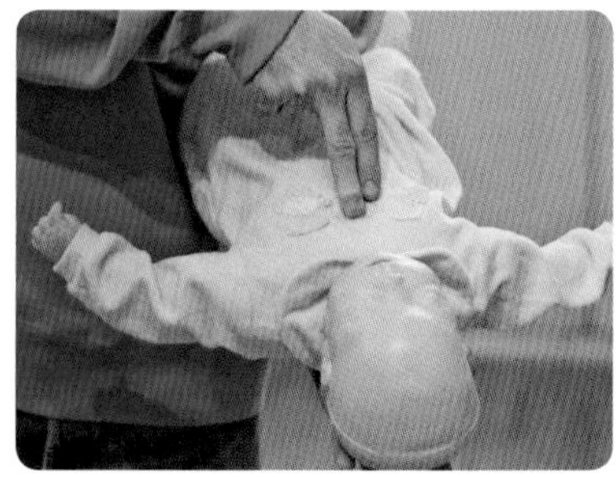

4 **Repeat chest thrusts** If the airway is still not clear, give chest thrusts. Repeat steps one and two three times. If he's still choking, call an ambulance. If he loses consciousness, see pp.210–11.

Choking child

If your child is choking, but attempting to cough, encourage her. Don't interfere until she is unable to cough as your action could also cause the blockage to move further down her throat into her lungs.

1 **Give five back blows** Start by letting your child cough to try to clear a blockage. If she can't speak, cough, or breathe, bend her forward – supporting her chest with one hand. Give five sharp back blows between her shoulder blades with the heel of your other hand. Look inside her mouth and remove any obvious obstructions. Don't put your finger in her mouth in an attempt to find an object.

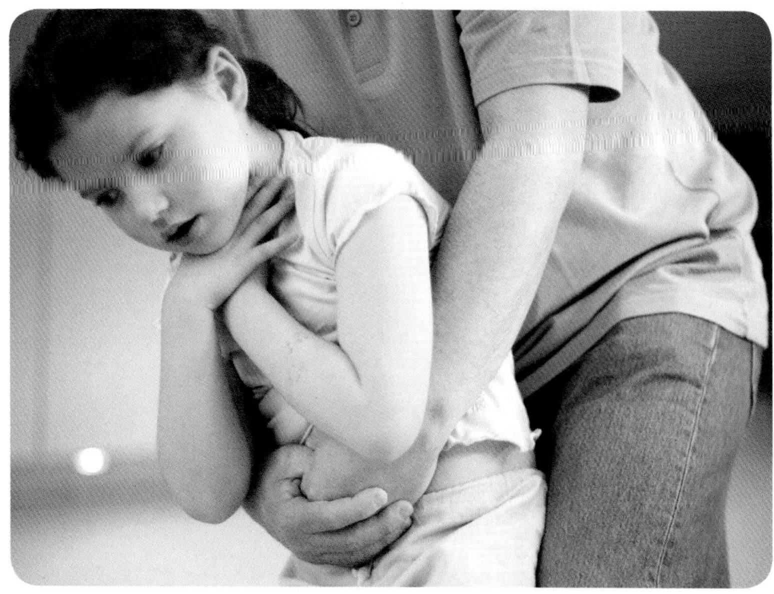

2 **Give five abdominal thrusts** If the airway is still blocked, stand behind your child. Make a fist with one hand and hold it against the middle of her abdomen (halfway between her tummy button and the bottom of the breastbone), and put your other hand on top. Pull sharply inwards and upwards up to five times. Check her mouth again.

3 **Repeat back blows** If the obstruction has still not cleared, bend your child forward again and repeat the five back blows. Check her mouth again.

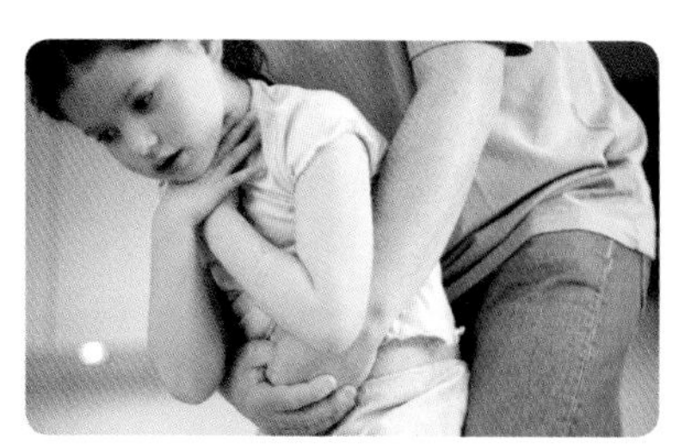

4 **Repeat abdominal thrusts** If the airway is still blocked, repeat steps two and three up to three times. If she is still choking, call an ambulance. If she loses consciousness, see pp.212–13.

REMEMBER

Make sure your child always sits down when she is eating or drinking. Don't let her play with toys that are not recommended for her age group.

Serious bleeding

Most injuries are minor and bleeding stops quickly. Controlling serious bleeding can prevent shock developing, which is a life-threatening condition. If a wound is large, stitches may be needed.

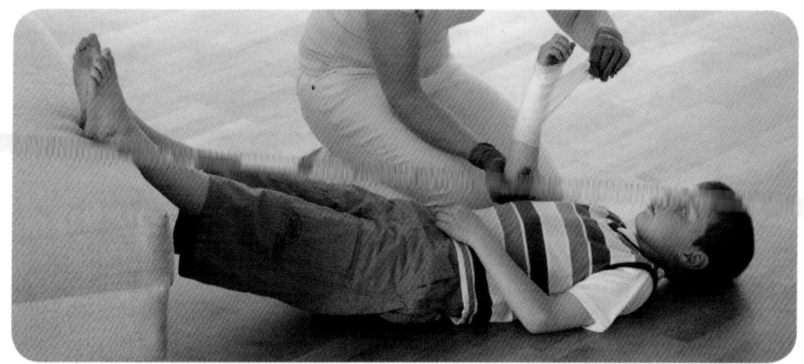

1 **Apply direct pressure** Press firmly against the wound, over a pad if you have one. Raise the injury above the child's heart to slow the blood flow to it.

2 **Lie child down** Reassure your child. Continue pressing against the wound, securing the pad with a bandage if you have one, and keep the injured area raised high. Help your child to lie down and raise his legs as high as you can; support them on a chair or pile of cushions. Call an ambulance.

Severe burns

Burns allow fluid to escape from the body and germs to enter. Seek medical advice for any non-minor burn on a child. For a deep or extensive burn, call an ambulance. Never put creams or oils on a burn.

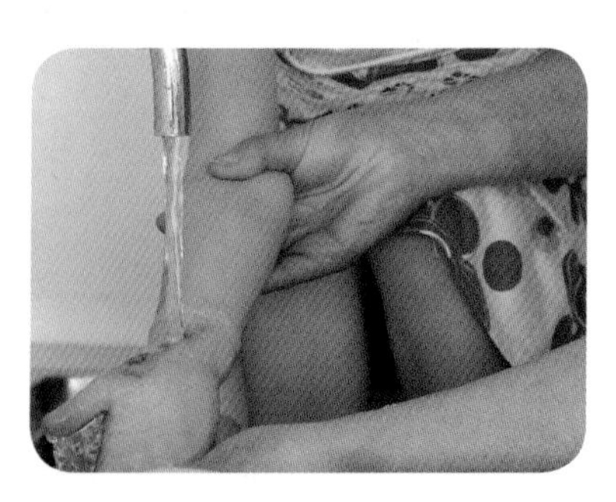

1 **Cool the burn** Hold the burned area under cold running water for up to 10 minutes. Remove clothing from the area before skin starts to swell. Don't touch anything that is sticking to a burn.

2 **Cover the burn** Lay clingfilm or a plastic bag or non-fluffy dressing over the injury to prevent it from drying out. Seek medical advice.

Poisoning

A child can be poisoned after eating a range of items, including berries, leaves, cleaning products, pills, and medicines. Look for clues such as an empty container nearby or unusual smelling breath.

Call the emergency services Find out what your child has taken and, if possible, how much. Seek medical advice or call an ambulance and give them as much information as possible. Stay with your child and keep talking to her. Depending on what she has taken she may vomit (don't try to make her sick though). Don't give her anything to eat or drink. If she loses consciousness, see pp.212–13.

Heat exhaustion

This is caused by dehydration. Your child will be sweating and have pale clammy skin. He may have a headache, feel dizzy and sick, and have cramps.

REMEMBER

Call an ambulance if your child develops a sudden headache and hot, DRY skin – this is heatstroke. Start to cool him by wrapping him in a cold, wet sheet.

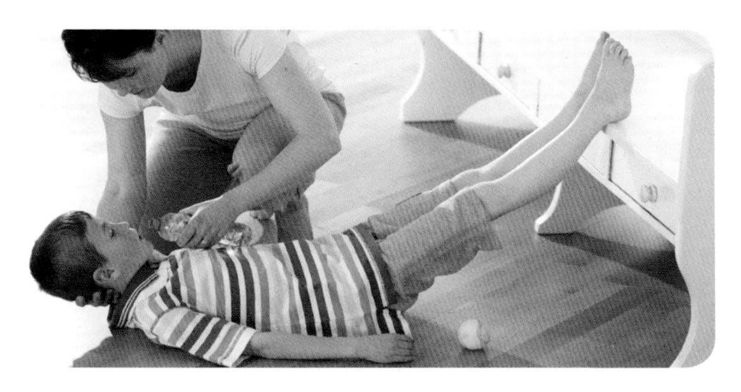

Take child into the shade Move the child into a cool place. Lay him down on the floor and raise his legs to improve blood flow to his head. Give him some water. Let him sip as much water as he can; don't let him gulp it down too quickly. Monitor him while he recovers and let him sit up gradually. Call for help if his condition worsens.

Anaphylactic shock

This severe allergic reaction can happen quickly. Call an ambulance. Children with a serious allergy often have an injector for use in an emergency.

REMEMBER

If your child is at risk of anaphylactic shock, she should always have her medication with her. Show her teachers and friends' parents how to administer it too.

Emergency signs

If your child has any of the following symptoms, ask someone to call an ambulance while you attend to her:

★ **Difficulty breathing and rapid pulse** Child suddenly starts wheezing or even gasping for air.

★ **Blotchy skin** Skin becomes red and blotchy, often all over.

★ **Swelling and puffiness** Eyes may be puffy; face, neck, and tongue can swell.

Give medication if you have it Sit the child in a comfortable breathing position. Hold the injector with your fist, remove the safety cap and place the end against the child's thigh (over clothing if necessary). Press firmly to release the medication.

Strains and sprains

This type of injury can be painful, but it usually heals relatively quickly. Your child should rest it initially. Then encourage gentle movement. If you are in any doubt about an injury treat it as a broken bone (opposite).

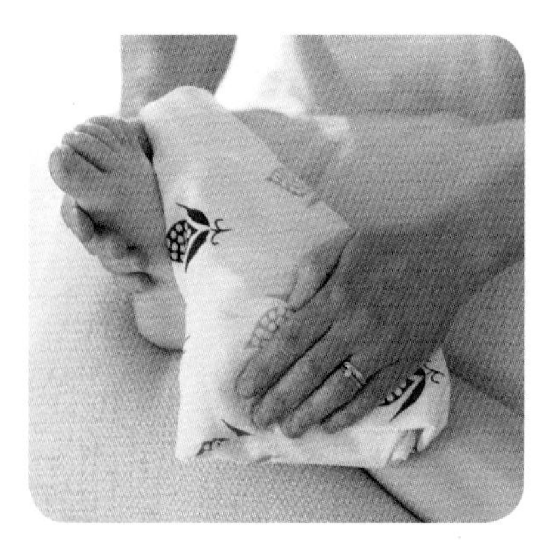

1 **Rest the injury** Sit your child down and raise her leg. Cool the injury for up to 20 minutes by placing a cold compress on it. Ideally use a bag of ice or a pack of frozen peas wrapped in a towel.

2 **Support with a bandage** Wrap some padding, such as a roll of cotton wool, around the injury, then cover with an elasticated bandage. Start the bandage at the joint below the injury, and continue as far as the joint above it.

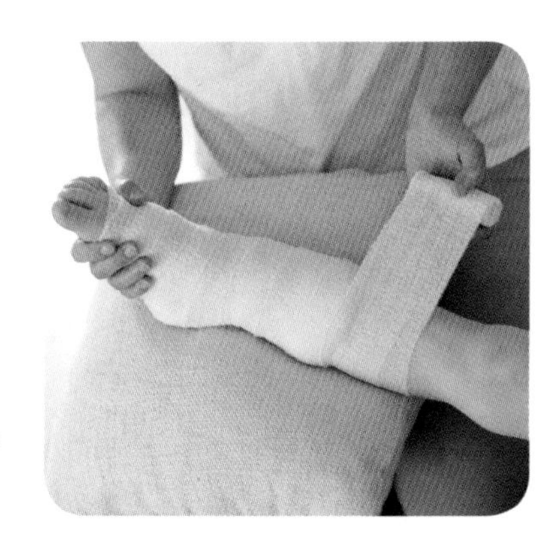

Broken bones

If you suspect that your child has broken a bone, he will need an X-ray. Immobilize the injury to prevent the broken bone ends moving, which can damage nearby blood vessels, nerves, or muscles. Seek medical help.

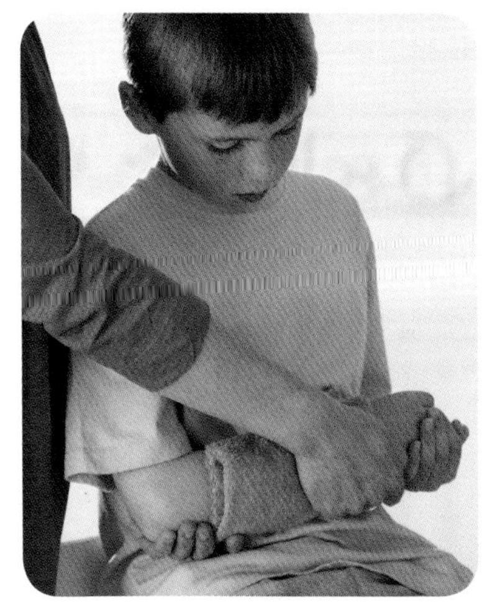

1 **Support the injury by hand** Reassure your child. Use your hands to support the joints at either end of the broken limb. Help him to sit down. Wrap a small towel around the injury for padding.

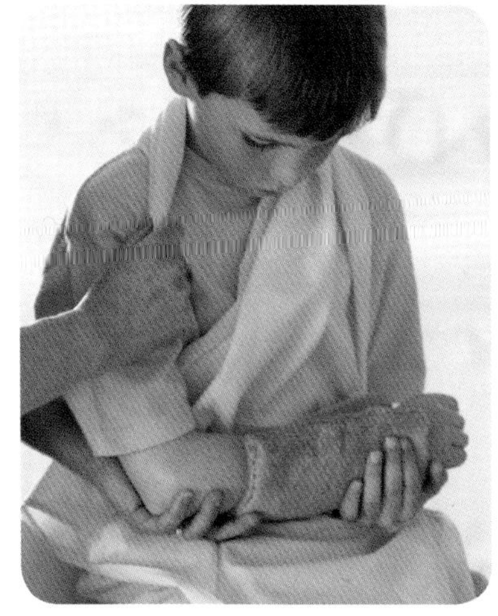

2 **Put a sling on** Slide a triangular bandage between the chest and arm. The long edge should be against the uninjured side, then take the top point around the back of the neck.

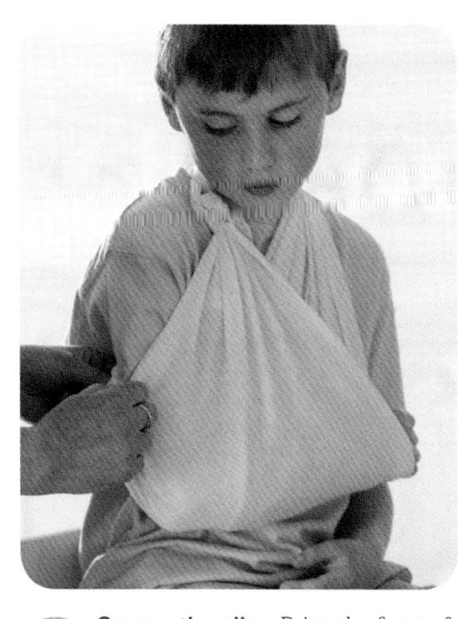

3 **Secure the sling** Bring the front of the bandage over the injured arm and tie a knot in front of the collar bone. Tuck in the bandage at the elbow. Take the child to hospital.

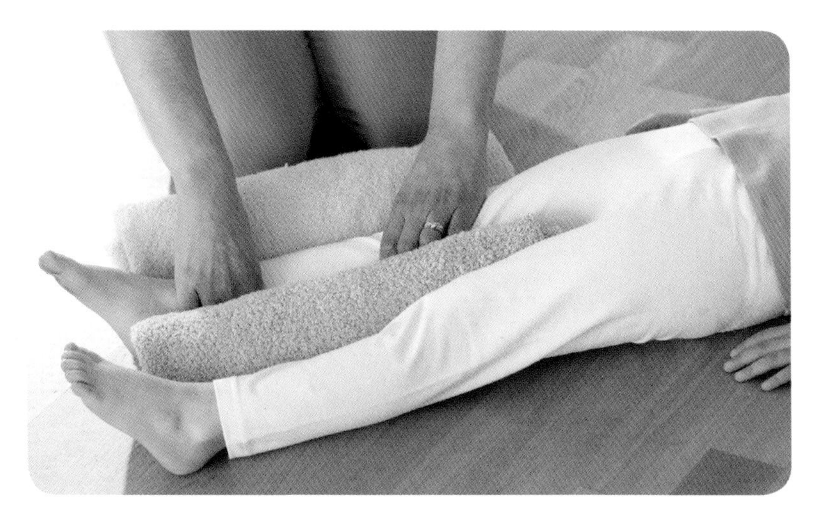

For an injured leg Support the joints above and below the break with your hands. Ask someone else to put rolled towels on either side of the leg for extra support. Call an ambulance as the child needs to be taken to hospital on a stretcher.

Useful resources

Adoption UK
www.adoptionuk.org
0844 848 7900

Afasic
An organization for those with speech and language impairment.
www.afasic.org.uk
08453 55 55 77

Allergy UK
Information and support for people with allergies
www.allergyuk.org
01322 619 898

Asthma UK
www.asthma.org.uk
08457 01 02 03

Attention Deficit Disorder Information and Support Service (ADDISS)
Support and information for parents and sufferers.
www.addiss.co.uk
020 8952 2800

British Dyslexia Association
www.bdadyslexia.org.uk
0845 251 9002

Change 4 Life
Information about healthy eating and exercise.
www.nhs.uk/Change4life

Diabetes UK
www.diabetes.org.uk
0845 120 2960

Dyspraxia Foundation
www.dyspraxiafoundation.org.uk
01462 454 986

ERIC (Education & Resources for Improving Childhood continence)
Information for parents on children's wetting and soiling.
www.eric.org.uk
0845 370 8008

Food Standards Agency
Information about healthy diet.
www.eatwell.gov.uk

Gingerbread
advice and information for one-parent families
www.gingerbread.org.uk
0800 018 5026

Great Ormond Street Hospital for Children and the UCL Institute of Child Health
www.ich.ucl.ac.uk

Home Start
support for families in local communities
www.home-start.org.uk
0800 0686 368

I CAN
Information and support for children with speech, language and communication difficulties.
www.ican.org.uk
0845 225 4071

IPSEA (Independent Parental Special Education Advice)
Advice for parents of children with special educational needs.
www.ipsea.org.uk
0800 018 4016

Mencap
For people with learning difficulties, their families and carers.
www.mencap.org.uk
0808 808 111

Meningitis Research Foundation
Information and support for people with meningitis or septicaemia.
www.meningitis.org.uk
080 8800 3344

National Autistic Society
www.nas.org.uk
0845 070 4004

NHS
Information about local GPs, accident and emergency services, and dentists, as well as information on a wide variety of conditions.
www.nhs.uk

NHS Direct
24-hour medical advice
www.nhsdirect.nhs.uk
0845 4647

National Eczema Society
www.eczema.org
0800 089 1122

NSPCC
www.nspcc.org.uk
0808 800 5000

Parentline
Charity providing support for those caring for children
www.parentlineplus.org.uk
0808 800 2222

Psoriasis Association
Information and support for people with psoriasis.
www.psoriasis-association.org.uk
0845 676 0076

Royal Society for the Prevention of Accidents
www.rospa.co.uk

TAMBA (Twins and multiple birth association)
www.tamba.org.uk
0800 138 0509

Index

Page numbers in **bold** refer to the main entry for a disorder, health problem or emergency.
Page numbers in *italics* refer to symptoms charts.

O

P

R

S

T

U

V

W

Acknowledgments

AUTHOR'S ACKNOWLEDGMENTS

A very special thank you to Karen Sullivan, the consultant editor, for her help, and everyone at DK who made the book possible, especially Mandy Lebentz, Andrea Bagg, Sara Kimmins, Louise Dick, Penny Warren, Glenda Fisher and Peggy Vance.

PUBLISHER'S ACKNOWLEDGMENTS

DK would like to thank Jemima Dunne, Angela Baynham and Viv Armstrong for editorial assistance, Becky Alexander for proofreading; Susan Bosanko for the index; Jo Godfrey-Wood for assistance at photo shoots; Victoria Barnes and Roisin Donaghy for hair and make-up; Carly Churchill, the photographer's assistant, and our models: Sabrina Batten and Bailey Latimer; Ember Bush; Susan Contoe and Faith Adekunle; Roisin Donaghy and Tilly Young; Tessa Evans and Jassy D[illegible]; Isabel Harlock; Julie, Kyle, and Rebecca Johnson; Sid and China Li; Emma and Chloe McKenzie and Harry Smyth; Hema and Himini Patel; Neelima and Lucas Pearce; Misha Pellova, Daisy and Eloise Johnson-Ferguson; Emily Smith; Tanya and Charlotte Stevens; Jai and Tulsi Varsani; Nicola and Elliot Ward; Sharon, Mia, and Jorja Walsh; Colin and Marcus Weekes; Oskar Graham-Taylor; Karlyn and Darcy Westwood; Natasha Garry and Solstice River Davies; Danielle Valliere and Dylan Baird; Hayley Sherwood; Shuna Frood and Joe Sutcliffe

The publisher would like to thank the following for their kind permission to reproduce their photographs:

(Key: a-above; b-below/bottom; c-centre; l-left; r-right; t-top)

8-9 Alamy Images: MBI. **10 Mother & Baby Picture Library:** Ian Hooton (bc). **15 Alamy Images:** John Powell Photographer (tl). **Getty Images:** Design Pics (tr). **16 Corbis:** JLP/Jose L. Pelaez (cr). **Getty Images:** Emely (br). **17 Getty Images:** Tatjana Alvegard (bl). **20 Getty Images:** Peter Cade (bl). **23 Corbis:** Hannah Mason (bc). **Getty Images:** Kikor (tc). **Mother & Baby Picture Library:** Paul Mitchell (bl). **24-25 Getty Images:** Jose Luis Pelaez, Inc / Blend Images. **26 Corbis:** Mina Chapman (br). **Mother & Baby Picture Library:** Paul Mitchell (clb). **27 Corbis:** (bc). **Science Photo Library:** Samuel Ashfield (cla). **28 Mother & Baby Picture Library:** Ian Hooton (c); Angela Spain (cl). **Photolibrary:** moodboard RF (cr). **29 Alamy Images:** Westend 61 GmbH (bl). **Corbis:** Frederic Cirou/PhotoAlto (c). **Science Photo Library:** Claire Deprez / Reporters (bc); Damien Lovegrove (cl). **30 Alamy Images:** Bubbles Photolibrary (c). **Corbis:** Bloomimage (cr). **Mother & Baby Picture Library:** Ruth Jenkinson (cl). **84-85 Getty Images:** Tetra Images. **86 Alamy Images:** Bubbles Photolibrary (br). **Mother & Baby Picture Library:** Ian Hooton (bc). **Science Photo Library:** Paul Whitehill (bl). **102 Mediscan:** (bl). **103 Corbis:** Ariel Skelley/Blend Images (cr). **104 Mediscan:** (bc). **Viewing Medicine:** (bl). **105 Alamy Images:** Celia Mannings (c); thislife pictures (br). **Science Photo Library:** Paul Whitehill (cl). **106 Alamy Images:** Bubbles Photolibrary (bl). **Corbis:** Sandra Seckinger (bc). **Science Photo Library:** CNRI (cl). **107 Alamy Images:** Craig Holmes Premium (bc). **Corbis:** Sandra Seckinger (br). **Viewing Medicine:** (bl). **108 Alamy Images:** Real World People (br). **Science Photo Library:** Bluestone (bc); Dr P. Marazzi (bl). **109 Getty Images:** Jupiterimages / FoodPix (bc). **Science Photo Library:** Ian Boddy (br) (bl); Dr P. Marazzi (c). **110 Science Photo Library:** Dr H.C. Robinson. **111 Alamy Images:** Scott Camazine (cr). **Corbis:** Brigitte Sporrer (bc). **Science Photo Library:** CDC (cl). **112 Alamy Images:** Angela Hampton Picture Library (c). **Corbis:** Hola Images (br). **114 Alamy Images:** Bubbles Photolibrary (bc). **Science Photo Library:** John Radcliffe Hospital (br); Dr P. Marazzi (bl). **115 Getty Images:** (br). **Science Photo Library:** Gustoimages (c). **116 Mother & Baby Picture Library:** Ian Hooton (bl). **Science Photo Library:** Dr P. Marazzi (bc). **117 Science Photo Library:** Dr P. Marazzi (bl). **118 Science Photo Library:** Dr P. Marazzi (cl). **119 Science Photo Library:** Dr P. Marazzi (bl). **120 Science Photo Library:** Dr P. Marazzi (cl). **Viewing Medicine:** (cr). **121 Viewing Medicine:** (cl). **122 Science Photo Library:** Dr P. Marazzi (cra). **123 Mediscan:** (bl). **Science Photo Library:** CNRI (c). **124 Mediscan:** (bl). **132 Corbis:** Beau Lark (cla). **133 Alamy Images:** MBI. **134 Alamy Images:** Trinity Mirror / Mirrorpix (br). **Science Photo Library:** Dr P. Marazzi (cla). **135 Science Photo Library:** Dr P. Marazzi (bl). **136 Science Photo Library:** Western Ophthalmic Hospital (cr). **137 Masterfile:** (br). **139 Getty Images:** Science Photo Library (bl). **140 Corbis:** Michele Constantini/ PhotoAlto (cr). **141 Getty Images:** Monashee Frantz (bc); Jupiterimages (bl). **144 Alamy Images:** Tomasz Niewęgłowski (bl). **Mediscan:** (cr). **145 Corbis:** Christine Schneider (cr); Terry Vine (c). **Mother & Baby Picture Library:** Ian Hooton (cl). **147 Alamy Images:** Real World People (c). **Science Photo Library:** Paul Whitehill (bl). **148 Corbis:** Ken Seet (bl). **Getty Images:** Jose Luis Pelaez Inc (br). **150 Alamy Images:** Angela Hampton Picture Library (bl). **151 Corbis:** LWA-Stephen Welstead (bc). **Getty Images:** Blend Images / Andersen Ross (c). **Science Photo Library:** Adam Gault (cl). **152 Mother & Baby Picture Library:** Ian Hooton (bl). **153 Getty Images:** Comstock (bl); Nicole Hill (br). **Science Photo Library:** AJ Photo (bc); Ian Boddy (c). **154 Alamy Images:** Celia Mannings (br). **155 Getty Images:** Amana Images / Kazuo Kawai (br). **Science Photo Library:** Tek Image (bc). **156 Alamy Images:** Ian Hooton / SPL / Science Photo Library (cb). **158 Corbis:** Don Hammond / Design Pics (br). **160 Getty Images:** David Crausby. **161 Science Photo Library:** Dr P. Marazzi. **162 Science Photo Library:** Dr P. Marazzi (cla); Lea Paterson (crb); Paul Whitehill (br). **163 Getty Images:** Cecile Lavabre (br). **Science Photo Library:** AJ Photo (bl). **164 Corbis:** Tetra Images (bc). **Wellcome Images:** (c). **165 Mother & Baby Picture Library:** Ian Hooton (bl). **166 Getty Images:** Jose Luis Pelaez Inc (bl). **168 Getty Images:** Flickr / By Jekaterina Nikitina (bl). **169 Science Photo Library:** Courtesy Of Crown Copyright FERA (tc). **171 Corbis:** Image Source (br). **172 Corbis:** Rick Gomez (br). **173 Alamy Images:** Steven May (clb). **Getty Images:** AKIRA/A.collection (br); Digital Vision / Siri Stafford (bc). **175 Corbis:** Roy McMahon (c); Alexander Scott (br). **Getty Images:** Hola Images (bc). **Science Photo Library:** Paul Whitehill (cl). **176 Getty Images:** Image Source (crb). **Mother & Baby Picture Library:** Ian Hooton (bl). **178 Science Photo Library:** Paul Whitehill (br). **180 Getty Images:** Pascal Broze (br); Ebby May (bl).**184 Getty Images:** Comstock Images / Jupiterimages (br). **185 Corbis:** Heide Benser (bc). **188 Science Photo Library:** David R. Frazier (bl). **189 Getty Images:** Meg Takamura (bc); Tetra Images (br). **192 Getty Images:** Image Source (bl); RK Studio / Dean Sanderson (tr). **193 Corbis:** Ron Nickel/Design Pics (cb). **Getty Images:** Nancy Brown (tr); Paul Debois (tl). **194 Getty Images:** Lo Birgersson (tr). **Mediscan:** (bc). **195 Corbis:** Ingrid von Hoff (tr). **Mother & Baby Picture Library:** Ian Hooton (bl). **196 Alamy Images:** Catchlight Visual Services (bl). **Corbis:** Steve Prezant (br). **Getty Images:** Beverly Logan (bc). **198 Getty Images:** Cheryl Maeder. **199 Alamy Images:** Catchlight Visual Services (br). **Corbis:** Nossa Productions (bc). **Photolibrary:** Rubberball (bl). **200 Corbis:** Nicole Hill/Rubberball (br). **Getty Images:** Joey Celis (bc). **201 Getty Images:** Riser / Meredith Heuer (bc). **208-209 Getty Images:** Stockbyte